Teaching Children Tennis
the Vic Braden Way

Books by Vic Braden and Bill Bruns:

Vic Braden's Tennis for the Future
Teaching Children Tennis the Vic Braden Way

Teaching Children Tennis the Vic Braden Way

VIC BRADEN AND BILL BRUNS

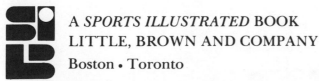

A *SPORTS ILLUSTRATED* BOOK
LITTLE, BROWN AND COMPANY
Boston • Toronto

First Edition

Photographs by Vic and Melody Braden and Dr. David Powell

Drawings by Moe Lebovitz and Marge Anderson

Sports Illustrated books
are published by
Little, Brown and Company
in association with
Sports Illustrated magazine

LIBRARY OF CONGRESS CATALOGING IN PUBLICATION DATA
Braden, Vic.
  Teaching children tennis the Vic Braden way.
  "A Sports illustrated book."
  1. Tennis for children. I. Bruns, Bill, joint
author. II. Title.
GV1001.4.C45B7   796.342'2   80–20364
ISBN 0–316–10512–0

BP
Designed by Susan Windheim
Published simultaneously in Canada
by Little, Brown & Company (Canada) Limited

Printed in the United States of America

This book is dedicated to a young girl who died shortly after giving birth to her only child, Joey. I think of her often, for she would have been today's perfect mother. Her name is Donna.

—VIC BRADEN

To my mom — for her encouragement and optimism; and to my dad — my first and best coach.

—BILL BRUNS

Acknowledgments

THANKS

. . . To those who helped me during my youth: Lawrence Alto, the Ernie Caslers, Hap and Agnes Funk, Dr. A. B. Hodgman, "Cap" Leighton, Al and Cora Riedmayer, Dr. A. B. Stowe, and Fielding Tambling.

. . . To those who helped me a little later in life: Russ Adams; Dr. Gideon Ariel; Phil Bath; Dick Boultinghouse; Bob Briner; Bill Bruns; Chuck Cobb; Dr. Irving Dardik; Mike Davies; Greg Harney; Al Hill, Jr.; Lamar Hunt; Bruce Juell; Dr. Pat Keating; Jack Kramer; Myron McNamara; Manuel Orango; Vic Palmieri; Dr. Ann Penny; Bill Phillips; Nelson Rising; Charles Silverberg; John Temple; Dr. Bert Tesman; Eddie Toler; Dr. Barry Unger; George Wise; and John Zimmerman—and the AMF/ Head Corporation, the Arvida Corporation, the Connecticut General Insurance Company, the Great Southwest Corporation, the PennCo Corporation, and Johnson-Nyquist Productions.

. . . And to those who help me every day: My wife, business partner, and best friend, Melody; and our five children, Kelly, Troy, Kory, Kristen, and Shawn.

Thanks also to Mary Ley for her organizational talents, and to the following people who agreed to appear in the photographs for this book: Brian Babbitt; Lisa Bates; Brooke Benedict; Shawn Bishop; Pam and Alan Bruns; Marylou and Christa Coutlee; Kent, Lane, and Mark Elliott; Mandi Fransen; Mike Hatch; Barbara, Stefanie, and James Honell; Tim Houston; Vic Linden; Luis Luna; Kelly and Courtney Lynch; Mike and Marianne Maiolo; Heidi and Lisa Powell; Rich Robison; Clinton Rowihab; Pam, Karrie, Kim, and Kelli Schott; Otis Smith, Sr. and Otis Smith, Jr.; Michael and Toby Stewart; Amy Stubbs; Joel Trejo; Sue Ann and Greg Warrington; Pat, Karen, John, Kevin, Michele, and Kenneth Wright.

A reflection: There wasn't much money in our house when I was young, but I was the luckiest kid in the world. In addition to having three great brothers and three fantastic sisters, I had intelligent and loving parents who knew exactly when, where, why, and how to jump into my life to do those things only parents can do best.

—VIC BRADEN

Contents

1/A Good Beginning Lasts Forever

I'VE always joked that tennis has done everything for my life except make me 6'3" and thin, and it's true. I was one of seven children in a coal-mining family that moved from Kentucky to Monroe, Michigan, during the Depression. When I was eleven, my time away from school was spent with guys who knew only three seasons: football, basketball, and baseball. Tennis, when we gave it any thought, was simply a game for rich kids or those who weren't good enough to play the "major" sports. Yet, as I watched people play the game at Navarre Field on my way to the athletic grounds, something about it intrigued me, and that was the ball itself. I started hiding outside the courts and stealing tennis balls that occasionally came flying over the fence. I'd take the balls home and save them—not with the idea of later selling them or actually playing the game, but just to have a collection in my room. The idea of owning something almost-new from a game played mostly by the apparently affluent was a symbolic thing for a youngster who was poor: that was about as close as I thought I would come to being rich.

One day, however, I was caught in my petty thievery by Lawrence Alto, the city's tennis director. Alto is a pleasant, soft-spoken man, but he told me quite frankly: "You've been stealing these tennis balls, so I'm going to give you a choice. You can either learn how to play tennis or you can go to jail." Neither option was appealing, but Alto handled the situation in such a warm way—with almost a twinkle in his eyes as he talked—that he made me really want to join him out on the tennis court. In fact, within ten minutes he was teaching me how to play (with a used racket from his office) and I was running after that doggone ball, trying to hit it over the net.

Within a week or two I was hooked on a game that would shape the rest of my life. After having played only team sports, I loved the one-on-one aspect of tennis—the fact that you don't have to rely on teammates to pull you through and that your rewards are based solely upon your own individual efforts. As I got into competitive play, I also began to realize that though I had to save up even to buy a pack of chewing gum, nothing could stop me—in tennis—if I had the talent and the drive to succeed. Yet it took a long while before I gained this same perspective about life in general. I had proud, loving, intelligent parents, but I still felt that my economic background made me a lesser human being.

Then I got lucky again. When I was thirteen, Hap Funk, a local newspaper writer, raised money to send me to an important junior tournament in River Forest, Illinois, where I stayed in a private home with two older players named Tut Bartzen and Glenn Bassett. Although they were two of the big stars in the tournament, I noticed how courteous and friendly they were to everybody, and I liked the fact they were in many ways just like me—at mealtime they ate whatever they could reach. But what impressed me the most was that they talked about going to college. Nobody in my family had ever gone beyond high school, and most of my friends never mentioned furthering their education; we basically wanted to graduate from the ninth grade so we could get a job on the railroad and maybe buy ourselves a car one day. That's as far as my horizon stretched—until I heard Bartzen and Bassett talk about college as they reached for another helping of potatoes.

In high school, I played football and basketball and summer baseball with reasonable success, but the only contact I had with any college was a tennis coach, Dr. Allen B. Stowe, at Kalamazoo College, 140 miles away. He saw me win the state high-school tournament three years in a row and he "recruited" me to Kalamazoo, where I ended up playing No. 1 on his team. More important, I found an academic interest that fascinated me—psychology—and I began to think about the future and how I might make a career out of that and tennis (in an era when teaching pros had most of the jobs that were available in the sport).

I actually started giving lessons after my junior year in high school, when I spent the summer in Kalamazoo, site of the junior nationals. I first taught three children from one family in exchange for tennis clothes, and then some other parents saw me at work and offered to pay me to teach their children. I came back to Kalamazoo every summer after that (I slept on a cot in a ball closet in the Stowe Stadium tower) and I worked my way through college teaching the game—on the sly, of course, since I was an amateur. I was so booked up with lessons that I even had to skip my graduation ceremonies.

After graduating in 1951, I became a teaching pro at the Toledo (Ohio) Tennis Club and began working on a graduate degree in psychology. I

Here I am (far right) with my three younger brothers and our first coach, Lawrence Alto, in the early 1940s.

also played in a few pro tournaments as they then existed, teaming up with Pancho Gonzales once in doubles, and losing in the first round of the World Pro Championships to Bobby Riggs, Frank Kovacs, and Frank Sedgeman. Then, in 1955, after spending two winters teaching at the El Mirador Hotel in Palm Springs, I decided to move out to California year-round to get close to the modern serve-and-volley game.

Again, I was busy on several fronts: giving tennis lessons, teaching school, working on my Ph.D. in psychology, and helping Jack Kramer promote several of his pro events. Jack, who's the greatest player I've ever seen, hired me full-time in 1959 and I began going on the road to promote his four-man tour. Our second stop was in Seattle in the middle of winter and there were only about seventy-five people in the stands shortly before the first match. I felt so sorry for the players—the best pros in the game at that time—that I went out on the sidewalk, in a rainstorm, and started shouting, "Tennis here tonight!" to anybody who happened to come along.

When Kramer built his tennis club on the Palos Verdes Peninsula, near Los Angeles, in 1965, I became the head pro and I organized the junior program with a lot of important support from Kramer, Jeanne Austin, and Del Little. This is where Tracy Austin got her start, hitting balls against a cinder-block wall when she was two, taking group lessons at three, and advancing from there.

For nearly six years at the Jack Kramer Tennis Club, I gave private lessons from 7 A.M. to 7 P.M., six days a week, and then spent most evenings working with the juniors. Everything I earned I poured into instructional films, while plotting my dream of a "tennis college" where I could (1) teach a large number of people on a sustained basis over a two- to five-day period, (2) work with teaching pros to improve their effectiveness, and (3) conduct tennis research. (The dream became reality in 1974, when I started my tennis complex at Coto de Caza in Trabuco Canyon, California, about seventy miles south of Los Angeles. The scientific, computerized study of tennis being done at the Sports Research Center at Coto helps substantiate what I say in this book about hitting a tennis ball.)

While I was getting started in my career, my younger brothers—Paul, Dan, and Ralph—all followed me on to college, and then found successful careers of their own. And I trace it all back to a tennis coach who caught me stealing tennis balls and who had the sensitivity to turn a bad situation into a propitious experience. Lawrence Alto knew I was athletic and competitive—he said he had seen me around, carrying a football or my baseball glove—so instead of dismissing me with a retaliatory move, he had the patience to take all my energy and channel it in the right direction. He simply gave me a chance to get close to the tennis ball where it counted—on the tennis court.

Throughout my own career as an instructor and coach, the memory of Alto's action has always made it easy for me to work hard at trying to give every youngster I teach a good attitude about tennis. I know that the approach I take, something I say or do, or perhaps just one tiny incident may trigger an interest in tennis that profoundly affects the youngster's life. In addition, my own teaching philosophy has drawn considerably on what I remember best about Alto in the years that we worked together before I went into high school: his sensitivity, his patience, and his constant encouragement. You couldn't be around him without the feeling that he really cared about you as an individual. You knew he could look past your weaknesses and say, "This kid's a product of certain things and he has a few problem areas but I'm going to tackle these problems and stick with him." He didn't talk a lot, but he tried to say little things that would give you a lift. During a tournament he'd point out a player and say, "You know, I think you can beat that guy." I'd watch the guy hit and I'd think: "Who's the coach kidding? I'll never be able to beat that guy." But it got me to thinking—positively—and usually he would be right.

Alto also taught me some lasting lessons about having respect for the individual worth of each person learning the game. Some tennis coaches today are actually spoiled a bit, working in an environment in which their sport is now well-accepted as a tough, demanding game—even by pros in other sports. Yet back in the 1930s and '40s, a tennis coach was generally saddled with the less-gifted athletes—often the ones who were told by a coach in another sport, "Why don't you try tennis, kid"—and it was his job to motivate them to stay with the game and to learn how to play up to their potential. Alto and (later) my terrific high-school coach, Fielding Tambling, knew I was taking a lot of ribbing from some of my football pals, but they both asked only that I put in a hard, honest effort and give the sport a fair shake.

That's the spirit I want to convey in this book. I hope you have the same objective—as a paid instructor, as a school or playground coach, or, especially, as an involved parent—as you help to pass this sport along to the next generation of tennis enthusiasts. Let's strive to teach youngsters in such a way that no matter what their natural athletic ability and regardless of how well they ultimately play, they gain a warm affection for tennis, exasperating as it might be to master. The game can give them a ton of enjoyment and self-satisfaction as they go through life, and expose them to opportunities they never dreamed about—if only somebody will help give them the right kind of start.

My goal is to help you keep that chain going as you work with children and teenagers to get the most out of the tennis-playing experience, whether their goal is simply to have fun with their friends or to strive for the top levels of junior tournament play—and beyond. I'm addressing teaching pros, coaches, school instructors, and recreation professionals, but my primary focus in this book is on parents. You may not know much about the game and you may play like a hacker, but I'm convinced you can teach your children the most important fundamentals of the game if you have a positive outlook and a willingness to do your homework. In fact, you may discover that you can help provide them with the advanced techniques and tactics needed in junior competition.

Obviously, I disagree with people who want to "insulate" youngsters from their parents when it comes to learning a sport. These critics argue that parents shouldn't even watch their youngsters take tennis lessons, let alone try to teach them the game—that everything should be entrusted to a "trained" instructor. Certainly it's true that teaching your child any sport is not a piece of cake; it can be a volatile undertaking, depending on the approach you take and the relationship the two of you have already established around home. However, the immediate and long-range benefits are potentially so great that I want you never to underestimate the influential and enjoyable role you can play as your child's tennis instructor. After all, most of the philosophies that make a good parent are the same basic ingredients needed to make a good instructor in any sport. And to abdicate involvement because someone says "only teachers can teach" is to miss a great opportunity with your child. If you have a keen interest in being a part of his—or her—development, then assert yourself; don't automatically leave this responsibility to others. (By the way, to avoid any hint of sexism, I'll hereafter alternate the gender of pronouns from chapter to chapter when I refer to your child; in chapters where the child is "he," I'll use "she" for references to the parent or coach, and vice versa.)

My belief has always been that if you have an optimistic attitude and a desire to make the game fun, you can't have a bad time teaching your child tennis. The point may come when you realize it's time to pass along the teaching responsibility to somebody else, but up until then you certainly should have the confidence that you can help your child grow in many ways—as a tennis player and as a person. The time you spend together, even if it's just an hour or two a week, can yield numerous rewards for both of you—on and off the court—regardless of how well he eventually plays the game. For example:

• Tennis may be the first sport your child attempts to learn. The approach you use as a teacher and the philosophy you try to instill in him as an athlete can generate a confidence and an enthusiasm for trying numerous other sports.

• This one-on-one relationship will provide important insights into your child's personality, such as his learning ability, his competitive drive, his ability to handle stress, and his willingness to work toward goals he has set. This knowledge—and what you learn about teaching—can lay the groundwork for a similar rapport in other sports you might pursue together, such as skiing, golf, soccer, or baseball. Whatever the activity, a good teacher will always draw on the same fundamentals.

• Sharing a tennis-learning experience will help draw the two of you closer together and should enhance your relationship. Successful teaching relies on two-way communication, and this can build a bridge for contact that will be treasured as your child grows older and communication in other areas of life becomes more difficult.

• You'll save a lot of money by doing the teaching yourself (especially if your child wants instruction more than once a week), and the two of you will gain far more than if someone else does the teaching. For example, in a relaxed parent-child teaching situation, you can gear the instruction to your child's interest span—which may be only ten or fifteen minutes—whereas a hired teaching pro is under pressure to fill up all the lesson time you've paid for, even if no real learning continues to take place. In addition, even though a lot of pros really care about their students, they have to make a living and may not have much time for casual contact with your child after or between lessons ("Sorry, I've got another lesson now—see you next week").

Only after you get involved as an instructor will you actually discover just how rich an experience it can be—whether it's the enhanced interaction you have with your child (not just on the court but around home), the positive changes that you see occurring in his personality, or the thrill that comes when he finally starts to hit the ball right, the way you've been teaching. You'll be telling yourself, "Hey, that's it!" and he'll be all pumped up with those pleasing sensations that accompany a solid hit. The satisfactions certainly don't end there, for the challenge always exists to solve problems together, to try new strokes, and to keep striving for improvement—no matter how many years you work together.

Since most of you parents have never had any formal training as tennis instructors or coaches, I've organized my approach into a teaching system that can take you from your first day out on the court all the way through advanced junior play—without slighting those of you who are already active in the field and who are always looking for methods that might improve your effectiveness.

I'll describe the many aspects of how to actually teach tennis to children, whether they be natural athletes or the kind who seem to continually trip over lines on the court as they run to hit the ball. An early chapter talks about how to prepare yourself for a teaching role, such as by establishing a teaching philosophy, knowing the different ways youngsters learn a motor skill, and planning the first lesson.

To help once you're out on the court, I include advice on how to keep motivation levels high throughout a lesson; how to cope with typical problems that arise in a teaching situation; how to communicate technique to youngsters of different ages and ability levels; how to conduct drills that provide fun, action, and stroking challenge; how to maintain discipline and foster your child's respect for etiquette; and how to develop an independent youngster who can think for himself as he works to improve his strokes. Later chapters cover what to teach (and why) in the way of strokes and match-play tactics.

Everything is here—to help take youngsters as far as their talent and competitive hunger will allow, whether it's a club title in Pismo Beach or the finals at Wimbledon. Just as in my first book, *Vic Braden's Tennis for the Future*, I use photo sequences and evaluative drills to show you how each stroke should be executed, how to focus on key checkpoints, and how you can detect—and correct—problem areas.

One warning here: Don't look for "kids' strokes" in this book. My approach is to have children strive to learn exactly the same stroking patterns as adults, though on a level with their strength and coordination. I've found that even four- and five-year-olds are capable of grasping the fundamentals of sound strokes that will help them a lifetime—which is a nice motivation for anybody who teaches the game. Moreover, by teaching adult strokes to little kids—without trying to go beyond their ability level—you never have to apologize to them later. You're not using a comedown teaching system in which a youngster is taught to swing a certain way for years and then is told, "Okay, now that you're older and stronger, we'll start swinging like this"—and a totally new motion is introduced. That's unfair to the child, who has thus, in effect, wasted his early years of learning the game and must now try to break grooved "muscle-memory" patterns. (In using the term "muscle-memory"—which I discuss more fully in chapter 9—I'm not giving a physiological definition, since researchers are still arguing the issue; I'm only saying that tennis players have a tendency to repeat whatever pattern they've been following on a particular stroke. By the way, the glossary explains many tennis and teaching terms that may be unfamiliar, including some of the slang expressions I like to use.)

In case your child progresses so well under your guidance that at some point you realize he deserves the expert attention of a trained coach or a teaching pro (or in case you decide not to teach your child tennis but you want to do the right thing for him), the final chapter discusses how to find a qualified instructor and how you can remain actively involved in the whole process. Even if you don't know much about tennis, there are many things you can contribute as an interested parent by getting involved. In fact, learning about tennis can be a growth experience for both you and your child when you take the attitude "Let's explore this game together." Instead of thinking of tennis as "only a game," parents should learn about it, as they learn math and reading—because the virtues of the game are often underappreciated. Tennis can provide a fantastic experience for kids and, as I've seen in my own life, it has a carry-over value many times greater than just the game itself.

Whatever role you play—and I hope it's as an instructor for your child or for other children—just set out to *make the game fun* in the learning and in the playing. For I've found that when that happens, everything else tends to fall into place: your approach as an instructor, your attitude as a parent, and your child's eagerness to master a good tennis game. As an instructor, you are in a position to affect important attitudinal and physical changes in a youngster. That's a great challenge, and I want to help you take advantage of the opportunity. I know what a fantastic feeling it is for me to see little kids who I started out years ago—grown up now, married, still playing the game, and teaching their own children tennis. It's wonderful to know that I have contributed something to generations to come.

I just hate to see kids miss out on tennis as they are growing up. That's why it's always a bittersweet feeling for me when I meet adults who are just learning the game in their thirties, forties, or fifties and who tell me: "You know, Vic, this is a terrific game; I never knew it could be so much fun. I just wish the heck I had learned to play when I was a kid."

2/Getting Your Child Started

A major controversy in the area of junior tennis involves when to start a youngster in tennis, and with what kind of approach.

Personally, I love to start kids swinging at tennis balls as soon as they show an interest in learning how to play, even if they're only three or four years old. My intention is not to rush them into competition or to identify early talent that I might develop into future champions, but to introduce children in a positive way to a game they can enjoy now—and for a lifetime. If a youngster's willing, I'll start right in on the proper stroking patterns with a "keep-it-fun" yet organized approach. The important thing is that I underplay any competitive aspects and the sense of having to "look good," while emphasizing the joy of running about the court with a giant racket and trying to hit that fuzzy yellow ball. I know that if I get a youngster hooked on the game, her competitive urge will surface naturally—when she's ready to start playing matches with her friends and, perhaps eventually, to enter junior tournaments.

Some teaching pros feel that eight or nine is the optimum age to learn tennis in an organized fashion, and they discourage parents from starting children any earlier. Many of these pros argue that they're little more than baby-sitters when they try to give lessons to children under eight—and thus they refuse to do so (which is another reason why you ought to consider doing the teaching yourself if you have a young child). They insist, for example, that five- or six-year-olds lack the necessary coordination and strength to learn proper strokes and that this will discourage their interest in tennis—perhaps forever. Another fear is that youngsters who start competing too early will be "burned out" by the time they are teenagers and will leave the sport just as they are entering their prime.

Here are some arguments to counter these charges and suspicions:

The little four-year-old girl at the net may be the youngest volleyer in Chinese history, according to coaches from the All-China Sports Federation. When I conducted junior clinics in China in 1979, I told the coaches it would be fun to have some youngsters who were five or six years old participate. The coaches were shocked. "You won't find a player this young in China," they told me. "We like to start them when they're about eleven." After I returned home, my interpreter wrote to say, "I decided to teach my daughter, age of 8, to play tennis exactly as what you taught me."

For one thing, adults tend to underestimate the physical and mental capabilities of children aged four to six. I've found that tennis is a physical comedown for most little kids compared to the way they play in the backyard and at the playground. Hitting a ball 78 feet from baseline to baseline on a tennis court is not really the problem—it's control, and control bedevils a beginner of any age. And regarding kids' mental capacity, I've found that six-year-olds, after six months of weekly lessons, can repeat over a hundred facts about technique and strategy; very often they know more about the game than parents who have played for years.

Second, if you're wondering what a first-grader can actually get out of tennis lessons, I can think of many benefits: she's relating to an adult; she learns to listen, to follow directions, and observe the rules of good behavior; she's discovering the fun of hitting a ball with a racket and what it means to learn a physical skill; she's gaining some confidence in what her body can do; she's developing an interest in sports and physical activity; and she's learning a game the big kids play. (Additional socializing benefits can be gained from learning in a group situation, as I describe later.) Sure, she may not be ready to play a match yet—and may not be for a year or maybe longer, after she acquires sufficient control and coordination to hit a serve. But in the meantime there are numerous ways to keep her motivated and competitively challenged, as we'll see.

Tracy Austin was as intent on the ball here, at age three, as she was about fourteen years later, in 1980, when she became the No. 1 player in women's tennis.

Third, I've found that youngsters don't get turned off to tennis by an early start itself, but rather by overzealous adults—parents and coaches alike—who "encourage" them to get into local competition or tournament play before they are actually ready, and who have a need to build champions. These adults exert so much pressure on kids to win and to devote their lives to the sport that eventually a youngster's only recourse is simply to quit.

Fourth, another advantage in starting children as soon as they show an interest is that they don't have many of the hang-ups afflicting teenagers and adults. For example, it's much easier for youngsters to focus their attention on the ball—instead of on their opponent. If they're properly motivated, they really zero in on what you're trying to teach; they're not thinking about problems away from the court, or about who's watching. Thus, with proper instruction, children can begin to "groove" sound strokes at a faster rate, before typical bad habits are ingrained by a haphazard approach to learning. In turn, they learn to play better at an earlier age and are able to have more fun for that many more years. Think about all the adults who are struggling to learn the game today because they never took it up or were never exposed to it as youngsters. Many of them work up the courage to attend my tennis college—and they have a great time discovering that they aren't as uncoordinated as they thought—but they often admit that they lived in fear and trepidation about putting themselves on display as beginning players at the age of thirty-five or fifty.

Fifth, even if a little kid gives up tennis, a lot of what she gains from learning the sport should help her in other sports and activities as she grows older—especially her experiences in working with an adult instructor, in training her body for a specific physical activity, and in striving toward specific goals she might have set.

Finally, tennis itself—as a sport—is a great activity for kids. Why deny them the chance to get involved in an enjoyable growth experience if it's something they want to pursue, whatever their age?

The key question for me has always been: What kind of attitude does a youngster develop for the sport? If you can introduce your child to tennis in such a way that she always has a good feeling about the game—even if she leaves it for something else—then you've done a great job. She'll always remember the fun she had playing tennis, and the chances are good that she'll eventually try to find the racket she stashed away in her closet. Meanwhile, those youngsters who get a positive start at an early age and who keep playing will nearly always develop a nice feeling about the sport—and about themselves. By the time they're eleven or twelve, they're confident out on the court and they're so good they can handle most adults. More important, they seem to slide through puberty because they have an activity that provides self-confidence, motivation, exercise, and experience they can fall back on. I've found that as kids play more tennis and gain some proficiency, they carry themselves better, they have a good body image, and they always have something they can talk about with anybody they meet.

Although the "recommended" starting age appears to be getting lower, the fact remains that most children learn to play tennis around the age of ten. That's when most parents feel their kids have the strength and coordination to play the game properly (that is, by getting involved in match-play competition) and—not incidentally—an appreciation for how much each lesson is costing, if a teaching pro is involved. A great many youngsters are even in junior high school before they're exposed to the sport, normally during physical-education classes.

Unfortunately, the ages from about ten to twelve can be the toughest time—*psychologically*—for starting out in a sport like tennis, as I'll describe in chapter 4. Not that I want to discourage you if your child is already this age or older and suddenly wants to learn to play, or if you've waited until now to give her lessons. Just be ready for an oftentimes tougher, more delicate job of teaching and parenting.

Determine Your Child's Interest

In starting a youngster out, at any age, the crucial determinant must be *the child's interest level*, not the ambitions or hesitations of the parents. Thus, if your five-year-old is driving you crazy because she keeps asking you to let her hit tennis balls against the garage door, why hold her back? She may be ready for some basic instruction. But if your twelve-year-old isn't a bit interested in going out on the court—despite your cajoling—she shouldn't be forced, because she isn't ready to learn.

This doesn't mean you must sit by idly, waiting for your child to express a desire to learn the game. Some kids never really visualize themselves playing tennis until their parents happen to introduce them to the sport. Many youngsters will even claim to hate sports and not even want to try, but if you can talk them into hitting a few balls and they have some "success experiences"—anything that gives them an emotional lift—they nearly always want to come back. I think kids have a natural instinct to be physically active and a strong drive to want to achieve something in a sport. So I believe you should help bring to the surface whatever interest there might be for tennis by exposing your child to the game and offering her the opportunity to hit balls. If she doesn't want to go beyond that—into organized teaching sessions, or even just to rally with you once a week—that's her choice and you should back off. At least you've met your responsibility as a parent by alerting her to a lifetime sport she could enjoy one day.

One way to develop your child's interest is to watch a televised match together or actually attend a pro tournament—if she's agreeable. You can use this opportunity to explain how the game is played, to identify the different strokes, and to point out some basics about strategy so that she can begin to appreciate what's involved. Afterward, you can casually ask questions, such as, "How did you like this game?" and "What seemed to be the most fun?" If her curiosity seems to be piqued, then you should offer her the chance to hit balls. Another method is to bring your child along when you go to play a match, providing you can reserve a court for a specified length of time and there's a nearby play area to keep her happily occupied if she tires of watching. Save about five minutes at the end of your session and let her come onto the court to hit some balls herself. Very often, you'll find that she's begging for ten minutes the next time, and pretty soon you're reserving a court just to work on her game.

I remember how little Trey Lewis would just hang around the Kramer club every week while her folks played tennis. When I pointed this out to her father, he asked me what I suggested he do.

"Hit some with her," I said.

"But she's only seven years old," he replied. A leading psychologist in Los Angeles, he certainly wanted the best for his daughter, but he just didn't feel tennis was quite yet appropriate.

"Just give her a chance to hit and you'll see," I said. So they started setting aside some time each week, and pretty soon Trey asked to join my junior group. Today she's on the pro circuit.

Out on the Court the First Time

Once a youngster expresses an interest in learning how to play, I like to get her into organized teaching sessions as soon as possible, for I've found that *within ten hits* an untutored beginner is already picking up bad habits that have a tendency to stay in her game. Yet before taking this step, you must first determine if your child likes the basic premise of the game by actually taking her out on the court to hit. All this requires is:

• Any old racket, though ideally one that complements her size and strength.

• An available court, or any large cement or asphalt surface.

• As many practice balls as possible, since the more you have, the more continuous you can keep the action and the less time you waste retrieving them. Even soft old balls are fine, since they bounce lower and are thus easier to control as you "feed" them to your child to hit.

• Your patience, enthusiasm, and constant encouragement.

In starting out, I know that kids want action *right now*, so I get them swinging at the ball as soon as possible. First I demonstrate the forehand stroke, then I guide their arm through a couple of practice swings, and then I back off about 15 or 20 feet from the baseline and start "feeding" them balls.

Unless you have excellent racket control, just toss the ball to your child

When starting out, stand about halfway between the service line and the net as you "feed" balls to your child on the baseline. Accuracy is what counts, whether you toss the ball underhand or gently throw it overhand at a speed that won't put pressure on the child. It will take some practice to master the method that works best for you. Take along a laundry basket and plenty of balls — plus something to elevate the basket so that you don't have to lean down every two or three swings.

with an underhand motion so that it bounces once and comes up to around her waist level, allowing her plenty of time to take her swing. A good cue is to have her start her forward swing as the ball bounces. Don't worry about form or where the ball goes; just let her whack away and see if she likes that feeling—infrequent as it might be—of striking the ball. It's crucial that you come prepared with a flexible "reward system," for if she misses practically every ball and rarely gets it over the net when she does make contact, you can still keep her enthusiasm high by praising her for such things as her effort, for trying the right swing, and for really concentrating on the ball. There's always *something* you can find good in what she's doing.

If your child is obviously enjoying herself after five or ten minutes this first day, you might want to move right into some basic stroking fundamentals. So be prepared. But if you notice her interest starting to wane or her frustration mounting because of her inability to hit the ball—despite your encouragement—then simply call it quits for the day, and have a low-keyed talk about what *she* wants to do about the game.

Does she want to give it another try next week? (Perhaps a lighter racket that has a smaller grip would help.) Or would she rather just skip it and try something else? After all, some kids just don't thrill to the idea of hitting tennis balls or playing an individual sport; they'd much rather spend their free time reading a good book or shooting baskets with friends. Other kids, from a growth-and-development standpoint, are just not ready when you first try to introduce them to the game. If you sense this is true with your child, don't worry—just wait six months or even a year or two, until she seems better prepared to start again or until she brings it up herself. You might even raise the question one day by saying: "Remember when we tried tennis when you were six? I think one reason you didn't like the game was because you didn't have the strength. But now you're eight and I think you might bomb the ball." If she still says no—that she's tried it once and she's not really interested in the game—then don't force the issue.

Should You Do the Teaching?

Given an interest by your child in trying an organized approach to learning the proper strokes, together you must now decide upon an instructor—either yourself or an outside person.

Despite the advantages I've pointed out that can be gained by teaching your child tennis, I'm certainly not advocating that every parent should try it. All I ask is that you be honest with yourself—and your child. You want her to learn the game, but you may already realize that you don't have the motivation, the proper temperament, or perhaps the necessary rapport with her to handle the instruction yourself. For example, some of you parents may have a few important questions to ask me:

I can't even communicate with my kid at home—how can I hope to relate to her on the tennis court?

My feeling is that teaching your child tennis gives you a perfect opening and a fresh environment in which to establish some rapport and mutual understanding. Even though communication may have broken down around home, you may discover that you can communicate with your child in an activity at a "neutral site," such as the tennis court.

What if I don't have the kind of personality you ask me to project during a lesson? Suppose I have some weaknesses in the way I describe things?

Fine. As a parent/instructor, you're going to make mistakes right along with your child. You may not have a "coaching" personality, but you can start with what talent you have and it can be improved—providing you have an open mind and can learn from your mistakes. You're asking your child to start from scratch as a player, so why should you have the right to avoid testing your ability as a teacher? If your answer is, "That's the way I've been and I'm never going to be able to change," then how can you fairly ask your child to mature, to change, to be flexible, and to "give it a try, you'll like it"? It's also important to remember that although coaches are stereotyped as rah-rah personalities, some of the most successful ones are basically calm, quiet people.

Keep in mind that if you're weak in certain areas, you can work to improve these traits as you go from lesson to lesson. Teaching the game and learning how to play should both be growth experiences. In making the decision about whether to teach or not, think about the following questions so that you have a better understanding of the responsibilities involved.

• Are your motives sincere? If your dream is to have a rich and famous tennis player in the family, and you intend to give your child every possible advantage toward that end, this pressure—subtle as it might be—can cause irreparable harm if she doesn't wholeheartedly share in your dream. Basically, your attitude should simply be that you're going to accept your child as she is right now, listen carefully to her comments, and then take her beyond that point. You should have some idea of her natural athletic ability, of course, but try to avoid preconceived ideas about how far that talent should take her.

• Can you go out and have fun with your child in leisure activities? Do you enjoy being with her, just the two of you? You owe it to her to have experiences together that are positive, so if the two of you can't have a good time on the tennis court, you shouldn't be the instructor.

• Are you an emotional person, to the point that it might interfere with the on-court learning atmosphere or disrupt the parent-child relationship once you return home?

• Can you communicate with your child on *her* level?

• Are you prepared to put in the time required—not just in giving a lesson (which could last from fifteen minutes to an hour or more), but in preparing for and critiquing each lesson, and studying how the game should be played?

• Can you be consistent in setting aside time for lessons? An eager youngster is going to look forward to each lesson and will be disappointed and hurt if you frequently cancel out.

• If there are other kids in the family, can you offer them your involvement and interest in something *they* want to do?

• Are you eager to investigate the game of tennis and to start seeking answers to whatever may puzzle you and your child about technique and strategy—by reading books, by talking with knowledgeable players and instructors, and by watching the pros play?

If you indeed decide you want to try teaching your child, the first thing you should ask yourself—obviously—is: *Does she want this relationship with me?* If you already play the game, simply ask her, "Would you like me to teach you how to play?" Or, if you are a newcomer, you might say, "Would you like to learn with me?" Chances are she will go along with your suggestion, but if she says, "I think I'd rather take lessons at the club," you should certainly honor that request. (Chapter 16 will discuss how to go about selecting a teaching pro.)

Playing Ability versus Teaching Potential

A typical reaction at this point might be: "Hey, Vic I play like a hacker—what makes you think I can teach my kid good strokes?" My answer would be: You might be a crummy tennis player, but you may have the ability to be a great instructor, so never let the falsehoods about teaching tennis hold you back. Good teaching doesn't stem from your ability to hit a backhand down the line, but rather from how well you can perceive the fundamentals and communicate what you perceive, while keeping your child eager to learn and improve.

Certainly it can help to have excellent strokes and a keen knowledge of the game—*if* you have the other qualities of a good teacher—yet some of the best coaches on my tennis-college staff are not experienced tournament players. They can interpret what others are doing wrong and communicate the possible corrections, but they really have to struggle to effect desired changes in their own strokes.

Moreover, a number of the teaching pros and prospective instructors who go through my tennis academy are still learning to play the game themselves. Some advanced players will look at them and tell me, "Jeez, I can beat that guy—how can he possibly coach?" But I've found that these relative beginners often have a keener interest in learning the correct principles of good strokes than many tournament players. The latter have a tendency to ignore careful analysis of what actually happens during a stroke. Even some of the leading pros promulgate misconceptions about how the ball should be hit, because they play by reflex—and very often what they teach is not actually how they play, only how they *think* they play. For example, pros will often talk about how they "roll the racket over the ball" to impart topspin, when in reality this is a physical impossibility (as I explain later).

Another reason excellent players are often less effective as instructors is that most of them took to the game naturally, and thus they have trouble patiently sticking with a youngster through difficult learning situations. They can't understand why she is unable to execute a basic technique that came easily to them when they were starting out. Conversely, adults who can't play the game very well are often more successful as teachers because they better understand a youngster who is having trouble learning to hit the ball properly and are more complimentary of good effort.

So forget the fact that you haven't been invited to Wimbledon. With the help of this book, you can still make valuable contributions as an instructor. You can learn the five or six key checkpoints on a specific stroke and you can train your eyes to see whether your child is actually swinging correctly. Then the key becomes your ability to communicate and motivate.

Still, whatever your playing ability or experience in the game, you have three obligations as an instructor:

First, you must recognize your limitations as a player and just be yourself. Be honest with your child and say: "I'm not a great player, but I've been studying how to play the game right. Here's how the pros make this stroke. Now let's see if you can swing like them."

Second, learn perfect form for the sake of demonstration, even if you can't actually hit a moving ball this way under pressure.

Third, let your child know that you're going to be working on your own strokes right along with her. Why should she be the only one motivated to improve?

Private versus Group Lessons

In deciding to teach your child tennis by taking an organized, week-to-week approach, you should consider the relative merits of working with her alone or with several of her friends or siblings. Although this book concentrates mostly on the one-on-one approach, your child may actually learn better in a small group.

For example, in a private lesson, all the instructor's attention focuses on one youngster, but when the child makes error after error after error, it's easy for the teacher to fall into the trap of saying, "Wrong . . . wrong . . . wrong." Pretty soon, the chemistry deteriorates and the coach and the student find they can't laugh, they can't interact. In a group situation, this youngster would realize that the tennis court is a "mistake center" for everyone. She won't feel so discouraged if she sees other kids struggling to learn the game and doing things wrong too.

A youngster who always takes private lessons will sometimes say: "I just can't do it. I've tried in this lesson, I've worked hard, but I just can't do it right." The instructor might answer, "Don't worry, it will come," but it takes a confident kid to believe that. In a group setting, she would have already taken heart by watching other kids facing disappointments before they improved.

Also, though your child is learning an individual sport, she gains many of the socializing benefits of a team sport by working with a group: she learns to interact with other kids, to follow directions, and to wait her turn to hit; she discovers how youngsters can motivate one another to improve; and she shares the learning experience. When kids are taught in a group they're exposed to identical instructions, so it's easier for them to help one another in practice sessions between lessons.

Even if you opt for a relaxed, one-on-one teaching situation, I think it's a good idea for your child to be also involved in group lessons with another instructor at some point. Not only will she benefit from the different perspective and environment, but you'll gain some insights by watching how another instructor works on the youngster's strokes and relates to her.

Of course, you may decide that your child is better suited to private lessons. She may be a loner or a particularly shy kid who's inhibited about learning in front of other children. Perhaps she's too easily distracted by commotion and is unable to concentrate on learning the task at hand when other kids are around. Or it just may be that she has an insatiable curiosity, a long attention span, and a tremendous need for individual attention. A youngster like this often can't function as well in a group situation, where she must share the instructor's attention; she needs a direct, one-on-one relationship with the teacher because there are a lot of things on her mind she wants to discuss. Given this opportunity in a private lesson, she will take all the comments and information from the instructor and then work hard to assimilate what she has been told.

I mentioned that one advantage of a group lesson for some youngsters is that they feel encouraged when they see other kids having trouble with the game, because they know they're not alone. Yet I've also seen kids who are terribly frustrated in a group situation when they can't measure up to their peers; they can't hack this loss of face and they start feigning illnesses and injuries in order to avoid lessons. Some kids will even tell you flat out, "I don't want to be in there because they're all good players and I'm terrible." So in that regard, a private lesson can be much less threatening.

Now that you know about getting your child started—when to do so, how to assess her interest level, whether you should do the teaching, and how to choose between group and private lessons—you're ready to consider what goes into teaching well.

3/Crucial Elements of Good Teaching

Since most parent/instructors lack formal training in physical education or child psychology, they tend to go out onto the tennis court relying basically on their prior experiences learning sports and raising children. Perhaps this seat-of-the-pants approach can work effectively for you, but my assumption is that you'll need some help to meet the challenges of working with your child and getting the most out of this experience. There are responsibilities inherent in good teaching that go well beyond merely knowing the tennis strokes, and I'll explore these basic concepts in this chapter.

I want to stress throughout this book—as a goal for instructors and learners alike—the importance of developing an independent-thinking player. To me, effective teaching boils down to doing all you can to help your child teach himself. He must want to learn tennis for himself—not simply to please his parents, or to meet the expectations of his peers. Just attending a series of lessons won't make him a good player unless he's taking the information you're giving him and trying to put it into practice. This means, of course, that good teaching also depends on how well you establish and maintain an atmosphere—on and off the court—in which your child *enjoys* the game of tennis and is eager to keep learning.

All good teachers want to motivate students to think for themselves as they learn rather than look to an authority figure who is somehow going to solve all their problems. Yet I find that most adult tennis players don't really understand what they're doing—or what they're supposed to be doing—when they hit a tennis ball. An instructor has no doubt told them, "Swing this way"—and that's how they're going to play, without any further investigation into what is actually happening during a particular stroke. The problem is not only instructors who are comfortable with dependent, nonchallenging students, but students themselves who are content to have the game spoon-fed in weekly thirty-minute doses.

I hope you adopt a different approach. Instead of fostering dependent thinking by your child (which is the tendency if you say, "Do it because I said so"), strive to create a self-motivated player who continually digs for his own interpretation of how a stroke should *feel* when properly executed—and who can eventually thrive without a parent or coach around. You might even explain to your child what the learning process is truly all about, on and off the tennis court: it's gathering information, analyzing it, keeping what's important and discarding the waste before moving on to the next stage. This process is hardly ever explained to kids when they go into a learning situation—all they know is that they're supposed to accumulate information, not necessarily understand it. So warn your child that not everything you tell him is going to be meaningful to him; some of it will seem confusing or may even be wrong at times. Let him know that you want him to tell you when he feels that way, and that you also want him to realize that it's going to be his responsibility to figure out what works best for him.

In other words, your goal from the very beginning should be to avoid a "traditional" teacher-student relationship. And your child should know from the beginning that this is the goal for both of you—he's not simply on the receiving end of a parent-child feeder system.

In certain areas of your child's life, it's clear that in the role of authority figure you'll call most of the shots, but out on the tennis court a different philosophy should prevail. What you want to have your child understand is this: "I'm teaching you tennis, but you're the one who counts out here. I'm going to study this game and give you the best information I can, and I'm going to help you think about your strokes. But what I'm really after is to have you learn to be your own teacher so you teach yourself. I'll be the happiest person alive if you can do that. And you'll be happy too, because you'll know that you're doing it on your own."

Respect Your Child as an Individual

When you have respect for the sport and respect for your child as a unique individual, then all the good aspects of teaching tennis tend to fall into place: you weigh everything in terms of what you think is best for your child; you try to make each lesson fun; you keep your tone positive; you communicate; you ask for feedback; and you always evaluate the teaching relationship in terms of your child's growth and enjoyment.

My psychological training has helped me enormously as a tennis instructor, by emphasizing how crucial it is to be concerned about my students' needs, not my own. This is vital at any level of teaching, but particularly with youngsters, because every child perceives himself as the center of his universe. The whole world revolves around him and there's nothing more important than: "What will *I* be doing today? Where am *I* going? Who will *I* be seeing?" Obviously, you'll want to help him grow out of any unhealthy absorption in himself, but this doesn't negate the responsibility you have—as his parent and as his instructor—to enter his world instead of always expecting him to relate to yours.

Before you go out to teach, you need to step back and get perspective on your child so that you can objectively see him as a student and respect him as such. Observe him, try to sense what he's going through, communicate with him on his own level, and appreciate him on that level so that you'll be able to judge him in terms of questions such as: Who is this kid I'm teaching? How well do I really know him? Why is he playing tennis? What does he hope to gain from the sport? What fears does he have? What are his concerns?

This responsibility you have to relate to your child's universe might seem axiomatic, but I've found that many parents and professional instructors alike tend to forget that kids really do have rights—rights that are violated all the time. For example, a parent might talk to her child about maturing and learning to respect another person's feelings, yet then make no real effort of her own to understand what the child is really feeling about something. Or, the parent will take it upon herself to answer questions that have been directed to the child by another adult. I've had parents ask me to assess their child's tennis game, but as I ask a few preliminary questions, I can already tell where much of the problem lies. I'll ask the son, "How do you perform in tournaments when the pressure's on?" and the parent will say, "He chokes a lot." Then I'll address the boy again: "Well, how about your serve? How's it working?" Once again the parent interjects: "He's having a lot of trouble with his serve—that's why I brought him here." The parent is talking as if the child weren't there and the child may become dependent on such treatment; pretty soon he'll be waiting for his parent to answer all questions asked of him.

Another important teaching quality is your ability to recognize and appreciate individual differences. It's an old cliché, but certainly true, that no two kids are alike, and you need to respect this fact when dealing with your own child. Don't compare him with his siblings or his friends on the street, nor judge him by any standards other than what he is capable of doing according to his own physical strength, agility, quickness, coordination, ability to concentrate, and other mental processes. In this regard, firsthand observation is especially valuable before your child gets into tennis. A lot of parents are so busy raising and supporting a family that they aren't as aware of their child's rate of growth and development as they think they are. They're not really listening to the child or looking at him, and the result very often is shock at what the child can—or can't—actually do and comprehend on the tennis court.

Develop a Learning Theory

I find that many instructors—parents and professionals alike—are quickly scared off when I start talking about "learning theory." Others tell me, "I already know how my kid learns—I'm his mother." This may be true in your case, but if you haven't really studied how your child learns best and considered the various approaches you might try, then you're not teaching—you're just hoping that he manages to learn by hitting a lot of tennis balls. That may seem a bit harsh, but if you lack such knowledge about how your child learns or if you don't seek feedback to insure that he's actually understanding what you're teaching, you may be structuring a series of lessons based upon a system that doesn't work. Even most teaching pros lack a flexible teaching system that can adjust to how an individual happens to learn best. These pros can tell a student, "Here's how I teach," but they can rarely add, "And here's how I think you learn," so that the two systems match up. As a result, the student is out of luck if he can't learn effectively the way the pro teaches. Many youngsters even begin to think they themselves are at fault.

Three Methods of Learning: Touch, Visual, and Auditory

One important measure of a sharp tennis instructor is how quickly she discovers whether a person learns best through *kinesthesis,* through *visual* receptors, or through *auditory* receptors. Everybody (except some physically handicapped students) learns in part through each of these methods, but the instructor must decide where to place the emphasis.

• Kinesthetic learners rely on touch, on feeling what they're supposed to do on the swing. They need to have a physical awareness of what different parts of their body are doing during the swing. For example, if they can actually feel the stroking pattern recreated with their fingers, they will generally associate that correct sensation when they take a swing. So you might draw the proper stroke pattern on paper, cover it with something that has a distinct texture, such as velvet or felt, pin it to a wall or a tennis-court fence at a level appropriate to your child's height, and then have him run his fingers over the pattern, tracing the stroke you seek. Another approach is to take his arm and guide it through the appropriate motion as he swings. A true kinesthetic learner will tell you

Here's a mother trying a combined teaching approach. She has taped a yardstick to her son's shoulders and is turning them so he can feel what it means to rotate the shoulders to initiate the forehand backswing (and the take-back on the serve). Seeing the yard-stick move gives the child a visual idea of what should be happening to his shoulders. Verbal instructions also help, especially when the child responds well to the auditory teaching approach.

something like, "Oh, I get what you mean," and will start doing it himself. Whenever possible, have him do these drills first with his eyes open and then with them closed.

Even on the first day of lessons, a kinesthetic learner is often able to make the gross stroking movements pretty well. He still may have trouble actually hitting the ball—since other abilities must be coordinated—but he'll have some success experiences when you say, "Show me how to do it," and he goes through the overall stroking motion of the swing. Eventually this learning ability will pay off, for once a kinesthetic learner has a feel for the desired movement, he tends to stick with it, practicing it over and over again until generally he falls into a nice hitting groove.

• Unfortunately, kinesthesis draws nearly a complete blank with some youngsters. They have to learn by visualizing what it is they're supposed to do, first by seeing the desired movement demonstrated, and then by imagining themselves doing the movement. So instead of trying to guide such kids through the stroke, just show them what it looks like and they'll try to do it themselves. I find that kids who are imitators very often make the fastest learning gains, once they get the visual pattern fixed squarely

The instructor should stand in front of his student to demonstrate technique, enabling the student to imitate from the proper perspective. Shown here is the loop backswing on the forehand, before the racket drops.

in their head. "They steal with their eyes," as one soccer coach put it. In fact, most of the champions I've known have been great imitators. If you're at a party with pro tennis players and they start to imitate other players on the tour, you'll see they don't miss. They can mimic perfectly all the little hitches, quirks, and mannerisms—and the other players can quickly recognize them.

So watch your child carefully, because he may tip you off early that he's a natural visual learner. If you attend a pro tennis match together, notice whether he copies the gestures and movements of a particular player when you get back out on the tennis court. If he's suddenly hitching his shorts a certain way and walking about the court with a particular gait, then you'll know he has some class and he's on his way to becoming a good player. Just don't get upset if you learn that he's also imitating your own peculiar mannerisms behind your back! When you spot him doing that, have a good laugh and then get a fun exchange going by mocking *his* idiosyncrasies.

• Auditory learners are those who learn best by hearing instructions. They need to have everything carefully explained, and they must be able to discuss it with their instructor before they can clearly understand what they should do. I like to have these youngsters close their eyes as I talk so they can concentrate completely on what I'm saying. I also have them repeat the instructions aloud, which enables them to hear them again and lets me know how well they understand what I've been saying.

• Researchers are working hard to find out exactly what's happening inside a person who's learning tennis. For example, what triggers the brain to send the impulses that make him move in a particular way? What causes him to be more of a visual learner than a kinesthetic learner? But until there's some proven data on exactly what the coding system for learning is, you should cover all three systems with your child if you're not sure which is most effective.

Anticipate Which Learning Method Will Work Best

Before you even go out on the court, there are a number of ways you can determine how your child might learn best.

First of all, just ask him how he likes to learn a new skill and how he likes to be taught (assuming here that he's already in school and has played at least one other sport). You don't want to overwhelm him with questions, but your questions might include: "How do you want me to act when I give you a lesson? Do you want me to be tough on you or easygoing? Should I talk softly or shout a lot or just speak normally, the way I do around home? Do you get upset when I start yelling at you, or does that make you work harder and concentrate better? Do you want me to demonstrate everything so that you can see what you're supposed to do? Should I take your hand and show you how the stroke should feel? Maybe I should just talk about it?" Most kids (and adults as well) have never been asked these questions, but I find they'll try to answer them—if you ask.

Second, try to keep such questions in mind as you observe your child in everyday life, and as you recall how he has acquired skills in the past. For example, if he is involved in activities such as swimming lessons, basketball, or gymnastics, firsthand observation and a talk with his instructor will provide important insights. Your child's schoolteachers should also be able to offer important observations about his learning abilities.

Third, although it's true that how *you* learn best might be totally ineffective with your own child, it's helpful to think about what you've always wanted in the way of instruction when learning a new skill. This self-questioning will remind you to be more understanding of what your child is going through and it should help you avoid the negative aspects of the learning experience that drove you crazy as a student. For instance, what kind of person were you? Did you want reassurance and encouragement from the instructor, or did you need somebody to take a hard line and always challenge you in some way? Did you want somebody throwing a tremendous amount of printed matter at you, or did you prefer just to have everything explained? Did you want to get it all in one day, or were you ineffective when swamped with too much information?

Fourth, use a teaching system that can be adjusted to how your child learns best. Remember that every youngster learns in a slightly different way—even those in the same family. How an older brother learns best may only alienate or confuse his younger sister.

Create the Right Atmosphere for Learning

Once you get involved in teaching tennis, you'll find that nearly everything you do depends upon how well you can encourage your child to stay with the game and to strive for the proper strokes. I know that if I had to choose between having all the technical knowledge about the game or having the ability to motivate people to run through a brick wall, I would opt for the latter. A properly motivated youngster will love the game so much that he'll find the right techniques, somehow and somewhere. But if he lacks the motivation to learn—to become an independent-thinking player—then you can give him all the knowledge possible and he will seldom do anything with it.

Ideally, in developing an atmosphere for learning, you may only need to tap the interest your child already has—if he's eager to learn and wants your instruction. In other cases, you might have to provide the spark. Or, the eagerness might be there initially, but may need to be properly guided through the frustrating stage when he discovers that the game is not as easy to learn—or to play well—as he might have envisioned. It may also be that your child is willing to learn tennis, but in starting out doesn't see the possibilities down the road or the fun he's going to have as you go along. Whatever the situation, the following sections discuss several important approaches involved in good teaching.

Emphasize the Here-and-Now

When I run across the kids who were in my junior program at the Kramer club in the 1960s, I'm stuck by how clearly they still remember their initial experiences in the game. They reminisce about the nicknames I used to give them and the games we used to play in practice—not about the junior tournaments they eventually won. Instead of bringing up their Wimbledon experiences, they remember the bus trips we used to take to places like Bakersfield and Glendora to play other junior groups. They had to wrestle with this crazy game and they worked their tails off, but they have lasting memories of how much *fun* they had.

Try to have this same perspective when you start out with your own youngster. The good times for both of you are not two or three years away, when he's good enough to play matches; they're going to start with the first lesson and continue through all the ups and downs the two of you have in the quest for good strokes. Strive to have your child develop an attitude that the whole process of learning tennis is something to look forward to, and that the rewards are not only going to come from better strokes but from the self-satisfaction of having worked hard at something for thirty or forty-five minutes.

My goal is to establish an attitude in youngsters that each lesson is going to be a fun and rewarding experience, that what they learn *today* is going to be meaningful to them *today*, not just in six months or whatever. I tell them at the beginning that learning tennis doesn't always come easily, because I don't want them to later feel that I've misled them by my enthusiasm. Yet I also emphasize how much fun they're going to have learning the fundamentals, and that once they master them, the game is going to be even more enjoyable.

Never let your child think that it's going to take a long time for him to amount to anything on the tennis court. Kids need the here and now, even when they're old enough to appreciate the long-term benefits that result from working hard today on proper strokes. You can talk to them about how important it is to lay a solid foundation, but it's much more meaningful to say, "If you can do this correctly, you're going to see changes right away in how you hit the ball." A youngster needs to laugh and have a good time today—when he's six, eight, or ten years old—and not just in a distant, undetermined future. That's why I hate parents to think, "Start them early in tennis if you want to develop a champion." What they really should be saying is, "Start your child now—if he's eager—because your nights are going to be better, knowing your child had fun playing tennis today."

Here's another warning: If you've instilled the sort of atmosphere in your family in which your kids feel a pressure to excel in everything that they do in order to meet your high expectations, weigh very carefully how this can influence the lessons you give—and face the fact that you might be trying to "live through your child." Are you enjoying each day? That's the key. If you've learned how to enjoy each day, you're going to help guarantee that your child will too, on and off the tennis court. But if you're basically dwelling on the past and living for your child's future, then you're probably trying to put him into a mold: you're actually thinking ten or fifteen years down the road and not about today.

Stress the "Mistake Center" Concept

Instructors everywhere have to fight the tendency to make their students fearful of making mistakes while learning the game. Such fear spoils much of the fun people should have on the court and it can make them hide from their mistakes, instead of recognizing them and going to work on solutions. That's why I feel it's crucial to let your child know that the tennis court is a *mistake center* for everybody. I like to tell kids: "You're going to make a lot of mistakes out here, but don't worry about them. Even adults miss the ball a lot; their shots go everywhere. So your mistakes aren't going to bother me, because I make them too. I have all the patience in the world, and I know that when you make mistakes, we can find the cures and you'll just keep getting better." With older kids, I try to get across the philosophy that successful players—and people who are successful in life—are not those who fail to make mistakes, since everybody makes them, but those who recognize their mistakes and try to make the necessary corrections. In fact, I've always felt that trying to find solutions that work is one of the most enjoyable parts of the game.

If you want your child not to be inhibited by his mistakes, you must back up your philosophy by showing that you can be relaxed about those mistakes and can still laugh when nothing much is going right. One way to do this is to learn to talk in a voice that's happy and supportive, projecting the spirit that "making corrections is fun." Your vocabulary while giving lessons and the tone of your voice should be exemplary; there's no place in tennis for an instructor who swears at a youngster or who uses abusive language of any sort.

By remaining refreshingly optimistic and by proceeding with patience and a positive approach, you will establish a learning climate in which your child understands that you have a genuine desire to help. He'll welcome your corrections because he knows your intent is not to hurt him in any way but to offer solutions that may help him hit the ball better and thus have more fun. In doing so, you will help overcome the tendency— of both the instructor and the student—to confuse constructive criticism with hostility. Adults fall into this trap by projecting a negative mood as they correct their children ("You're still doing it wrong—aren't you listening?"). This in turn leads children to react stubbornly rather than cooperatively when their mistakes are pointed out.

Easing your child's fear of making mistakes will also serve to reduce anxiety levels on the court, which in turn will set a better atmosphere for learning. You want your child to get into an easy rhythmical pattern as he hits the ball, but this rhythm can easily be disrupted by the fear of "looking bad." Most children are actually no different from adults in their apprehensions about tennis. At the tennis college, I constantly see adults who are proven successes in life, yet who are terrified that on the court they're going to embarrass themselves in front of everybody, and that people will laugh if they miss the ball. These fears may stem from human nature and show up at most any age—we all want to look good when doing something—yet I've found that many kids seem to pick them up early in life from their parents. So be sensitive to this fearfulness in your own child, and try to break that parent-child cycle if you notice it surfacing.

Balance Positive Reinforcement and Constructive Criticism

My teaching style has always stressed positive reinforcement, constant encouragement, and a lot of enthusiasm. But I never discount the importance of constructive criticism when working on a student's technique. I know that every time he swings incorrectly he just reinforces what he is doing wrong. Most of the desired techniques in tennis do not come naturally but must be learned, so if a student is making the same mistake over and over again, the problem is unlikely to correct itself without a conscious effort.

What you want to strive for here is a balance in how you critique your child's technique, so that he feels pretty good about himself even as he's being corrected. As I learned from my old coach Lawrence Alto: if you have to deck an individual with some tough criticism, make sure you give him a lot of support underneath. A youngster needs to know what he's doing wrong on a particular stroke in order to work toward the proper sensation. But he also needs to know what he's doing right—not only to help him "groove" the stroke, but to keep his morale high.

You can't expect your child to stay involved in the learning process if, in your desire to have him learn good strokes, you fall into the trap of repeatedly saying, "That's wrong." A steady stream of negatives will only undermine learning and eventually lead to a disgust with the game. Instead, remember to *balance good and bad points* when correcting technique and to be positive while working toward the proper strokes. Let's say your child can rotate his body and get his racket back properly on the backswing (part one of a good forehand or backhand), and can then lower the racket to about knee level as he steps into the ball (part two). If you've clearly described the overall stroke, you could tell your child: "You've got the backswing right and you've got the drop. Now you just need the forward movement into the ball, which is part three. You still have a tendency to pull across instead of moving low-to-high, so let's work on that. But I can't believe it—you're already zeroing in on a perfect swing. That's fantastic!"

Provide specific input like this whenever possible. For instance, instead of simply saying, "Your swing wasn't right," try to point out, "You had a nice backswing, but then you started forward too late, and that's why the ball went off to the right." Kids get a much clearer picture of what they're doing wrong when you give them a very clear picture of what they're doing right, and vice versa. Also, by always drawing such comparisons, you won't mislead your child into thinking he can do no wrong, or into feeling he's an absolute klutz. He will develop a trust in what you tell him.

In developing this concept of balance in your teaching, an important step is to consider carefully various aspects that might please you about your child's performance during a lesson. I find that many parent/ instructors fail to give this much thought. They simply put all their hooks into one criterion—how well their youngster keeps the ball in play—and thus establish an unrealistic situation in which most beginners can't win. Afterward, you'll hear such parents mumble to themselves, "That wasn't much of a lesson—he couldn't even hit the ball." Yet if they had asked themselves beforehand, "Okay, now what are my objectives? What will I be happy with?" they could go into the lesson with many ways to praise their child, no matter how much trouble he had hitting the ball. For example, did he try hard? Did he have a nice attitude? Was he willing to experiment? Did he keep trying to work on the correct stroking pattern, regardless of where he hit the ball?

Be Honest with Your Child
From the very start of your tennis relationship with your child, you should have him know that you think so much of him that you're always going to be honest and not lie to him about anything, even if it means having to get tough with him about his strokes. When you tell him, "I'm always going to let you know what's right about your game—and what's wrong," you can always look at him and know that you're doing the fair thing all the way along. Besides, he will learn to see right through false praise.

When I was a psychologist in the Los Angeles school system, a second-grade teacher divided her students into different reading levels and gave each group a name—the Blue Jays, the Robins, and the Cardinals. I remember asking one child, "What group are you in?" and he said, "I'm with the dummies." He didn't fall for that stuff, even at the age of seven, and neither will your own child out on the tennis court. Once he gets around other kids, you won't be able to put much over on him because he'll know exactly how good he is. He'll start telling you, "Alan can do it, and Allison can do it, but I can't do it." So if you keep telling him that he's great, but he knows he can't beat anybody, you're stretching your credibility as an instructor. It's also important to remember how quickly most kids tune in on phoniness. For example, if you're not really paying attention as you give a lesson and you just pass out the praises in a monotone—"Great . . . that's the way to go . . . nice swing"—then your child is going to sense a snow job. Suddenly he may blurt out, "You're always saying 'Good try,' but I'm missing every ball." This is where your attitude and the trust you've established are very important. If you say "Great effort!" only when your child *really* works hard, you're not lying and it will show, even if he fails to hit the ball.

You can actually turn a bad situation into a good one by sitting down with your child after a frustrating lesson and talking to him honestly about your feelings. I sometimes make my best gains by leveling with a youngster: "We couldn't put it together today, I'm afraid. Either I wasn't saying it right, or you weren't listening carefully, or maybe it was a little bit of both. But what I really liked is that you never quit trying and I didn't quit trying. We worked hard. I just want you to know how much I appreciate your effort, and I guarantee you we're not going to have two of these days in a row."

It's also important for your child to realize that the relationship is an open exchange—that he can always tell you the truth about anything that may be bothering him. Let him know that you're never going to hold back and that you expect the same thing from him, because you want to grow and improve yourself.

The Benefits of a Positive Approach

I've always stressed that learning to play a better game of tennis should be fun, not drudgery, from the first day on. When a youngster enjoys his tennis lessons, he has more incentive to improve his strokes, and this eventually increases his chances of winning matches, which leads to more enjoyment, self-satisfaction, and motivation. So a beautiful circle is created. I'm not saying that you have to crack jokes repeatedly or that your child constantly must be laughing and in high spirits in order to learn a skill like tennis. After all, there are serious youngsters who respond favorably to an equally no-nonsense instructor. Yet I've found that the learning environment is always enhanced when kids are relaxed and enjoying themselves, and the instructor is setting the right tenor.

Once you get into teaching, I'm sure you'll find that your ability to keep your child motivated is just as important as the fundamentals you dispense week after week. Ideally, if your relationship grows as it should, the major part of his motivation will come from within. But in reality, a lot of kids aren't self-motivators, and they need constant reinforcement from adults. Most all top athletes will tell you that there were times when they

I used to hold Tracy Austin up at the net to volley when she was about three, but it wasn't long before she stood up there herself and whacked at the ball. She certainly thought tennis was fun, and worked very hard, too.

wanted to quit, but one or both of their parents found some way to remotivate them.

Following are some concepts to keep in mind as you try to nurture your child's motivation by emphasizing a positive approach:

• As you give a lesson, many pleasant thoughts will cross your mind that can inspire your child, but it's common to get so wrapped up in teaching that you forget to say them. So continually remind yourself about one of my golden rules: *If you're thinking something nice about your child, say it.* He needs to feel good about himself now, as well as later when you return home. I've also noticed how some instructors come off the court and tell another adult, "Did you see how well that kid hit the ball?" but fail to give this same kind of praise to the youngster himself. He's the one who should hear it.

• When a child ceases to find rewards and reinforcement in a lesson or during practice, the learning process will stop. You must develop an effective "reward system." In using that term, I don't mean money ("Practice this for ten minutes and I'll give you a quarter"), but comments or facial expressions you make that give your child an attitudinal or emotional lift. Kids really respond to an adult who encourages them with kindness, warmth, and enthusiasm about what they're trying to accomplish.

• The instructor who can enhance a youngster's self-esteem and make him feel at ease during the lesson will normally speed up the learning process. At any learning age, the student's need to protect his self-image is great. So plan on meeting with psychological resistance if your child deems your criticism harsh or unfair. The dignity of the human being doesn't start at a particular age, nor is it suspended during a tennis lesson. You're violating your child's rights if you use degrading language ("Look at the ball, dummy," or "You must be stupid—I've told you the same thing ten times") or if you downgrade by comparison: "Your friends understand this—why can't you get it?" Body language and facial expressions also play a big role. Some parents don't have to say one word, but the look on their face tells a youngster, "You're a failure."

Communicating as an Instructor

You'll discover soon enough that effective communication on the tennis court requires much more than your ability to explain the proper strokes. A number of factors are involved, including your preparation, the confidence you have in what you're trying to teach, the enthusiasm in your voice, and your willingness to seek feedback from your child.

First of all, realize that communicating tennis technique is not easy and rarely comes naturally. You may be an effective communicator on one level—such as in your profession—but if you're not prepared when you get on the tennis court with your child, you're going to find yourself groping for meaningful things to say. So to begin with, have an overview of the game clearly in mind at all times—as dictated by the physical realities of the court dimensions, the net, the ball, and the racket. These realities (which are detailed in chapter 9) are going to determine the stroking patterns you try to teach your child. Then learn *why* a particular stroke is important and *why* your child should try to execute this stroke in a specific fashion. One reason parent/instructors often have trouble explaining tennis technique is that they really don't understand the rationale behind what they're trying to teach. Thus they find themselves stumbling through a lesson or inclined to take a dogmatic, do-it-this-way-because-I-know-it's-right approach.

Study in advance what you're going to teach your child in a particular lesson, and then actually rehearse aloud how you are going to describe whatever stroke or strokes you are tackling. Know the stroke well enough so that you can describe it from different viewpoints should your child not understand a particular approach or explanation; an alternate perspective can also deepen his understanding of the stroke. Always ask yourself, "Will my youngster know what this means?" As motor-learning expert Diane Ross stresses: "When you say something, does it mean the same thing to your student as you intend it to mean?" After playing tennis or studying the game, you may feel quite comfortable with common tennis terms and key aspects of stroking techniques, but the terminology can initially draw a blank with children (although you'll be amazed at how fast most kids catch on). Thus, you must be ready to explain—and often demonstrate—every new term and phrase that comes up in your teaching dialogue, and you must repeatedly ask your child if he understands precisely what you are saying. Those of you already in the teaching field who have only given lessons to adults will find that your grown-up lingo sometimes has to go out the window when you start to teach children. Not that you have to talk down to them, but you must speak a language they can understand, on their own level.

Another crucial element is the manner in which you talk to your child and explain things during a lesson. Boredom is easily detected from the speaking voice, so make sure yours is full of enthusiasm. In fact, remember that the tenor of the entire lesson can be set by the tone of your voice. Little kids react to a monotone just like adults—by tuning out or falling asleep—and they are equally motivated by verbal exuberance. I've watched instructors talking in a monotonous tone, "Racket back, step, swing . . . Racket back, step, swing," and I know their students are thinking, "Boy, I've got to dump this game fast." Then you have the instructors who treat everything matter-of-factly during the lesson and who have no real eagerness in their voice. They'll say, "Fine, Johnny, now we'll go on to this," and poor Johnny is so put off by the starched-shirt approach he's almost afraid to express any emotion. That's why I love to hear an instructor who really sounds like he's enjoying the experience.

Teaching Is a Two-Way Street

Your child's growth in tennis and as a person is going to be greatly enhanced when you make every effort to involve him in the learning process—by seeking out feedback, encouraging his questions, and inviting him to challenge anything you're teaching that doesn't make sense. Only then will you know just how clearly he understands what you're saying and what might be bothering him about the game or your teaching methods. He may never become a great tennis player, but what he learns about communicating and verbalizing will help him enormously in school and everyday life.

Unfortunately, a number of parents who try to teach their children a sport fail to realize the importance of encouraging a free exchange of ideas and feelings. Instead, these parents try to establish a sense that they're the last word in the game by simply taking a youngster out on the court and saying: "Okay, I want you to keep quiet and pay attention. Just do what I say and concentrate on hitting the ball." By turning communication into a one-way street, they never really know what's going through the child's head and eventually the learning process reaches a dead end.

One of the clearest memories I have of my first coach, Lawrence Alto, is that he never seemed to overreact. There was a calmness about him that I liked, and when I went to him with questions he would give me a chance to get my ideas across in a nice way. He looked at things and analyzed them in such a way that I could really think about what I was saying. As a teenager I had other coaches who cared about me, but we'd often end up in a war because the prevailing attitude then was "I'm the coach and you bow to the coach." I never had those wars with Alto. Thus I always found myself going back to him because I had the feeling he would really listen and discuss something with me—much as he might disagree. Alto really knew that teaching was a two-way street.

Seek Out Feedback

I forgot my own advice about feedback one time a number of years ago, and I still remember the embarrassment it caused me. I was giving a series of lessons to a group of secretaries, and one of them just couldn't contact the ball, no matter what I said. She was very nice and she really wanted to hit the ball, but she whiffed it every time. I started out saying, "Betty, you're not watching the ball," and then I tried everything I could to direct her attention to the ball: "Try to watch the seams come into focus. . . . See if you can read the lettering." Nothing worked.

The next week, Betty didn't show up, and I felt bad because I thought she had given up on the sport. But she came to the third lesson, and I couldn't believe it—she hit every ball that came her way.

I told her: "Betty, I don't get it; that's absolutely terrific. What happened?"

"Well, I don't want to hurt your feelings or anything," she said, "but I was gone on a little trip and I took a lesson from a real pro. He solved my problem."

"What was the problem?" I asked, dying to know what this other pro had seen that I hadn't seen.

"You won't believe this," she said, "but I wasn't watching the ball. Just a little thing like that."

Obviously, I had gone through all my tricks and either she hadn't heard a word I said or it simply never registered. I realized it was my fault for not asking if she understood what we were trying to work on. For all I know, she was just wondering when I was going to explain how to keep score.

In working with your child on his technique, your goal is to provide the correct cue systems that will enable him to teach himself how to play. He should know why he wants to swing a particular way and what it feels like when he does it right. Only by asking questions—and listening carefully to the answers—will you know if he is accurately absorbing what you have been saying. Be persistent and keep dissecting his answers ("Yes, that's right, but this is wrong—here's what I mean") until he has a clear fix on what he is trying to achieve. This constant verbalization will also help him recognize what's wrong and what's right in his stroke, and thus what he must do to improve on his own. When he's continually answering questions such as "How did that hit feel?" and "Did you know the minute you hit the ball that it was going over the net?" he will become attuned to the sensations he must cultivate in trying to groove proper strokes. And he will learn to concentrate on what he's doing—and striving to do—as he takes a particular stroke.

Constantly explore what your child feels as he hits the ball. Let him know that you're going to count on him to give you some important clues about what he senses he's doing wrong or what he can't do. For example, if you can get him to say, "I'm not very confident on this stroke because I feel like I'm going to turn the racket face too early," you can now respond to this problem. Instead of always setting up the problem yourself and supplying the answer, you can ask him to analyze what he thinks went wrong on a particular shot, and pretty soon he'll be providing his own criticism and reinforcement (for instance, "I stepped into the ball right, but the racket face was tilted back too much"). Here again, by soliciting feedback you're encouraging a teaching environment in which your child is not afraid to recognize his mistakes or to admit confusion. By all means, remember to thank your child for raising these issues, especially in the early going when he may be reticent to do so. You might say: "Good for you, I really like it when you speak up like that. Now you've given me a chance to work on some possible solutions."

As you gain experience in teaching, you should try to determine how many times your child needs to describe a particular technique himself before "learning extinction" sets in. Instructors often overlook this point, but it's a key issue to me because most repetition in teaching tends to come from the instructor, although it should come from the student as he verbalizes what he is trying to do.

Unfortunately, some instructors make it too easy for students to hide uncertainty. The teacher will ask a youngster, "Do you understand this?" and if he says, "Yeah," she will move on to something else. Instead of this approach, learn how to phrase questions that elicit a detailed response and not a simple yes or no. You might ask your child, "What are the things that you understand about this?" If he can't respond with a clear explanation, you can discuss the technique from another angle. Also, be sure to ask him directly: "What confuses you about this?"

Another virtue of feedback is that when you keep asking your child questions, you also expand your reward system, since he doesn't have to perform a physical task to please you. He may not be able to hit the ball properly, but he can still feel successful by giving you all the proper verbal responses. (Of course, as I discuss later, there may also be a frustration point to deal with if your child begins to say, "I *know* what I'm supposed to do, but I *can't* hit it.")

In seeking feedback, you'll probably find it productive to use a cooperative tone—"Let's talk about this"—instead of using a more threatening approach, like, "What have I told you so far about the backhand?"

Encourage Questions

Make sure your child knows that you're living off his questions and comments. Give him the confidence to ask you about whatever doesn't make sense, or is bothering him, or arouses his curiosity, and make it clear that you'll take the time to discuss it without criticizing him. I'm always telling my students, "I don't care how simple your questions might sound, you've got to ask me about anything you don't understand or is bugging you—because that's the only way I can help you." I emphasize this philosophy because I myself remember sitting in classrooms as a kid when the teacher wasn't making something clear. My fists would be clenched and I would be thinking: "Doggone it, I don't understand what she's saying. Why doesn't she explain it better?" But I was afraid to raise my hand and ask, because school to me was never a "mistake center" until I got into graduate school; there was always that fear of being ridiculed by the teacher or having the other kids snicker if you asked a "dumb" question.

Even if your child is smiling and looking pretty confident, his frustration may be mounting under the surface because he's unable to grasp a concept that you're teaching. To help him speak out in such a situation, you might suggest a one-line code that he can use, such as, "That doesn't make sense," or "I don't understand this," or "I've thought about this and it still doesn't make sense." This way he won't feel threatened, since you yourself have given him the words he might normally be afraid to use with you, and since he's only doing what you've encouraged him to do.

Also, take a tip from learning theorists who claim that you will generate more responses from a child by saying, "I need your questions," instead of asking, "Do you have any questions?"

Solicit Challenge

The crucial point here is to have your child understand that you're not running a dictatorship on the court. He should feel free to challenge anything that you're trying to teach, and should know that he can do so without being hostile. Set it up by saying, "I want you to have an inquisitive mind, so if you disagree with anything I'm teaching, you can bring it up in a nice way and I'm not going to get mad." Have him know that you'll discuss his questions and that perhaps the two of you will investigate further, by researching several books or talking to a qualified teaching pro—all in the spirit of "Let's have fun and take a look at this concept together and we'll come up with the right answer in the end." Make it clear that if you together discover that you were wrong—or if your child supplies the evidence himself—you'll face up to the proof and make the appropriate correction. In fact, you want him to know that you really enjoy the chance to change and grow yourself and that you appreciate his contribution.

Establish Respect for the Lesson

I've always found it interesting that when I ask teenagers about the teachers they've enjoyed best, they never bring up those they pushed around. Instead, they usually recall the ones who were tough and who demanded good work—but who also generated an enormous amount of enthusiasm by making the subject fun and interesting. The students were motivated to read extra literature at home, they got involved in lively discussions, and in the end their work output was far greater than in other subjects. Such teachers were invariably well prepared and they loved their subject. If it was government, their attitude was "Government is interesting, darn it, and I'm going to show you why" (but there was never a spirit of pushing it down somebody's throat). Less-effective teachers would say: "I don't care—if you want to learn, fine. If you don't, you can just flunk." But the dedicated teacher would say, "I want you to learn as much as you can about government and I'm going to love the challenge of teaching you."

It's great to see tennis instructors who have the same kind of drive and dedication, for if you motivate your child properly and make it clear you care about him as a person, he's going to enjoy the learning process and feel good about working hard to acquire good strokes. Both elements—enjoyment and hard work—can and should be present in a healthy teaching relationship. Some instructors, for example, can get the fun pitch high but their students goof off and fail to make a concentrated effort on perfecting their strokes. Conversely, other instructors will work their students into the ground but you never see their students laughing during a lesson or hear them talking about the fun they had.

By taking the right approach—again, a balanced one—you'll find you can be relatively tough on your child by insisting on proper behavior, good hustle, and a concentration on the task at hand, yet still have him look forward to each lesson. Some kids, in fact, recognize that they're inherently lazy and that they need to be brought into line by a strong instructor who's dedicated to having them learn to play tennis. Other kids even discover they really like to be worked into a sweat, providing that they know why they are being driven so hard on a particular aspect of the game and that they can see tangible evidence of their improvement. I remember how parents at the Kramer club were often shocked to see how long and hard their children were willing to work at tennis. They'd tell me: "This is like a revelation to us. At home, our kid used to just sit in front of the television all afternoon. He'd never get off his tail to do anything physical."

There are several ways you can help instill a respect in your child for the lessons you are giving, and thus a greater motivation on his part to pursue sound tennis strokes. For one thing, lessons should be regarded as a privilege—not a right. They should be given on the basis that your child earns the chance to keep going out on the court with you. If he tries hard, then he earns them; that's all that you ask for. Of course, you don't want to be preachy and say, "This is a sacrifice I'm making for you," but you want your child to realize as you do that lessons are a two-way street: "I'm giving up a lot of my personal time, but I want you to know that I love doing it because it's fun to teach you the game." When I coach I like to tell kids: "If there's just an effort from you, I'm the happiest guy alive. I care about your strokes—don't get me wrong—but I care much more about effort. But I guarantee you, if there's no effort, I'm going to get mad and you're going to know it. I won't be getting mad because I don't love you, but because you think so little of yourself that you don't work hard. I know on those days that you're going to go home and feel bad even about looking at yourself in the mirror, because you didn't put out. So let's don't let that happen." Tracy Austin really understood that philosophy. When it was time to work her tail off, she never backed off. Even after she started getting good, she still kept showing up for the free classes I gave to kids every Saturday. Most of these kids were just starting out and could barely get the ball in play, but Tracy simply focused on her own strokes and never horsed around.

Second, instill respect for the lesson by establishing that there's a shared obligation in the relationship the two of you have, based on the premise that you're a teacher, not a servant. One essential step is that before you give the first lesson, your child must understand that both of you will retrieve balls. I've watched parents who give lessons collect all the balls while their youngster just sits on the bench or practices serves. It's as though the kid is saying, "When you've picked up all my shots, we can start again." I hate to see this happen, for not only does the youngster fail to learn about responsibility, he gains a distorted idea of the instructor's role. At the same time, one of your obligations is to make time count for your child. Don't tolerate unproductive moments or let yourself use "busy time" to fill out the lesson. Instead, look for ways to squeeze everything possible out of each situation by taking the attitude that you never want any shot to be wasted. For example, your child might complain, "I don't want to run for that volley—it's going out anyway." But so what? He can still stretch for the ball, try to keep his racket head up, and then punch the shot deep.

Third, make it clear that there's a commitment required from both of you. I always let kids know that we are going to work hard together but we are also going to have a lot of fun at the same time—and it's all going to pay off in good tennis. I really mean it when I tell a youngster: "You stick with me and together there's no way you're ever going to be a bad tennis player. I'm not going to let you be bad, and you're not going to keep yourself from improving, because it would hurt our pride too much. We'll hang in there and work things out together. So I can tell you right now—you're going to be good."

Fourth, your own attitude toward each lesson is crucial. A good starting point is to think about the atmosphere you want to maintain during a lesson and about ways that you might keep it fun and fast-moving.

Remember, it's going to be your time too, and the lesson should be enjoyable for both of you. I never find it hard to motivate youngsters, because they always seem to pick up on my enthusiasm for teaching and my love of the game. They know I'm really engrossed in the lesson and I think they respect that; I doubt if many of them even think about horsing around or not applying themselves. A good way to keep this motivation high for both of you is to stress the here-and-now, as suggested earlier, for this forces you to make each lesson as enjoyable and productive as possible. Before a ball is even hit you can establish or reestablish an attitude that will give the lesson quite a boost. For example, let your child know beforehand how eager you are to get out on the court. You might say: "I'm really looking forward to hitting today. I thought about you last night and I had this idea about your forehand that I'm positive will work." You can also talk to him about the fun he's going to have during the lesson and how he's going to enjoy running all over the court and working on his strokes—emphasizing that this is going to make him faster and stronger each week. Meanwhile, you'll have set up drills that will indeed enable him to have fun today and you'll reward him right then for the effort and progress he shows. Don't push the payoff into the future with an attitude that says, "If you keep working hard on these strokes, you're going to be a good player in a year or two."

Fifth, learn to sense when learning extinction is taking place and put a stop to it. Keep the action moving, but know when your child needs a breather—physically or psychologically. If I find that I'm pushing too hard on a particular drill or that a student is starting to lose interest, I'll say: "Okay, take two minutes to get a drink and catch your breath. Then we'll start up again." If you try to force kids to stay interested in a lesson or if you don't know when to ease off, you simply hurt your effectiveness and spoil the fun they should be having. Let your child know that you're always willing to give him a needed break during the lesson and you'll find it much easier to keep him hustling and his learning motivation high. Similarly, if you're working on a stroke like the serve or backhand and your child starts complaining, "Jeez, I can't even hit the ball," or "Do I have to keep serving?" it could be time to jump to something else fast. But if he's keenly interested and zeroed in on what you're teaching, even though he may not be hitting the ball well, then I would stick with the stroke for as long as learning seems to be taking place.

Your Rewards as a Teacher

Your basic objective as a coach is to teach somebody to play better, at the fastest possible rate for that individual—and for that person to enjoy the learning experience. If you can always keep this goal in mind as you work with your child, and pursue it with flexibility and understanding, you can look in the mirror and pat yourself on the back a thousand times.

Along the way, don't count on your child to verbally recognize how hard you're working, the time you're spending, or the patience you're showing on the tennis court. If he's like most kids, he won't sit back and think about the benefits derived from learning tennis from one of his parents. Nor will he recognize the long-term value of all you're trying to nurture, such as what it means to work hard toward certain goals, to listen carefully and evaluate what he's being told, and to formulate his answers and his questions in a logical way while relating to an adult. Right now he's primarily going to reward you through his physical actions—by his hustle, his effort to swing correctly, and his manners. If you go into the relationship with the right approach, this should be all the gratification you need.

If you have this perspective, no money in the world can buy you such rare moments as those you'll share with your child in the tennis experience. The funny things he says will make you laugh and he'll stun you with his unique little insights into the game. And you'll never forget the look of self-satisfaction on his face as he starts to hit the ball in bounds, then begins to hit target areas, and eventually beats you for the first time—with the strokes and tactics you've taught him.

4/The Challenges of Teaching Children

ONCE you've decided to get involved as your child's tennis instructor, an important part of your preparation is to anticipate potential trouble areas and what you'll do when problems arise as you give your lessons. I've found that when coaches are well prepared and they have a teaching system that incorporates the principles I've suggested in preceding chapters, they rarely have catastrophes out on the court. Their system takes care of any major problems before they ever have a chance to fester and erupt. As I've always said: "The best lessons don't have a lot of surprises—except for pleasant ones."

Your child is unique, growing and changing in different ways, and you won't be able to predict ahead of time all of the negative incidents that are likely to arise as you go along. But you can anticipate many of the one-liners every coach gets ("How do you know that's right?", for instance) and thereby have a better chance of dealing with them calmly and effectively. By reading this chapter with your child in mind, you should actually be able to mentally rehearse how you'll respond when certain situations arise—or when you see them coming.

Get Into Your Child's World

You're on your way to a rewarding experience as an instructor when you do all you can to get into your child's world—and not force her into yours. This approach will help you develop a close, understanding relationship, while leading the way to better tennis strokes. Following are some pointers for staying abreast of your child so you can relate to her on her level:

• *Do some thinking about your own experiences in learning sports as a youngster.* Try to recall the positive things instructors did that left a warm impression, and the negative aspects that drove you crazy—the instructor who never explained things carefully, the one who made you afraid to ask questions, the one who never asked you for feedback, and so on.

• *Ask a lot of questions about what your child is thinking instead of declaring what you think is going on inside her head.* For example, instead of saying, "You're not concentrating," and thus committing yourself to an attitude, ask her, "How's your concentration? Are you able to stay with what I'm teaching?" She might tell you, "I'm so confused I can't even hear you talk," and this will enable you to discuss the issue in an open, nonthreatening way. Or, let's say you find her daydreaming during the lesson. Instead of responding angrily, "You're daydreaming—stop that and start concentrating," go the other way and ask, "What are you daydreaming about?" She might tell you, "Well, I was thinking about gliders and airplanes," and a subsequent discussion could reveal that instead of learning how to volley, she'd rather learn how to build model airplanes.

• *Listen carefully to everything your child says, on and off the court.* I've found that kids will tell you who they are, how they feel, what they're worried about, what makes them happy, and what their fears and hopes are—providing they're encouraged to open up and that you stay tuned in. My experience has been that too often parents tend to ask the same questions over and over again because they're not really listening, while all the time their youngster is revealing exactly what they want to know. You need to be a good listener all the time, but this talent is especially crucial as your child comes into puberty, for kids at this age have grown more skilled at developing defense mechanisms and veiling cues. For example, a six-year-old will generally come right out and tell you her fears and dislikes about tennis, but a twelve-year-old may conceal her specific apprehension by saying, "I can't play sports," or "I'm not coordinated in anything." Thus you have to get at what she really means.

• *Try to stay in tune with your child's athletic interests.* Observe her level of interest in the sport. Is she reading about tennis in newspapers and magazines? Does she check out tennis books at the library? Pull things out conversationally: Does she have any heroes in tennis? Does she want to go to a tournament? What does she like best about the game and what bores her? What makes her feel good about the way she plays? Are there other sports she'd like to learn? Once you've raised these key questions, return to them only when you notice that her attitude toward tennis seems to be changing in some way. Meanwhile, stay on top of what's happening in tennis yourself, so that as she gets more involved the two of you can talk intelligently about the sport. Then you're unlikely to hear her say, "Oh, Dad, you don't know what's happening."

How to Start the Ten- to Twelve-Year-Old

As I mentioned earlier, the ages from about ten to twelve can be the toughest time to learn how to play tennis, and can present the instructor with an especially difficult teaching challenge. Kids this age have the strength and mental capacity to learn quickly, and they're bursting with energy, but oftentimes their bodies are changing rapidly, which leads to coordination problems out on the court. More important, they also have a lot of self-doubts, impatience, and a tendency to view themselves only in terms of "good" or "bad." A sixteen-year-old who's just starting may still have some of these problems, of course, but the chances are good that you can tell her: "Don't worry that you've never played tennis before. You don't have any bad habits to get rid of. All you have to do is take it slowly and you'll have this game wired." Most older teenagers can accept that, but it doesn't mean much to warn a typical ten- to twelve-year-old. You can tell her how tough it is to learn good strokes and that she must be patient, but as soon as she gets out onto the court she's saying, "Let's hit, let's hit." She's so anxious to "do it right" that if she can't get the ball to land in bounds quickly, you hear her start mumbling, "Jeez, stupid game."

Most youngsters can't afford to lose face at this age. They're acutely sensitive and concerned about how people see them. It's humiliating for them to miss the ball completely, and if they hit it over the fence, they look around to see who's snickering. These same fears carry over to when such adolescents start playing matches. If they're not too good and they keep losing, their defenses quickly surface and it doesn't take long before they give the game up because it kills them to be identified as losers. They may eventually return to tennis when they're feeling secure enough, but meanwhile they never forget the humiliation that once came from playing the game.

In viewing themselves at this age, most youngsters can see very few gray areas: they either look good playing tennis or they look lousy, they're either fat or they're skinny, they're attractive or unattractive, popular or unpopular. A typical statement would be, "I'm really good," or "I'm really crummy." This again is a big reason why I like to see kids get an earlier start in tennis, because the longer they live in our society, the more they become influenced and victimized by our emphasis on the importance of winning and "looking good" when playing a sport.

In addition, the pubescent child may have had negative experiences in other sports that she's bringing to tennis. She may even be afraid to feel excited about the sport because she doesn't want to have another disappointment. Or she'll come in with enthusiasm that lasts until she discovers she's not going to be able to play the game well overnight; then she starts working up defense mechanisms, such as "I didn't even want to come out here in the first place."

If you hope to counter these attitudes and to keep a youngster like this in the sport until she starts to have some self-motivating "success experiences" (which you can guarantee her will come if the two of you just hang in there together), you'll have to call on all the qualities of a good teacher: sensitivity, patience, the ability to give positive reinforcement. Be ready to throw in support mechanisms at every stage in the learning process, because it's too tough for a youngster this age to keep taking corrections without plenty of encouragement.

How to Deal with the Competitive Instinct

You will have to cope with your child's competitive instinct on the tennis court long before she actually plays a match. The key is to take the middle road between (1) denying her this competitiveness until you feel she's old enough to handle the pressure and (2) rushing her into match-play competition. What you must do is watch and listen for the cues that let you know how competition-oriented *she* wants to be during a lesson (does she want to emphasize ball-direction, targets, and drills?) and when *she* wants to go beyond competition with herself and actually start playing other people. Just let these competitive tendencies surface naturally.

From the first lesson on, don't be surprised if your child is downright competitive, no matter what philosophical approach you've tried to instill. Let's say you've told her, "I'm not worried about where the ball goes; I just want you to have fun and learn good stroking patterns. Everything else will fall in place." She nods her head, but once she starts swinging at the ball she wants desperately to knock it into her opponent's court and she gets mad when she can't. Instead of trying to fight her inclination, use it to advantage, since ball direction is obviously important to her and will ultimately become a crucial factor in her success. Continue to place your main emphasis on producing good strokes, but at the same time give her incentives for controlling the ball—for instance, by suggesting, "If you do this right on the backswing, it's going to produce a more accurate shot." Another example: When she's working on her forehand stroke, have her try to hit everything into an imaginary opponent's backhand corner with a reminder that "if your palm moves toward that corner, so will the racket—and the ball." Then she's working on her stroke and ball direction at the same time. Another ploy I use with youngsters who have gained some proficiency is to point out, "If your opponent's in this corner, you can make him run a lot of steps—all the way to that corner—if you can control your shot." Then I have them alternate hitting into each corner.

Actually, a highly competitive youngster will set up almost everything for you along the way. For instance, after a couple of lessons you might mention a certain target area—"It's really hard to hit the ball inside this five-foot circle, but later on you'll be able to do it"—and your child might respond, "I could hit it in the circle right now." Terrific. Give her the chance to take her shots and put herself to the test; don't bottle up this competitiveness. Then, if she can't do it, don't knock her back by saying, "See, I told you." Instead, tell her: "You're really a competitive person and that's great. You're going to be a fine player because you really want to be good. But as you can see, this game's a little tougher than you think and it's going to take some time to master. But I know you're going to be smart enough to find a way to lick this thing because you're competitive."

Of course, you may have a youngster who appreciates a low-key approach to competitive aspects until she gains some confidence in her ability to play the game right. I remember a group lesson in which I explained to the kids that once they started playing matches they would want to keep the ball out of the net and inside the boundaries. Before we started hitting, a six-year-old boy came over to me and said, "Let's don't play to keep it inside those lines today, okay?" Obviously, the boy was already aware of winning and losing, and he was telling me he just wanted to have fun swinging at the ball without feeling any competitive pressures.

Ideally, although I'm certainly in favor of match-play competition when the time is right, I love to have kids wait until they've acquired proper stroking patterns that will stay with them under pressure. This book suggests many fun, instructional drills that can help your child master the basics of good strokes while also appealing to her competitive nature—before she ever plays a match. In my view, the problem with having any beginner move too quickly into playing matches is that in her urge to win, she immediately goes for what's comfortable (yet often incorrect) in the way of technique. Instead, she should just concentrate on the fundamentals she has been trying to master, regardless whether she wins or loses the match.

How to Work with the Left-Hander

Our society forces left-handers to view nearly everything from a right-hander's perspective when it comes to learning or teaching a sport. So wherever possible in this book, I describe technique and tactics using terminology that should make it a little easier for you to teach if you're left-handed yourself or if your child's a lefty.

If you're a righty with a left-handed child, keep in mind two rules I have for the coaches on my tennis-college staff. First, learn to demonstrate all the strokes you teach left-handed. And second, practice actually hitting left-handed—even your serve—so you can give your child a better interpretation of what should be happening. But also remember that the game itself is not going to be any tougher for your child to play just because she's left-handed. Good tennis strokes must be hit exactly the same way off both sides of the body, because the physical laws that dictate the most efficient stroking patterns are absolute—the same for right-handers and left-handers.

If your child hasn't yet established her dominant side, be careful not to force her into automatically playing right-handed. Let her start with whatever hand she wants to play with and develop from there. If she prefers to switch her racket back and forth so that she hits a forehand off both sides of her body, she may be a true ambidextrous player who never has to worry about learning a backhand stroke. There are precedents for this, such as Beverly Baker Fleitz, a national champion in the 1950s.

The great player Kenny Rosewall, a natural lefty, rues the fact that his dad, who thought tennis was basically a right-hander's game, taught him to play right-handed. Kenny has had a pretty fair career, but he told me: "My dad did a great job on my groundstrokes, but he couldn't teach me to serve right-handed. [Rosewall's weakest stroke over the years has been his serve, which he hits right-handed, as he was taught.] I think if I had it to do all over, I'd serve left and play right."

How to Work with the Less-Talented Youngster

It's easy to become charmed by the child who displays a lot of natural ability when learning tennis. After all, she's going to impove rapidly and make you look good as an instructor. Yet this isn't reality in most families. The odds are good that your child is going to lack certain of the physical or mental abilities, or both, that are necessary to make the learning process an easy one, and you're probably going to be called on for patience and hard work, with little evident payoff in the early going.

This is where your positive approach to teaching will really show through. If you can provide your child with the attention and support she needs, then the two of you can keep dogging the game until she makes the breakthrough to good strokes. In fact, your goal should be: *Never give up on your child*, no matter how little physical ability she seems to have. Be enthusiastic and keep positive reinforcement at the forefront, because her determination alone may bring her through—especially if you've established a trusting relationship.

I try to give all the youngsters I teach the hope that they can learn to play good tennis, even as they're struggling almost hopelessly with the game. I tell them: "Even if you buy an ice-cream cone and stick it in your forehead, I think you have a great future. We can do it. Honest." Then as we work together I keep reiterating: "I know you're having trouble, but don't worry. Just have faith in what I'm telling you, because if you can hang in with me on this thing, you're going to be super one day. You'll make it, I know you will. One day we'll be laughing out loud together, looking back on these days."

Often, that's all the motivation kids seem to need to stick with the game. It's not false motivation, either, because I always have other students around who are transforming into smooth, talented players after years of being tall and gawky or short and lead-footed. If your own teaching situation is taking place in relative isolation, make sure you have your child see other kids learning the game so that she knows she's not alone. She can even benefit from watching adult beginners taking lessons, for there are many similarities.

If your child has very few "success experiences" in learning any of the strokes, the positive approach you take may be the crucial factor that keeps her coming back for more lessons until finally things start to fall in place.

Every time you go out onto the court, make sure you have ready a reward system that doesn't rely on your child's actually hitting the ball or keeping it in play. She may miss every other ball, but she can still enjoy herself if you continually praise the little things she manages to do right on the swing—the way her eyes trace the ball perfectly as it approaches, her good footwork, a terrific ready position. I like to say things like, "That's super, Jimmy—you really stepped into the ball beautifully," or "Great eye contact on the ball, Mary—you followed it like a hawk." Youngsters really pick up on this kind of encouragement, and I'll often see them look over at their mother and just beam, or give a knowing grin, as if to say, "See, Mom, he noticed."

Remember, you may have to look for things besides the stroke itself to praise, such as the fact your child always has a nice attitude and is willing to try anything you suggest. Or you might say: "I know you haven't started playing as well as you'd like, but I notice you're always eager to go out for another lesson. That's super with me." Traits such as determination, staying power, and enthusiasm should always be rewarded, for they will eventually pay off in tennis—and in other areas of life as well. Unfortunately, some parents are so obsessed with how their youngster hits the ball that they fail to recognize the effort she puts into the game or to appreciate the fact that she keeps coming out for lessons when she can't play very well. They'll even tell me: "I tried to find something nice to say to my kid during the lesson, but there was nothing I could see. She couldn't hit the ball and she looked angry the whole time." What a shame they hadn't learned to focus on the positive.

How to Deal with Your Child's Frustrations

When your child gets overly frustrated by her inability to hit the ball properly, there are several ways you can help her keep her emotions on a more even keel and thus make your lessons more enjoyable.

First of all, remember that you're working in a "mistake center" environment. Strive for an atmosphere in which your child is not afraid to "look bad" as she learns the game and as she works on improvements; if she tries something new and she doesn't get it right, throw support her way so that she's eager about trying it a second time and a third time—until she starts to acquire the proper sensations. When she's focusing on a specific area of technique like this, you'll find that the rest of her stroke almost always suffers. You should expect this to happen, and even warn her: "Remember, we're focusing on your footwork, so you may not even hit the ball."

Second, if your child is just starting out, remind her that frustration is part of the game for everybody, and that every beginner in history has gone through a period when nothing goes right. You might tell her: "You're probably thinking, 'How can I swing a big racket like this and still miss the ball?' The answer is: *easily*—even the best athletes in the world often swing and miss."

Third, let her know that since frustration is a normal, human response in any learning situation, there's no need to deny or hide it. Your point could be: "I know you're frustrated, but everybody gets that way. There's nothing wrong with it—as long as your behavior is good and your frustration doesn't interfere with what you're trying to do on your stroke." That's true. I never tell a youngster, "Don't be frustrated—that's stupid," because then I might be encouraging her to lie about her feelings. Besides, frustration can sometimes be turned into a positive force, channeled into motivating a youngster to want to master a particular skill—the "I'm-going-to-get-this-right-even-if-it-kills-me" type of determination.

Fourth, if your child's frustrations boil over in every lesson, you need to spend time getting at what seems to be causing such intense feelings. Ask her questions such as "Why do you get so angry over this game? Is it because you're disappointing yourself? Or do you feel you're letting me down?" You can remind her that progress is slow and patience is always necessary in developing sound tennis strokes.

Fifth, when she becomes overly frustrated on a particular stroke, don't keep feeding her balls to hit, hoping for a magical breakthrough. All that's going to do is reinforce negative attitudes and incorrect "muscle-memory" patterns. Instead, go back to how you taught the stroke on the very first day and just slow everything down so that the two of you have time to review the fundamentals and your child has a chance to chalk up some success experiences. She has to sense that positive things are actually happening, and this will give her the motivation to build what I hope will be a stronger foundation.

Sixth, let your child know that when you recognize she's uptight about something and in need of a release valve, you'll tell her to take five minutes to get a drink of water and cool off. Moreover, she should know that she herself has the freedom to ask for such a break when her strokes just aren't working right and it's pressure-cooker time. Knowing that she has this "out"—even if she seldom needs it—will tend to dissipate most of the anxiety that can build up.

How to Address the "I-Can't-Do-It" Attitude

When a youngster is struggling with the game, it may be that she's just not ready to learn according to her natural growth-and-development schedule. But I've also found that many beginners are held back instead by a defeatist kind of attitude that, in many cases, echoes their parents' own experience with tennis or sports in general. When I have a youngster who warns me before the first lesson, "I'm not going to be very good—you'll see," or one who starts saying, "I can't do that" as soon as the instruction begins, then I make sure to see her parents afterward. Invariably, they don't play tennis themselves ("I'm too uncoordinated to learn now") or they played years ago but "never very well." Even a six- or seven-year-old will pick up on this negativism, and thus the earlier you can reverse this kind of thinking, the faster your child will make strides in learning the game.

Try to bring up the subject of negative attitude with your child before you get into the lessons, or at least when it first surfaces. You might suggest: "It hurts me to hear you say, 'I can't do that.' I know that's the way you feel, because you're honest about yourself, but I need to know exactly what it is you think you can't do. If it's your forehand, are you saying you can't get your side turned to the net properly? That you don't have the right grip? That you can't keep your head still? That your hips don't turn at the right time? These are the kind of answers I want, then we can go to work on them."

By taking this approach, you keep your child from transferring her "I-can't-do-it" attitude about her forehand into one of "I'm no good at tennis," and eventually into an attitude of "I'm a no-good person." This commonly happens with older kids, so whenever a youngster tells me, "I'm so dumb I can't do anything right," I try to disarm her by saying: "Hey, look, we all have certain limitations, but the fact is, you're smart enough to eventually learn to play the game right. So instead of thinking you can't do anything, let's be more specific: What is it you can't do?—and what don't you understand?" I'll have her tell me all the things she's picked up about playing the game, so that she realizes she's really not dumb about tennis at all. Then, when I throw her some balls to hit, I point out how many things she can actually do right. I'll say: "You're holding the right grip, you're very good at turning your side to the net, and you're stepping into the ball just fine. But you're having trouble making the ball hit the center of the racket face, so let's go to work on that."

Of course, some youngsters don't want to be logical or rational about the skills they might already have; they just want to vent hostility by saying, "I can't play this dumb game." When that situation arises, I never turn it into a confrontation. I'm not looking to win a war with a twelve-year-old by fighting over this issue. Instead, I simply say: "Hey, look, I don't think you feel too good today. You've got some problems with your tennis game and I'm willing to help out, but I have a feeling that even if I try, you're not going to listen today anyway. So why don't you think about it this week and then tell me when you're ready to try again, because I don't want to fight with you. I like you too much to do that."

Here's another psychological twist to consider when dealing with negativism. When you're asking your child for feedback and saying, "Fine, now show me," then it's pretty hard for her not to grasp at least part of what you're trying to teach, and to understand what she's after on a particular stroke. But she may be saying she's totally confused anyway—because she's afraid to admit she understands. Certain kids think that if they claim they don't understand something, they can't be held responsible for being unable to do it properly. Their attitude is: "If I understand everything I'm supposed to do, I don't have any excuses for not hitting the ball right; it's all up to me, then." And they just aren't prepared to shoulder that kind of responsibility. A youngster like this needs your encouragement—or perhaps another sport.

How to Deal with the "I-Won't-Do-It" Attitude

When you have a youngster who won't listen to what you're teaching—who says, "I want to do it my own way"—it's not necessary to get into a squabble just to assert your authority. Disarm her by going in the other direction; let her try her own method of hitting the ball, because until she works this out of her system, you're not going to make any progress. You might try this approach: "I've showed you how I think this stroke should be hit and I've given you a lot of reasons why it works. I know I can help you, but I also know that in the end you have to teach yourself how to play. So let's take a look at your system. I'm interested to see if it can help you hit the ball better."

At this point, or after she has had a chance to work on her stroke her own way, you can put her to the test and see how effective she is. This is one of the nice things about tennis—that it allows you to measure a youngster's strokes objectively. Both of you can see the results and judge them together. One simple test is to make a circle at one end of the court and have her stand at the opposite baseline while you feed balls to her to hit. "All right, let's see how many balls you can land inside that circle." (It can be a 10-foot-diameter circle—or about one-third the court—in the early learning stages, eventually shrinking to about 4 feet across.) After she's had twenty or thirty hits, or whatever number you decide upon, ask her, "Now, do you really feel you can control the shot with your swing?" If she defends the stroke even though she didn't come close to the target ("Aw, I had a bad day"), you can set up another test when she's feeling right, or it may be time to bow out of the relationship. You've given her a chance to be logical but apparently she's motivated in a different direction. You should also question your own personality. If you find yourself telling friends, "She's just like me—she wants to do everything her own way," don't fight it out with her on the tennis court. It could be far more enjoyable and productive just to throw all your support behind her as she learns tennis from somebody else (see chapter 16).

The key throughout all this instructional interplay with your child is that *what you try to teach must make sense to her*. She must understand your rationale and accept it, for if she really doesn't believe what you have to say about technique—or she just doesn't feel comfortable playing your way—then she's not going to work on your suggestions between lessons. You might be telling her, "I can see you're trying to make the right changes in your swing," but the moment she gets into a match-play situation she's going to rely on her own instincts. She'll tell herself, "I know what Dad said, but I can swing my way and still beat this kid easily."

How to Handle Behavior Problems

If your child is misbehaving or having an emotional outburst around home, you can always say, "Go to your room until you're ready to act nice again." Also, a lot of outsiders aren't looking on as you try to deal with the problem. But when you're out on the tennis court giving a lesson, you're stuck with every personality trait your child has—right out on center stage. At a private club or on a public court, people will almost always be waiting for your court, or watching from an observation deck, or listening to the sounds coming from your court as they play nearby. Thus, if your child is acting like a jerk, you not only feel bad for her because she's embarrassing herself in front of everybody, but you think, "She's making me look bad—and she's stealing my free time doing it."

This is why, for the sake of more enjoyable lessons—and your child's growth—you should try to run a tight ship when it comes to dealing with behavior that is spoiling the lesson, disrupting players on adjoining courts, or is out of line with desired tennis etiquette. From the first lesson on, your child should understand that *the lesson will end* the moment she violates any of the rules that you've set up together and have agreed upon.

Following are some of the rules you might suggest:

• No racket throwing and no slamming the racket against the fence or the court.

• No swearing. (It's hard to explain to kids today that swearing is an unseemly habit, but I still insist that learning to control their language in public is a part of growing up.)

• No hitting balls over the fence *intentionally*. (Let your child know that you can tell the difference between when she does this by accident and when she does it out of anger or just to goof off.)

• Anger and frustration, though normal traits, must be kept under control so they don't bother adjacent players who are trying to have a pleasant time.

• Both of you must share in picking up the balls.

After explaining your rationale for each rule, encourage your child to raise any questions she might have. Ideally, she'll agree with the code of behavior you've proposed so that you're not simply imposing your value judgments on her—she's imposing them on herself. Then make it clear that you don't want to get into arguments out on the court that will bother other people. Make an agreement that if she breaks a rule, you both understand what happens next—"The lesson ends and we go home." It's always best to have a preliminary discussion about rules at a relaxed time before the first lesson, when rational thinking can prevail and nobody's mad.

If your child begins to act up once the lessons are under way, I think it's crucial for her to know that you are strong enough to act decisively, as you promised. In fact, I view it as positive reinforcement when you stop the lesson and say: "Hey, look, you've stretched this thing too far. You're being unfair. I love you, but I'm a human being just like you, and what you're doing is not fair to me, to yourself, or to others. So that's all for today." Why continue to put up with behavior you don't want to see in your child?

I also think it's tremendously important for kids to understand that their parents have the same kind of emotions and hurts as they do. For example, kids are always telling parents, "Don't embarrass me in front of my friends," but when these kids act up on the court, they tend to forget that they're embarrassing their parents in front of other people. So have your child know that even though you're not part of her gang, you *are* her parent and you still have the same feelings that all her friends have.

As a final note, it's important to realize that when your child displays a certain behavior problem on the court—for instance, a tendency to cry easily at frustrating moments, such as when she can't hit the ball the way she thinks she should—it means you'll probably have to combat a behavior pattern she has used successfully previously, especially around home. If your child cries easily on the tennis court, it's likely to be a defense mechanism that also surfaces in other activities when she can't do something right or she loses. This is a common problem, of course, but rather than reprimanding her for crying, take time to calmly ask her about why she does so. Explore it on that level and you may find that she's filled with self-doubt and really needs your constant support, or that she feels rejected by her friends when she plays poorly, or perhaps that she has unstated goals that are totally unrealistic.

How to Control the Length of the Lesson

I've found that it's inappropriate to plan a tennis lesson for children in traditional time blocks of thirty minutes or an hour. You have to be much more flexible than that, particularly in the early lessons as you try to determine your child's real interest in the game. Tennis should start out as a leisure-time activity, and if your child isn't having fun during a teaching session, you should reevaluate the lesson you are giving—or bring it to an end—however early that point comes.

Still, it's important, after you've given a lesson or two, that you try to have a discussion with your child about how long each session ought to last. Without some type of understanding, you're likely to find yourself confronted by a child who announces, after just five or ten minutes on the court, "I don't feel like hitting today; let's go home." You'll either have to agree to leave—and waste the time and effort spent traveling to the lesson—or you'll be forced into a hostile situation in which your gut reaction is to say: "What do you mean? I've given up an hour of my time to bring you out here, so we're going to practice." Either way, nobody will win.

By soliciting your child's input, you should be able to agree on a reasonable time schedule that matches her potential to keep concentrating on the lesson and doesn't try to force her to match your potential to do so. After all, if her concentration span is only about fifteen minutes, you can't expect to teach effectively much longer than that, enthusiastic as you might be. Instead of trying to force her to stick it out for thirty minutes or an hour just because you've reserved the court and don't want to waste the time, practice your own serve while she rests on the bench or helps you retrieve the balls.

The important thing here is for your child to know that though you're willing to compromise, you're not going to let her jockey you around. Let's say you've agreed on thirty-minute lessons, but she starts losing her interest halfway through or complains that she just isn't having much fun. If your evaluation of the situation indicates that she likes tennis but not the way you're teaching it (whether she says so or you sense it), that's something you have to work out. Yet she also needs to be reminded that a lesson involves sharing, whoever does the teaching—that you're giving up some of your free time to help her learn tennis and if she wants you as her instructor, she has a responsibility to give you her best effort.

Once again, as I've stressed throughout this chapter, prior discussions with your child will help you defuse—if not prevent—confrontations that can spoil the fun you should be having together out on the court.

5/Preparing for the First Lesson

EXPERIENCED instructors never slight the planning and thinking that goes into a good lesson, whether it's the first or the tenth in a series. Then there are those parents, buoyed by enthusiasm and years of playing experience, who think it's going to be a snap to teach their child tennis, so they skimp on preparation. These instructors fail to plan how to actually give the first lesson and out on the court quickly realize they aren't as smart as they thought: they don't know where to start, what to say, what to watch for, or how to keep things moving. In short, they don't know how to be effective.

This chapter discusses the important steps you should take to prepare yourself before you get out on that firing line with your child. You may question the emphasis I place upon preparation, but from what I've observed, the instructor who's most relaxed walking through the gate for a lesson is the one who's best prepared. When I go out to teach, I know exactly what I want from the student and how I hope to achieve it. Children aren't dummies; they know when an instructor isn't ready for the lesson—she doesn't have a basic goal in mind, she can't remember what was covered in the previous lesson, she stalls and floats along until the lesson starts taking shape by trial and error. Right away she's fighting to have her students learn what she's trying to teach.

Conversely, when you know exactly what you're looking for and you don't have to ad-lib a lesson, it really helps your confidence and the respect your child has for your teaching. It will take some time for you to feel comfortable and confident as an instructor, but in the meantime you're going to establish a much more successful teaching relationship by being prepared.

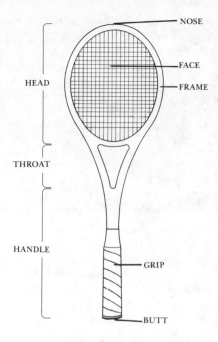

NOSE

FACE

FRAME

HEAD

THROAT

HANDLE

GRIP

BUTT

The Racket

Find the Right Racket

However far your child advances in tennis, keep one axiom in mind when you go looking for a racket: Buy what feels comfortable to him and what your pocketbook can afford. For children starting out, practically any racket will have enough energy in the strings to allow him to hit the ball very hard without swinging fast (though some of the cheaper models are prone to break). Even if your child gets into top tournament play, don't let yourself be snowed into buying the most expensive model available, for there's no proven correlation between a person's success in tennis and the quality of his tennis racket. You might want to give your child an expensive racket as a reward for working hard and being a good sport; it might also give him more confidence and thus help his play psychologically. But I've never heard a great player credit his success to his racket or blame his problems on his racket. Win or lose, the top pros know it boils down to the quality of their strokes. Most of them, in fact, chose the particular racket they use because of the endorsement income they receive. Some will even switch from a racket they've used all their lives—from a wooden one, say, to one made of metal or graphite—not to improve their games, but to fatten their bank accounts with royalties.

Researchers are trying to determine which racket characteristics are best suited to which kinds of player, but in the meantime here are some points to keep in mind as you try to find a racket for your child:

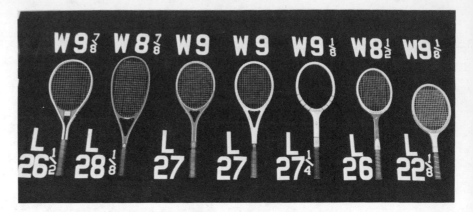

There's a wide variety of rackets available today, as indicated here by the width of the head (W, in inches) and the overall length (L, in inches). A junior racket is shown at far right. Rackets are made of various materials — such as wood, graphite, and aluminum — and can be strung with either gut or nylon. You can spend a lot of time worrying about which combination is right for your child, but he'll go a long way in the game with almost any racket that feels comfortable — providing he works on stroke production.

• My position—until research proves otherwise—is to have youngsters use *as heavy a racket, with as large a racket grip, as they can comfortably manage.* I don't want them adjusting their swing to compensate for a racket that's too heavy, nor do I want them to develop "wristy" strokes by playing with a racket that's proportionately too light for their strength.

• If older kids have the strength when they're beginning, I have them use rackets that are weighted "medium" (13½ to 13¾ ounces) rather than "light" (12 to 13 ounces), because physical laws benefit those who can use a little heavier racket. (A "heavy" racket—which is usually noted as such on the throat—weighs 14 to 15 ounces and is used successfully only by very strong teenagers and adults.) The energy produced as you hit a ball is equal to the mass times the velocity squared, which means that using the same amount of effort, if you hit a ball with a heavier racket, it will travel faster. In addition, when kids play one-handed with too light a racket, they tend to start using too much wrist and whipping the racket, which is lethal to good stroking patterns. Defenders of lighter rackets argue that a youngster can't get a heavier racket back fast enough on the backswing. However, this problem arises not because of the racket, but because most beginners and intermediates use only their arm and wrist in stroking the ball, rather than incorporating the rotation of their body. If your child learns to turn his body properly, the uncoiling of his torso will supply the power he needs to easily handle a heavier racket.

• Children under six or seven are often more effective with a shorter and lighter junior-length racket of the type first designed by Elaine

Mason, an innovative tennis coach in California. If you can't find one, simply let your child use the lightest adult-size racket in your closet (or cut about 3 inches off the handle of an old wood racket and replace the grip covering), then have him hit holding the racket with two hands on the forehand and backhand alike, unless he has the strength to use one hand. Proportionately, a shorter racket for a shorter arm makes sense, but a youngster can adjust to a bigger racket by learning to rotate his body properly and by playing with two hands (see photos on pages 77 and 224–225).

• In determining racket grip size, always consider the relationship between the size of your child's hand, the length of his fingers, and the gripping strength of his hand muscles. A kid with short fingers but a Godzilla handshake might best use the same size racket grip as a youngster with longer fingers but less strength. A good starting point is to have your child measure these three factors against kids already playing the game. Just knowing your child will also help you find the appropriate racket. If he's ten, has a slight build, and you've noticed that he's weaker than other kids his age, he likely will start with a 4½ or 4⅜ "light." (These numbers indicate the handle circumference in inches and are usually indicated on the racket throat.) But if he's one of the strongest kids in his class and his hand is big, he ought to try a 4½ or 4⅝ "medium," as long as he can maintain comfortable racket control.

• I agree with Jack Kramer, who believes that the smaller the racket grip (and thus, in nearly all cases, the lighter the racket), the more strength you actually need to use the racket effectively and the more energy you must expend to keep it from turning in your hand. I've seen this happen many times with juniors; they switch to a lighter racket because the one they're using is turning—but the new one, with the thinner grip, turns even more. It's like taking a screw out of a wall with a small screwdriver versus the ease of using a big screwdriver.

• Seek out a racket that will do pretty well when balls are hit off-center. Tennis instructors continually discuss the "center of percussion" in the middle of the racket, yet realistically most kids—and adults as well—hardly ever hit the ball with the exact center of the racket face. A thicker frame will do more to send the ball back solidly, while a light frame will relay much more torque into the hand and hitting arm.

• If your child finds a racket he likes, it doesn't matter whether it's made of wood, metal, or whatever—just so long as it feels good to him. But keep in mind that most wood rackets will be cheaper.

• I wouldn't start any youngster out with a gut-strung racket. Nearly all of the inexpensive rackets on the market come strung with nylon (which provides all the power your child will need), and gut requires better care.

However, as your child grows and you're looking for ways to reward him, you could buy him a gut-strung racket to give him a lift.

Play Down Clothing and Accessories

If you can afford proper tennis attire, it is common courtesy to have your child dress in a manner acceptable at your club, park, or playground. But you should never let a problem with "appropriate" dress keep your child from enjoying tennis. My philosophy has always been that clothes and accoutrements never make a tennis player. The "tennis dandy" may *look* like a player, but without some strokes he's going to play like a toad.

Stock Up on Practice Balls

Since inactivity will kill most kids' interest, a crucial element in good teaching is constant action: lots of hits, no standing around, and a minimum of wasted time and energy chasing down balls. The best way to insure this is always to have plenty of tennis balls on hand. I've seen parents bring only one can of balls to a lesson and then tell their youngster, "Hit it to me, hit it to me." Of course, the kid doesn't yet have that kind of control. Then the parent orders him to chase down the balls. It doesn't take long for the youngster to think, "Man, I'd rather ride my bike; that's where the action is."

Locate a Court

In many areas of the country, finding a court on which to teach your child can be a difficult and expensive problem, especially if you live in a climate where winter play is relegated to indoor clubs. However, whenever the game can be played outdoors, search around your neighborhood and you'll be surprised at the number of courts that are relatively unused at certain times during the day (especially in public schoolyards and playground areas). They may be a little old and dusty, with uneven surfaces and a drooping net, but they're perfectly fine for teaching the game. You can also explore schools and playgrounds for backboards, windowless sides of old buildings, and high walls that might provide a suitable hitting area. Tracy Austin got her start at the Kramer club hitting against a wall next to the clubhouse.

Also, don't worry about your four- to six-year-old being intimidated by learning on a regulation court (as opposed to a paddle-tennis court, which is slightly more than half the area and is used by some teaching professionals to start little kids). If he can't get the ball over the net from the baseline, just move him up to around the service line so that he can get those success experiences.

I prefer to start all youngsters on a regulation court, using the same basic stroking patterns they will always want to use. Then when they get into competitive tennis I know they'll be ready; they'll be familiar with all the court dimensions and their strokes will be attuned to these dimensions. I never like to have youngsters view the game—or a particular stroke—from one perspective, only to force them to change that perspective as they grow older.

One other court consideration: the problem of trying to teach when players are on adjoining courts and your child is causing havoc with numerous errant shots. One partial solution is to secure an end court, which leaves only one neighboring court to worry about and provides a side fence to catch stray balls. Then, if one stroke is causing most of the trouble (say, a pulled forehand), you can put your child on the most convenient side of the court—so that his pulled shots will go toward the side fence. Such a situation should motivate both of you to get to work on his stroking problem.

Develop Your Demonstration Technique

Whatever your playing ability, you have a responsibility to work hard at learning how to demonstrate the way each stroke you're teaching should look. You may not be able to produce the perfect swing when a ball is actually hit to you, but at least your child can imitate the correct form you demonstrate. (In my opinion, those of you who are already teaching pros or tennis coaches have a special obligation to learn perfect demonstration form. If you haven't worked hard enough on your game to do at least this, then how can you expect your students to be properly motivated?)

I've found that many parents, in two or three days, can learn to demonstrate all the strokes except possibly the serve (which calls for a more complex coordination of movements and requires a longer period of work for most people). But to do this, you must set aside time for concentrated practice. This book will show you how to teach yourself the correct stroking patterns. Then you should have your form critiqued by a qualified teaching pro, a coach, or a knowledgeable player. You might even pay for a "demonstration lesson," in which you have the instructor spend thirty minutes working on your "demo" techniques.

Of course, don't let an inability to master good demonstration form keep you from teaching your child. Just make sure he's somehow exposed to the proper techniques (perhaps through group lessons with a qualified teaching pro) and that you're honest about your stroking deficiencies.

Don't try to pretend you're Chris Evert Lloyd when you swing like Bertha Boondoggle, because your child will know you're a phony once he begins to play and starts to observe good players.

Set Up a Lesson Plan

Most people who are successful and who are going to be evaluated on their performance are accustomed to drawing up "plans of attack" for the next day's work. Business executives plot their company's operation, salesmen coordinate their schedules and priorities, and schoolteachers outline their curricula.

In teaching tennis, a good lesson plan will boost your confidence by providing a "road map" for your lesson, outlining what you're going to try to teach your child and how you plan to reach your objectives. However, don't feel you must hold to every little detail in your plan. You need flexibility, in case your child wants to work on an unscheduled stroke or you feel a particular problem needs extra attention.

You should have your child help organize each lesson. Before the first one, sit down and ask him questions such as: "How long do you want to practice? Are you going to gather up all the balls in the closet, or am I? I wonder if we should go in the morning or in the afternoon? Are you going to call and get a court or am I?" Then, after that first lesson, when he's a bit more familiar with the game, you can start asking him about the strokes he wants to work on (those you've already introduced and new ones he wants to learn) and the drills that interest him. Right away you thus let him know that you're going to involve him very closely in the learning experience and that you're not interested in dictating every step to be taken. Moreover, you're starting to develop a self-sufficient player by encouraging him to take some initiative. I find that too many youngsters refuse to take the initiative in anything, or that they often just don't know how. Your child's involvement in the tennis-teaching role can give him some valuable experiences that will carry over into the rest of his life.

In addition to your child's suggestions, use your own input and be methodical, resourceful, and realistic when you draw up a lesson plan:

• Know *why* the strokes you are teaching are important and *why* your child should try to execute them in a specific fashion.

• Review how you are going to introduce a new stroke and check to see that your demonstration form is as accurate as possible. Most children are great imitators and your child is going to copy your form, right or wrong.

• Continually update your insights into how your child learns a physical skill and the type of teaching approach he seems to prefer (kinesthetic, visual, auditory, or a combination) and adjust your methods accordingly.

• Draw upon visual and mechanical aids (many of which are illustrated or described in this book) that may help your child gain proper stroking motions, and have them available. For instance, a yardstick can be taped to the back of the shoulders to indicate how the body should turn on groundstrokes and the serve.

• Consider targets (empty tennis cans, balloons taped to the court) and target areas (using rope to mark off parts of the court) that can help motivate your child and improve his strokes.

• Plan to tackle specific trouble areas in technique. For example, you may write down: "(1) Show Pete how to take his first step toward the ball—he's been getting mixed up; (2) his head is lifting early on his groundstrokes, so we'll work on drills that keep the head down until the follow-through; (3) he's not starting his backswing early enough—I want him to turn his body before the ball reaches the net."

• Try to anticipate potential problems that can ruin the fun (such as your child's frustrations and your impatience when nothing goes right) and how you might deal with them. Prior thinking—even rehearsing what you'll say—will generally help you react more appropriately. In a more positive vein, think about ways to keep the lesson enjoyable and fast-moving so that learning is maximized.

Some Final Reminders for Parent/Instructors

Before you go out to teach this game, here are some final thoughts to keep in mind that will test your readiness and perhaps raise some issues you haven't yet thought about. Once you're into teaching, you might find it helpful to review this section periodically to see what improvement you're making.

• *Try to view the teaching experience as a healthy, ongoing aspect of child-raising, not simply isolated weekly lessons on the tennis court.* Some tennis-teaching parents fail to enjoy themselves as much as they should because they regard their role as an obligation instead of a great opportunity to develop rapport with their youngster. They'll say, "Aw, I promised my kid I'd teach him to play, so I'm going to do it," and then go out but resent the time they're spending. The youngster can sense this resentment, and the result is often a lot of bickering that quickly sours both of them on the whole deal.

• *Keep in mind that your responsibility is not only to help your child learn good strokes, but to help him develop favorable attitudes toward tennis.* Ideally, these goals are intertwined and mutually supportive, but too often I've seen nice kids lose all their enthusiasm for the game when their instructor places all the emphasis on technique—and forgets to make it fun along the way. So if you lose your sense of humor while giving a lesson and find yourself shouting to get your points across or using deprecating language, step back and think about what you're doing. Your child is going to form important, often indelible attitudes about tennis—and about you—so try to make sure that those attitudes are positive.

• *Remember that when it comes to the needs people have while learning tennis, the only real difference between adults and children is a lot of years.* If you're in doubt about your teaching approach, simply visualize yourself as a beginning player and this should give you a clearer perspective and some sensitive insight. After all, what type of instructor would you want? One who's considerate? Who understands your problems? Who respects you as an individual? Who can communicate clearly? Who really thrives on your questions? Who recognizes the fact that the tennis court is a "mistake center"? In short, an instructor who does everything he can to enhance your self-confidence and your enjoyment of the game?

• *Know your limitations as an instructor and learn to sense when the requirements have surpassed your ability to remain effective.* If and when that happens (as discussed in chapter 16), be ready to bow out gracefully and then find a qualified instructor for your child. Too often, parents fail to understand or face up to their limitations, and their child is the one who suffers.

• *Ask yourself if you've given your child an "out" in case the relationship, or simply the game of tennis, just isn't working out.* It's crucial for him to know that he has the freedom to tell you about his unhappiness—that he'd prefer to quit the game or go to another instructor—and that you'll abide by his feelings without getting into a war or using reprisals ("You quit tennis, so why should we let you play Little League baseball?"). If you want to take a tougher stand than this, first consider one of the inequities in parent-child relationships—the fact that most adults, unlike kids, can generally work their way out of a situation that has turned unpleasant, such as tennis lessons. Yet they'll thrust a child into the same type of situation but give him no real options short of just quitting the sport and then having to live with parental wrath and his own guilt.

• *Always remember that you're a parent first, and a tennis teacher second.* When that priority is reversed and you sense that your child is gaining a full-time tennis coach and losing a parent—when all you want to talk about is his tennis game—you should back off. It's okay to start afresh and simply teach him in small, incremental time periods, while encouraging him to pursue other sports and activities. However, if the tennis relationship repeatedly becomes an all-consuming involvement, bring it to an end.

As a parent myself, I feel there's no greater joy than sharing time with children. By electing to teach your own child tennis—using the guidelines I've suggested here and elsewhere in the book—you should have a gratifying experience that both of you will always enjoy recalling. Remember, the way you spend your time today with your child will be tomorrow's memories. So above all, prepare to have a good time.

6/Giving Your First Lesson

WHEN you go out to give your first organized lesson, be relaxed—you're not on a crash course for Wimbledon, nor are you setting anything in cement. Whatever mistakes you make in what you teach or in how you go about giving the lesson can certainly be corrected in future lessons. So the important thing is to view the undertaking as an exciting challenge and a chance to have a lot of fun with your child. If you have a friendly, reassuring voice and you're laughing genuinely and feeling good, she will pick up on this enthusiasm and will tend to have a relaxed approach that enhances learning. I've found that even when kids can't play well in the beginning, they tend to come back for more instruction *as long as they enjoy what they are doing* and the instructor takes a positive approach. But if the fun isn't there because of the instructor's attitude or his teaching style, then a lot of kids never want to return for a third or fourth lesson, even if they're making good progress.

Give Your Child an Overview of the Game

As a parent, you have an edge over the teaching pro or other instructors who are working with beginners: you can give your child an overview of the game before the first lesson, thus saving some explanatory talk that otherwise delays getting on to the action.

One way to present this overview is to take your child to the nearest tennis court and watch a match being played, so that the players illustrate the points you want to make. Bring along a note pad in order to draw a diagram of the court and to label the different lines (or use the drawing in

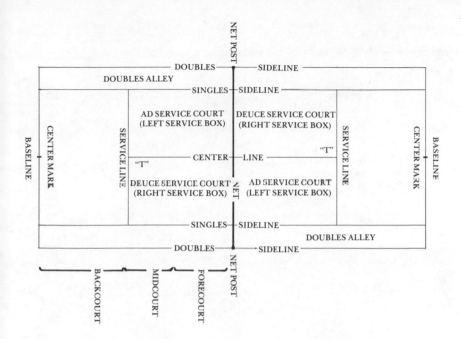

The Court

this book). You might start out by saying: "One player is the server and he tries to hit the ball over the net and into the service box. If he does, then the other player tries to hit it back—over the net and inside the lines." You can point out the singles sidelines and the baseline, both on the court and in your diagram. "Now watch how they play. The ball has to go over the net and it has to land inside the lines if allowed to bounce. A player can return a hit before it lands or let it bounce once, but he has to hit it before it bounces twice. If he doesn't reach it in time, or if he hits it into the net, or if he knocks it outside the boundaries, then he loses the point and they start again." You may prefer not to introduce the competitive aspects at first, but most kids will ask, "How do you win?"

So as you watch the match, be ready to explain how the scoring works, even though it won't make much sense to a child at first. For instance, the winner of the first point has 15 (not 1) and if he wins the next point he goes ahead 30–0 (traditionally called "thirty–love"). However, if he wins another point his score advances not to 45 but to 40. He wins the game if he wins a fourth point before his opponent reaches 40. But once the score is tied at 30 or 40 (called "deuce"), a player must win two straight points to win the game. As the score flops to one opponent's favor after a deuce point is played, that player is said to have the "advantage." Now, just as

Draping a blanket over the net shows these twin sisters, eleven years old, that they can't see their opponents' court when playing from the baseline unless they look through the little squares in the net. This technique reinforces the importance of a low-to-high stroke, in order to lift the ball over the high net.

your child is beginning to grasp what is happening, she may hear the server call out the score as he goes to serve: "Five–forty," or perhaps "five-all." He always gives his score first, but the "five"? He actually means "fifteen," but some players around the world have shortened it to five. Usually, the first player to win six games is awarded the set, but he must win by at least two games—6–4, 7–5, or some such score. (When the score reaches 6–6, there's now a "tie-breaker," which is explained in the glossary.)

I always stress the fact that the basic idea in tennis is to learn to keep the ball going back and forth over the net. "Most people win by hitting everything back and letting their opponent make the mistakes," I tell kids. "So I'm going to teach you some things that will help you hit the ball all the time, all kinds of ways, and be really good." Then, depending upon the child's interest and comprehension, I'll briefly introduce such concepts as the high net (see page 154), why players should learn to hit with a low-to-high forward *lifting* motion on their forehand and backhand groundstrokes (page 155), the importance of hitting the ball deep (page 156), and the advantages they gain, once they have some experience, by working their way up to the net (page 243). You should have an overview of the game clearly in mind at all times, because the realities of physics—how they involve court dimensions, the net, and the racket—are going to determine the stroking patterns you try to teach your child.

After you and your child have watched people play, you can acquaint her with the various lines on the court. If she's younger than seven or eight, find an empty court and walk with her single file along each line, calling out as you go: "I'm walking on the baseline . . . now I'm walking on the singles sideline . . . now I'm walking on the service line . . ." I've found that little kids (especially in a group) enjoy this game and that it's valuable from a kinesthetic and visual standpoint in helping them understand what all those strange lines mean. Although my primary concern at first is a youngster's swing and how well she contacts the ball, I like to have kids get a sense of court dimensions and the singles boundaries so that they don't simply stand on the baseline and try to knock the ball over the fence or feel they can hit in any direction they wish.

Another thing you can do at home before the first lesson is to acquaint your child with a tennis racket. You might start out by telling her how smart she's going to be when it comes to tennis: "You're going to know so much about this game, nobody'll believe it. A lot of grown-ups who have played for years don't know the different parts of their racket or what the lines on the court are called." Then hold up a racket and point out the head, the face, the frame, the throat, and the leather grip that covers the handle. I also show kids the center of the strings and say, "This is called the 'sweet spot,' because when you hit the ball here it's really a sweet shot, like candy." Now you can set a precedent for feedback by asking her questions about the racket. She will also become familiar with some important terminology for when lessons begin.

On the Court for Lesson 1

I know that the attitude I establish at the beginning of my first lesson with children (and adults as well)—before even one ball is hit—is absolutely crucial. So when we're ready to start, I kneel down in front of them to be on their level and I begin to tell them how enthusiastic I am about teaching them and how much fun we're going to have together. I explain my philosophy about the tennis court being a "mistake center" and point out that all I expect out of them is a good effort. As I've mentioned, I think it really helps youngsters relax when they realize they don't have to hit well to earn the right to keep taking lessons or to make me happy; they just have to try their best, because that's all I'm expecting from them. I also try to reduce anxiety by letting them know I care about them as individuals, and that I'm confident there's a place for them in tennis, no matter how uncoordinated they think they are. "If you can walk to the water fountain without falling over, you have a great chance with me," I tell them.

I then go into my overview of how the game is played, explain the parts of the racket (if I haven't done so already), and then turn to the first stroke I teach—a forehand groundstroke. Like most coaches, I prefer to start with the forehand because it's the most natural stroke to learn, if not the easiest one to master. Compared to the backhand, the forehand motion is much more similar to the motions kids make while doing things in everyday life, and they feel more comfortable hitting off their dominant side—which gives you some natural motivation to work with.

Before you demonstrate the desired stroking pattern, explain what a "forehand groundstroke" is. Remember, take nothing for granted in what you teach your child or in the terminology you use. One definition might be: "This is a forehand because 'fore' means front and you're hitting with the front of your hand—the palm—moving forward into the ball. It's also a groundstroke, which is any ball you hit after it touches the ground."

When I describe and then demonstrate the forehand, I stress about five or six main points the first day. "Here's how the good players hit a forehand," I'll tell a child. "They want to get the ball up and over this high net, so their stroke looks like this: as the ball is coming, they turn their shoulders so their nonhitting side faces the net and they draw their racket head back at about eye level until the racket points to the back fence. Then they lower the racket, down to about knee level, so that they can bring it forward and up to meet the ball, like this. They always try to finish with their upper arm under their chin, and the racket face aiming toward their opponent's back fence and raised to the sky. This is called the follow-through." I then go back over the stroke slowly, stopping at key points and adding other elements to my description, depending upon how much I think the youngster can absorb.

For example, turning the shoulders to initiate the backswing is such an important concept that I try to say: "This first part of the swing is called the backswing because you turn your body like this, which takes the racket back automatically. Don't let your arm do all the work. Try to visualize that you're taking your racket over and around a giant beach ball. When you bring the racket down before starting your forward movement, you want it to be about twelve inches lower than where you're going to contact the ball. This forces you to swing low-to-high. It also means that you have to watch the ball very carefully before it bounces, so that you know how low to get the racket."

To demonstrate, I hold a tennis ball at about waist level and I ask my students, "How low do you have to get your racket when the ball's this

1

2

high?" Then I lower the ball to about knee level and ask: "Now, how low do you have to get? Notice how I have to bend my knees to get my body down so that the racket can be lower than the ball? I don't want to simply drop the racket head without bending my knees because I want the racket to be just about even with my arm—parallel with the ground—when I hit the ball."

I also have the child notice that the racket face is straight up and down (vertical) when I contact the imaginary ball. "This should make the ball go up over the net and come down in my opponent's court." Right about here, the kid's brain is churning and she's very likely thinking (quite sensibly): "If I want to hit the ball up over the net, shouldn't I tilt the racket face back?" This is a big point, so I stress that even though the racket face should stay vertical at impact, the low-to-high swing is going to elevate the ball properly. If the youngster is old enough, I also explain that a swing like this will produce topspin on the ball if she swings upward at a steep enough angle (greater than about 17 degrees). Topspin and the downward pull of gravity enable her to hit the ball hard and have it clear the net safely, but still come down deep in her opponent's court. (See chapters 9 and 10 for detailed analyses of topspin and the forehand.)

Once you've provided the key concepts on the forehand, start asking your child questions (and encourage her questions as well). She'll gain a much quicker understanding of what she should be trying to do, because

The Backswing Loop

1. To help your child understand what it means to have a loop backswing and then a low-to-high forward motion, hold a large beach ball at about the youngster's waist level and tell her, "Start at the top and go around the ball." As shown here, the beach ball forces the student to bring her racket back properly at about eye level.

2. After pointing her racket to the back fence, the student bends her knees and lowers the racket so that she can bring it under the beach ball and upward as she goes out to make her hit.

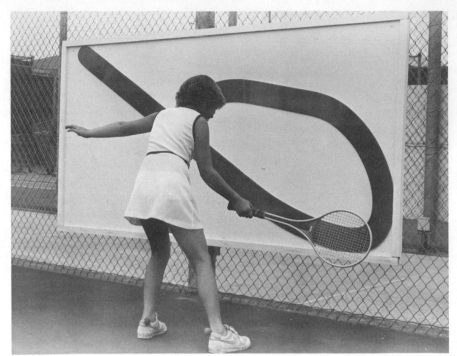

Another way to help your child master the loop is to trace her desired stroking pattern on a large piece of wood or cardboard. She can then practice taking her racket along this pattern, as the player is doing here. If there's a wall nearby, you can sketch the guideline pattern with chalk.

each time she answers a question, she's reinforcing the concept in her mind. And very likely she'll love to display her knowledge about the game. If you present information to her patiently, in language she can understand, you'll be amazed at how quickly she absorbs—and feeds back—the basic tennis techniques, terminology, and catchphrases.

In demonstrating the stroke (by dropping a ball and hitting it after it bounces) swing easily and don't try to hit the ball hard; just give your child a chance to visualize the proper flight pattern. This will also emphasize an important tennis concept that you should reinforce early: she doesn't have to swing hard to hit the ball hard and deep—she merely must make her body segments work together properly. When you demonstrate, make sure that you stand so that your child will have the same perspective as when she tries the swing herself. UCLA physiologist Dr. Bryant Cratty points out that people often learn faster by observing such a motor skill from behind, since they can visualize themselves making the movement without having to reverse the image mentally.

Now that it's time to start hitting, show your child how to hold the proper grip, and stress how this will help her hit better shots. I teach the Eastern forehand grip, in which the racket head and the palm of the hitting hand are straight up and down at the point of impact. My

The Two-Handed Forehand

Once out on the court, don't worry if you discover that your child is not yet strong enough to hit a forehand with one hand. A smaller, lighter racket might help; otherwise let him grip the handle with both hands. He'll have more fun and he'll develop some nice habits, since a successful two-handed stroke, like the one-handed version, depends on good upper body rotation. This youngster is demonstrating the proper forehand grip, which has the dominant hand on top, using an Eastern forehand grip (see photos on page 174). The non-dominant hand generally uses the same grip. Also notice that the racket face is vertical at impact and that he contacts the ball out away from his body and off his front foot — which are the proper techniques for players using one hand, too.

approach is to say: "Just take your hand and open your fingers so that the palm is straight up and down. Now, put the racket in your hand and close your fingers. Is your racket face still straight up and down? That's how you want the racket to look when you contact the ball. This is also what I mean by a 'vertical racket' at impact."

Then I add: "I only teach one grip on the forehand because I think it's the best one, and I've studied all of them. If you think another grip feels better, you're free to try it, but I'm going to be watching your swing closely

Before going out to hit the first ball, have your child imitate the form you seek. The mother here is demonstrating the desired follow-through on the fore-hand. Imitating her, the seven-year-old assumes exactly the same position, keeping his head down and his eyes focused on the point of impact until his upper arm touches his chin.

and if you're having trouble hitting the ball right, the problem could be your grip." (See chapter 10 for more details on the Eastern, Continental, and Western grips. Also, if your child is going to start out by holding two hands on the racket, her dominant hand should be on top and both hands should use the Eastern forehand grip.)

Swing Into Action

At the beginning of this first lesson with children, I spend no more than ten to fifteen minutes explaining the game and preparing them for the first stroke—then we're in action, whatever their age, because that's why they're out there. I know that some instructors are more relaxed starting kids out with isolated learning games and a rigid sequential progression; perhaps the entire first lesson is spent on everything but hitting the ball. But why delay all the real fun? A youngster is armed with a big racket and he's eager to start whacking at that little ball. Another reason why I go for the real thing much sooner than some coaches is that no matter how many lead-up drills you might use to prepare kids for actually hitting a tennis

When hitting groundstrokes from the baseline with a low-to-high stroking motion, youngsters should actually aim for an imaginary point about 6 feet over the net — not just a bit above the net tape. This mother is giving her child a visual target by holding her racket high; he can then try to relate this target to a point just above the back fence for future reference. The key is to have your child concentrate on aiming high over the net, even in the beginning, before you actually concentrate on how to impart topspin rotation. A seven- or eight-year-old who has a low-to-high forward motion can swing hard, hit the ball on a high arc, and still have it land in play thanks to the pull of gravity. He will have to increase topspin rotation, however, as he gains more power on his stroke.

ball, most of them are still going to have trouble making good contact at first. So I go for reinforcing the motivation that comes from tackling the game itself.

Once on the court, I first have my student take two or three practice strokes at an imaginary ball to gain a better feel for what she wants to try to do. I'll stand between her and the net and say, "Just try to imitate my stroke: turn your nonhitting side to the net as you take your racket back, drop the racket down low as you bend your knees, and bring it forward and up, contacting the ball here and finishing like this." Then I set myself up between the service line and the net and start feeding balls to her to hit from the baseline. Once again, I make sure to throw the ball softly and to a point out in front of the student, to allow her every opportunity to make contact.

The basic forehand that I described above is as detailed as you ought to get with your child in the early learning stages. Just take it all slowly and concentrate on these key fundamentals so that you don't overteach. Save the more detailed critiquing for when she has gained some proficiency with the basic pattern of the stroke. However, since she will start acquiring "muscle-memory" patterns within ten or fifteen swings, you should be prepared from the very start (1) to have her strive for the proper technique and (2) to try to keep her from reinforcing incorrect techniques. This can all be done in a positive atmosphere if you simply balance your comments and use the right tone of voice. A typical line might be, "That's the way, you're watching the ball like a hawk, but your racket head is a little floppy, so tighten your grip some more." You've already established the fact that you're out there to help her learn to play the game as well as she can, and this means the two of you must work together to correct her mistakes—that it's your job to help point out these mistakes, not to keep overlooking them, and it's her responsibility not to deny them or try to hide from them. So during this first lesson you might want to remind her: "Just because I'm telling you what you're doing wrong doesn't make me a dirty rat; I never want to make you feel bad. I just want to help you learn to hit the ball better so you can have even more fun."

As you get into the lesson, you should also occasionally stop the action to ask questions such as, "Do you take the racket back at eye level, or belly-button level, or knee level?" and "When you contact the ball, how should the racket head be—straight up and down or tilted back?" Questioning like this keeps your child involved in the learning process and reminds her about key checkpoints she might want to think about on her next swing. In addition, remember, she doesn't have to perform a physical task to please you or to have a success experience; if she can't hit the ball but she knows all the answers, you can still applaud her for being smart. (During this first lesson you should remind your child that you'll always be asking her questions—"Not to put you on the spot, but to see whether you really understand what we're working on and whether I'm doing a good enough job making it clear.")

Here it's very important to reiterate one of my underlying concepts of teaching tennis: that hitting the ball with the racket is not the important immediate goal—form is. Just practicing long enough will eventually produce the hit. As I tell the students at my tennis college, "If you have perfect form but you're eight feet away from the ball when you go to swing, don't worry—we're down to just one thing to work on (getting to the ball), and that's easy." Most youngsters put a lot of pressure upon themselves to make the hit—to contact the ball and hit it somewhere. If you as an instructor now add more pressure to make the hit, by saying, "Come on, you're not watching the ball," or by emphasizing ball direction, then you have to be very careful that a concern for ball direction doesn't take precedence over your child's stroke production—to the point that she's always saying, "Yeah, but the ball went in," whenever you try to

Whether your child plays right-handed or left-handed, show him where the ball should be contacted on the forehand: off the front side, just ahead of the front foot. Also notice that the racket face here is in the proper position — straight up and down (vertical) at impact.

correct technique. You can acknowledge the fact that when she eventually plays a match the object will be to land the ball inside her opponent's court, but the only thing the two of you should worry about in these early lessons is her form.

Following are basic approaches I've found useful in helping beginning youngsters grasp the various aspects of good forehand technique.

• Show your child where she wants to contact the ball in relation to her body—off the front side (see photo), and out away from it. (When her body is turned sideways to the net, "off the front side" refers to the side closer to the net and "out away from it" means the direction in which her belly button is pointed.)

• As the ball approaches and before it bounces, have her turn the shoulder of her hitting arm toward the back fence so that her nonhitting side is toward the net. This is an elemental move in starting the proper backswing, and there are a number of ways to get the concept across. With little kids I might say: "This is my belly and this is my side. Now watch what happens when I put my side to the net. See where my stomach is facing now? That's what you want to do when you see the ball coming."

Older kids can visualize what it means to rotate their shoulders if you face them head on and tell them, "Pretend your name is written on your left shoulder blade [assuming they're right-handers] and as you turn to hit the ball, make sure I see who you are." Some kids even call out their name as they turn—"Hi, I'm Jimmy." One important reason why I emphasize shoulder rotation: research shows that the trunk of the body turning back into the shot is the primary source of power on groundstrokes.

• Encourage your child to take the racket back in a loop pattern (over the "beach ball," at eye level), but if she prefers, you can also let her take it straight back on a downward diagonal—providing she can get the racket low enough with knee bend to swing low-to-high. I point out that the more loop players have, the more they generate natural power with their swing. (See page 180 for a fuller discussion of these two backswing styles.)

• At first, don't worry about your child stepping forward in to the ball. Just let her stand in a comfortable, fixed position while she first concentrates on swinging *slowly*, low-to-high, and then on making good contact. (When kids swing fast, they don't know what they're doing.) But once the swinging motion is firmly established, have her try to step foward as the ball bounces—without transferring all of her weight forward—so that she can then use the power of her body as she shifts her weight and strokes up through the ball. (Kids with baseball or softball batting experience will already know the importance of "stepping in to the ball.") On nearly all types of playing surfaces, a good rule of thumb is to have your child start her forward motion on the swing when the ball hits the court. Certain pros find it effective to use a "bounce-hit" technique, in which the student actually says "bounce" as the ball lands, and then "hit" as she strokes the ball. Some players, however, find this verbalizing distracting as they try to swing. Whatever approach you use, the key is for your child to be ready to swing when the ball bounces—and to think only about that task. (In the first day's "run-and-hit" drills along the baseline, you'll let your child know that when she stops to hit, that's also her cue to step forward in to the ball.)

• Nearly all beginners have a timing problem when it comes to contacting the ball, so make sure your child at least strives to be early rather than late. You can't help a youngster who's consistently late, except to get her to start her swing sooner. Plus, there's no last-second correctional factor she can make on a late hit; she's dead. But if she concentrates on a good, methodical follow-through (and early preparation), she increases her hitting zone and thus her margin for timing errors. In turn, she enjoys more success.

• One of the most important concepts you can stress with children, at a very early stage, is "Take care of the shot you're on." Kids are often so eager to get to their next shot that they rush their stroke, or they lift their head too early around the time of impact, or they fail to complete their follow-through properly. One good way to teach your child patience on her stroke is to place a penny on the court, out in front of where she normally contacts the ball (because of inflation, some parents use dimes). Then have her focus on the coin—after she hits the ball—until she completes her follow-through. She'll discover that she has plenty of time to then look up to see where her shot is going, well before it reaches her opponent.

• Coaches like to say, "Think of the racket as an extension of the arm," but that's not a natural feeling for many youngsters as they try to contend with all that extra length and weight. They can *see* what they're supposed to do with the racket during the swing, but they can't relate to this image once the racket is in their hand. This is why I like to have kids stand *without a racket* and practice stepping forward when the ball bounces, as if they're going to hit it with the palm of their hand. After all, as I later point out: "As the palm goes, so goes the racket face" (when a player uses the Eastern forehand grip). I also run through this drill without a ball, instead saying "bounce" to initiate the student's forward swing. This helps her concentrate on her stroke or footwork without worrying about the racket or about hitting the ball. Yet another approach is to demonstrate the stroke with a racket while your child imitates your hand-and-arm motion by tracing a perfect swing without a racket. (It's a good idea to have your child practice *all* strokes without a racket—and also with her eyes closed.)

• Even though most kids have a marvelous ability to zero in on the ball as it approaches and to rule out other distractions, I still talk to them about how important it is to ingrain this as a habit, because as they grow older they'll have a tendency to start focusing attention on everything but the ball. "It's really fun to hit the ball," I tell little kids, "and if you watch it closely, you'll hit it even more than you do now." I even have them place their racket face at the intended point of impact and then I walk the ball right into their strings from about 10 feet away. "Here comes the ball . . . watch it . . . watch it . . . watch it—bang! Did you see it hit the strings? That's what I want you to try to do with your eyes every time. Just follow the ball right into the strings." I assure them that this is optically impossible, but it's a nice approach to develop.

Then I have them hold a ball, run their fingers over the fuzz and along the seams, and study the writing (if they're old enough to read) so that they become familiar with this new friend. "The ball's your pal, so get to know him well," I tell them. "Once you're on the court, it's just you, your racket, and the ball. Don't worry about anything else."

The name of the game is action, so even on the first day of lessons I try to have youngsters run over from the baseline center mark to hit a ball near the fore-hand corner. After the student hits, I have him run back and touch the center mark with his foot, then return to the forehand corner for another try. When you try this drill, remember to "lead" your child; aim the toss so that he has a chance to take the best swing he can.

This will also ease apprehension among kids who seem to fear getting hit by the ball. (Some kids go up to volley at the net holding their racket in front of their face as a shield.) I let them know that such fears are natural and there's nothing wrong about having them. Then I demonstrate how a player can easily avoid a shot coming right at her simply by stepping forward on a diagonal. "This will keep you from getting hit and also set up a proper swing," I explain. I even lob the ball softly toward a nervous kid's face a few times to let her get used to the sensation and to give her a chance to practice dodging.

Let Your Child Run to Hit the Ball

Kids learning tennis are no different from those learning any sport: they love to be active. Thus, even on the first day I like to give them a chance to run and hit the ball—on the forehand and on the volley. Whether they're successful or not makes no difference. The important thing is that they learn there's a lot more to tennis than standing at the baseline and hitting balls that come right to them. Plus, "stand-and-hit" drills can quickly become boring.

Once your child starts to become familiar with the basic stroke, or if you just sense a need for variety, you might suggest: "You're getting the right idea, so let's try something new. Remember the players we saw playing at the park? They stood back here at the baseline, which we'll call home base, and sometimes they ran out to a corner to hit the ball. Then they would run back to their home base and wait for their opponent's next shot. Do you want to give that a try?" If so, have her stand at the center mark on the baseline and then run toward the forehand corner as you bounce the ball in that direction, out ahead of her and about waist-high. Once she follows through—even if she misses the ball completely—have her run back and touch the center mark, then return to the forehand corner as you bounce another ball to her there. Stand close enough to this corner so that you can toss the ball on a bounce (generally with an underhand motion) to a spot where she has a good chance to take her swing; if you use a racket it will take a practiced touch to deliver the ball into a youngster's ideal hitting area consistently, so it's best just to toss the ball.

You shouldn't really worry about your child's footwork in the early going, since most kids need to concentrate simply on their stroke and on contacting the ball. She may catch on fairly quickly, or she may not get her swing started until the ball has bounced two or three times; little tykes will even drag their racket across the court as they run for the ball. But whatever happens, stay enthusiastic and be ready to laugh right along with her because the balls she does manage to hit are likely to go in every direction. If she keeps missing, find little ways to praise her, such as, "You really were fast getting there," or "I can't believe how hard you're working." With constant encouragement like this, she'll still want to come back to this drill at the next lesson.

Another reason I like to have kids run for the ball on the first day (and in every lesson) is that they get some exercise and work up a little sweat. As you retrieve balls together, you have a chance to say, "That was terrific; you were like a real athlete out there today." Kids love to hear this kind of praise, especially after they've worked hard at a "big-person's" game— and have had fun doing it. Moreover, you learn more about your child's real interest in tennis. Maybe she doesn't really enjoy running around and exerting herself on a tennis court. She may tell you, "Just throw the ball straight to me," in which case you can question her about whether she even wants to keep taking lessons. But after the drill she may respond, "Just let me rest a minute, then start again, okay?" You always want to look for clues such as these, because you may have a youngster who's hungry for the game from day one—or you may be rushing the nonathlete.

How to Introduce the Volley

You may want to concentrate only on forehand groundstrokes during the first lesson, but I love to introduce the volley also—whatever age group I'm working with. Again, this is not because I'm eager to prime children for competition, but for these benefits: (1) youngsters gain a more realistic feel of what the game offers, (2) you have another opportunity to introduce some little running drills, which means action, (3) you can help eliminate early on some possible fears and apprehensions about this stroke that might arise later in the learning experience, and (4) you don't have to rely on a youngster's groundstroke in order for her to gain the success experience of hitting the ball over the net.

To introduce the volley, you might tell your child: "You've been hitting the forehand groundstroke, right? And why is it called a groundstroke? Because you've been hitting the ball after it bounces off the ground. Now we're going up to the net and you can hit the ball before it bounces. We call it a forehand volley and here's how the stroke looks—just a short punching motion like this." At this point, I briefly explain why the volley is important—"When you can hit this stroke from up near the net, it's easier to hit the ball away from your opponent"—though I also let them know that a volley can be hit from anywhere on the court. (See chapter 13 for a full description of the stroke and its value to the all-around game.)

Obviously, I'm not talking about introducing hard-nosed volleying here, in which you pepper your child with drives from the baseline. Simply take your youngster up to the net and have her hold her racket up in the proper position. If she has been hitting her groundstrokes with one hand on the racket, she may have to use two hands in order to volley with sufficient racket control. Toss the ball underhand, on a fly, from about 5 or 10 feet away, as close as possible to the racket strings. Most kids can at least hit the ball over the net from up close, which is a nice feeling if most of their shots have failed to clear the net from farther back. In fact, you can actually score more successes up at the net with a youngster who's really having trouble with the game; if her racket is held up properly and you can aim the ball there, it's going to bounce back over the net—she doesn't even have to swing.

After your child has had some swings up at the net, have her move back to the service line and then run up to the net and assume her ready-to-volley position with the racket up. Again, simply toss the ball from a short distance away and aim for a spot as close to her racket strings as possible. This gets her moving, just as in a match, and she quickly learns that tennis is not going to be a game in which she stands around all day, on the baseline or at the net. If you have the right attitude, that's all the motivation most kids need to keep their enthusiasm high this first day.

Here's how close a parent ought to stand when starting a youngster out on the volley. You want to be able to direct the ball as close as possible to your child's racket face to help insure "success experiences."

How to Work with a Youngster Who Can't Hit the Ball

Throughout this book I suggest ways that you can motivate less-talented youngsters, boost their self-esteem, and keep their interest level up. This should help, but let's say that you're on the court and your child is floundering—you're saying all the right things but she's missing more balls than she hits and her swing isn't even close to the one you're trying to teach. What then are some practical tips that can help give her some success experiences and a chance to feel those important sensations of actually hitting the ball?

First of all, you may be standing too far away from your child, feeding the balls to her at too fast a speed, or bouncing them inconsistently, too low or too high. Get closer so that it's easier for you to bounce the ball right to where she has the best chance to make contact.

Second, get her to shorten her backswing, which will give her more control and consistency in the hitting zone. Besides, if she's like most beginners, she's taking too long a swing anyway, by letting the racket come back too far. If a little kid is really having trouble, I'll even have her take just a 10- or 12-inch swing. I'll stand right next to her, hold the ball in the

air, and then let it bounce so it's almost guaranteed she'll make contact. Gradually I back up, but I have her continue to take that tiny stroke until she gets a better idea of what it means to hit the ball.

Third, if your child's having trouble coping with a moving ball, teach her how to throw the ball up gently with her free hand (about 4 or 5 feet high) so that it bounces and gives her time to take a proper stroke. This should help give her some confidence in hitting the ball and is something she can practice by the hour against the garage or a backboard.

Fourth, if she lacks the strength or coordination to get the ball over the net from the baseline, you can let her move up and hit from the service line.

Fifth, demonstrate several "lead-up" drills that might give her a better "feel" for the ball and the racket. (See pages 101–102 for a discussion of such drills.)

How to Wind Up the Lesson

Despite your child's apparent eagerness, she might be afraid to come right out and tell you she wants to go home, so keep looking for the little signals that indicate diminishing interest, such as when her effort begins to lag or her attention wanders. It may be that there's not enough action, or you're repeating a drill too many times, or you're having her volley when she would prefer to stand on the baseline and slug the ball. Take a different approach, and then if she's not almost totally engrossed in what she's doing, call it quits for the day.

Even if she's still going strong this first day and is pleading for more hits, cut the lesson off after an hour or so and give her something to look forward to the next time. You might tell her: "I can't wait to do this again. You're fantastic. Next time I'm going to teach you a new stroke, too—the backhand." Then on the way home you'll have a lot to talk about: the lesson just completed and the one coming up. However, if your child's interest in the game never takes off and even seems to disintegrate as the lesson progresses, you should point out an aspect that did seem fun for her, then tell her, "The next time you want to go out, just let me know." She may have found that tennis wasn't exactly what she had in mind—but you thus leave the door open should she want to try again when she's a little older.

Whatever happens during the first lesson—and this should apply to every lesson you give—it's tremendously important that you (1) seek your child's feedback and (2) end the day on a positive note.

You've offered your child a lot of important information and, if things went well, she's responded with enthusiasm to new sensations. Give a last

Opposite:
When a youngster is having trouble contacting balls approaching from a distance, he needs some success experiences. I simply stand right in front of him and drop a ball so that he can hit it on the first bounce. The emphasis here should be on a short backswing and an easy forward stroking motion. The object is to make contact, not to hit the ball hard. If the ball goes over the net, the instructor can say, "See how gently you swung, and still the ball went over?"

quick review of the forehand and volley, since summarizing aids retention, and then have her recap what it is she's doing right and what it is she's doing wrong. This helps her maintain a healthy, balanced perspective about her game, by realizing her strokes are not all black and white, good or bad, but that there are many gray areas: she does certain things right on the forehand, but other things give her trouble. Also, her feedback will enable you to know if she has assimilated the lesson carefully and properly, and whether she has gained something that will help her. You should then try to summarize points of technique for her to think about—and, ideally, practice—before the next lesson (this process is explained more specifically in subsequent chapters).

Remember, your child's motivation and self-satisfaction are so important that you should never let her leave the court without your having said something good about the way she hit the ball, or how hard she worked, or whatever you can think of that will give her a lift. If you've had a reasonably successful lesson, she'll already be feeling pretty good about herself just for having worked up a little sweat, and she'll love to hear extra encouragement from her instructor—not to mention her parent. And you can be sure she'll be ready to throw herself into the next lesson.

What to Cover in the Next Lesson

As suggested earlier, in developing an independent-thinking player who has a mature approach to the game, you must have your child help you organize every lesson. Let her know that you're counting on her input, and that you want her to eventually provide the direction for her learning process—in a healthy manner—while you basically act as the resource. Don't fall into the authoritarian rut of saying, "Today we'll work on this . . . this . . . and this." Consult your child, for she may have entirely different notions about what she'd like to practice. Not that you should simply let her work on her strengths while ignoring problem areas—but do incorporate her suggestions into the lesson plan.

For example, you might want to concentrate on the backhand and volley, but if she says, "I've been thinking about my forehand and I'd like to try something new," then you should be flexible and work on forehands for ten or fifteen minutes. Moreover, once she gets into competitive tennis she'll probably know what she wants to work on at the next lesson as soon as she finishes a match. She'll have a sense of which strokes need special attention, and, preferably, somebody will have "charted" her match (as explained in chapter 14) to provide objective information on problem areas.

When you start asking your child questions like "What are some things you want to accomplish today?" before every lesson, this makes her *think* about her tennis game, and she's going to come up with specific answers because she knows you're counting on them. If this becomes a nice routine, it's nearly always clear what the two of you feel needs to be covered. But when you fail to encourage her input, you may ask her what she wants to work on and she may just shrug her shoulders and say, "I don't know; whatever you want to do." This might drive you up the wall, but it's a good indication that something has bogged down. It could be that she just doesn't care that much about tennis. Or perhaps you're too intimidating and she needs to be reassured that you really want feedback. Maybe she just has to learn how to explain herself better. A lot of kids want to provide feedback to an instructor—or a classroom teacher—but they have trouble focusing on what they want to say. So use tennis as a way to help your child gain greater skill and confidence in expressing herself and you'll help provide her with a tremendous asset.

7/Teaching the Game from Week to Week

You've given your child his first lesson, and now your obvious concern is "Where do I go from here?" This chapter covers the practical aspects of teaching the game to a youngster from week to week—from the sequence to use in introducing new strokes and how to work on technique, to evaluating and improving yourself as an instructor. It's here that I help you and your child establish goals that will allow both of you to objectively evaluate the progress you are making, and I discuss the ways you can keep him closely involved in the teaching process so that you maximize his growth as an independent-thinking player.

The Sequence of Strokes

One advantage you have as a parent/instructor is that you have the freedom to expose your child to new strokes according to his physical readiness, the improvement he is making, and his eagerness to tackle something different. Most paid professionals are under pressure from fee-paying parents to introduce children to all the important elements of the game within a certain time frame (generally six or eight weeks)—whether a youngster is ready or not.

My own teaching approach is built on the premise "How can I give kids the most success experiences early?" Thus, if I don't have a time obligation, I try to adhere to the following sequence when introducing strokes. (All the strokes and concepts mentioned in this sequence are discussed in detail later on, as listed on the contents page.)

Lesson 1
Every instructor has adopted the approach that seems to work best for him. As I explained earlier, I've found there are psychological and

physiological advantages to starting with the forehand. I also like to introduce the volley because it (1) adds variety to the first lesson, (2) introduces more running, (3) lends itself to numerous drills involving the other strokes in future lessons, and (4) enables a youngster to start gaining confidence and ability in a stroke many adults try to avoid.

Lesson 2

At the beginning of this lesson (and all subsequent ones), I spend about five minutes reviewing what we did the week before, demonstrating the strokes again and highlighting a couple of the common problems the student seemed to be having. I also ask if he's tried to work on the forehand between lessons, and if so, what questions does he have? Then we get out on the court to hit. If you don't have your youngster hitting within about five minutes, you're going to start losing his interest and attention, because he'll want action—not a lot of talk. With older and more-talented children, I like to introduce the backhand in this second lesson, while continuing with the forehand and volley.

Lesson 3

Depending upon the child I'm working with, I may save the backhand for the third session—or until I know he's ready. I find that children can have more success concentrating on the forehand groundstroke and volley during the first couple of lessons, without having to worry about the backhand. Although the ideal stroking pattern (the path the racket face takes) on the backhand is identical to the forehand, it does present some learning problems—such as, hitting off the nondominant side (like the sensation of swinging at a baseball from the opposite side), confronting weakness in the forearm extensor muscles, and, for many youngsters, having to hit with two hands.

When I do introduce the backhand, I tell kids: "If you can hit a forehand, I know you can hit a backhand. You just have to start your swing earlier, because as you can see, you must contact the ball farther out in front of your body than you normally do on the forehand. You also need strong muscles right here on your forearm, but I have some little exercises that will help." By introducing the backhand soon after the forehand (whenever possible), I can draw on important relationships between the two strokes that my students can understand. If I bring the backhand into this third lesson, I also include the forehand volley and drills that use the forehand groundstroke.

Lesson 4

After introducing the backhand, I like to keep everything loose and flexible in future lessons. I continue to pick up the running with a number

Baseball Tennis

Many of the ingredients of tennis are found in baseball tennis, a drill in which the ball is kept in play without a racket. This boy is starting a point by "serving" with a baseball-throwing motion. His mother must then field the ball before it bounces twice and throw it back in play to keep the rally going. If your child has trouble catching the ball, alter the rules so that he's allowed to try to catch it again on the first bounce after he drops it. You can also shorten the playing area by using the two service lines as boundaries. Meanwhile, he's learning how to keep score, to keep his eyes on the ball, and to respond quickly. He's also grasping a basic tennis strategy: aim the ball to where your opponent isn't.

of little drills, but I save the serve and other strokes until a youngster indicates to me that he's ready. Nevertheless, lesson 4 is not too early to have children at least try the serve, as long as the intent is simply to introduce them to the basics of the stroke so they have a sense of what's involved.

Trying to coordinate the service toss with the stroke itself is a totally alien movement for children, but there are a number of ways you can scale everything down and attack the basics while keeping your child interested. For example, since the ideal service motion simulates a baseball pitcher's delivery, help your child learn how to throw a ball properly. One way to make it fun is to play "baseball tennis," which involves throwing the ball over the net instead of hitting it with a racket (see drill, page 107). If he already knows how to throw, then he's likely to grasp the basic service motion in a short period of time.

A second choice is to have your child try some half-swings, in which he holds the racket over his shoulder before tossing the ball up. If he lacks the power to hit the ball over the net from the baseline, let him serve from the service line so he can at least get the feeling of landing the ball in his opponent's service box.

Most children don't seem to mind a scaled-down approach to the serve, but if I run into a loss of interest or too much frustration, then I go back to forehands and backhands and volleys.

Lesson 5

If a youngster's ready, I like to start expanding my approach to the volley about now. Having observed his efforts in the opening lessons, I know whether he's still afraid of getting hit by the ball, how well he grasps the techniques involved, and how his footwork, agility, and reactions at the net measure up. It may be that I have to continue tossing the ball to him softly from a short distance away, but he may be eager for the challenge of drills that incorporate volleying at the net against my groundstrokes from the baseline.

Lesson 6 and Beyond

Basically, if you listen carefully and observe, your child will give you the best indication of when it's time to move on to a broader approach. On his own, he'll start throwing the ball up and trying to serve the way he has observed other players. Or he'll start asking questions such as: "How do you lob? Will I ever be able to hit the overhead smash? What's an approach shot?" Even when a youngster doesn't reveal this kind of curiosity, I like to take time at about this point to talk more about strategy and to provide a brief introduction to these other strokes. The youngster may not be ready (or willing) to tackle them yet, but he'll realize the variety tennis offers.

Set Objectives and Goals

Many people tend to regard goals as cold, distant objects way off in the future. I like to treat them as something immediate and practical—warm, fun, and exciting to deal with—for a tremendous amount of motivation can be generated in youngsters when they learn (1) how to establish short-term objectives that lead toward long-term goals, (2) what it means to strive for these objectives, and (3) how to evaluate these objectives, whether they're achieved or not. What your child learns from this process of goal setting will have lifelong value, I've found, because youngsters tend to flounder if they don't have a sense of where they're trying to go, how to go about setting that direction, and how to articulate it. Moreover, goal-oriented people seem to be the ones who make the best gains in life.

Following are some guidelines I recommend to help keep goal-setting and evaluation in a healthy perspective, so that your child's personal growth will benefit along with his tennis-playing ability.

• *Your child must be deeply involved in the goal-setting procedure and subsequent evaluation.* Some of his goals may be self-imposed and even kept to himself, but the others should never be set by the adult involved without the child agreeing to them. You might go about this by sitting down with your child early in the tennis relationship and saying: "I think it's important that we have a few objectives to shoot for in these lessons. So let's talk about some things you might be able to do in another month or two. Maybe we'll be unrealistic, because we don't really know what's going to happen, but let's at least see what happens. We're not going to be rigid about it; we'll grow together. If we don't achieve these goals we won't be disappointed, but maybe we'll find we've set our sights too low and you've gone way beyond them. Let's just set them somewhere and this will help us be more realistic the next time we do this."

What are some reasonable objectives? First, to learn the rules and some basic things about strategy and how the game is played. Second, to understand the important strokes (not that your child has to hit them properly right away, but he should know the key principles involved and why each stroke is needed to play a sound game). A third objective could involve a list of favorable traits and attitudes you'd like to see him display: having fun, showing courtesy to you on the court, being cooperative, having a nice attitude about learning, trying hard all the time, listening carefully, and feeling at ease about asking you questions or challenging what you've said. Of course, the understanding here is that you will simultaneously be adhering to the principles of good teaching and striving for self-improvement yourself.

• *No youngster should be overburdened with goals.* They should be set in a fair manner and they should be undertaken in an easygoing spirit: he can try to shoot for these things if he wants, but you don't want him to worry about them all the time or constantly be looking over his shoulder. The message should be: "We'll write down these goals, seal them in an envelope, and then forget about them. Let's just have fun and learn as much as we can about the game. Then one day we'll open the envelope and see how things came out."

• *In learning to set goals properly, it's crucial that your child knows he has your support and understanding, and that you will help him maintain a realistic perspective.* For example, have him realize that he can't necessarily expect to set just any goal the first time and definitely meet it. Also, when he's fallen short of certain goals, help him learn how to pull back and become more realistic in setting up new ones. And without sounding like you're putting him down, let him know when you feel your own expectations have been unreasonable: "It looks like I got carried away. You were giving everything you had and I know that's the best we can expect."

• *Not everything he's attempting has to come out on the table*—although the more things that do come out in a nice way, the better. If your child has self-motivating goals that he prefers to keep to himself, that's fine. For example, he may secretly want to be the best player in the world, or he may simply dream about beating that kid at the club who keeps clobbering him, 6–0, 6–0. In fact, his unstated goal may be to defeat you one day in tennis. Most youngsters harbor that dream about a parent or other adult coach, so I always try to bring that desire out into the open by telling the kids I coach: "Boy, the happiest day in my life will be when you can beat my brains out. But I'm not going to lose without a fight." I find that this takes away any guilt feelings youngsters might have and it also gives them a nice incentive.

• *Set goals together and evaluate them together so there are never any surprises.* This means your child knows from the very start what he's going to be evaluated on at a later date, and that he'll be able to learn from that evaluation. He'll discover that this is the fairest way to have his progress analyzed, for he's being assessed only in terms of what he originally set out to do—as documented on paper.

• *If the teaching relationship is properly handled, your child will gain a respect—instead of a fear—for setting goals and seeking evaluation.* For one reason or another, some people go through life without ever setting goals, and though they thus may never have to feel accountable, they deprive themselves of a sense of accomplishment. Other people may want to evaluate themselves, but they can't objectively do this because they originally failed to set goals. Your child will learn that these two criteria, setting goals and evaluating performance, go hand in hand in attaining maximum performance on the tennis court—and in life.

How to Work on Your Child's Technique

Before I tackle the specific aspects of each stroke (chapters 10 to 13), there are some important overall concepts and suggestions to keep in mind that should help you make greater progress when you work on your child's technique.

Try the "Whole-Stroke-First" Approach
Earlier I stressed my preference for starting children out with the same stroking techniques they ought to use as older, advanced players. Even five- and six-year-olds are capable of learning the correct *overall* stroking

patterns I seek (though it certainly takes years to master the crucial details that are needed to produce sound, consistent strokes). Thus they later never have to change long-grooved "muscle-memory" patterns in order to play championship tennis.

I like to demonstrate the entire stroke to a youngster and then have him try to match the pattern of that stroke as he swings. I find that if he has the correct overall picture of the stroke fixed in his head, we can go to work on the isolated parts and he has a much better idea of what we're striving for and why a particular part of his swing may be getting him into trouble at impact.

Now, some instructors like to have students start out by learning little isolated parts of the stroke first, step by step by step, progressing toward what they hope will become one smooth, complete stroke. I'll agree that most children who learn by this rigid approach can often make a few immediate gains the first couple of lessons. However, though research may some day prove otherwise, I've found that when kids start out by trying the tennis stroke in its complete form, the end result is normally better than if they first learn the isolated parts. Their respective "learning curves" quickly even out and those children who have spent their time working on the desired, overall task from the beginning will generally go way past those who have learned by a point-by-point method such as "Racket back, step, swing."

Of course, a progression is involved even in trying to teach the whole stroke from the beginning, since a youngster must focus on specific parts of the stroke in order to eventually produce a coordinated motion. But when your child has an understanding of how the various parts relate, it should make him more receptive to your advice in tackling specific problems. Another built-in virtue of the "whole-stroke-first" approach is the motivation your child gains knowing that the strokes he's trying to learn now are exactly what the pros are using. I like to say to young kids: "These are the strokes that can make you famous. I'm giving you exactly what Tracy Austin does and Bjorn Borg does, because I want to treat you as an intelligent human being. I'm not going to come to you when you're fourteen and say, 'Okay, now you can go to the fourteen-year-old system.' I'm giving you the championship stuff right now." This approach has always worked well for me, because kids respond favorably when they know they're not learning "comedown" strokes and you're not going to change directions on them somewhere down the road.

One warning here: If your child simply can't handle the overall stroke—if he needs to begin at point one and progress from there—don't give up on the stroke, or on your child. Just try to teach the advanced system as much as possible, but on a level he can handle, so that he's always having fun. Here's the kind of approach I'll take with a youngster who's trying hard, but who just can't seem to grasp what I'm teaching: "Jimmy, I know you're not hitting the ball the way you want, but your attitude is exactly what I love to see. You're trying to swing the way I teach and that's the important thing right now. I've known a lot of kids who couldn't hit the ball when they first started—just like you—but they kept trying to do it their way, and they never became very good. So even though this is causing you a lot of pain now, you're sticking with my system, and I guarantee you'll see the day when you're beating all these guys who are killing you now."

Put Stroking Form Ahead of Ball Direction

Once your child manages to get the ball into his opponent's court, it's hard for him not to be influenced by where the ball lands on every shot. Yet he'll make far better strides in this game and ultimately derive greater self-satisfaction if he knows from the very beginning that a concern for *proper stroking form*, not for where he hits the ball, is his primary goal at first. Try to emphasize this and then reinforce it with the right teaching approach. Remember the following important points.

• Assure your child that once he acquires good stroking patterns, direction and distance will come easily, and reliably.

• Just the slightest alteration in the racket face at impact—away from a vertical position—can affect the direction of the ball dramatically, even when the stroke has been perfect up until that point. This can prove discouraging to a youngster who puts all his early attention on ball direction, instead of realizing that it takes time to acquire the consistent racket-head control that brings about good aim.

• Letting the end (where the ball lands) justify the means (how it was hit there) will unfairly mislead your child if his stroke pattern was incorrect. Your job as instructor is to keep him from repeating—and thus reinforcing—incorrect movements, even if the ball sometimes does go in. Let him know that in the long run relying on the right form will land a lot more balls in bounds than relying on lucky hits will. If you fail to establish this philosophy, you're constantly going to face situations in which you suggest an important correction but your child replies, "Yeah, but that ball went in."

• Initially deemphasizing ball direction will also help you maintain a positive teaching pattern. Let's say your child is making haphazard contact at best and spraying his shots in every direction. Instead of falling into the trap of saying, "Watch the ball . . . watch the ball . . . watch the ball," you can say: "Look, don't worry about where the ball is going; that's not important now. Just take a look at your follow-through and see if it's going to the sky . . . That's the way! It went to the sky."

As you work with your child, back up your emphasis on stroke production by never looking around to see where the ball lands. Just feed another ball for him to hit, and stay focused on specific aspects of his stroke. If you have a youngster who's competitive, don't deny this instinct but channel it toward better strokes. You can set up target areas to make learning more fun for him, but meanwhile, tend to the nitty-gritty: Is he turning his shoulders properly? Is he bending his knees and getting his racket head down low enough on the backswing? Is his rear end lifting as he strokes the ball on groundstrokes? . . .

Learn to Observe Technique

One of the biggest problems you'll have as a novice instructor is the fact that your eyes aren't trained to study technique; you may know that *something* is wrong with your child's swing—but not exactly what. You'll find you're smarter than you think if you can go into every lesson with two specifics in mind: (1) know what the overall stroke should look like and know key checkpoints along the way, and (2) concentrate on one little aspect at a time—either a part of the swing itself or a desired body movement. Later chapters will give you the important details to look for on each stroke.

Here's where a pro tournament can provide valuable insights for you and your child if you treat it as an educational opportunity. For the price of admission, you can check out the strokes you are teaching and your child can see for himself that the pros are doing the same things he's trying to do. This realization should pay off in subsequent lessons, especially if you're not a strong player in your own right and your child has tended to resist what you have been teaching. At the tournament, you might say: "I know I can't hit like these guys, but we can put my teaching to the test. It's all down there on the court for us to see." Even though the racket is moving so fast near impact that your eyes can't accurately record all that is happening, you'll be surprised at what you can learn by choosing one player and studying important, isolated movements (ideally with binoculars, or by looking through a pinhole in a three-by-five card so that you block out distractions). For example, how soon does the player turn to initiate his backswing? Does he take his racket head back at eye level or is it down around waist level? When he finishes the swing, has he come up from low-to-high or has he gone straight across with his racket? How do his feet move when he runs for a wide shot? What do you notice about his service motion? Is it similar to his overhead?

An important point here is that you keep validating your system by what you actually *see* the very best players doing—not by what you *hear* them say, for many pros do not actually do what they think they do as they stroke the ball (although a lot of them are starting to take a keen interest in what really happens).

Observe More Than Just Your Child's Stroke

Since fear or tension can inhibit proper or desired physical responses, not to mention a youngster's enjoyment of the game, be on the lookout for cues to anxieties that may be negatively influencing your child's strokes and sapping the rhythm you want him to have.

For starters, learn to study his face as he's hitting the ball. Does he look like he's having fun or does he look nervous? Is he obviously tense—even angry—or is that how he always looks when he's concentrating during a physical activity? Can you notice if his eyes are intent on contacting the ball, or is there a lackadaisical sense about them?

Second, look at his nonhitting hand during the stroke. Is it nicely relaxed, or clutched tightly—a dead giveaway for anxiety? Is the nonhitting arm locked against the body, or comfortably out away?

Third, study the rest of his body movements as he covers the court. Does he seem to walk and run differently than in other activities? Does his body tighten up as he prepares to hit the ball, or is it comfortably relaxed?

Consider "Lead-Up" Drills

If your child just can't make contact, or the ball simply dribbles off his racket in the early learning stages, you might want to show him some "lead-up" drills that might help his hand-eye coordination and provide a little fun—for instance, drills in which he sees how long he can keep the ball bouncing up off the racket strings, or down onto the court like a basketball dribble. From what I've observed, however, drills such as these are basically confidence builders, with no real carry-over value to regular tennis strokes (unless they simulate actual stroking requirements).

Now, I'm not opposed to showing a kid a couple of these drills during a rest break and letting him try them briefly, right then or later on at home. Also, by providing some success experiences, such drills can help motivate a youngster when he returns to the baseline. Lead-up drills also make some instructors feel more comfortable, since they can think, "At least the kid's doing *something*." Excess is the key issue—for if the instructor is spending an entire lesson on "non-tennis" drills, he's likely avoiding the real issue, which is stroke production.

In defense of those coaches who like to use a lot of lead-up drills in early lessons, I don't want to underestimate how important it is for every

In this popular "lead-up" drill, the youngster tries to bounce the ball up off his racket as many times as he can. Most beginners will get a better feeling for their racket and develop their hand-eye coordination. You'll also be able to tell whether your child's racket is too heavy; if it keeps falling as he tries to keep it up, he needs a lighter model. However, once he masters this drill, it's time to move on to another lead-up exercise — or to concentrate on stroke production.

coach to feel comfortable about his own particular approach to teaching the game. There are two people on the court—the student and the coach—and the coach, like the student, must have a nice attitude about what's happening during the lesson or he's going to lose much of his enthusiasm and effectiveness. So if lead-up drills get results for you, and your child can do them *and* enjoy them, then that's fine with me—even though the same drills might drive another coach crazy. Just be sure you don't use those drills only to give you some breathing time at the beginning of the lesson. I've noticed that when some pros are poorly prepared, they automatically start with such drills, even if their students have mastered them and are bored by doing them.

What to Do When Learning Bogs Down

At some point in the teaching relationship with your child there probably will be learning extinction—a point when, for any number of reasons, he becomes overwhelmed by what you're trying to teach, loses interest in learning, or simply refuses to swing the way you teach. Here are some ways to help keep those problems from arising and to deal with them if they do.

First of all, before learning apathy sets in, try to sense how much instructional repetition (in the way of stroke demonstrations and verbal explanations) your child can absorb or needs. In a similar vein, know the quantity of information he can effectively handle. One way you can discover this is by seeking feedback. If your child can accurately describe everything you've been telling him about a particular stroke, you should ask him: "Well, do you want to go for more technique? I'm really shocked by how much you already understand." He might want to dig deeper into the stroke, but he could beg off because he just wants to concentrate on what you've already given him. Even adults who come through my tennis college for the second time are amazed at what they realize they didn't hear the first time because they tried to gulp in too much at once. They'll say, "Vic, I was so worried about trying to do things right that I didn't hear half the stuff you were saying." Forty-five-year-old corporation presidents admit this, so imagine the eight-year-old's perspective.

The key is that you must be careful not to overteach. Before moving on to new concepts, always ask your child questions such as, "What's confusing about what I've told you so far?" and "What's the reason for this—why does it happen?" This gives him a chance to relay important feelings and attitudes. Don't get bogged down in details. The minute an overload of detail begins to interfere with enjoyment of the learning process, slow everything down and refocus on just one basic fundamental. It's easy to get wrapped up in teaching and forget that you're bombarding a youngster with advice about his racket, his wrist, hips, knees, thighs, trunk, feet, palm, hands, elbows, eyes—and he can't handle it all. He may in fact be getting a grasp on the stroke in question, only to lose it as you continue to barrage him with information.

What you want to do as you correct technique, especially in working with beginners and intermediates, is to stress the gross movements on a stroke and not all the little nuances that might need attention. Keep your list of corrections and solutions as short as possible, because your child is going to bog down if you try to have him concentrate upon three or four things all at once he strokes the ball (for instance, "Eyes on the ball, head down, wrist firm, bend the knees"). If you overteach, you're also going to destroy his motivation, so just take a specific goal you have in mind and try to refer only to the right or wrong aspects of that single goal. And remember the cardinal rule: You can be *positive* and work toward the proper strokes at the same time. Learning is not going to take place when you negatively try to force his interest with threats such as, "If you're not going to concentrate on what I'm telling you, we're not going to come out here again."

If you start finding yourself in situations in which your child just can't hack the instruction you are giving and you fear the point is coming that he might leave the game in frustration over his inability to execute the "proper" strokes, remember: his enjoyment of the game must come first, not your ego as a tennis instructor. If he just won't accept the concepts you're teaching—"It just doesn't feel comfortable your way"—or he can't seem to learn the appropriate techniques needed for improvement, then you must let him adapt a playing style that is natural and comfortable to him, even though you know it may severely limit his eventual success as a player. But before giving up, try my suggestions for addressing the "I-Can't-Do-It" and "I-Won't-Do-It" attitudes (pages 54–56), and perhaps consider some role-playing, as described in the following section.

Try Switching Roles

My students are always reminding me that the teacher-student relationship is an exchange system: if I remain alert and nondefensive, I can learn from them while they are learning from me. This was never made clearer to me than the time I was practicing my serve at the Kramer club and one of my students, Wendy Appleby, called out from the next court: "Hey, Vic, do you know you have a hitch in your serve?" She was about fourteen, and my initial reaction was to say, "Come on, Wendy, you've got to be kidding!" But when we videotaped my swing and watched it on a TV screen, I realized that Wendy was really being gentle with her coach. Instead of having a continuous motion on my backswing, I had developed an awful-looking "hitch" that I hadn't noticed myself.

This is an example of unrehearsed role-playing in which the student becomes the instructor. You can structure it right into your lessons with beneficial results. For instance, you may have the talent to evaluate technique and communicate what you perceive, but you likely can't check yourself hitting; even top coaches have to go to another coach to improve their strokes. So give your child a chance to test his ability to evaluate technique, free of pressure to actually execute what he teaches. Set aside time regularly (perhaps five or ten minutes at the end of each lesson) for him to be the instructor, feeding balls as you work on your stroke. While your game improves, he'll gain a better appreciation for your role as the instructor and he'll find he has to think hard about what he's teaching and how to get it across. This in turn will improve his ability to express himself and give him a fresh perspective on the strokes he's learning.

If you listen carefully, trading roles with your child will offer a revealing method of self-evaluation. He'll tend to give his true feelings away when he imitates a parental role and you'll discover the attitudes you're projecting as an instructor and how much knowledge he's picking up about technique. He'll even give you some of the same unfortunate lines you may have been using under stress, such as, "Run, dummy, run!" or "Aren't you listening to anything I tell you?"

Role-playing can also provide a healthy release for your child if he's having trouble on a particular stroke or with the game in general and you sense the tension building up. You can tell him: "I understand what you're going through, so let's switch this thing around. I'm not playing well myself, so you teach me for a while." Most kids enjoy this change of pace and I find they're often more demanding than their instructor. Right away, your child may tell you, "No, Mom, you're not doing it right." This gives you a chance to respond—in a nice way—by saying, "You know, it's funny, but you say I'm not patient with *you*." Take a nonthreatening approach and you'll open up some fun, honest dialogue that should result in a more productive relationship when you go back to being the instructor.

Use Stroking Drills for Fun and Improvement

An experienced instructor will gradually acquire a bagful of trusted drills that enable his students to have a lot of fun while they work on their strokes—whether they're beginners or advanced juniors. Properly selected and organized, such drills can help introduce competition and realistic pressure when you feel your child is ready to handle it and will give him a realistic understanding of how much progress he's making on individual strokes. Before presenting a couple of my favorite stroking drills, I want to stress the following considerations:

• Tennis drills do not guarantee learning; they merely expose a student to the possibility of learning. All the crucial elements of good teaching discussed in chapter 3 must also be present.

• You should carefully communicate each drill so that your child knows why the drill is being used and the rationale behind each shot in the drill.

• Keep your drills as realistic as possible—by having your child hit the kind of shot he would actually hit from a particular position on the court, and by encouraging him to *strive* to swing the way he's expected to in a match. Discourage him from swinging any way he feels just to "save face" by getting the ball over the net.

Dink 'Em

"Dink 'Em" is played using the service courts for boundaries, as indicated by the white cards. The drill is started by an underhand serve into the appropriate service box, and then proceeds like a regular point. Youngsters learn what it means to take the speed off the ball in a short-court game, how to anticipate an opponent's next shot, and how to force him to run to different places.

• Although you want a drill to move quickly, make sure your child completes each stroke pattern correctly before preparing for his next shot or moving on to his next hitting position. Also, check that he's in an actual ready position—and not already moving—as the ball is hit or tossed to him.

• As your child begins to acquire some control over his shots, station targets in appropriate positions (for example, tennis cans in the backhand corner at the baseline) to encourage precise shot-making attempts rather than random efforts. He should clearly understand which target he is aiming at.

• Although you don't want to shield your child from the facts, make sure you always give him plenty of support and encouragement when a drill brings home the fact that he still needs plenty of work on a particular stroke or strokes.

• If your child appears flushed or faint during a vigorous drill, immediately sit him on a bench, and don't be afraid to let him get a drink of water if he says he's thirsty. Despite the lingering myth that water will induce cramps, researchers tell us that it's better to let people drink too much water than not enough when they're exercising.

The drills that follow can also be used in group lessons, which are discussed in the next chapter, but they are included here to give you an idea of what you might try with your child.

"Dink 'Em"
For singles and doubles tennis alike, youngsters should eventually acquire a short-court game—in which they find themselves facing their

opponent up near the net or from within opposite service courts. Short-court shots hit from within these confines are normally considered "touch" shots and demand practice. Therefore, an excellent drill for you and your child is simply to play a regulation tennis game using only the service-court areas as boundaries. On the serve, the ball must be bounced first and hit from a position waist-high or below, over the net and into the appropriate service court. The server may attack the net, but the receiver who develops a softly angled crosscourt shot will usually equalize this advantage. This drill can be a great deal of fun, is tiring, and requires excellent concentration—but it should not be used in a group that has more than six kids, to avoid excessive waiting.

Baseball Tennis

This is a terrific change-of-pace game for any caliber of player, and can give a lift to baseball players who are having trouble in tennis. The idea is to have two people play for points, but without using rackets—by throwing the ball to one another over the net after either catching it in the air or fielding it before it bounces twice, just as in a regular tennis rally. A person is allowed only one second after catching or fielding the ball to throw it back over the net. Try this drill yourself and discover how quickly it wears you out and how it forces greater footwork and anticipation, since you don't have a 27-inch racket to reach the ball. Baseball tennis is also a great drill for youngsters because (1) they can actually rush the net, grab the ball out of the air, and "volley," (2) they pick up a throwing motion almost exactly like the one they want to try for on the serve, (3) they have to learn to anticipate where their opponent is going to throw the ball and must concentrate intently when fielding the ball, and (4) they learn to look for an opponent's vulnerability—not unlike the way they'll eventually learn to look for a tennis opponent's weakness (the way he runs, how well he throws, how he bends down for the ball, and so on). This drill is also the best way I know to teach kids how to keep score when they're not yet ready to play an actual match.

How to Evaluate Your Teaching

Most teaching pros have never subjected their teaching system to an objective evaluative process. They can give lessons for years and claim they're terrific, but how effective have they actually been? Did they achieve their original goals with a particular student, or were objectives ever established at all? Have they periodically critiqued themselves? Have they sought evaluation from their students and objective observers? Have they learned to enjoy the evaluation sessions? And have they tried to make the changes suggested by such evaluation?

These are questions you should ask yourself once you get into teaching, for I've always felt that the mark of a good instructor is her willingness to evaluate her teaching and to try to learn from the results of that evaluation—without feeling threatened. Following are some ways you can assess the progress you are making with your child and evaluate weaknesses you might have in your teaching approach, plus some methods to help you improve.

Check Your Child's Progress

The fairest way to evaluate the lessons you give your child—and thus his progress—is in terms of the goals and objectives that the two of you established at the beginning and which may have been readjusted along the way. The key is to document as many things as possible, so that you can objectively review what you've accomplished, without having to rely on a memory that is often faulty or self-serving. For example:

• By writing down your lesson plan beforehand, you can review the lesson afterward in terms of what you set out to do. Many weeks later, as you look back on your notes, do you find you're bogged down on the same strokes or are you amazed at how far your child has advanced? There may be a little of both.

• Maybe it comes from my psychological training, but I always make notes after giving a lesson and then take them home and review them. This forces me to document what has happened and gives me a clear notion of what I want to cover in the next lesson.

• Chapters 10, 11, and 12 include "Stroke-Production Charts" that you can fill out after every lesson and then use as a way to note your child's specific improvements over a period of time as well as the problems that still exist. You can say: "I've been teaching you for six weeks and here's what we've covered on this stroke and here's what you are doing. You've improved here and here but you're still making the same mistakes here and here. Maybe it's my fault, maybe it's yours—but I think we can both do better. Perhaps I should change my approach a little."

• Try to take home movies of your child's strokes in the beginning, and then periodically after that. You'll have some good laughs and both of you will notice the improvements over time.

Check Yourself

Let's assume you've evaluated the progress your child is making, as a tennis player and as a person, and you know where you're trying to go. But what about your effectiveness as an instructor? Is there anything about your teaching style that might be inhibiting your child's ability to learn? This is something you should be constantly asking yourself. After teaching all day, I force myself to take time every night—tired as I might be—to evaluate the kind of job I have done. I do this not only to keep myself from falling into bad habits but to try to come up with new little insights that might improve my overall effectiveness or my progress with certain students.

One of the most revealing methods of self-evaluation is to tape-record a lesson and listen to it when you get home. Painful as it might be, you'll find it's remarkably instructive to hear yourself talk. You'll find yourself thinking, "Jeez, what I said wasn't clear at all," or "I mumble too much," or "I went so fast, no wonder he had trouble understanding." You may sense that your child needs to hear more enthusiasm in your voice, since a certain amount of verbal enthusiasm really picks people up. Or perhaps you need to speak more softly, so that you calm him down and he's better able to concentrate upon what you're actually saying.

Another self-evaluative technique is to have one of your lessons videotaped so that you can see for yourself how you come across to your child. He's studying your face the whole time—but what does it reveal? Enthusiasm? Boredom? Hostility? Warmth? Here again, I've found that most people fail to have an accurate self-image. When students at my tennis college watch themselves hitting the ball on our closed-circuit television, they're usually amazed and often say, "I wouldn't have believed that's me unless I saw it for myself."

Finally, you might ask a friend to observe and critique one of your lessons, watching for points mentioned above as well as your ability to keep things moving, how well you solicit feedback from your child, and so on. If he likes the way you teach, perhaps you can give him a free lesson in return for his scouting report.

Seek Your Child's Assessment

Perhaps the most valuable feedback you can receive is to have your child evaluate the lesson you have just given. In a trusting environment, when you've made it clear that you're ready for criticism and you can accept it, kids will give you honest opinions if you simply ask them questions such as: "Did you have a good time? Did you feel you learned something? Did I work you too hard—or was I too easy on you?" Little kids, especially, will almost always forget themselves when you start asking them questions, and their answers will often reveal any hostilities they might have. For example, say you ask them, "What about the tone of my voice—was I too hard on you?" They might answer: "Yeah, why did you have to get so mad? I was *trying* to do what you said."

Ideally, if you've established the right climate, your child's opinions about your teaching style will surface naturally, in a nice way, without any real prompting on your part. In fact, you sometimes have to be careful not to create a problem by asking too many negative questions along the line of "Did anything bother you about the way I gave the lesson today?" You may be doing a terrific job, but your child will respond, "Yeah, I'll tell you what bothers me—when you keep asking me if it bothers me."

In establishing a healthy process for seeking your child's feedback, try to form a reciprocal understanding so that you might ask your child nicely: "Do you want to hear my feelings about the lesson? Well, I liked what you did there and the way you acted here, and you really seemed to be concentrating. But all of a sudden, when you started losing your temper, I sort of lost my interest. It wasn't as much fun for me after that." By taking this approach, you share some honest feelings back and forth. This is such an important thing to nurture, not just for the tennis lessons you give, but in strengthening the parent-child relationship.

8/Giving Group Lessons

In giving your child lessons, you may have the opportunity to include other children from your family or some of their friends. This chapter will help you handle that challenge by addressing those situations unique to group lessons or which you may not often encounter when giving individual lessons. However, for the sake of organization, approach, and reality—since most adults involved in giving group lessons are teaching pros, phys-ed teachers, or parks-and-recreation personnel—I'm primarily addressing myself in this chapter to those who are working with children professionally.

There's no denying the fact that giving effective lessons to a group of children is a constant challenge to your teaching ability. Not only must you try to impart sound fundamentals to each individual student, you also have to deal with them as a group of individuals with varying levels of physical ability, learning skills, and athletic background. You may have one seven-year-old who's happy just to be on a tennis court ("Look, Mom, I'm playing tennis!"), while his buddy the same age is wondering how soon he can start playing in tournaments. One nine-year-old may just smile a lot and never say a word, while her friend tries to tell you all her problems. Or you may have an eleven-year-old who has never played a sport before versus one who has already been through five years of soccer, baseball, and swimming. Moreover, you have to work harder when giving group lessons, especially if your goal is to maximize the attention you give to each youngster and the number of times each gets to swing at the ball. You have to keep the balls coming to them while providing a stream of encouragement and advice. It's easier in a private lesson to think, "I'll tire the kid out and then I can loaf for a while as we talk across the net" (though I certainly don't recommend this attitude).

Still, you can gain an enormous amount of self-satisfaction from

In group lessons some kids will let you know immediately that they don't enjoy waiting around in line to hit. So be organized and keep the balls coming.

well-run group lessons. I've always enjoyed knowing that far more children gain the benefits of instruction in groups: instead of starting 20 or 30 kids a year, an enthusiastic, well-organized pro might start 250 or more. The talented instructor will also see quicker gains by more youngsters because they are learning in a *positive* group setting. This is especially true in regard to attitudinal changes; some youngsters, as they acquire some strokes and a knowledge of the game, go from feeling incompetent and uncoordinated to reaching a point where they have a nice sense of accomplishment and self-worth. (You'll recognize the same changes in private lessons, of course, but group lessons offer more of the socializing benefits that can help speed attitudinal changes.)

Some pros think they're going to develop more "champions" by concentrating on private lessons, but I haven't found that to be true. Junior tournament players need concentrated work on their problem areas and can certainly benefit from an occasional private lesson, but they can meanwhile derive valuable motivation by belonging to a good group program. Many juniors think they work hard on their own, but when they join a group, they often discover other kids working much harder, and this gives them tremendous impetus.

A one-on-one relationship in tennis (either between a coach and student or a parent and child) can rarely equal the sustained energy generated by peer group influence—if the coach learns how to harness this energy and use it effectively. In my days at the Kramer club, for example, I found that in a group lesson it was easier to motivate kids to work harder to improve because they fed upon one another's enthusiasm. One of my former students, Mary Ley, recalled: "We were always trying to excel and stay up with the group. It really hurt our pride not to hustle and work hard during the lesson, and not to practice between lessons." Although I was giving Tracy Austin private lessons when she was five, one important reason why she built such a solid base for the future was the opportunity she had to drill with high-school and college kids on Saturday afternoons. She insisted on going to the net and taking her turn in all the volley drills. They'd pound that ball at her, too, and sometimes it would hit her, but she hung in there. Pretty soon she was hitting winners, and when she did well, all the other kids would cheer and give her a lot of encouragement. Group experiences like that provided her with a toughness and a love of volleying that she still has.

Important Concepts in Teaching A Group of Children

In my opinion, the talented and qualified instructor devises lessons that reflect the basic philosophical concepts I discuss in earlier chapters— respect individual worth, strive to get inside the child's world, and so on. Following are some ways to apply or adjust these and other concepts in a group teaching situation with children. For those who have yet to get into group teaching, this section is intended as an overview, to prepare you for the first lesson.

Create a Positive Learning Environment
I've always tried desperately to build a positive respect for learning among my students—children and adults alike. I talk to kids about being at ease and feeling free to laugh at things that happen during the lesson,

but also about the work that must go into learning and improving tennis skills. I remind them that a lesson is a *learning* opportunity, not a devil-may-care hour in which everybody horses around but nobody really improves. Learning about tennis usually costs money, and I want them to see a relationship between the effort that has gone into earning the money to pay for the lesson and the effort they exert. "Don't waste your parents' money with a halfhearted effort," I tell them—because I've seen so many youngsters who think it's their right to take lessons, when really it's a privilege.

Then, by the way I run my lessons, I show kids that I'm sincere in wanting them to learn and improve. I convey this by my approach to behavior and discipline, by the close attention I give their technique, by my efforts to keep the action going so they can get as many hits as possible, and by my constant encouragement. I also let them know that when they pay me for a lesson, they're getting a lot more than just the actual time I spend with them: "I think about each one of you between lessons and how you're hitting the ball. So when I see you next week, if you haven't practiced the things we work on today, I'm going to be disappointed. You'll just be wasting my time—and your time." I want kids to know that I have a concern for them all the time—not only because it makes them feel good, but because it tends to give them more self-respect and incentive for learning the game. They know that I'm in there with them, pulling for them to become good players.

Of course, by taking this approach I'm forced to evaluate my lessons in terms of "Was it worth that much money to the kid?" At the Kramer club, I would occasionally have to answer no when I felt I didn't give enough diversification or I didn't drive home an important point. Then, if I had a break between lessons and I noticed the student still hanging around, I'd say: "Give me five minutes. There's something I didn't try in the lesson and I want to see if it works."

Also, remember that the attitude you bring to each lesson is crucial. Be positive. If you fall into the rut of thinking that you're teaching "the same old thing" every day, you're probably not working to recognize the individual differences in your students (and perhaps you ought to consider trying your hand at a different aspect of the sport). I have many interests in and beyond tennis, but I never grow bored with teaching forehands and backhands and all the other strokes, even after more than thirty years as a pro. I always look forward to the challenge that each student presents, because no two people are alike in the way they learn to hit a tennis ball.

Show Concern for Each Student

In my view, the good instructor devises lessons that reflect a concern and respect for the individuality of each youngster in his group. My teaching system reflects such personal orientation in a number of ways.

• *Try to get through to each student in a nice way from the first lesson on, so that you're sensitive to her needs and aspirations.* Some teaching pros fail to get to know a youngster until the third or fourth lesson, and that's too late.

By questioning, listening, and observing you'll discover fears and anxieties she might have about tennis lessons (perhaps she feels she's under pressure to "show results" for the money her parents are spending or to meet their high expectations); you'll determine how she learns best; and you'll gain an understanding of her life away from tennis—her athletic background, other activities she's involved in, brothers and sisters she might have, who else plays tennis in the family, and so on. This information will certainly reflect how she feels about tennis and how you might adjust your teaching approach to suit her needs better. A good way to gain these insights beforehand is to have parents fill out a questionnaire that covers the areas mentioned above. Then, once lessons are under way, take advantage of those moments when students are picking up balls to talk with them informally. Also remember to set aside time for questions and feedback at the end of every lesson.

• *Try to recognize—and enjoy—the challenge of teaching each child at her own level of understanding, experience, and ability.* This implies several responsibilities: to attempt to view every situation from the child's standpoint; to remember that you're dealing with a youngster, who has limited experience in life; to empathize with what she is going through in trying to learn tennis; and to encourage feedback so that you can better understand what is happening from her point of view. If you try to be interested in each person and treat each as an individual, you'll soon discover who needs to be motivated, who already has an eagerness to learn, and who needs to have this eagerness cultivated. For instance, an enthusiastic youngster may suffer a rude awakening when she discovers the game is harder to master than she ever envisioned, and she'll need your support to help pull her through a rough transition.

• *Be flexible in your thinking so that you can adjust your teaching to the way you feel a youngster learns best, instead of forcing her to adjust to how you teach.* Most instructors I've seen have such a rigid teaching system that the student who can't follow it or learn from it is simply disregarded. The instructor's attitude is: "Here's the way I teach and if you don't like it, you can leave." Sure, it's frustrating when you have a pattern for teaching that works for five kids in a group, but not the sixth. But instead of saying, "This kid will never learn," you must investigate all the approaches that could work.

This also means that you provide appropriate rationale for your instruction while encouraging your students to challenge the reliability and validity of your system. A weak instructor suggests that students should follow his system because he has the "final word" on the subject. He is threatened by inquisitive students, especially when he doesn't know the answers to their questions, and is likely to respond, "Just do it the way I told you."

• *It's easy to favor the youngster who shows a lot of natural ability over the clumsy one—but avoid that temptation.* The gifted young athlete represents only a tiny percentage of the kids who learn tennis every year. If a prodigy monopolizes your attention, those who really need individualized help are being slighted in favor of someone who already has a lot going for her, and the "slow learners" are thus being made to feel even less capable than they are. So be sensitive when you look at a youngster who appears to be hopelessly uncoordinated and think: "Ouch, this kid couldn't walk through the gate without bumping it three times. How's she ever going to learn to play?" It's easy to feel that way, but remember: she probably feels ten times as bad as you do. And clumsy as she might appear, she's in important ways no different from any of her more-talented peers—she wants *something* out of tennis, and it's your responsibility never to give up on her. (I discuss how to deal with the less-talented youngster later in this chapter.)

Overcome Your Personal Biases

Tennis instructors are human, just like their students, and their personal biases come out very clearly unless they learn to deal with them effectively. For example, in a typical group situation, kids who are fat, excessively skinny, homely, or burdened with unattractive features such as bad skin seldom get much attention from an instructor. These youngsters tend to be touched less, talked to less, looked at less (and rarely in the eyes). Conversely, most instructors tend to strive harder and more enthusiastically with children who have more agreeable physical traits, especially when they show some talent.

You must recognize when such biases are surfacing and learn to deal with them objectively before they interfere with the teaching relationship. This is not an easy task, for there's a tendency to overlook certain prejudices that might be keeping you from treating a particular student fairly. In fact, you may find yourself getting irritated or losing patience with a youngster without realizing what's really bothering you. So think for a moment: if you have some negative feelings toward a certain "unattractive" student, very likely other adults are treating her hostilely in other areas of her life. At least give her a refuge out on the tennis court.

Opposite:
As an instructor, you've got to be ready for all kinds.

Let's say that a youngster in your group is fat and you don't like fat people. Then make an especially strong effort to encourage her during the lesson, no matter what your personal feelings. Use any excuse you can think of to help her with her swing by holding her wrist or guiding her arm through the desired stroke pattern. If you do this, you'll often find that you're one of the first adults to have done so. Kids have told me: "Nobody has ever touched me during a lesson before. My other instructors just talked across the net all the time."

Still, there's one caution here about physical contact with your students. I've always been close with the kids I coach; I hug the girls and slap palms with the boys, and I always let them know I'm happy to see them. But I know that some kids can't handle too much of a display, such as a hug, and I learn to back off. Also, those of you instructors who are male may start teaching a girl when she's eight or nine and be hugging her all the time, and she counts on that kind of close support. But when she's twelve or thirteen you really have to be careful that the hugging is still for her, and not for yourself.

You should also try to deal with the biases you might have against certain personalities. For example, if you're a blood-and-guts type of competitor, it's unlikely you'll have much patience with passive and noncompetitive kids, but they deserve as much encouragement as the hard-nosed youngsters who better reflect your athletic ideal. Similarly, children who are starting to deviate in a way that's offensive to you will normally tend to get less of your attention—when they really need all the positive support you can give.

Don't feel ill-at-ease or defensive with an independent child who constantly challenges what you're teaching, and don't take retaliatory action to get even. I've always found the negative, hostile, smart-aleck youngster tough to deal with. I don't like to feel that I'm in a war with somebody like this, but I always wish she wasn't in the class, because it takes a lot of time and hard work to go after what's causing her problem—at the expense of all the other students. It may be that her whole goal is to test and retest my ability to discipline the class. Perhaps her bluster is a defense mechanism. Or maybe she is having a rough home life. Whatever, I accept that she *is* in the class and I must overcome my bias and deal with her. I'm always motivated by the knowledge that when I take time to figure out a youngster like this, to stop her from acting the way she does and to channel her energies into tennis, she very often turns out to be one of my best students.

It's also important to learn to recognize when you're taking out on a youngster feelings that you have for her parents or other members of her family. Over the years I've taught a number of nice, well-mannered, hardworking kids who, unfortunately, had a parent (or parents) who was unpleasant to have around. When people ask me, "Why do you want to work with this kid when her father is so obnoxious?" I tell them: "I'm not worried about the father; he's already had his chances in life. I just want to give this little kid her chance. Why should I penalize her just because I happen to dislike her father?" Admittedly, it's hard to look at a youngster without thinking about her parents or perhaps an older sibling who was once your student. Yet she's an entity in herself, and you must put on blinders when you're an instructor so that you only look at her and her individual needs.

How to Deal with the Reluctant Student

You occasionally must deal with the youngster who really doesn't want to be out on the court taking tennis lessons, or who apparently would prefer taking lessons from somebody else. In either case, the problem can arise as easily with a four-year-old as a fourteen-year-old, but in different guises.

When I give group lessons for children of mixed ages, I invariably face a preschooler who starts crying when the gate closes behind her on the first day, or a slightly older youngster who suddenly decides she doesn't want to hit. When either situation comes up, I quietly tell the kid: "No problem, I can understand how you feel. Why don't you just sit on the bench with your mom and watch the other kids have some fun. You don't have to learn this game until you're ready." If I can manage to keep the youngster on the court watching, I later go over to her as the other kids are picking up balls and ask her if she wants to help out. Or I'll say, "Here, do you want to try to hit just one?" Very often she'll give it a try, having seen that the lesson is no big deal, but that's as far as I "push." I never try to motivate kids to play tennis by saying, "Oh, come on, you'll love it," or "I'll buy you a candy bar if you can hit five in a row." Once a kid has been handed the opportunity, she has to show me there's an actual interest on her part to get involved.

Occasionally, parents will only make matters worse by trying to embarrass their youngster into taking a lesson, with a taunt such as, "Come on, Johnny, don't be a crybaby." Or they'll get mad at me for refusing to use my own influence on the child. I always try to pull these parents aside and tell them: "Don't force your child to take the lesson. I'd love to have her, but let's face it: she's not ready for tennis yet and we'll only do her, and the game, a disservice by trying to ignore her fears. Wait until she's ready—maybe next week, or next month, or even next year. You can offer to bring her out here just to watch the other kids if she wants—but don't do so only on the basis that she must agree to play."

Very often, of course, a fourteen-year-old who's coming out to play tennis for the first time is just as fearful as a little kid. She's scared to death of looking clumsy or doing something wrong, but her defense mechanisms will be a little more sophisticated than tears or simply refusing to go onto the court at the last moment. She may come up with lines such as, "I just thought I'd try tennis, but I don't really like it much," or "I don't even want to be here, but my parents made me come." My response in these situations is not to get in a war with the youngster, but simply to let her know that basically I'm on her side. For example, I might tell her: "If you decide to stick with these lessons, you may be right—you might not enjoy this game. But I'd like to have you at least give it a chance. Go through six lessons with me and if you really don't like tennis by then, you shouldn't keep playing. I'm the first to admit that not everybody loves the sport. All I want to do is expose you to the game. If I do that properly, and if your folks have helped, then you can never accuse them of not giving you the right opportunity." I've found that this approach nearly always works well for me.

Similarly, if a youngster tries to use her parents as an excuse for being there, I try this tack: "I really want you to be here because *you* want to learn tennis, not because your parents sent you. To me, a tennis lesson has to be a two-way street. I'm going to throw a lot of things at you and you're going to have to receive them, just like a quarterback working with an end. If we don't work together, I'm going to feel lousy. So, if you don't want to be out here, I don't want to give you lessons."

Most kids will then say, "No, no—I want to learn," since very often they were only setting up a defense mechanism for the way they were playing the game, or were simply acting hostile in retaliation to a strong push from their parents. Then I ask them: "Are you sure this is *you* talking? I don't want your mom or dad talking. But if *you* want these lessons and you're ready to learn, then I want to give them to you." Again, I find that this approach fosters a lot of respect for my lessons. The youngster is forced to think hard about why she's out on the tennis court; she knows that an instructor is keenly interested in helping her learn the sport, and she realizes—perhaps for the first time—the responsibility she has to that instructor.

I always try to talk to a youngster *alone*, either before or during the first lesson, to determine that she is the one who wants the lessons and that they weren't solely her parents' idea. I ask, "Why are you here?" and if she fails to convince me of her own interest in learning, I tell her, "I appreciate your honesty, and you're a terrific kid, but I've got to be very honest with you: I don't want to give you lessons because I don't want to steal your family's money." Then I get together with the parents and explain my reasons for wanting to wait until their daughter is properly self-motivated. Some parents will try to argue, "Look, you're the club pro and I want my kid to have lessons now." But I say: "I appreciate your position, but my professional code of ethics is to do what's best for your child, not for you. And I can assure you, if your daughter doesn't want to learn, she's not going to learn. You can't force it, so why waste your money and her time?"

In the same vein, I go into each new teaching relationship with an understanding that not every student will accept me. So if a youngster doesn't want to abide by my ground rules or if there's something about me that interferes with her enjoyment or her ability to learn, I let her know: "If you don't want to be in this particular class, that's no problem with me. I don't really care to fight you on that issue. But maybe I can help you find a pro who's right for you." I always want to give a youngster the freedom to get out of the relationship, just as I want her to understand that I never have to take her as a student simply because her parents are paying me.

How to Work with Less-Talented Youngsters

In earlier chapters, I suggested many ways in which parent/instructors can motivate less-talented youngsters and keep them from losing their self-confidence and their interest in the game. Here are some other points to keep in mind as you work with a group:

• Learn to sense when a youngster can handle a large amount of additional information, when a small dosage is more appropriate, and when it's best to return to point one. For example, if I notice that a youngster is getting discouraged on a particular stroke, the last thing I want to do is tag on more instruction and advice. I simply back off and say, "All right, Chris, let's take one thing at a time . . ."

• If you're using a ball machine, remember that the tendency is for these machines to be set up to fire balls too fast. So if a student is working on a particular stroke and keeps missing, don't let her just go through all those failures and reinforce a negative attitude. Slow the machine way down or stop it completely and feed the balls by hand so she can have some success experiences.

• If a student is unable to get the ball over the net from the baseline, you might let her move up and hit from the service line—but only, for safety's sake, if there's not a hitter on the baseline. Perhaps another student having the same problem can join her. Yet keep in mind that kids who are struggling with the game generally prefer to stay with everybody else on the baseline; they don't want a comedown treatment.

• When a youngster is having trouble making contact with the ball, I generally stop the class and demonstrate several "lead-up" drills (see pages 101–102) that can give her some success experiences. I have everybody try these drills for a few minutes so that the youngster who's struggling won't feel singled out, but then we go right back to tennis. Be careful that these drills don't become a way of procrastinating about getting to the heart of a youngster's problem; and don't dwell on them to the point of turning the class into a contest. If lead-up drills are something your students want to do on their own before or after practice, fine. Otherwise, keep them to a minimum or you'll have parents complaining, "My kid can win all of your ball-bouncing drills but he can't hit the ball."

• When running a stroking drill, never isolate a student with harsh criticism for making a mistake. Just let her get back in line, and if you then suggest a correction, always include something positive. More than enough pressure will be placed on a youngster—pressure from within herself and from her peers. She needs to know you're on her side, from the tone of your voice and by your constant encouragement: "Wow, you got to the ball so fast, I don't believe it," or "Your follow-through was perfect," and so forth.

• Always remember that a youngster's self-image can really become wrapped up in tennis, irrespective of how well she can hit the ball. Thus, you must constantly search for positive things to tell each student during the lesson and afterward. This can be a difficult task at times, but you can always find something nice to say, even if you have to go beyond her tennis strokes. For example, I often reward kids for being polite and having a nice temper or just for being reliable and showing up at every lesson. I'll say: "You know one of the things I like about you? I know that every Saturday you're going to be here, unless you're sick or something." Other times I'll say how impressed I am by a youngster who looks neat and clean when she comes out onto the court. She may not hit the ball very straight, but I think it's important to encourage a concern for one's appearance, and so I'll tell her: "You know what makes me feel good? You always look nice when you come out here; you're not sloppy." Very often, she'll turn up even cleaner the next week, which shows you how much some kids thrive on just a little praise from an adult.

• When a kid's having trouble with the game, I invite her to watch some of my other lessons. "Come early next week if you can, or stay late today and just sit and listen," I'll tell her. When she doesn't have to worry about hitting a ball herself, she'll often start hearing some things that suddenly make sense, and she'll come up to me and say, "I get it now—I understand what you're saying." Then, if I have time, I'll even get her out on the court for five or ten minutes to hit, while her enthusiasm is high.

Equipment and Clothing—What's "Proper"?

I never want a youngster to feel there's anything funny about the way she's dressed or the racket she's using; I want her to feel she's as good as anybody else out on that tennis court, whatever her economic background. Thus, if a kid comes out for her first lesson carrying an old wood racket that obviously is too large and heavy for her to use properly, I won't try to get a laugh by saying, "Where did you get that old war club?" Why should she feel she has two strikes against her before she even swings at a ball? Instead, I'll try to encourage the parents to consider buying an inexpensive junior racket when their child shows sufficient interest—if I sense they can afford one. If I know they're disadvantaged, I won't even bring it up, or I'll suggest they cut a couple of inches off the racket handle. Most parents quickly discover what the other kids are using, and if they then want to purchase a more appropriate racket, that's their choice. In the meantime, a beginner who enjoys the game will rarely complain about having to use an old, heavy racket. It's the youngster looking for defense mechanisms who latches on to her racket as an excuse.

Another reason why I tread carefully here is that peer pressure can be brutal in group situations. If a disadvantaged youngster doesn't have the instructor on her side, she's going to feel even more strongly that "the other kids have some nice things and I have nothing." You can't always prevent insensitive remarks by other kids (such as, "How can you play with a crummy racket like that?"), but you can tell the whole group, "It's not the racket you use—it's how you swing it that counts." Then, when there's a break in the lesson, you can pull the culprits aside and give them a quick one-liner. You might say, "A champion never criticizes somebody who doesn't have everything going for him," or "One thing I've always liked about you was that you had big-time manners, but today you really slipped." That's all you have to say to get through to most kids.

Once youngsters start to play matches and learn about the game's tradition, I try to coax them into wearing regular tennis clothes (if I think they can afford them), because I want them to have pride in how they look and a respect for the sport. But again, I handle this sensitively, because I always remember how I started out myself—wearing cutoff jeans, a white T-shirt, and black sneakers.

Encourage Parental Involvement

Unlike some teaching pros and coaches, I love to have parents watch the lessons I give—providing they act sensibly and refrain from criticizing their youngster. I even hand out a photocopied sheet that lists the ways parents can help their child improve between lessons (such ways are discussed in chapter 16). Most kids want their parents to take an active interest in their pursuits and to observe the progress they're making—as long as the parents represent a positive influence. Well-meaning parents shouldn't be cut out of this involvement by a defensive instructor who lets it be known that he doesn't want them hanging around during the lesson.

By encouraging parents to stay abreast of what their youngster is learning week to week, you will likely avoid the conflict between parent and instructor that often arises now that so many adults are playing the game. For instance, when a father attends his youngster's lessons and takes notes, he can then go out and work constructively with his child between lessons, without contradicting what you're trying to teach. But the tutoring parent who misses your lessons, for whatever reasons, will quickly fall behind his youngster in what she is actually learning about the fundamentals of sound strokes. He may then take her out to practice, only to provide—perhaps insistently—incorrect or at least differing instruction. When this happens, the poor kid can often find herself caught in what Dr. Thomas Tutko calls an "Athletic Triangle"—she must decide between listening either to her parent or to her instructor, or else she must try to incorporate what both of them are saying (at the risk of becoming totally confused). Whatever she does, she can't really win.

So to avoid being contradicted by a parent who insists on incorrect technique, try to prevent the problem from ever arising. Meet with parents before lessons even begin and tell them: "You have every right to challenge whatever I'm teaching. All I ask is that you first discuss it with me and then we'll discuss it with your child." If this preventive approach fails, I tell the interfering parent: "I can't go along with your theory about this stroke. If you can justify your rationale, fine. I'm always willing to change what I'm teaching if somebody can prove me wrong. But otherwise, what you're telling your child is only going to cause her problems learning to play the game correctly." This discussion, which should always include the child, is in itself a good object lesson. And of course, if the parent proves to be right in what he's saying, show that you have the same flexibility you're asking from him (and his child) by making the necessary changes in what you're teaching.

Another way to get parents involved in a positive manner is to enlist their help if you're giving free or inexpensive weekly clinics for a large number of youngsters. You can generally find parents who are eager to assist, but the key question is: Can they help competently? You should first have them watch you give a group lesson, so they can observe how you feed the balls and how you react to the kids. This provides a positive example. Then show them how to feed balls in rapid succession to two or three kids along the baseline. If they can do this properly, you will be free to teach while they run the hitting procedure. If they can't, you're going to fall behind. They can still help, however, if you make sure they're versed in what you're teaching so they can watch for key checkpoints and monitor a youngster's technique.

Preparing for and Giving the First Lesson

When a group of youngsters comes out on the court for their first lesson, they're understandably a little nervous and apprehensive—perhaps even intimidated—as they enter your domain. Moreover, they're already formulating opinions about you and the learning situation based on first impressions. These conscious and unconscious feelings may not be reliable or valid—but you must realize how they can make your job more difficult or much easier, depending on your personality, your facial expressions, the tone of your voice, your approach to the lesson, and the rapport you establish with each person.

Such first-day impressions are crucial, so give special attention to the way you greet a new group and do all you can to make them feel comfortable and at ease from the very start. I say hello as they come in the gate, and then when they're all together, I either kneel down in front of them to talk, or I stand, depending on their age. Some kids are less threatened when you get down to their physical level, while others want to look up to an adult, so I always use different approaches during the lesson.

In the opening minutes, I tell them my name and I let them know that I already know their names—and especially their nicknames (which I've obtained from the parents). Then I go into my philosophy about the game and about learning. "You're going to miss a lot of balls at first," I warn them, "but that's not important to me because this is a 'mistake center.' Everybody makes a lot of mistakes hitting a tennis ball, even after they've been playing for years and years. So all I'm going to watch for is that you *try* to swing the way I show you. I'm not worried about where the ball goes. Just try as hard as you can and have a good time." After that, I talk to them about the concern I have for each one of them as an individual and how I know they all can learn to play a good game of tennis if they have

When talking to your students as a group, try to get down to their physical level as often as possible. Don't create a threatening atmosphere by hovering over them and pointing a finger at their faces. This instructor is having a question-and-answer period at the end of the lesson. The youngster at the far right is either shouting the answer or thinking, "Oh no, I'm wrong again!"

the right attitude. "Honest, we can do it—and we'll have fun, too," I tell them. "You're also going to learn a lot of things that will help you in school, in other sports, and in other situations."

Establish the Rules for Behavior

I'm basically a happy-go-lucky person whose fundamental theme is that fun and learning can, and should, coexist. I strive to have kids adopt this philosophy when they're taking tennis lessons. However, I run a very tight ship when it comes to their behavior on the court. I know that if I want to function effectively with a group of children and have learning take place, then I need to control the atmosphere that prevails during the lesson. And that atmosphere is one in which my students are concentrating on tennis—and nothing else. They're not goofing off by hitting balls over the fence, or reacting to other kids causing trouble, or thinking about what they might do the next time my back is turned. I won't tolerate back talk (as opposed to feedback) at any point. The moment I get back talk from a student, I think: "Individual conference after the lesson." It's vital that the students have respect for their teacher.

Many adults dread teaching a group of children because all they can visualize are little monsters who are too distracted to listen carefully, who are not going to work hard on desired techniques, and who will behave however they want. Sure, some groups have disruptive students, but whether or not they ruin your lesson will depend on how well you establish and enforce the ground rules for behavior from the very start. Here's the approach I take:

After talking to youngsters about enjoying themselves out on the court ("If the game makes you want to giggle or laugh out loud, that's great—I love to hear it"), I let them know: "I'm here to teach and you're here to learn, so there are certain things that I don't want to see happen. If you do these things, you'll have to leave the lesson until I decide you can come back—if you want to come back." I then go through the rules (which I've already written down and given to them and their parents before they even arrived) so that everybody knows my expectations.

Following are the rules for group lessons that I generally stress the first day; they can be added to those I provided earlier (page 57).

• Listen very carefully.

• Once I start talking to the group, stop what you are doing—immediately.

• Don't throw balls at each other.

• If I say to swing slowly and just barely hit the ball, don't try to slug the ball just to be funny or to show off.

• Do not poke fun at kids who might be having trouble learning the game. Nobody likes to be ridiculed.

• Everybody must share in picking up the balls. [This is a crucial concept to get across, because some kids will start avoiding that responsibility fast. They want the good part (lots of hits) but not the work involved (constantly policing the balls), so you must explain that there's a price for everything.]

After answering any questions, I let them know why I have set up these rules and I ask them some questions to see how clearly they understand what's involved—thus alerting them that I like to have people respond and discuss as much as possible. In some situations, it can be fun to have kids help you make out the list of rules—usually they are tougher on themselves than you are—but don't let this bog down the lesson.

I next make it clear that I'll ask kids who violate any of these rules to go sit on the bench or even leave the court until I tell them they can return. If they act up again, they're finished for the day and won't be allowed back into the class until I've talked to their parents. I also point out that I don't want to get into a shouting match when they know they've broken a rule. "I don't want to embarrass you in front of the others," I tell them, "so I'm just going to give you the thumb—like this—and I want you to leave the class quietly." This sometimes works so well that during a busy lesson, a youngster will get the thumb and head out the gate, but the other kids think she's just going for a drink.

Maintain Discipline

Once you've established the rules of behavior, you have to back them up. If you fail to enforce your rules, then you're forced into shouting threats ("Look, if you do that again, I'll knock your head off!") in order to maintain discipline, instead of having an atmosphere in which you simply give a troublemaker the thumb. Believe me, the situation will rarely get out of hand if you clearly articulate your rules and then always act decisively when they are broken. Not that you should set up a totalitarian atmosphere in which kids are afraid to breathe—but be fair, firm, and consistent. You'll find that your students will respect and appreciate this approach.

When a young child goofs off the first time, you might give her one warning, or you might say: "You're going to have to sit on the bench and think about what you've done. You're going to be a terrific tennis player, but I've set up these rules and you broke one of them." An older child who obviously misbehaves in some way (for instance, throwing a racket or a temper tantrum) should be disciplined immediately, because she's old enough to know she has it coming. I also tell the youngster why I'm cracking down hard: "I would be doing you a disservice if I let you continue acting like that, because you're going to get worse and you're not going to have any respect for the sport, for me, or for yourself. Not only that, people are paying for this lesson and you're stealing their money by the way you act. So I want you to sit on the bench and think about what you've done. If I give you a chance to come back in, and you still don't want to follow the rules, then I'll have you go over there and wait for your parents to pick you up."

One drawback of a group lesson, if you're unable to deal with group dynamics, is that *one* misbehaving youngster can destroy the atmosphere you seek. If you try to keep such a person who demands special attention in the class, you're going to spend the entire lesson saying, "Susie, stop doing that . . . Susie, cut that out." Meanwhile, all the other kids in the class suffer. So my approach has always been simply to remove this person from the scene, but also to tell her that I'll save a few minutes after the lesson to talk with her. I let her know that I still care about her, but that she has to leave the class because that's the only fair thing to do for everybody concerned. I also tell her, "Maybe you can come back next week; I'll call and talk to you about it." This gives her an opening to return, but it also lets her realize that it might be the end of the relationship. If the youngster is sassy and obviously a behavior problem, send her well away from the lesson. Don't let her sit on a nearby bench where she can make faces and continue to distract the other kids. By acting decisively, you'll find that in most cases she'll shape up. After all, she wants to be where the action is, and very often her primary goal was to see if you were strong enough to control your class. Knowing that you are, she may become one of your best students.

A similar example is the child who manipulates her parents at home and who quickly tries to jockey you around once the lesson begins—by acting up, breaking the rules, or giving you lines such as, "I don't want to do that," or "I want to hit from *right here,* not over there." When this happens, remember that you're very likely talking to a youngster who gets away with similar behavior with other adults, so act sensibly; don't let her drag you into an emotional, retaliatory reaction. Just firmly tell her, "Okay, Jennifer, we love you and everything, but if you don't want to follow directions, then sit here on the bench away from the other kids." If she says, "No, I'm not going to sit on the bench," simply escort her outside the court. If you let her stick around and get away with sassing you, she will think she can pull any behavior she wants, just as she does at home. Her reinforcement will be the attention she gets by causing trouble, and in the process, she'll ruin your lesson.

Uncompromising action like this not only removes a disruptive influence, it rewards those kids who are being nice and working hard. Most children hate troublemakers just as much as adults do, and they'll even point out the culprit when they think you haven't noticed. Of course, an experienced instructor sees and hears nearly everything going on during a lesson; he can even smell trouble brewing. Therefore, a youngster bent on mischief is eventually going to get caught, even if the instructor's back happens to be turned during one incident. So if a reliable student complains to me about something Susie did that I didn't notice, I might pull Susie over, out of hearing range of the others, and say: "Hey, look, I didn't actually see you goofing off; it may even have been someone else. But if you're doing these things, you're going to get caught eventually and you're going to have to leave the class. So let me save you the trouble by warning you now."

By setting up and enforcing rules of behavior, you also help motivate youngsters to learn to cope with anger and frustration. For example, when a student has an emotional outburst and curses or slams her racket against the fence, you have a chance to address all your students about how important it is for them to control their temper—though they shouldn't feel guilty about getting angry. Let them know that it's okay to find a release valve for expressing their anger, as long as they don't destroy equipment or make somebody else pay a price. You might tell the youngster who blows up: "I know how frustrating it is to learn this game—that's human nature—but you're going to have to leave the court and cool down. You have the right to get angry, but you don't have the right to throw a racket or to say things that are going to spoil the fun for these other kids. That's selfishness. I'm not saying that you have to keep your anger all bottled up. But when you let it get out of control, you hurt the way you play and it's also unfair to the other kids."

One of the unfortunate aspects of group lessons in any sport is that you can't completely shield less-talented youngsters from being hurt by the belittling, sometimes cruel remarks of other students. However, you can exert a tremendous influence by letting your students know from the very start that you're not going to tolerate such put-downs. When I hear a kid cutting up someone having trouble with the game, I tend to want to say, "Hey, let's show some class out here—any toad can criticize somebody." But I think it's much more effective to pull such a kid aside and remark: "Look, I heard what you said to Johnny. It's not the right thing to do and I think you know it. You were in a position where you could really help him, but you chose to hurt. You know he looks up to you, and just a few nice words from you could have made his day." You can also discourage razzing by keeping students busy, occupied with their own tennis strokes. When you hit to only one student at a time and the waiting line is moving slowly, kids will start focusing on those who are having the most trouble and slowing things down.

Finally, it will be easier to maintain discipline if you make sure all the parents involved know all the rules and how you will enforce them. You can meet with them beforehand and give them a list of the things you will not tolerate and explain how you will handle the discipline, or you can invite them to listen from outside the fence as you make your opening talk. Then there are no surprises for anybody should you have to remove a youngster in the opening five or ten minutes of the first lesson. If the parents come over and complain, "You mean we drove all the way out here and our daughter can't play?" you can tell them: "Yes. Remember the rules that we all agreed upon? You saw what your daughter did, and I'm simply honoring our agreement. Believe me, I'd love to have her back in the class next week—if she wants to come and she feels she can follow the rules."

Set Up Safety Guidelines

Always talk to your students beforehand about safety—not just for their own sake, but because coaches now run the risk of lawsuits stemming from on-court injuries. Kids tend not to think about the possibility of getting hurt or of hurting somebody else, and it's easy for them to get so absorbed in trying to hit the ball that they walk right into the path of another racket. Therefore, I space them about 10 feet apart and I make sure they maintain that distance, because a racket can fly out of a child's hand or she can finish with a unique follow-through. To bring home my point, I have a student show the group that she can extend her racket quite far in every direction if she takes just one step as she swings.

You'll learn ways to space out your students, depending on how many are in the class. If there are four kids, have two hit and two either stand behind each hitter as "coaches" or retrieve balls. With six students, have three hit and three either coach or retrieve. I allow as many as four hitters at a time along the baseline, with each person getting about five or six hits at a time. Then everybody shifts to a different position. (One drawback of having four students spread 10 feet apart along the 36-foot baseline is that hitters on the ends don't get the proper orientation for their shots, so remember to keep alternating the hitting positions.)

Here are some other safety guidelines every instructor should observe during the lesson:

• Continually caution students picking up balls to watch hitters and thus avoid being struck by rackets or flying balls.

• Have students waiting to hit be responsible for clearing balls from around the hitters' feet between shots. For example, if volleyers are stationed at the net, their shots will occasionally wind up near the feet of hitters stationed across the net at the baseline; players waiting in line to hit from the baseline should help clear these balls.

• Always arrange left-handed hitters in relation to right-handed hitters so that there's maximum hitting space between the players.

• Teach players to avoid running in front of the ball machine; kids positioned on the same side of the court as the machine should stay low in their ready position to avoid being hit in the back of the head.

• After each hitter completes her shot during a drill, have her run *outside* the nearest alley to reposition herself in the waiting line. Students who forget this often cause major crashes on the court as new players run into hitting position.

• When a student appears flush or faint, immediately have her sit on a bench. If you've set the right atmosphere, youngsters who feel the slightest bit ill or dizzy will of their own accord go sit on the bench—without asking first—and then tell you they're feeling bad. It's important for kids to learn to take care of themselves, and for coaches not to regard this as a sign of weakness or as a competitive failing in the youngster. The great athletes heed their body's warning signals and take them very seriously.

How to Introduce the Game and the Strokes

With groups of youngsters just starting out in the game, I go through the same routine that I use in private lessons (see chapter 6), briefly describing the game, the racket, the court, and then the first stroke I teach—the forehand groundstroke. I'm careful to explain every tennis term I introduce, using language that each youngster in the group can understand, and I ask for feedback at each stage of my overview, so that from the very start my students know I expect them to listen carefully and that I want their input. I also make sure they know that I anticipate that they'll progress at different rates: "Some of you have played other sports and you may quickly catch on to tennis. But those of you who haven't had such experience may have more trouble at first. If so, don't worry about it, because in the end you'll be able to play this game well if you're ambitious and work hard." This is a very important issue to bring up, for you thus give support in advance to youngsters who don't learn quickly and who might otherwise feel like failures.

Remember the importance of having a lesson plan when you come out on the court. If you don't have an overall approach organized on paper or in your mind—and an idea of how you're going to implement it—you'll quickly discover how fast your class can break down. Once you start hesitating and saying, "Well, maybe we should do this next," you're going to lose the attention and respect of most of your students.

Once I've provided the basic concepts, I start asking questions geared to the age of my students. For example, I like to ask young children: "As you go to strike the ball, should you swing high-to-low?" And the ones who have been listening will answer, "No—low-to-high!" I also ask, "On the follow-through, do you finish with your racket wrapped around your neck?" When they respond, "Nooooo!" I follow up with, "Well, where do you go?" And they answer, "Straight toward the sky." We turn it into a little game and it pays off by reinforcing key concepts. Plus, the youngster who didn't hear me the first time because she was watching to see where her mother was can pick up what she missed. Pretty soon all the kids are yelling out answers. They've begun to feel knowledgeable and more comfortable about the game—and we haven't even hit a ball yet. In fact, you'll find that most kids soon know more about the fundamentals of good tennis strokes than their tennis-playing parents. This can raise a few problems, as I mentioned earlier in this chapter, and it's one reason why I love to have parents sit in on lessons and stay on top of what I'm teaching.

Before moving my students out onto the court to start hitting, I have them imitate my forehand stroke and I check their grips. If you have a group of young beginners, don't assume they're all right-handed; give

them an option to do what seems most comfortable by saying, "Put your racket in the hand you like to use." Then we swing into action.

Starting out, I have two to four players hit from the baseline. I stand between the service line and the net and "feed" each hitter balls in rapid succession, focusing on just one or two aspects of their respective strokes and making suggestions. This rapid-fire procedure takes practice, experience, and concentration, but it's a talent you'll need to develop to keep the action moving, particularly with a large group.

As we get into the lesson, I occasionally stop the action to ask questions, and if I notice that a certain youngster is acquiring the overall stroke pattern that I'm seeking, I have her demonstrate some swings in front of the group. I like to say: "Watch what Lisa's doing on this stroke. She really is good." This not only encourages the other kids to imitate good form, it gives Lisa a tremendous reward.

Next, just as in a private lesson, I have my students start running to the forehand corner to hit the ball. Even if they swing and miss every time, I can compliment them on their hustle and they can begin to appreciate the challenge that tennis presents. Movement is the key. Kids don't want to stand on the baseline the entire lesson; they want to be in action, whether they can hit the ball well or not. Just knowing they're part of a group effort is in itself a big motivator, and very often they'll give one another a lot of verbal support. When they're running like this and the action is fast, you'll hardly ever hear any complaints.

We then move on to the volley. As they take a breather, I explain that they're now going to move up to the net to try volleys. What I like about introducing this stroke on the first day—even to the youngest of players—is that I can bring my students up close and give all of them that nice sensation of being able to hit the ball over the net. The next step is to have them run up to the net from the service line and try to volley a ball that has been softly lobbed from a short distance away. Once again, they're in action and they're getting an idea about how to play the real game.

How to Wind Up the First Lesson

By the end of the first day's session, we've gone through a lot of technique, so I bring my students together for some final questions. In asking them, "Is a volley a ball you hit after it bounces?" I've had little kids pipe up with, "No, that's a grounder." But this gives another youngster the chance to say, "No, it's a *groundstroke*." I also try to point out individually two or three key concepts for each student to think about—and, I hope, practice—before the next lesson.

A Six-Lesson Sequence of Instruction

Given a typical six-lesson series, the sequence below is how I suggest you introduce strokes and strategy to a group of beginning players, regardless of their aptitude. Even if there are wide discrepancies in natural ability within the group, you can tackle this first series of lessons without holding back the talented kids or discouraging those who are struggling every step of the way. In a subsequent series, however, try to draw on other youngsters in your program to form groups that are more balanced according to interest level and ability. Very likely you'll find you have some kids who need six more weeks just to work on groundstrokes and volleys, while others are eager to practice everything.

The following approach is what I use as a teaching pro, since most parents expect their child to get an introduction to all the strokes and an overview of how the game is played in six weeks. This sequence obviously differs in several ways from what I recommend to parents teaching just their own child (chapter 7, pages 92–95).

Lesson 1

I introduce the forehand groundstroke at the baseline and the forehand volley at the net, plus some little drills involving each stroke alone and together—along with running. Some teaching pros want youngsters to be proficient hitting from the baseline before they allow them to work on volleys, but I don't think that's necessary. Although I emphasize groundstrokes as the basic foundation for good tennis, I like youngsters to see the overall picture right away so they don't develop a fear about playing at the net and they don't hesitate to attack the net when their stroking ability catches up with their knowledge of tactics.

Lesson 2

I introduce the backhand, and then work again on forehands and volleys. If you start right in on the forehand this second day, you'll tend to get into the same problems you ended with in the previous lesson, so it's better to give your students a new challenge, using a supportive approach. You can ease a lot of fears by showing your students that the stroking patterns for both strokes are identical. I'll say: "We're going to learn the backhand today, and what's nice is that you take the same swing as on the forehand, but on the other side of your body. Notice how I turn my body and how I step out toward the ball—but I'm stepping out with my other foot." As I demonstrate the stroke and make my key points, students realize that I'm not introducing a totally new technique.

You may want to teach the traditional one-handed backhand, but you had better know the two-handed stroke as well, because you'll have to teach both. Some kids simply lack the necessary strength to hold the racket with one hand, while others want to hit two-handed to emulate pros like Bjorn Borg and Tracy Austin. As I point out in chapter 11, it's okay to let older, stronger kids play two-handed as long as the trunk of their body is supple.

Even though the backhand will present new problems, many kids learn something during their backhand lesson that they can also apply to their forehand. A knowledge of the backhand also enables them to go out and try to rally with a friend between lessons. If you have young students, under about seven years old, who are genuinely not ready for the backhand, don't force the stroke on them during this six-week sequence. But when an older student tells you, "I just want to hit forehands," remind her that when she goes to play, there's no way she's going to get away with hitting just forehands against a smart opponent.

Lesson 3

Depending on the group, I either concentrate on the volley (forehand and backhand) or introduce the serve, while continuing to work on the groundstrokes. If the group is having trouble with groundstrokes, I now tackle the volley in greater detail, because it gives kids a few more success experiences and enables me to put together more involved drills. (For example, I'll have a youngster start at the center of the baseline, run over to hit a forehand groundstroke, then hurry back past the center mark to hit a backhand groundstroke, then rush up to the net for a volley.) However, if I have a group in which the kids are saying, "We want to learn to serve so we can play," I may teach the serve third and save the concentrated work on the volley for lesson 4.

Lesson 4
I now introduce either the serve or the volley (depending upon what I covered in the previous lesson), while I continue to work on ground-strokes—using drills and simply having kids hit five or six shots in a row from the baseline. When introducing the serve, I show students that the motion they are striving for is the same one they'll use on the overhead (which helps reduce anxiety when they move on to that stroke).

Lesson 5
I spend most of this lesson working on the four different strokes I've already introduced and incorporating them into drills. For example, while two kids practice their serves, two other students can start to learn what it means to return serves, which at this point generally involves a regular forehand or backhand. During these early weeks of instruction I try to keep the motivation high by telling my students: "Hey, what I'm telling you is true—you have to have a little faith in me; I'm throwing a lot of information at you and you're going to have a million frustrations along the way, but we'll laugh and have a lot of fun as we go along, and it will all start coming together. All of a sudden you're going to be so good in tennis it will scare you. It's going to take some time, but I know you're going to be good at the end of all this."

After six lessons some youngsters can go out and play a decent game, which is amazing to them, but the average youngster shouldn't expect that six lessons are all that's needed to play the game. That may be all her parents can afford or want to spend, but if I've done my job right, she'll be motivated to find other ways to keep learning, such as free clinics and watching a pro give lessons to other beginners.

Lesson 6 and Beyond
I briefly demonstrate some of the other strokes kids will one day want to use when they play (such as the lob, the overhead, and the approach shot), and I give them an overview of strategy and tactics and how to keep score. I've plunged them into the game in six sessions; if they like it, they realize without any prompting on my part that they need to sign up for another series of lessons.

One thing that concerns me is the youngster who wants to come back for more lessons but who never goes out to play between lessons—even if it's just to rally or to hit against a backboard. A youngster like this may become a professional lesson-taker, so I warn the parents: "I've encouraged your daughter to go out and at least practice between lessons, but I never see her around, and she told me she doesn't hit. So at this point I think it's a waste of money to have her take any more lessons. You've paid thirty-six dollars and she's been exposed to the strokes and to how the game is played, but that's all you owe her. Now she should earn the next series of lessons by showing that she actually wants to play the game."

As an instructor, half the ball game with kids is just to get them to start hitting the ball with a friend between lessons. If they go out and start becoming familiar with the bounce of the ball and with changing grips, their anxiety about the game will ease and they'll get wrapped up in chasing after the ball and getting it back over the net. Even though they may not yet know all the strokes, they'll want to keep playing—as often as possible.

Divide the Group

Even with youngsters the same age, practically every group of beginners will have striking differences in native ability. These differences have never really bothered me as an instructor, since I want kids to learn how to adjust to varying ability levels—such as in drills in which there is actual head-to-head competition, or when two players are feeding off one another's shots (one player volleying at the net, say, against a player hitting groundstrokes from the baseline). Yet problems can certainly arise, and when they do you must know how to divide the group in such a way that differences in ability don't discourage a weaker player or bore the stronger one.

Even though kids are going to be competitive anyway, I try to have them realize they don't need to feel they're competing against anybody else in the group. "I'm not going to compare you against the other kids," I tell them. "I only care about you, and how much you're improving. So just worry about your own strokes." In reality, of course, kids will observe one another all the time and they soon know exactly where they fit into the group ability-wise.

So when I notice that a youngster is feeling intimidated by peer comparisons or is overwhelmed by having to cope with major differences in skills, I divide the group so that each student is hitting with or against those of comparable ability, if at all possible. All the kids remain on the same court, going through the same lesson, but by grouping them well I avoid the complaints that commonly arise when players of unequal ability play opposite one another in a drill. The weaker player can't return the ball in the other player's direction, and thus the drill is basically wasted.

The better player isn't getting any practice and the weaker one is dwelling on how crummy she thinks she is.

Use Kids as Coaches

From the first lesson on, whatever their age, I have youngsters act as student coaches for those who are hitting. Even when they're beginners, all in the same boat together, I can show them key checkpoints on a swing (for instance, head down at impact on the forehand and backhand, follow through to the sky, and so on) and as they await their turn they can then watch to see how the hitter is doing. When introducing kids to "coaching," I make the point that it's a cooperative effort, not a competitive one, and that the aim is not to hurt another youngster but to help her improve. "Remember," I tell them, "the kid you're coaching is going to be coaching you."

Over the years, I've been an advocate of student coaching for a number of reasons:

• Inactivity is my pet peeve in group lessons, and "coaching" helps keep kids mentally involved when they're waiting to hit. Meanwhile, the hitter is receiving additional instruction.

• Most kids assume a more professional attitude toward lessons and the game itself when they're called on to coach. They're forced at least to understand the proper techniques involved, even though they may be struggling to effect those techniques themselves. Having to verbalize technique—by telling another youngster what she's doing wrong and what she should be striving for—also reinforces the learning process.

• Kids gain a much better appreciation for what the adult instructor goes through and what the instructor-student relationship should involve: mutual work toward a better tennis game. When a youngster tells me after a lesson, "Boy, Johnny really made me mad; he wouldn't listen to me," I try to have her realize that adults also feel frustrated when their students don't listen, whether it's on the tennis court or in the school classroom. Insights like this are really important for youngsters to gain, and yet few of them are ever encouraged to coach another person. Most athletes, in fact, never really share the learning experience as they're growing up in sports. Thus, when they eventually try to coach, they often have a tough time learning to invest their time and patience and understanding in another person.

• The adult instructor is presented with beautiful teaching opportunities when kids are allowed to coach each other. When discrepancies arise between what I'm trying to teach and what a student coach is advocating, or if two kids get into argument over technique, I'll quietly step in and turn the situation into a learning experience for both of them. For

Encourage kids learning tennis to "coach" one another in fundamentals and you will all reap the benefits. Here, an older brother is showing his sister that her dominant hand goes on top during the two-handed forehand volley and that she should keep the racket head high as she swings.

example, if the coach is saying, "That's not how you're supposed to swing," and her student replies, "Yes it is—that's what Vic said to do," I can tell them: "You both may be partially right, or you both may be wrong. Let's take a look at Jimmy's swing and see."

• A student coach can often help me convince a youngster that what I'm telling her about her stroke is actually happening. For instance, I can be standing behind a youngster and telling her repeatedly, "Mary, your racket's going back too far," but she often doesn't really believe me until I have another student stand next to me and yell "Now" whenever her racket goes past the proper checkpoint (which is straight to the back fence on the forehand). When she hears *both* of us saying "Now," my point suddenly seems to hit home.

Bringing Lessons to a Close

I always like to finish a lesson with some sort of enjoyable running-and-hitting drill that leaves the kids puffing, because this is what they usually remember best. Then afterward, as they're sitting on the bench resting or while they're gathering up the balls, I can tell them: "I'm really proud of you kids. You worked hard but you were still going strong at the end. I can't wait for next week's lesson." Before they go out the gate, I also try to give each of them some kind of positive statement and personal recognition. A positive ending comment makes a student feel good and motivates her to strive for additional improvements. It may even provide the impetus that gets her back for the next lesson. (If a group is too large for this kind of individual attention, I try to pick out those youngsters who were having the most trouble and give them encouragement, because it kills me to have anybody drop the game without giving it a fair chance.)

In addition, I talk to the kids about what a nice gesture it is to thank their instructor for the lesson, even though he is getting paid. "It's not for me," I tell them, "and it's not just in tennis. It's simply a polite thing to remember to thank people who have tried to help you or give you a good time, like when you go to somebody's house for dinner or a birthday party." This is such an important social courtesy for kids to develop, yet one that many parents fail to stress or even bring up. As a result, many youngsters finish a lesson thinking, "My folks are paying this guy—I don't owe him anything." But if they come up and thank the instructor, this gesture leaves a nice feeling and it enables the instructor to say something nice in return, such as: "Thanks for trying hard today—you were super. See you next week."

I've always felt that sports instructors should consider themselves educators in a wider sense. I know that parents will be forever grateful for the little social courtesies you teach their children, and the youngsters will one day appreciate how you helped them grow not just as tennis players, but as people.

What to Cover in the Next Lesson

At the end of each lesson, make sure you allow time for your students to evaluate the day's lesson—and to help plan the next one. Let them know that your goal is to develop independent-thinking students, and that you thus want them to get closely involved in the teaching process.

You might ask them after the first lesson: "My goals were this and this today—how do you feel we did? Do you think you're ready to move on to another stroke?" Also question them about what they liked most about the lesson, and what they liked least. Soliciting these attitudes will help you organize more-effective lesson plans. For example, if one youngster says, "I didn't like to do all that running," try to find out why. Then ask the other students for their opinions. You may realize that you overdid the running or you failed to keep it fun, in which case you need to make necessary adjustments in your approach. But also remember that running is a part of the game, and that the youngster who complained may actually be veiling the fact that she just doesn't like tennis, or exercise.

Next, spend a few minutes listening to what your students would like to work on in the next lesson. You'll have to guide them in the early stages, until you've covered all the basic strokes, but then you can become more flexible—not to the point that you allow them to work only on their favorite strokes while avoiding their trouble areas, but so they contribute their input and shape each lesson as much as possible, in a healthy way.

Finally, give yourself enough time to tape-record or jot down notes about what you covered in the lesson and specific points about each student's strengths and weaknesses. This refreshes your memory from week to week and helps you document growth. You won't get caught in the next lesson saying, "What did we cover last week?" and you can periodically review your notes to find persistent problem areas in a youngster's game and to check how well she is progressing. When you take this kind of care after each lesson, the succeeding lesson plan falls easily into place, and you can plan an appropriate overall program to bring about desired improvement.

Evaluate Your Own Teaching

The methods of evaluation that I offered parent/instructors in chapter 7 (pages 107–110) are certainly applicable here, with one important addition: When you have an impartial person evaluate one of your lessons, make sure he watches what happens to the class when your back is turned. This is a crucial test, for if most of your students forget about tennis and start goofing off, then you haven't been very effective in establishing discipline and fostering a desire to use the entire lesson time to learn tennis. At the next lesson, you can bring up the issue, and perhaps tell the class: "I know what happened last week when I had to leave the court for a couple of minutes. No problem, but if I see it happen again, the lesson is over, because I'm only interested in working with people who are here to learn. I love you kids, but you can hit balls over the fence on your own time."

On the other hand, if your evaluator notices that when your back is turned only one or two kids act up (such as by throwing balls at other students or by making horrible facial expressions in your direction), you should talk with these youngsters alone, without showing any hostility for what happened. You might say: "Look, I want you to know that I had a friend watch my class to see what kind of a job I'm doing, and he noticed that you horsed around whenever my back was turned. I'm not mad at you, but apparently you're not getting anything out of the lesson unless I look right at you. So maybe you need a private lesson, or you need to find another instructor, or maybe you don't even want lessons. What's your feeling about this?"

If you're concerned about upgrading the teaching profession, you'll let your students and their parents know that you're keenly interested in their evaluation of your teaching ability. You'll also solicit this feedback in the spirit that the teacher-student-parent relationship is an exchange system, and that the more effective you can become, the better the chances are for permanent gains by the youngster. In keeping to this philosophy, you won't avoid what your evaluators (or your own self-evaluation) turn up. You'll admit to your shortcomings and try to make the necessary changes in your approach. A dedicated instructor is not defensive; he knows his strengths and weaknesses and accepts himself as he is—but it never stops him from trying to grow.

Stroking Drills and Games

Drills and games can provide a number of excellent experiences for youngsters of all ages and ability levels, even when they are in the same group. In addition to the virtues pointed out in the previous chapter (see page 105), such diversions provide a way to get less-talented youngsters actively involved in the game, and they teach the better players how to adjust to those not as capable or as lucky as they from the standpoint of native ability. Just incorporate the following guidelines and your students will have a lot of fun while improving their strokes and court movement.

• Handpick each drill according to difficulty—considering the age and ability levels of your students—so that each youngster can at least successfully *attempt* what is required. Be ready to scale down certain aspects of a drill to give weaker students a chance, but don't deny the capable ones their chance to go all out.

• Design drills to move quickly, without confusion or excess waiting time between hits. Your students should learn the drills so well that they can move into their respective positions without your aid; this keeps the drill moving and frees you to teach.

• Stress the fact that when students listen carefully, they're spared the embarrassment of fouling up the drill—by not knowing where they're supposed to aim a particular shot or where they're supposed to run.

• All drills should activate a good-hearted spirit, even when there's a competitive aspect involved. "Winning" will be important to many kids, but your focus should be on hustle and stroke production and the fun of putting skills to the test. If there are to be any penalties, such as laps around the court by the losing team, they should be agreed upon in advance by all the players.

• If you set your program up properly, you won't have to rely on rewards (such as candy bars or ice-cream cones) or the threat of punishment to motivate your students to work hard. I've found that the only thing kids really need in the way of motivation is to know that you're watching them, that you care about them, and that you occasionally call out their name—not to chew them out for something but to give them verbal rewards: "That's super, Alan!" or "Wow, I can't believe it, Allison—you played that shot like a pro!" Be sure not to overlook the less-talented players; address them by name in an encouraging manner. The better players will gain some inner rewards from their good performances in front of the group, but don't overlook any kid's need for praise from the coach.

• See that all students have equal opportunities to participate in every drill, unless the rules make an exception (such as when two students play a point and the winner stays on the court until she loses).

• Don't allow players to skip shots while hitting or to take a breather by waiting in line and skipping a turn. Encourage them to go all out during the drill; if they become overly tired they should get off the court and make room for the other players.

• Encourage orderly waiting lines—formed without bickering and kept safely away from drill participants who are in action.

• Be alert to variations during a drill that will suit individual needs. For instance, if a youngster is in a volley drill that moves to the right and she hits great moving in that direction—but poorly moving to the left—you should switch gears and have her move to the left and work on her weakness, while the other players keep moving to the right.

• Make sure you provide actual instruction during a drill, and that it's not simply "busy time." If you don't have a ball machine, try to have somebody else feed the balls so that you can remain free to teach.

• When using a ball machine (as when feeding balls by hand), it's far better to have balls fired at too slow a speed than too rapidly, until your students have gained some expertise. Ball-machine speeds and trajectories should be checked before the class begins.

• Since discrepancies in talent are likely to exist in nearly every group, drills can help youngsters learn to play against stronger players as well as against weaker players—a basic situation they'll confront when they go out to play matches. But in selecting drills, make sure the strong player doesn't suffer from a prolonged lack of realistic competition and that the weak player isn't unduly outclassed and embarrassed.

Around the World

In this game the emphasis is on hustle, stamina, and an ability to keep the ball in play under pressure. After a student hits, he is immediately replaced and play continues as he runs around the right net post to join the waiting line at the opposite baseline. The two lines gradually shorten as players who miss a shot are forced out of the game and watch from the back fence. In this photo, there's no longer a waiting line at the opposite baseline, which requires the player at position 3 to really hustle, because she's the next hitter on that side.

Ping-Pong Tennis

In this drill students form two lines, one on each side of the court, behind the baseline. The first player in one line stands near the center mark and begins the point by bouncing a ball and hitting it over the net. He then scurries to the end of his waiting line. The opposing player now returns the first shot after one bounce and hustles to the end of his line. The player now first in each line continues this sequence—the hitters alternate as the rally continues—until an error has been committed by a player of either team. Then the winning team puts the ball in play to start a new point (and a running score can be kept). This drill encourages waiting players to be prepared and to anticipate an opponent's shot. Each player also has a feeling of responsibility to the team and seems to try a little harder.

Around the World

Students form lines at the center of the baselines, as in Ping-Pong tennis. The first person in one line bounces the ball, hits a playable shot to the person across the net, and then immediately runs to the end of the waiting line on the *opposite* side of the court. Meanwhile, the opponent hitting the second shot returns the ball, using any kind of stroke she wants (as long as it lands inside the singles court), and then also runs to the end of the opposite waiting line. Each person runs around the net post on the right (as she faces the net) to prevent possible collisions. A player who misses a shot drops out, and the game continues until only two players are left on the court. These two opponents then play a point to determine the winner. The competitive aspects of the game provide a good deal of excitement, while those players who last in the game receive a tremendous amount of exercise as they sprint from one side of the court to the other. Because of the running involved, it is important that the side having the greatest number of players always starts a new point.

King or Queen of the Hill

Students form two waiting lines, one at each baseline, and two players take the court. The first starts a point by bouncing the ball and stroking it over the net, down the middle and not too hard, to the waiting player. If she doesn't hit the ball in this manner, it must be played again. (Each "server" soon learns to hit the ball deep—which is a key fundamental in tactics.) The first two players rally and the winner of the point remains on the court as the loser returns to her waiting line and a new challenger from that line replaces her. Play resumes and continues in this manner until every player has had at least one turn (ideally, several turns). The player winning the most points is proclaimed king or queen of the hill.

This drill offers an opportunity for students to experience a competitive situation and presents a chance to help them learn about performing under pressure. When a player has won two or three straight points, he'll find himself under pressure from players in his waiting line; they'll shout at him, trying to distract him, because they don't get a chance to move up until he loses. Sometimes a problem can arise over the question of playing time. One youngster might win five or six points in a row, while another one lasts for just one point at a time and thus spends most of her time watching. There's no denying the fact that the person with the best strokes will get the most action in this drill. Here's an instance when it can help to divide the group so that students only play against those of fairly comparable ability. Remember, however, the nature of competition: the talented win out. This is a rude awakening for some kids, but it can also provide them with excellent motivation if you handle the situation properly, with sensitivity and support. For example, if a youngster comes up and says, "This game is no fun—Kelly's getting all the hits," then you can say: "Right, and when you get as good as she is, you're going to get a lot of hits, too. That's what competition is all about." But boy, if she can't

The Groundstroke-Volley Drill

The groundstroke-volley drill, shown here with one player hitting from the baseline and two players volleying at the net, is an excellent way for youngsters to practice strokes against their peers. The instructor (left foreground) feeds balls to the baseline player, who then tries to drive the ball past her opponents at the net. They in turn work on anticipation, on moving quickly forward, and on volley technique. This is a flexible drill — you can station either one to two hitters at the baseline, as well as at the net — and it's very useful for doubles practice.

hack that realization, you've got to back off and find a drill that will offer her some success experiences.

The Groundstroke-Volley Drill

An important virtue of group drills is that kids can hit back one another's shots. Instructors (not to mention ball machines) tend to get into a rhythm of feeding balls to students at a constant speed and into the same hitting area. But when kids also have a chance to go against their peers in a drill, they learn to cope with shots that bounce at different heights and arrive at varying speeds, just as in a match. Plus, they get used to playing against a real opponent. To set up a typical drill for this purpose (assuming you have four students), place two youngsters on one baseline, hitting groundstrokes as you feed them balls while standing at the *T* formed by the opposite service line and center line. Station the other two students at the net, volleying shots back to the groundstrokers. If you're stuck with just one court but ten kids, let two students be coaches (watching as they wait their turn to hit) behind the baseline hitters, have two more retrieve balls that get past the volleyers, and let the remaining two load the ball machine or relay balls to you. Give each hitter about five or six swings, and then move everybody to a different station.

The One-against-One Volley Drill

In the one-against-one volley drill, players in opposite lines volley against each other until one player misses. That player moves to the back of the waiting line while the winner remains in the game until she misses. The ball cannot bounce — all shots must be hit as volleys — and players must keep the ball inside their respective service courts by hitting in the general direction of the white cards. (Here the court has been divided in two to accommodate a large group.) Volleys should not be "babied" over the net, but hit with control and good stroking form. The instructor, behind the ball basket here, puts the ball in play to each line.

One-against-One Volley Drill

This drill helps players develop quickness and anticipation at the net as they practice their close-range volleys. The group is divided into two waiting lines, each stationed at the *T* on opposite sides of the court. Two players face off across the net and you start the action by feeding a ball to player 1 at about waist level. She must volley this first ball from the *T*, after which she may move forward. As soon as you put the ball in play (station yourself off to the side of player 2), player 2 must lean forward and try to anticipate the volley. If she returns it successfully, the players continue volleying until there's a winner. The winner stays in and the loser moves to the end of her line. You start the next point the same way. This can be a fast-moving drill, so all players must pay strict attention and be ready to move in immediately. Have the teams change sides midway, so all players get a chance at the first volley. You can keep score for added

The Four-Corner Volley Drill

The instructor (center background) starts the action by hitting to the player at position 1. This player must volley to player 2, straight ahead (roughly along the path marked by the white cards) and inside an area bounded by the singles sideline and the center line. Player 2 then volleys on the diagonal to player 3, but can hit as far to the side as the doubles sideline. Player 3 then volleys to player 4, who can volley to anywhere on the court. Nobody returns player 4's shot, but if it's properly hit, the same players get to play again as the instructor starts a new ball. No ball is allowed to bounce — all shots must be hit as volleys — and balls lobbed over a player's head are not acceptable.

The brainteaser begins when someone makes an error. That player is out and must go to the end of the waiting line (foreground), while the first person in line hustles into hitting position at either 1 or 3 to fill a vacancy. A player in position 1 or 2 stays until making an error, and a good volleyer can remain there for the entire drill. When player 2 makes an error, players 3 and 4 both shift clockwise one station to fill the vacancy, so that position 3 opens up for a new player. If player 4 makes the error, only player 3 must shift. Ideally, the instructor is already hitting to player 1 as player 4 volleys, so that the action is constant. Kids in the waiting line are allowed to add a little verbal pressure — "Miss it, miss it!" — which gives this drill extra excitement.

fun and interest. What counts, however, is volleying form and trying to predict where the opponent is going to volley; there's no time for second-guessing. This offers you a nice opportunity to reward kids for guessing and going with their original decision or instinct—even if they go the wrong way.

With larger groups, you can run two games simultaneously by dividing the court in half and using the center line as the side boundary. You can then feed two waiting lines from the middle of the court. At the end, the top point-getters from each group can form a new group and go head-to-head on one half of the court. Or, you can have your top girls go against your top boys.

The Four-Corner Volley Drill

This fast, exciting game challenges a player's ability to volley under stress, while helping to develop quick hands and feet. Concentration and alertness are crucial for everyone involved. The players must volley well and always be ready to rotate quickly into hitting position as other players miss and hurry to the end of the waiting line. Those in line must dash into vacated volleying positions at a moment's notice. Some groups like to increase the competitive aspects by setting a goal: if the same four players stay in for a predetermined number of rounds (say four to five), everyone else must run a couple of laps or pick up the stray balls.

Vic-O-Rama

Here's a fun, competitive game that has a greater purpose than most people realize at first. I often end my large group lessons with this drill, and the kids really look forward to it. Two teams of four or more players line up at opposite baselines. The first person in each line plays a complete point; one player starts by bouncing the ball and hitting a playable shot down the middle. The loser goes to the end of her line and is replaced by the second person in line. The *winner* brings in a partner to help her play the lone new opponent on the losing side. It's now two players against one, and the winning player—the "captain" as long as her team keeps winning—starts the point. If the same team wins this point, the loser is again replaced, and the winning side adds a third player and again plays against just one opponent. But if the single player is able to defeat these three players, she sends them all off the court, and then brings in a partner from her side to help play a single opponent. The object is for one team to win a point while all of its players are on the court.

If it's established that the losing team has to pay a penalty, such as running laps around the court, the lone youngster who must play against

1

Vic-O-Rama

1. This drill starts out with the first two youngsters in each waiting line playing a complete point.

2. The loser is replaced by the next person in line (foreground) while the winner (at far baseline) gets to bring in another player. The winner puts the ball in play and they complete the point.

3. To win a game, all members of one team must be on the court at the same time and win a single point. (The losing team may have to take a lap around the court, if this is what you've previously agreed upon.) If the girl in the foreground wins the point, she wipes out the other team and brings in one of her teammates to play against a single opponent.

the entire opposing team has a chance to become a real heroine if she can manage to win the point; if she fails, she has a pretty sound excuse. I've seen this game expand to the point that there are fifteen kids on one side, playing against a single youngster. It once happened when I was giving clinics in China, and when the lone player won the point, everybody went crazy, even the people who were watching from house balconies nearby.

Since a youngster can find herself competing against four or more players, important game tactics are constantly stressed, such as shot selection and placement, and determining the strengths and weaknesses of other players. For example, a lone player realizes how crucial it is to lob the ball deep—beyond the net players—or to drive it close to the net tape to make her opponents' volleys more difficult. She learns she must attack the net at every opportunity, especially when she sees an opponent start to hit the ball high into the air, since this likely will present her with a good overhead or volley opportunity. She also learns to try to capitalize on an opponent's particular weakness. (Keep in mind that no shot-hogging or "poaching" is allowed in this drill, nor may a weaker player avoid a shot by saying "Yours"; each person must play any ball that clearly comes in her direction.)

Although the opening shot of each point must be playable and down the middle, youngsters quickly learn the advantage of hitting it as deep as possible. The captain of the team that wins the point is allowed to position her teammates on the court, which encourages her to assess their specific ability levels so that she can put a strong volleyer at the net while keeping a steady groundstroker on the baseline. This, too, will help her learn how to determine future opponents' strengths and weaknesses. Meanwhile, everybody learns about teamwork—and pressure, since a youngster's mistake can clear her entire team off the court. Obviously, coping with such peer pressure is tough, but it's something every young player must eventually learn, not just in tennis but in any team sport. Your responsibilities as the instructor are (1) to see that teammates are fair to those who make mistakes, (2) to insure that all your students know they have your support and understanding, no matter how poorly they might play, and (3) to watch carefully for signs that a youngster just isn't ready for this kind of competitive effort and should be held out of the drill. I've never seen an injury occur in this game, but as a team expands on one side of the court, you should also remind the players to stay clear of the person hitting.

A successful coach in group lessons is nearly always an excellent motivator. If you have that talent, your enthusiasm and constant encouragement can help maintain a very fast pace from start to finish, even with kids who are struggling with the game. You may even hear a youngster say afterward: "Are you kidding me—the lesson's over? We just started!" Then you'll know you've given a good lesson.

9/The Key Fundamentals of Sound Strokes

THOSE of you who read my first book already know that my priorities as an instructor are to keep the learning fun and to have players "groove" sound stroking patterns. There's a time and place for working on a youngster's court coverage, mental toughness, and shot selection. Yet, whether he plays the game recreationally or on the tournament level, the basic question always remains: Does he have the consistent stroke that's needed to hit the shot he wants under pressure?

On most groundstrokes, for example, the problem for nearly everybody is not in reaching the ball with enough time to take a swing, but in failing to hit it back in play because of an unsound stroke. Balls go into the net not because a player's thyroid activity is low, but because tennis balls are round and they go where the racket is aimed. A lot of people have sensual movements and long, flowing strokes, but their racket head is often crooked at impact and thus they find themselves finishing second in a field of two.

That's why I like to tell all my students: "Try to learn perfect form first—and then worry about getting to the ball. If you develop a nice swing but you're always about eight feet from the ball when it lands, don't worry. I can call a cab to get you there in time."

Before I explore the individual strokes, I want to introduce some of the crucial elements that influence the stroking patterns I teach. These underlying fundamentals never really change, for they derive from *physical laws* that dictate the movement of the body and the action of the racket. Meanwhile, the strokes themselves must respect the realities of the court dimensions and the net. This doesn't mean that the style you teach must exactly follow what I advocate in this book; your child can have a different look in his overall approach to the ball and on his follow-through, but if he hopes to master reliable strokes, he cannot violate physical laws, particularly in the "hitting zone" (normally, an area about 6 to 12 inches long in which a player can contact the ball and still hit it in the desired direction).

In reading this chapter, don't feel bad if you discover you have a number of incorrect impressions about how a tennis ball should be hit. You're not alone. Scientific research into the game is finally exploding some long-treasured misconceptions about tennis strokes and is bringing us into a marvelous era for instruction. Everybody is growing in tennis knowledge, and nobody has really licked the subject. Even after all my years of teaching, I'm continually gaining new insights into technique, thanks to the availability of high-speed photography and computer technology, and thanks to researchers like Drs. Gideon Ariel and Ann Penny, my partners in the Coto de Caza Sports Research Center, and Dr. Pat Keating, a theoretical physicist. I hope this book will motivate you to continue investigating the sport and to stay abreast of the research that comes out, so that your child's strokes can always be built upon well-founded techniques.

The Realities of the Court and the Net

Obviously, whatever I have to say must make sense to you before you'll try to incorporate it into your instruction. So I'll first present my rationale for why a low-to-high forward motion on forehand and backhand groundstrokes makes sense, and why I therefore emphasize a reliance upon topspin as opposed to underspin or swinging on a horizontal plane.

The Court Is Like a Long, Narrow Sidewalk

Although the tennis court may seem to be a gigantic expanse at first, children (and adults) should learn to visualize themselves playing on a long, narrow sidewalk. This helps them develop groundstrokes with a follow-through that keeps their hitting arm on line with the target area, instead of pulled toward a side court. A good teaching aid here is to have your child stand anywhere on the baseline, extend an arm, and point his finger—first to one of his opponent's baseline corners, and then to the opposite corner. He'll see how little he has to move his arm. You can then point out that this is all he has to vary his follow-through when he hits from the baseline and tries to run his opponent from corner to corner.

The Net Is Higher Than It Looks

The high net is a fact of life for little kids, yet as they grow older and taller, they tend to forget how high it still remains in terms of hitting the ball hard and keeping it in play. As you might imagine from the

These two players illustrate my concept that the court is like a long, narrow sidewalk. One player has hit down-the-line and the other has gone crosscourt, but notice that their rackets are almost identical on the follow-through. People tend to imagine a wide change, but there should be no more than a 19-degree variation in the direction of your child's swing as he hits from the baseline to any point near his opponent's baseline.

photograph on page 72, a person must be 6'7" tall in order to stand at the baseline and see his opponent's baseline while looking *over* the net. This means that nearly everybody in tennis is looking at his groundstroke target areas *through* the little squares in the net. The physical reality of the surprisingly high net also has a significant influence on the serve, the volley, and the approach shot.

Tennis Must Be Envisioned as a Lifting Game

Since the net is actually a high barrier, it follows that your child should learn to *lift* the ball on his groundstrokes with the right amount of spin, speed, and elevation, so that the ball can clear the net safely and still come down deep in his opponent's court. When he can elevate his ground-strokes like this, he'll rarely hit into the net; the ball may still go long or wide, but he might get a lucky line call. Very few opponents will give him the point when his shot hits the net.

In studying this game, you may come across instructors who tell students to "stay down with the ball" on groundstrokes. That advice

Since there's a tendency for youngsters to want to hit low, hard "net-skimmers," these coaches have tied balloons to a thin rope that is stretched across the court 6 feet above the top of the net. This provides their students with some fun targets and the correct visual orientation as they learn to lift the ball with a low-to-high forward stroking motion.

amazes me, because all the great players I've seen always get down to the ball and then *lift* their bodies in synchronization with their forward and upward stroke (if they are going to hit with topspin). Simple physics dictates a bodily lifting motion here, since the upward energy flow of the hitting arm is so great that the player who tries to stay down with the ball simply fights his own swing by making these forces work against each other.

One fun and effective teaching method is to have your child aim for a string of balloons stretched across the court about 6 feet above the net. This orients him to how high he actually wants to elevate the ball in a baseline rally and gives him some nice feedback when he manages to hit a balloon (assuming that he's also using topspin, as discussed below, to bring his shots down in bounds—not smacking them into the back fence).

Depth Is a Crucial Element

If you want your child to maximize his success in tennis, at any level, you can never overemphasize the fact that few players will give him trouble if he consistently hits the ball *deep* (and in bounds). For example, in a groundstroke rally, deep shots that keep an opponent pinned behind his baseline give a hitter the following advantages:

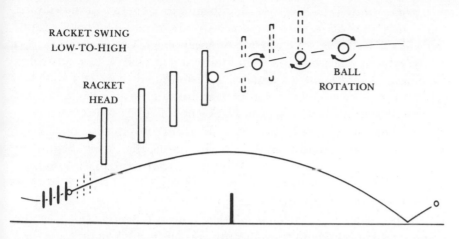

Topspin

- They prevent his opponent from trying to rush the net.
- They give the hitter more time to prepare for his next shot, because the ball is in the air longer.
- They make it much more difficult for the opponent to hit short, sharply angled shots that can force him off the court.
- They insure that the opponent's drives (baseline-to-baseline shots) will seldom move him more than two or three steps along the baseline, because of the angles involved.

To put it another way, players who continually hit unintentional short balls wind up losing. In fact, a main goal in good tennis is simple: Don't be the first one to hit a short ball in a rally, unless it's intentionally designed to run an opponent off the court, tire him, or set him up for a passing shot (a shot driven to one side, beyond reach of an opponent charging or already at the net). Otherwise, a short ball allows a smart opponent to move up to the net, thus gaining a tactical advantage in most cases.

The Importance of Topspin

Since a young tennis player will eventually want to hit his groundstrokes hard—either deep or on a sharp diagonal—he must learn to capitalize on topspin. Imagine a dot on top of the ball that moves forward and down toward the opponent, then backward and up toward the hitter; spin in this direction is topspin. (A nice teaching aid is to paint a large black mark on a ball to make its rotation visible.) To impart topspin properly on the forehand and backhand, a player must contact the back of the ball with a racket face that is vertical or near-vertical at impact and traveling low-to-high in the direction of the target. When the racket face brushes against the ball, the ball is lifted, and it travels upward until gravity and air pockets caused by the spinning begin to generate a downward force—after the ball has safely cleared that high net. The ball's overall path will generally resemble the arc of a rainbow.

I've always emphasized a low-to-high stroking motion on groundstrokes as the basic requirement for imparting topspin, and that's still true, but there's an important qualification to keep in mind as you teach. Recent research has shown that an upward swing of 17 degrees, against a waist-high ball, will actually produce little or no topspin rotation. This is not a very steep upward angle, but it means that most beginning youngsters—conscientious as they might be about swinging low-to-high—will not generate much spin on the ball until they acquire a more vertical forward and upward stroke.

With this in mind, remember another crucial warning: Don't let the common falsehoods about topspin scare you off or put you on the wrong track. Hitting with topspin is not a skill that youngsters have to save for when they're older and stronger. Some pros confuse the issue by arguing that a lot of whipping action in the wrist is needed to hit topspin, and that this requires a strong wrist (which is true). However, topspin doesn't really require whipping action by the wrist—not at any age, and particularly by youngsters. Extra wrist action may help generate a bit more power, but very often at the expense of accuracy and consistency. (I'll more fully explain the importance of playing with a firm wrist a bit later in this chapter and in the following one.)

A more damaging concept is perpetuated by pros who claim that a person must "roll the wrist" in the hitting zone so that the racket face can "turn over" the ball and impart topspin. The effort to achieve this rolling-over action by the wrist ruins more forehands—and leads to more cases of tennis elbow—than anything I know. Fortunately, research is helping us scuttle this misconception. In photographically studying the strokes of pros like Rod Laver and Ilie Nastase at over ten thousand frames a second, I have discovered that although these players use a lot of wrist action before the racket reaches the hitting zone, the wrist locks at that point and is firm at actual impact. It then relaxes again on the follow-through. Remember this the next time you watch a pro tournament, because your naked eye will trick you into thinking some players are hitting with a big wrist-roll. Even the pros themselves are sometimes fooled. They tend to describe what they *feel* they are doing as they hit the ball, and if they have a "wristy" forehand or backhand, they tend to think they are "coming over" the ball at impact. But think about that for a second. If people actually turned the racket face over the ball at impact, the ball would have to rise up through the racket strings in order to clear the net.

I place an emphasis on topspin because I want kids to play this game right, with stroking patterns that should never become obsolete (though I'm always open to what ongoing research might prove). Certainly underspin is an important element in good tennis, particularly on approach shots, volleys, and service returns. But basically it's a defensive technique in a game in which winning groundstrokes are built primarily around topspin—from junior tennis through the pro ranks.

I'll explore the ramifications of this in greater detail later, but if your child can learn to hit forehands *and* backhands with topspin, he'll have two things going for him the rest of his life: (1) the ability to hit the ball down-the-line or crosscourt with velocity and a greater chance to hit safely over the net than if he tries to hit the same shot with a horizontal swing or with underspin, and thus (2) the flexibility to beat both an opponent who camps at the baseline and one who likes to rush the net. (Of course, topspin doesn't guarantee that the ball will always land deep when hit hard. Your child must still calculate the upward angle of his stroking pattern, and misjudgment can result in shots sometimes landing too short. But even then, shots hit with topspin tend to jump at an opponent after they bounce, keeping him pinned to the baseline.)

If your child insists on hitting the ball hard and "flat" from the baseline (that is, if his racket starts and finishes on about the same horizontal level, rather than moving low-to-high), you should at least teach him the two major limitations of such a style—assuming you accept my basic premise that successful groundstrokes must blend speed, safe clearance over the net, depth, and accuracy.

First, there is, I'll grant, some research to show that a child can plant his feet firmly, turn his hips into the shot, and hit balls harder swinging horizontally than when hitting with topspin. Yet simple physics dictates that he must also play the game with a slim margin of error using this horizontal stroke, for the harder he tries to hit the ball, the closer it must come to the net in order to land inside his opponent's baseline. He thus must acquire unbelievable accuracy in order to hit the ball hard and keep it in play. This method also means having to take the speed off his short diagonal passing shots, which in turn limits his ability to hit the ball past good players who come to the net. By contrast, topspin would give him the confidence to hit hard always, either down-the-line or on the diagonal.

Second, hitting with a horizontal swing makes timing more difficult, because there's only one point in the hitting zone where your child can contact the ball on line with his intended target. He's in theory trying to hit the ball down a narrow sidewalk but centrifugal force is driving his hips around like a spinning top, and his racket is following. Conversely, a low-to-high forward swing would give him a natural "bowling" motion

You can help your child understand what it means to have a vertical racket head at impact by taping a yardstick across the racket face and having him hold it against a fence, as shown here. Then when he's out on the court you can tell him: "Remember how that yardstick was straight up and down against the fence? That's how you want your racket to be when you meet the ball." When you have him try to fix a vertical racket face with his eyes closed, he will often tend to lay back the racket head. Using the fence and yardstick, he'll kinesthetically learn to push his wrist farther forward instead, to the proper wrist position, and thus eliminate the layback. This is a good exercise because it helps make your child his own teacher.

and lengthen his effective hitting zone, by allowing the racket face to travel toward the target over a longer range.

The Overall Goal: An Efficient Stroke

No matter how sophisticated we might become in teaching this game, a successful stroke still boils down to one thing: *the position of the racket head at impact*. People can approach the ball differently and do some crazy things, but to produce the desired speed, trajectory, and accuracy, the racket face must (1) contact the ball at the proper (vertical) angle and (2) be properly synchronized with the body and the racket arm. In other words, nothing crazy can happen when the racket is in the hitting zone or contacting the ball.

The more I study this game, the more fanatical I become about the importance of the racket's position at impact, because it dictates an efficient stroke. For one thing, the instant the ball hits the racket strings, it's gone; and thus wherever the racket points at impact is basically where the ball is going to go. Moreover, research has also shown us that just the slightest variation in the angle of the racket face at impact will produce dramatic changes in the ball's trajectory and the length of the shot.

Since the necessary timing mechanisms are so sensitive—for kids and adults alike—and since the key in tennis is to keep the ball in play, I teach stroking patterns that, though they may at first seem rather rigid, are intended to hold up under playing pressure. To me, good stroking form eliminates all extraneous movement while producing maximum power with minimum effort. Thus, on all strokes but the serve and the overhead, I advocate (1) a firm wrist position that remains as unchanged as possible throughout the swing, (2) a short, controlled backswing, and (3) a follow-through that "tracks" toward the intended target. "You may feel a little stiff at first," I tell my students, "but winning will loosen you up."

Following are some of the important factors involved in developing such a stroking form.

The Question of Power and Fluidity

In subsequent chapters I stress certain movements and body positions that will help your child acquire strokes that are biomechanically efficient—that supply the power and control he needs (especially if he aspires to junior tournament play) with the least amount of strain. The key here is for both of you to realize that he doesn't have to swing hard to hit the ball hard *if* he has an efficient swing. This means syncing his body movements and coordinating them with his racket-arm position and swing. The more efficient he becomes from the standpoint of human movement, the less he will have to put muscular effort into a shot to hit with similar power.

Fluidity is a term that must be properly defined, for I find that it is not necessarily synonymous with successful stroke patterns. To me fluidity (and good form) means that a person's body segments are moving correctly—at the right time and in the proper sequence—*and* that the racket face is meeting the ball at the proper angle: a person with sound stroke production generally looks fluid because everything is in sync.

Now, other people ascribe "fluidity" to a player who simply looks smooth as he swings. But, unfortunately, the "slick" look has nothing to do with being a good tennis player if that person's movements are not properly in sync. A lot of fluid players can't play worth a lick, because their racket face is in the wrong position at impact, hit after hit after hit.

What your child should strive for—biomechanically—is a sequence of forces, starting from the ground up. In other words, on groundstrokes, power starts with the feet firmly planted on the court. This allows the knees and then the thighs to make their turn into the ball, followed successively by the hips, the trunk, and the shoulders. Each body segment should in turn slow down (decelerate) and stop, which makes the immediately following segment move faster (accelerate); this series of actions must occur in the right sequence to deliver maximum power with minimum effort. This is what I mean in the book when I refer to the positive and negative effects of deceleration-acceleration.

When players lack this coordinated stroke on the forehand and backhand, it's almost always because of excess movements, primarily on the backswing. Most beginners and intermediates, in fact, are unaware that a synchronized body turn with a short arm swing will generate more power than very little body rotation and a long arm swing. They think they have to lengthen their backswing to gain greater arm power ("The longer my swing, the harder I can hit the ball"), but arm power will never match trunk power. This is why I'm such a stickler about students *limiting* their swings from the very beginning. I want them to start out with a short backswing and stay with it, keeping it stripped of extra movements that might feel stylish but are absolutely damaging to an efficient swing.

The Ball and the Racket at Impact

Since tennis all boils down to how the racket is meeting the ball in the hitting zone, it's important to understand exactly what is happening and should be happening at this point.

First of all, I want to clear up some popular misconceptions. Perhaps you've heard playing pros claim they can "feel" the ball on the strings when they hit, or that a good follow-through enables them to "guide" the ball toward their target. Or maybe you've read about certain rackets that allow you to "carry" the ball on the strings longer than with a competitor's model, thus giving you "more time to do what you want with the ball." This all sounds intriguing, but it is simply impossible to consciously control the ball by touch in such a manner. By using highly sensitive sensors and sophisticated electronic equipment, Dr. Gideon Ariel has determined that at impact the ball is on the racket strings for only 3 to 6 milliseconds, and since it takes 50 to 70 milliseconds for the nervous system to relay sensation to the brain cortex, the ball is on its way toward the net by then. So there's nothing a person can do to affect the direction of the ball once he feels it hit the strings; it's all in how his tennis racket was aimed at impact. Therefore, when you talk about a person having a good "touch," you're really discussing what takes place *before* impact—his ability to move the racket at a particular speed and to have it facing in the right direction and at the correct angle at impact. Dr. Ariel's finding also undermines the idea that a player can consciously affect the speed of the ball the instant he feels it touch the strings. I'm always amused by pros who grimace as they contact the ball, particularly on volleys and service returns, and who later explain that they were "taking the speed off the ball." We filmed one top pro as he returned serves with an underspin motion, and it showed that while he was making his facial expressions, the ball was already crossing his service line, 18 feet away, on its way back to the server. (In view of these realities, the follow-through may seem unimportant. But as we'll see, a good follow-through is the end result of a good stroke and it increases the effective hitting zone, thus insuring a greater "safety margin" for contacting the ball.)

A second important factor here is that in order to hit groundstrokes with topspin, your child must learn (1) what it means to have the racket face straight up and down at impact, and (2) how to know—without looking—that it's in this desired position. If he slights this detail, beautiful footwork and a perfect stroking pattern will be wasted, for a mere 10-degree tilt in the racket head produces drastic changes in ball direction. Once your child sees what it means to have the racket face vertical at impact and learns how it "feels" in the wrist and forearm, have him close his eyes as he takes a practice swing. Tell him to stop the racket where he normally contacts the ball, and then ask him if he thinks the racket face is vertical. If he says "yes," but you can see that he's mistaken, move the racket to the proper position. He'll likely say, "That feels terrible," but you can assure him: "Remember this crummy feeling; it will help you beat me some day." A similar test is to have him place his racket near the contact point, close his eyes, and try for a vertical racket face. Then say, "Tell me when you think the racket face is straight up and down." When he says "Now," have him open his eyes and see for himself just how much the racket is actually tilted. A wall or fence can also be used for this test, and will offer positive proof that the racket face is vertical (see photo on page 160).

A third point to remember is this adage: If you err in timing your stroke to coincide with the arriving ball, it's better to be early rather than late. A player who has his racket traveling on line with his target before impact can hit the ball a little early and still maintain good direction. But if he's late contacting the ball, nothing can really save his shot.

"Keep Your Eye on the Ball"

Tennis instructors put such unquestioned faith in the line "Keep your eye on the ball" that you may wonder if research has exposed it as an overblown concept—particularly when you see photographs of the pros hitting groundstrokes while their eyes are focused out ahead of the ball. There's a reason for their doing so (as I'll explain), and there's also a related misunderstanding to discard—that a player can actually "see" the ball hitting the racket strings. Yet still, an effort to track the approaching ball with the eyes not only helps a youngster develop better concentration, it leads to more consistent stroking patterns.

In order to get my students to focus their attention on the ball, I used to tell them cute things like "Watch the fuzz on the ball when it comes through your racket strings." I've since been corrected by ophthalmologists who point out that the eyes can't actually track a ball all the way into the racket, due to a sudden head shift just before impact. So now I tell people, "Follow the ball as long as you can and then try to see the racket or your racket arm as it comes through at impact."

What you're actually striving for as an instructor is twofold. First, you want your child to become ball-oriented rather than opponent-oriented when he goes out to play. Most people lack the ability to remain glued on the ball as they go to swing, and as a result they are easily distracted by what their opponent is doing across the net or by other external stimuli.

This leads into the second goal, which is for your child to keep his head steady and his eyes down *through impact*. This helps insure consistent contact on or near the center of the strings. If, as is natural, he lifts up prematurely—to see where his shot is going, or out of curiosity at what his opponent is up to—the racket also lifts, and can produce a missed hit. One way to help him acquire the desired sensation is to have him try the "neck-brace drill," in which he places his free hand behind his head to help hold it down as he swings. Two warnings: (1) some kids will still lift their head, even with the hand held behind it, so make sure the drill is serving its purpose; and (2) very young kids shouldn't use this drill if they need their free hand for balance.

I also try to nip this habit of looking up too soon by reminding kids: "You want to hit the *ball*, not your opponent, over the net. There's only one ball in play and it's come to you, so he can't do anything until you hit the ball back over the net." Another good way to help your child learn to keep his eyes down through impact is to say, "Keep your eyes focused on

The Neck-Brace Drill
An efficient stroke requires that a youngster keep his head down and his eyes focused on the point of impact. He can practice by holding his nonhitting hand behind his head and keeping his eyes on an X (or a coin) on the court until the shoulder of his hitting arm touches his chin. At that point in his stroke he can lift his head to follow the ball, which will still be on its way to the net. The lesson here is to be patient in completing the stroke. The student should remind himself, "The shot's not over until my shoulder touches my chin."

where you contact the ball and count to two—then you can look up to see where the ball is going." At first, he may be too eager to wait that long, or he even may be a little worried; very likely he'll be thinking: "Are you kidding me, Mom? If I keep my eyes down that long, my opponent's shot is going to hit me right in the ear."

If you sense such apprehension, simply have him hit from the baseline as you stand at the net. He'll then realize that his shots do not even reach you by the time he raises his eyes to focus on the ball again, and he thus has plenty of time to prepare for his next shot. Kenny Rosewall is the player to imitate here. Even his fellow pros marvel at his ability to keep his eyes down and complete a perfect stroke before he looks up, even under pressure.

You may be thinking, "If it's so important to keep your eyes on the point of impact, why do I see pictures of the pros hitting with their eyes focused out ahead of the ball?" The reason has to do with the fact that our eyes can only keep the ball in focus until it reaches a point 3 to 8 feet before racket impact. Thus the pros, through years of playing experience, have developed a cue system that enables them to sense exactly where they are going to contact the ball, well before impact. They don't have to consciously try to follow the ball into their racket. Some of them even prefer to raise their head immediately after impact, since their forward and upward inertia is so great. But in studying their technique, notice how they keep the head steady and synchronized with their body movement through impact. They've also learned not to look up until they actually feel the ball hit the racket strings, which is all the safety factor they need, since by the time that nerve impulse reaches the brain, the ball is already on its way toward the net.

The Importance of Playing with a Firm Wrist

A lot of people are enamored with "wristy" strokes, but my years of teaching and analyzing the game of tennis have convinced me that reliable groundstrokes and volleys are built upon a firm wrist position that remains as unchanged as possible on the backswing and through impact. Of course, there's no such thing as a perfectly fixed wrist; the forces that impinge upon the racket during the swing are so great that the wrist is going to move no matter how strong your child might be. But he can build a solid foundation for stroke production by consciously minimizing this movement, except on the serve and overhead.

If you're teaching a young child (one under seven or eight years old, particularly), he may tend to use too much wrist because he lacks the strength to stop or curb deceleration-acceleration on the backswing effectively. There's not much he can do about the physics at work until he gains some strength, but he can nullify the problem by shortening his backswing. He may complain that it feels too short, but he'll find that the effect of deceleration-acceleration on his wrist will bring his racket to impact right on the money. Don't let him take the easy way out by flailing away at the ball with a long backswing and floppy wrist.

Here are some reasons why I emphasize a firm wrist position:

• A youngster who rolls the wrist over in the hitting zone or tries to snap it through at impact is fooling with a critical element. The wrist is a radial point, and just a few degrees change in its position can lead to pretty substantial changes in the racket-face position and, therefore, the direction and trajectory of the ball.

• When your child learns to keep his wrist as firm as possible and the racket head locked in as it approaches the impact point, he has a much longer range in which to contact the ball properly. Conversely, the player who rolls his wrist must time that roll to produce a vertical racket head in those 3 to 6 milliseconds at impact, taking care to curb the inertia so that the wrist doesn't roll over before impact. Few youngsters (or adults, for that matter) have this kind of timing and muscular control.

The youngster on the left is demonstrating the desired backswing, with the racket high and the hitting elbow slightly raised and bent to help prevent wrist layback. The player on the right is committing a typical error by taking the racket back with a straight elbow and using an isolated arm movement instead of shoulder rotation. The result is wrist layback and a swing that's too long and thus less efficient.

• Playing with a firm wrist reduces the number of variables to contend with. Consider what your child may be up against when he starts out in tennis. Not only must he tackle coordination problems, he hasn't had any experience hitting a bouncing ball and hasn't developed the muscular system to keep the racket head as steady as possible during the stroke. If he's also trying to rely on wrist play, he's going to be so erratic at controlling the ball that he's unlikely to enjoy the competitive aspects of the game once he starts playing matches.

• The wristy player must throw out form in favor of a "touch" system. To play successfully, he must be strong and well coordinated, must have much more talent than the average player, and must play virtually every day in order to retain a "feel" for his strokes. Even then, he's developing an erratic style that is only as good as his timing on a particular day; when he loses his instinct, he loses everything. I want my students to develop consistent stroking patterns that will hold up even on days when they have Excedrin Headache number 38. They need a much more dependable system than "touch" if they hope to win a junior tournament by lasting through four, five, or six rounds.

• In a controlled test of tennis balls at my tennis college, we were not able to produce the same exact bounce two times in a row (even when new balls were fired out of a ball machine against a cement surface). Although the variations were very slight, this still means that the wristy player must continually modify his swing as he tries to roll his wrist at the right instant.

• The child who is allowed to play with excessive wrist action can't really turn to an instructor for help. He has to rely on instinct, and you can't teach instinct—you can only ask him how he feels. There's no way to tell him when to start his wrist-roll, or how to judge the amount he should snap his wrist.

Develop the Right "Muscle-Memory" Patterns

In striving for the appropriate stroking patterns, there's yet another element you and your child must confront, and that's the predictability and intransigence of "muscle-memory." In using this term as it applies to a tennis swing, I'm not using it in a true physiological or neurological sense, since researchers themselves cannot agree on what is actuallly happening. Some claim the swing is totally a reflex action, while others argue that the brain has to send an impulse through the nervous system to trigger a response—that a kind of cognitive thinking is involved. I simply use "muscle-memory" to mean that in performing a motor skill, we all have a tendency to fall back on patterns and techniques we've used in the past—especially when we're under pressure.

As a tennis instructor I can actually predict—in a statistical sense—how an individual is going to swing based upon past performance. If a youngster has swung 3,000 times in a row with wrist-roll, and I tell him, "Don't roll your wrist," I can bet my house that he's still going to roll his wrist on swing 3,001. He might admonish himself, "Okay, dummy, don't lay the wrist back," but it's not easy to prevent motor movements that have been "grooved" by months or perhaps years of improper play. It will take a long period of concentrated practice before he can groove new muscle-memory patterns and maintain a solid wrist position when he's playing under pressure.

In helping your child achieve the desired sensations on specific strokes, keep in mind the concepts stressed earlier in the book (among them, that the tennis court is a "mistake center," that it's exciting to discover problems and the appropriate cures, and that it's best to reward stroke production—how well he swings his racket and contacts the ball—rather then ball direction, unless the two are complementary). Good strokes result from grooving the proper muscle-memory patterns, and not simply from doing what feels "natural."

My experience with thousands of students has indicated that the most desired movements in tennis are not natural, but must be learned. Conversely, most of the initial movements that come naturally are undesired. To me, "natural" means first impressions and first movements. So if you have to teach a person something, it isn't natural. Look at some of the crucial techniques needed for sound strokes and you'll realize why tennis is such a difficult game to master—and why patience and sensitivity are so important as you teach your child.

For example, research shows that the body has a tendency to operate on a vertical axis, which means that it's "natural" to swing at the ball on a level plane, instead of low-to-high. It's also more natural to tilt the racket face back at impact (so it can lift the ball up over the high net), but that's a mistake when striving for topspin. There are other points: a natural inclination to use excessive wrist action on groundstrokes and volleys, instead of keeping the wrist as fixed as possible; it seems natural to watch your opponent out of the corner of your eye rather than to concentrate totally on the approaching ball; and it's natural to want to lift your head quickly, before impact, to see where the ball is going, rather than keep your eyes down until you reach a certain point on the follow-through.

Remember, however, that although the game might seem unnatural to your child in the beginning, he can certainly *learn* to play with fluid movements and what appear to be "natural" instincts. In this learning process, moreover, the two of you can take a relaxed, spontaneous approach by laughing together and having fun.

Foster a Respect for the Fundamentals

At the heart of my teaching system is a line I use with all my students: "Champions are those who pride themselves in just learning to hit the same old boring winner." This doesn't mean there aren't a variety of shots to master—at different speeds, depths, and trajectories. But if your child intends to master a particular shot—in terms of direction, speed, and elevation—then it's the *sameness* of his stroke that will make him famous (if indeed that's his goal). The physical laws that dictate what must happen on a particular shot don't vary, and once your child learns what always has to be done, then the goal is repetition. If he needs an incentive, remind him that he'll never get bored with winning.

As you try to lay this groundwork for sound strokes, keep in mind that tennis is a game in which nearly every point is won either by somebody's outright error or by a weak shot that sets up an easy return winner. Seldom will a player hit the ball so hard and so accurately, especially from the baseline, that his opponent can't reach it in time to take a normal swing. So as you and your child get into the game, if he's serious about improving, a realistic goal at first would be for him to work toward mastering stroke patterns that will enable him just to keep hitting the ball back over the net—and deep—under pressure. That's where the real fun and satisfaction comes in: when he realizes that he's not the one who's missing. Then, once he learns to keep the ball in play, he can become more aggressive because he has earned his way by first building a solid foundation at the baseline.

A perfect example is champion Chris Evert Lloyd. She helped raise the general level of play in women's pro tennis to such a degree that she found she could no longer simply hit the ball back from the baseline, hard and deep, and beat younger challengers Martina Navratilova and Tracy Austin; she had to start forcing the action by taking some gambles and occasionally going to the net. But she didn't have to make these subtle changes in her style until she had won Wimbledon twice and was No. 1 in the world.

This is why I always warn junior players that they're making a big mistake by trying to hit the cover off every ball and always aiming for the boundary lines. "Forget the fancy kind of thinking," I tell them. "Just be happy to keep the ball in play. Stick to the fundamentals and try to master them first, then you can get fancy." If a youngster buys my argument, he generally finds an interesting thing happening along the way to the Nationals: the better he plays, the more simplistic he becomes in his approach. He discovers he doesn't have to go for all-out winners on every shot in order to win and that it's usually the players who can't win who try to showboat.

If you and your child one day set sights on junior tournaments, college tennis, and the pros, don't be misled by a prevailing notion that he will eventually need to have a sophisticated style of play, or that once he masters the fundamental stroking patterns, he can then make a quantum jump to the big-time strokes. The quantum jump is not made by becoming fancy, but simply by honing better strokes. "How do you hit this shot in pro tennis?" is the question I often get from a student, and my answer is, "You hit it the same way I'm teaching it to you now—but you have to do it under stress." A lot of pros have all the right strokes, but you never see them in the finals because stress gets to them somewhere along the way. Nevertheless, what the game really always comes down to is mastering the key fundamentals of sound strokes.

10/The Forehand

USING the photos on pages 172–173, which show the desired forehand, you can analyze every important element of this stroke in detail. At first, of course, you should just focus on perhaps a half-dozen key concepts, until your child begins to implement the right overall motion. But since grooving a winning stroke is important, the time will come when you'll need to dig deeper into the finer points of forehand technique.

The Grip

As I pointed out earlier, a proper grip—one that helps insure a vertical racket face at impact—will strengthen your child's game for the rest of her life. Therefore, she should always know which grip she's using, why she's using it, and how to evaluate it periodically.

I actually prefer to have my students learn to play a two-grip game on groundstrokes, switching between an Eastern forehand and an Eastern backhand (the changeover requires a quarter-turn of the hand on the racket handle). Some pros advocate the Continental grip—a compromise between the two Eastern grips—since it allows players to hit all their strokes with the same grip. They argue, for example, that there's not enough time in top-flight tennis to switch grips. Yet I've found through timed experiments that this is untrue, even on the pro level. With a little practice and experience, most youngsters can learn to switch grips faster than they can take a first step toward the ball, and eventually switching grips becomes an automatic, subconscious movement. However, if your child can't seem to prepare for her stroke and change grips simultaneously, and if she seems frustrated by the problem, she should start out with a Continental.

3

5

The Loop Forehand

1. In the ready position, this player stands fairly erect, in a comfortable stance, looking over the top of his racket with his elbows out. He's not bent in a crouch waiting for the ball, since research shows that a higher center of gravity leads to faster lateral movement. Also, by having his nonhitting hand help support the racket head, the hitting hand can remain relaxed and his shoulders are ready to take the racket in either direction.

2. The nonhitting hand on the racket helps turn the front shoulder away from the net, thus initiating the desired body rotation. In fact, one of the first things to tell your child is, "Look over your front shoulder as you turn."

3. The player has taken his racket back at about eye level toward the back fence, and he's focused on the ball, waiting to lower the racket as he bends his knees and steps into the shot at the right moment.

4. He is getting the racket and hitting hand down below the intended point of impact, with the racket face slightly hooded so that it will be vertical at impact without any adjustments.

5. The player's eyes are focused on the point of impact and his hitting arm is extended for maximum power. He's not worried about actually seeing the ball at impact, since the eyes can't actually record what is happening, but he knows that watching the impact point keeps his head steady as his body lifts forward and up through the hit.

6. On the follow-through, the chin is touching the shoulder of his hitting arm, he's still looking down at the point of impact, and his racket face is directed toward the right of his intended target. To achieve this follow-through, he had to contact the ball comfortably out away from his body, which in turn freed his hips to rotate into the shot properly.

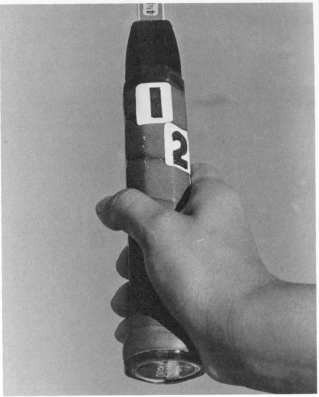

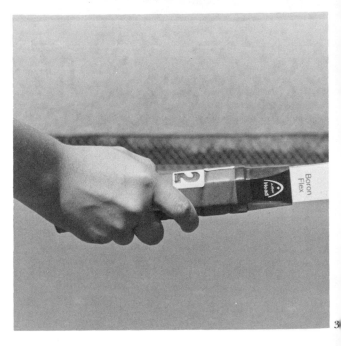

The Eastern Forehand Grip

This sequence shows the desired Eastern forehand grip from three perspectives:

1. There are eight beveled planes on a racket handle, and three are numbered here in order (but only two are visible). On the Eastern forehand, the center of the palm should lie against the outside vertical bevel (number 3, which is obscured) while bevels 1 and 2 both show when viewed from above.

2. Here's a close-up of the grip from the youngster's perspective. People always ask, "Where should the knuckle at the base of the forefinger go?" I have to tell them that everybody's hand is different, so the knuckle's position can't serve as a consistent guide. Instead, concentrate on the center of the palm; put an ink dot on your child's palm and have him press that dot up against the outside vertical bevel. You can add numbers yourself with masking tape and tell him to cover number 3.

3. This side-view shows the palm properly placed against the outside bevel, on the same plane as the racket face. Remember, with this grip the palm and the racket face travel in sync.

One important reason why I advocate the Eastern grip is that it demands very little wrist movement in order to produce a vertical racket face at impact. This helps minimize errors and produces more consistency in a youngster's shots. Jack Kramer, who was among the great players who used the Eastern grips, agrees that the Continental—by forcing a severe wrist-roll—demands perfect timing and thus greater talent in order to have the racket meet the ball properly.

This is not to say that everyone should use an Eastern. Some youngsters are more comfortable using a Continental or a Western or something in-between. If they can learn to play the game well, and they're having fun, who's to keep them from using the grip they prefer?—as long as they understand the ultimate limitations it may present. Once again, motivating a youngster to stay with the game should always come ahead of insisting upon the "right" techniques. If you try to force a grip and lose your child to chess, what have you gained? Besides, there's no uniformity among the pros in the grips they hold—only in the way they try to have their racket strike the ball.

Ultimately, what's important isn't the grip your child uses, but her ability to get the racket face vertical at impact as consistently as possible—and, in turn, how well she can learn to hit desired target areas under stress. Any grip will place some amount of awkwardness upon the forearm and wrist in order for the racket to contact the ball properly, but I believe a youngster's best chance lies with the Eastern.

The Eastern

In teaching this grip, have your child understand a basic premise: that the hitting palm and the racket face move in sync with one another, aligned on the same plane. In other words, "As the palm goes, so goes the racket head"—which means that if your child can learn to have her palm vertical at impact and moving low-to-high toward the intended target, the racket face is going to do exactly the same thing. So teach her to "play with the palm" and she'll be on her way to a trusted forehand.

Start out by having her hold the throat of the racket with her nonhitting hand so that the racket face is straight up and down at waist level and pointed toward her opponent. Then have her grasp the racket handle with her hitting palm vertical, flat against the back side of the handle, and her fingers pointing slightly downward (at approximately a 45-degree angle). When she closes her fist the thumb should overlap and lie next to the middle finger, with the index finger slightly spread. Next, she should hold the racket out away from her body and check to see that the top edge of the racket frame and top edge of her hitting palm are aligned. That's the relationship she wants at impact. Cradling the racket throat with her

The Continental Grip

On the Continental, the center of the palm is rotated to lie on bevel 2, halfway between the Eastern forehand and the Eastern backhand grip (in which the palm is centered on bevel 1; see photos on page 212). I recommend the Continental for the serve — but not for groundstrokes.

nonhitting hand, she can also test her palm position by unclenching her fingers and checking to see that the palm is on line with the racket face.

Once she starts to learn the forehand and is playing matches, she should know how to evaluate her own grip. She can check between rallies to see if the palm and the racket head are indeed vertical, but she can only rely on "feel" as she plays. So encourage her to learn the grip through repetition and kinesthetic testing. Have her balance the racket on edge on a flat, waist-high surface so she can visualize what it means to have the racket face straight up and down. Then have her practice until she can close her eyes and achieve the perfect grip.

The Continental

Using the Eastern grip as a base, the Continental is achieved by rotating the palm of the hitting hand inward an eighth of a turn (45 degrees), so that the center of the palm rests on the top outside diagonal bevel. Try the grip yourself and see how much the wrist must be adjusted during the swing in order to effect a vertical racket head at impact. This contortion necessitated by the Continental demands a stronger arm and wrist than the Eastern grip does.

A youngster must also be extremely talented and have excellent coordination to use the Continental and play a winning game. One problem is that every time she reaches out in front to hit the ball—especially on the forehand volley—she tends to hit crosscourt, because that's where the face of the racket is automatically pointed. It takes a difficult adjustment to hit down-the-line. Although the Continental is nicely suited for low-bouncing balls, it causes trouble on balls that bounce high. Try the grip and notice that as you raise the racket to contact a high ball, your palm turns up naturally and the face of the racket points more toward the sky. Thus, an adjustment is again needed to produce a vertical racket at impact.

The Western

With this grip, the palm rests mostly on the bottom half of the racket handle and points to the sky. Players using the more common semi-Western—halfway between the Eastern and the Western—will have the center of their palm basically on the same plane as the lower outside diagonal bevel. The Western is ideal on surfaces where balls tend to bounce high (clay, for instance) but is limiting against very low balls, forcing a strain on the wrist and forearm in order to hit with authority.

If your child has a natural semi-Western grip and doesn't want to switch to an Eastern, I wouldn't worry too much. After all, Bjorn Borg holds this grip, as do other top players, such as Chris Evert Lloyd, Guillermo Vilas, and Harold Solomon. The advantage here is that the racket face is automatically "hooded" at the lowest point on the backswing, which facilitates a natural topspin forehand. However, most of the players who rely on this grip have trouble volleying well because the racket face is pointed off to the outside of the court as they go to hit, thus requiring an adjustment before impact. Your child should also know that this grip may also limit her versatility on certain court surfaces, unless she has the strength and talent to make the necessary adjustments as she strokes the ball.

The Ready Position

I like to tell kids (and their tennis-playing parents): "Don't get wrapped up in your ready position because you'll seldom hit a ball from that position. Most shots are going to make you move." My only concern is that youngsters wait in a stance that will produce a smooth body-turn and the fastest possible first step toward the ball.

1

2

4

3

5

Footwork on the Forehand

The footwork of champions varies so much as they prepare to hit the ball that you shouldn't think only one method is "correct." What counts is comfort and efficiency as your child turns sideways to the net as the ball approaches and then has a good body position to step into the shot.

1. The student is in his ready position, feet spread comfortably apart.

2. He rotates the shoulder of his hitting arm away from the net, which takes the racket back naturally. Notice that his feet are now both sideways to the net.

3. As he begins to drop the racket head, he draws his feet together.

4. The student has first stepped forward and now shifts his weight as he goes out to make contact. On the forward step, the front foot should be planted on a diagonal to facilitate proper hip rotation and to prevent a twisted ankle.

5. On the follow-through, the heel of the back foot should come up off the ground to continue the body's upward momentum.

You can help your child find this ideal ready position by bringing a stopwatch to one of your lessons, once you've covered the forehand and backhand. Have the child face an imaginary opponent, racket in hand, while straddling the center mark at the baseline. Then say "Forehand!" or "Backhand!" and time her as she turns and runs to the appropriate singles sideline. Do this repeatedly, sending her randomly to both sidelines, until you find the ready position that gets her there the fastest yet with enough control to take her swing. Don't worry about how this ready position might look; I've found some people can make fast exits from unique stances. Even the pros assume different types of positions before the ball is struck by their opponent (though most of them stand fairly erect but relaxed).

The Backswing

There's a tendency to think that whatever happens on the backswing can be corrected with last-second adjustments before contact. Unfortunately, the racket head moves so fast that the success of your child's forward swing depends largely on her backswing. Unless her opponent's shot is traveling at an unbelievably slow rate of speed, there can be no positive adaptive behavior in the middle of the forward swing. And therefore, since she is basically locked in by her backswing, there are a number of important elements to consider.

The Loop versus Straight Back

The two most common backswing patterns are the loop swing and the straight-back swing. On the loop swing the player turns her body so that the racket goes back at about eye level. She pauses to wait for the ball and then drops the racket and racket arm to about knee level before moving them forward and up into the ball in a continuous motion. The straight-back hitter takes her racket back directly toward the court on a *diagonal* and then moves it up into the ball. Her swing thus travels nearly the same path on the backswing as it does on the forward motion. (Though "straight back" is common terminology, "diagonally back" might be more proper, since the racket should travel on a straight diagonal line going down, not on a horizontal at waist level.)

Of course, both stroking patterns present teaching problems, but I prefer the loop because it delivers a much bigger payoff—if properly executed. Not only does the overall motion give most players a better sense of rhythm, but the dropping action generates greater racket speed (and thus greater power), providing the motion is continuous through impact. The kinetic energy generated by the loop helps explain why little

If your child is having trouble visualizing the ideal loop swing, wedge balls into the fence to describe the path his racket should take as it goes back, makes the drop, and then moves forward and up. He can then practice perfect stroking-pattern form, and later incorporate this with the "Sit-and-Hit" drill (page 188–189) to perfect knee bend. This student is practicing his form against the balls arriving at chest height. The balls have been placed in the fence so that the racket goes back at about eye level, then drops below the lowest ball. The stroke here will generate only mild topspin; for greater ball rotation, set the bottom balls lower on the fence, to force a more vertical lifting motion.

kids can learn to hit the ball so hard while still so small. At five, Tracy Austin certainly didn't have a strong arm, but she could generate real power off the downflight of her loop.

In contrast to the loop, when the straight-back hitter reaches the low point on her backswing, her racket must begin moving into the ball from a dead start. She thus must rely on more muscular effort and a precise body turn in order to generate good racket speed at impact. Moreover, she's going to be a punch hitter, lacking the flowing motion and the rhythm that comes with the loop. The straight-back swing can generate sufficient power if there's a trunk turn, since the body supplies the real power in a stroke. But given the same bodily input, more power with greater ease is going to be derived from the loop than the straight-back.

Teaching pros who advocate a straight-back swing raise several arguments against the loop (though I notice that most of these pros prefer to loop when they themselves go out to play). One contention is that the loop takes longer than straight back, and thus can lead to timing problems. Yet research shows that both swings, if properly executed, bring the racket to impact at about the same time. I'll agree that a youngster can get into trouble by taking her racket back too high, but that's why I advocate taking it back at eye level.

Another argument is that the average player can learn the straight-back more easily. This again raises one of my fundamental concepts about teaching tennis: that the individual who takes the simplest, most "natural" approach to a particular stroke may make more immediate gains but may not end up with the most efficient stroke, while the individual who tries to swing the way I want may have a harder time at first but will eventually end up with much greater gains—providing I can keep her motivation high along the way. An important point to note is that virtually every player in pro tennis uses a basic loop swing (except when intentionally hitting with underspin). This does not in itself justify teaching the loop to youngsters, but they do have the ability to learn it and many of them take to it easily.

If your child can't get the hang of the full loop, don't worry. I've seen many youngsters effect forehands with topspin by using a straight-back swing, or even by taking their racket back at waist level and then adding a small loop at the end. Just be aware of two common problems: (1) your child will have to work harder to gain the equivalent power generated by a full loop swing; and (2) she must learn to take her racket back low enough so that it's below the intended point of impact as she begins to move into the ball. This will enable her to hit with a low-to-high motion, the same as a full-loop hitter. On many straight-back swings the racket goes back on a horizontal level and remains there throughout the backswing, even though the hitter is convinced she's taking it down low. As a result, when she leans into her shot and starts to raise her hitting arm low-to-high, the racket head moves higher than the oncoming ball. This forces her to make last-second adjustments just to contact the ball. Only if she's early in going out to hit can she quickly bring the racket down in time to be going forward and upward at impact—a very difficult maneuver. So she must learn to really take the racket back low.

Early Preparation

I try to ingrain in youngsters the attitude that they should work hard to get into position early so they can be absolutely calm as they take their swing. By doing this they avoid a mistake made by most beginners and intermediates: delaying the start of the backswing until the last moment —very often until their opponent's shot hits the court. As a result, they're consistently late or out of position as they rush to stroke the ball, and they seldom feel in charge of the situation when playing a match. I've also found that players who take their racket back late tend to be content with any kind of hit possible, whereas those who have an early backswing are concentrating on directing the ball to a target area.

A useful drill here—and a good periodic check—is to see whether your child can prepare for a forehand so early that she can stroke the ball in "slow motion." (This also reminds her that she doesn't have to swing hard to hit the ball hard, providing she uses the power in her body by rotating into the shot.) If she still has to rush her swing, check how soon she actually begins her backswing. The eye is capable of detecting the direction of an opponent's baseline shot before it has traveled 10 feet, yet many players fall into the habit of waiting for the ball to clear the net or even land on the court before they take their racket back. You can help your child prevent such hypnosis by telling her, "Start your backswing before the ball passes your opponent's service line, unless you're still running to get into position." Remember, the ideal loop backswing is taken in two distinct stages: the initial swing backward at eye level (which sets the racket and takes care of deceleration-acceleration forces on the wrist) and then the racket's dropping motion. Only when your child has to run wide for a ball and has no other choice should she have a continuous loop swing, from beginning to end.

Shoulder Rotation

Ideally, your child should move into hitting position the instant she detects the direction of her opponent's shot, and then initiate her backswing with one basic thought in mind: "body-turn" (rather than "racket back"). When she consciously rotates the shoulder of her hitting arm toward the back fence, the racket is drawn back automatically, in sync with her body. If she's kept the racket at eye level, she can now save the drop for when she's actually ready to hit the ball. Meanwhile, having pivoted her body, she can use the power that derives from rotating her trunk. This uncoiling action enables her to hit the ball very hard, using less energy than if she relied upon an isolated movement by the racket arm.

A good drill is to have your child imagine that her name is written across the shoulder blade of her nonhitting arm and that she wants to rotate this shoulder far enough to allow her opponent to read her name.

The Two-Racket Forehand Drill

I like this drill because it can help youngsters develop a kinesthetic sense — a "feel" — for the proper body and racket synchronization on the loop swing, while it enables an instructor to discover exactly where trouble starts.

1. The player starts out by standing sideways to the net and gripping one racket in his hitting hand (this is a left-hander) and propping the other against his front shoulder, parallel to the first, as shown.

2. He then goes through his normal loop swing by taking the hitting racket back, down (as shown here), and then up, while the front-shoulder turn moves the nonhitting racket through a "mini-stroke." The object is to keep both rackets nearly parallel until impact. Remember, body rotation must coordinate with the movement of the hitting arm; so when you see your child's rackets begin to spread apart, you'll know exactly where the trouble is starting. Another benefit of this drill is that your child must bend his knees properly if he hopes to keep his rackets in sync.

3. Just before impact, the front shoulder should stop its rotation in order to produce deceleration-acceleration on the hitting racket.

Running wide to hit a forehand, this player is carrying his racket high and out in front of his body, which is good. This keeps his hips in natural alignment as he runs, and facilitates a loop backswing.

Jack Kramer used to hold his left (nonhitting) hand on the throat of his racket as he started his backswing, since this would force his left shoulder to rotate properly.

The Racket

Using the loop swing, your child should turn her nonhitting side to the net until the racket points toward the back fence (or slightly farther if there is corresponding body rotation). She may feel restricted at first and may protest, since most youngsters believe they have to take a lengthy backswing in order to hit the ball hard and deep; but this is all she needs. In fact, some playing pros don't even take their racket back this far. They know that a short, controlled backswing (1) helps keep the racket arm moving in sync with the body, and (2) insures more accurate ball-racket contact, since a longer backswing activates excessive wrist motion and thus makes timing more difficult.

When your child has to run to get into hitting position, she should carry her racket at about eye level and pointed upward, just ahead of her body. (This holds true on the backhand also.) Then, as she reaches her ready position, she can lengthen her backswing with a little more shoulder rotation. Studies have shown that running to the ball with the racket trailing can cost a player speed.

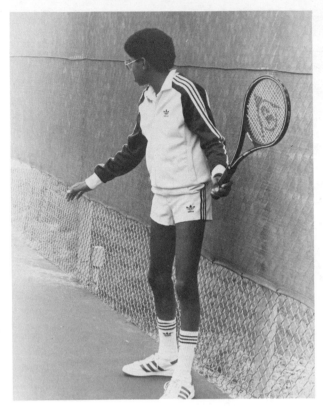

You don't need to rely on home movies to show your child that his forehand backswing is too long. Just have him stand with his back near a fence and rotate his shoulders to initiate his backswing. If the racket bangs into the fence, wrist layback is sending it back too far — unless he has deliberately used extra trunk rotation. Ideally, he should try to imitate the player here, by getting his arm into this position on the backswing before the dropping action on the loop.

How to Prevent Wrist Layback

The most persistent and damaging problem on the backswing—at any age—is failure to stop the racket when it is pointed roughly straight at the back fence. If the racket is allowed to continue around behind the body after the shoulders stop turning, it goes out of sync with the body when the player turns into the shot. She might have a fluid look, but if her racket face is trailing the rotating body or the racket arm at impact, she's in real trouble. She may get the ball back into play—if she's not too late—but without the power and consistency needed for good tennis.

The basic culprit here is wrist layback, and it occurs when an individual fails to maintain a firm wrist position, either out of habit or because she's late in taking her backswing. Here are five basic steps that can help your child prevent this from happening:

First, demonstrate what you mean by wrist layback and make sure she knows what it means to maintain a *firm* hitting-wrist position throughout the swing (a totally fixed or locked wrist is a physical impossibility). I make the point: "Don't let your arm go spaghetti. Keep it firm so that it's easier for the wrist to remain firm. But this doesn't mean holding a death grip on your racket."

Second, have your child learn how to set a correct wrist position at the beginning of her backswing—one that doesn't require any adjustments along the way to impact. One drill you can use is to have her stand sideways at a fence or a wall, with her front foot angled against the barrier. Have her hold her proper grip and place the racket face flush against the fence, at a point approximating where she normally contacts the ball (the elbow of her hitting arm should be several inches away from her body). She should close her eyes and concentrate on how this wrist position feels, then take a careful look at how the wrist is positioned. You might point out, "If you start your swing with the wrist like this, and it doesn't change its position along the way, your racket will be in a perfect position to smack the ball." Then have her slowly practice her stroke at the fence as she tries to sense what it takes to maintain a firm wrist and where a problem might exist. Meanwhile, she'll also be learning what it means to have the racket face vertical at impact.

Third, watch that she doesn't let her racket arm "take a solo" going back; body rotation should initiate the backswing, while the wrist remains firm. Check that you're not saying, "Take your racket back . . . ," since the imagery suggests an isolated arm movement.

Fourth, have her try to draw the racket back with her hitting elbow slightly raised and bent on the backswing, instead of maintaining a straight arm. When her elbow is in this position, she'll notice how difficult it is to lay the wrist back. Experimentation will tell her how much she must raise and bend her elbow in order to keep the wrist in its original fixed position.

Fifth, stress the importance of initiating the backswing early enough to counter the effects of deceleration-acceleration. If she's late taking her racket back, she can't suddenly stop her racket arm and proceed forward without the racket automatically laying back. The reason is dictated by the laws of physics: when her racket arm decelerates toward the end of the backswing, inertia causes the wrist and the racket to accelerate. Since a late backswing tends to be rushed, the increased backward momentum tends to intensify wrist layback.

How to Time the Drop on the Loop Swing

Through practice and experience, your child will learn how to pause at the end of her backswing and delay the drop of her racket and racket arm until she is actually stepping in to the ball. In a simultaneous action, she should (1) step out with her front foot—without shifting all her weight forward—and (2) bend her knees so that she can (3) lower her racket and

racket hand approximately 12 inches below the intended point of impact. Without pausing at the lowest point of this drop, she should then bring her racket arm and thighs forward and up together as she transfers her weight into the shot.

Your child can practice coordinating these movements by trying my "Sit-and-Hit" drill (see photos). Then have her work on timing these movements with an approaching ball. Just feed balls to her nice and easy, always in the same area, so she can concentrate solely on stepping out with her front foot as she bends her knees and lowers her racket with a fixed wrist. An important checkpoint: make sure her weight doesn't transfer forward as she steps into the ball, but remains equally distributed over both feet until the racket starts forward. Also remember that *timing* is what you're striving for here; where the ball goes doesn't matter. If she drops her racket too soon as the ball approaches, she'll have to hesitate at the bottom of the loop, thus losing the momentum and power gained by using a continuous motion from the top of the loop through impact. If she's late with her racket drop, she'll suddenly have to cut across her body with her swing in order to contact the ball in time.

3

4

The "Sit-and-Hit" Drill

In my opinion, the number-one error on groundstrokes is failure to bend the knees and get the racket low on the backswing, in order to insure a natural lifting motion. Most people also have trouble coordinating their loop swing with their step in to the ball. My "Sit-and-Hit" drill tackles these problems and strengthens the thighs at the same time.

1. The student is in her ready position for the forehand. She's going to use a chair here, but a bench such as those found alongside most tennis courts can also be used. (For this drill, most any size chair you use will require even a tiny youngster consciously to bend her knees.)

2. She brings her right foot back while turning her shoulders to initiate the backswing.

3. Her goal now is to try to sit in the chair for an instant as she steps in to the ball and lowers her racket and racket hand. Ideally, she should aim for a brief "three-point landing": her rear end should touch the chair at the same time that her front foot finishes its forward step and her racket reaches its lowest position (12 inches below the intended point of impact). However, like most people, she doesn't get low enough here to touch the chair and is thus reminded just how much knee bend and thigh lift are usually required to hit groundstrokes well. After making a proper "landing," the student should transfer her weight out onto her front foot as she comes forward and up to hit the ball, producing a proper low-to-high stroking pattern.

4. She completes the drill with the desired follow-through, keeping her head steady and eyes down on the point of impact as she comes up.

How to Bend the Knees and Get the Racket Low

Somewhere along the line, "Bend your knees!" became a trusted crutch for tennis instructors everywhere. Proper knee bend is important—but why? Well, when I talk about getting the racket head below the intended point of impact in order to hit with topspin, this doesn't mean that your child can stand stiff-kneed and simply drop the racket head by loosening her wrist. She must learn to bend her knees so that she can lower her hitting arm, wrist, and racket *as a fixed unit.* This allows her to hit with a natural lifting motion that is coordinated. Her body and racket can move in sync, and she doesn't have to make any adaptive movements as she comes through on the swing. Conversely, ineffective stroke patterns generally result when a person tries to play with stiff knees, especially on balls that bounce waist-high or lower. She must "bevel" her racket face (actually, lay it back slightly) in order to get the ball up over the net, and this "scooping" produces a variety of high or misdirected shots.

The bending action by the knees, which should occur simultaneously with the dropping of the racket hand, might be easy to visualize. But some curious phenomena are at work, and to put it into effect is not so easy.

For instance, what about youngsters who can easily lower themselves into a chair or do deep knee-bends, but whose knees seem to lock when they go to hit a tennis ball? Very often there's some laziness involved, but mental factors are also at work. One is the fact that when youngsters get their racket *lower* than the approaching ball, they tend to feel that they're going to miss it—particularly if they've played some baseball or softball, where the emphasis is on a level swing. Not only do the knees have to fight through an invisible psychological barrier, the racket seems simultaneously to encounter a shelf at about waist height that prevents it from going any lower on the drop. Then there are those players who can't seem to bend their knees and lower their racket in the same motion. A youngster may really concentrate and manage to bend her knees—only to leave her racket up high on the backswing. Or she'll drop her racket low, but remain stiff-kneed. Either way, her stroke will deviate from the ideal low-to-high motion that produces topspin.

Fortunately, there are several ways you can help your child learn to blend knee bend with the proper racket action:

• In addition to using the "Sit-and-Hit" drill (which brings home how much the knees should bend, even for a ball bouncing at waist level), place a large beach ball at about waist height and have her draw the racket back over the ball, then down (by bending her knees) and then underneath as she comes up to hit.

• Tell her to exaggerate in getting low—"Try to scrape your racket against the court"—because even when she thinks she's low enough, she's

I'm showing this youngster that his racket should be "hooded" — faced slightly downward — as he reaches the lowest point of his backswing. If he then keeps his wrist position firm on his forward and upward motion, the racket will automatically be vertical at impact. Most beginners and intermediates make the mistake of doing just the reverse. They let their wrist lay back, which causes their racket face to be "beveled" — turned up toward the sky — at the end of their backswing. This forces them to compensate by "rolling" their wrist forward in the hitting zone.

probably still too high (until she has acquired the proper swing). When hitting a ball that's approaching about knee level, some pros will often bend so low that they actually touch the court with one knee. Most people, however, won't bother to bend their knees on a ball that's knee-high; they simply lower their racket and try to scoop the ball up over the net—usually without success.

• Nearly everybody has trouble visualizing what their racket is doing on the backswing, once it is out of sight, so as your child takes her swing, have her tell you when she thinks her racket has reached its lowest point. You may find that when she says "Now!"—when she thinks the racket is down around her kneecaps—it's actually higher than her waist. If she doesn't believe you, have her stop her racket at the lowest point of her backswing and take a look. Or record her swing on film so that she can realize for herself how much lower she needs to get.

Racket Position at the Bottom of the Loop

Here's a crucial but often overlooked or misinterpreted point about the forehand, whether your child uses the loop or straight-back: In order to produce a vertical racket face at impact—without a wrist adjustment—the racket face must be slightly hooded (aimed facing down) at the lowest point of the backswing.

A good way to drive this concept home is to have your child place her racket face straight up and down where she normally contacts the ball, off her front hip. Tell her to fix her wrist position here and then, without moving the wrist, take her racket straight back to the lowest point of the downflight. She should notice that her racket face and the hitting palm are not vertical here, but are slightly angled toward the court. Although this hooded racket face can make her famous, her initial reaction might be, "I'm going to hit the ball into the net with this dumb angle." However, when she moves the racket forward to her normal point of impact—without changing her firm wrist position—she'll discover that the racket face is now vertical. (Leading slightly with the elbow on the backswing will help her achieve a hooded racket face.)

Also, point out what happens when her racket face is straight up and down at the lowest point of her backswing. If she keeps her wrist firm as she moves into the imaginary ball, the racket face will turn and face upward at impact. Unfortunately, rather than learn to hood the racket properly, most people who swing this way simply roll the wrist over in the hitting zone, hoping to achieve the proper vertical racket position at impact.

Forward Movement in to the Ball

As the ball bounces, your child should begin moving forward and up, and she should be striving to contact the ball off her front foot. This will facilitate her striking the ball as it rises or at the peak of its bounce, with the power she wants. Since she has already stepped into the ball with her front foot, it now provides a base as she transfers her weight forward. Never let her fall into the habit of hitting with her weight primarily on her back foot (unless she has been forced back by a hard, deep shot), for her only salvation will be the strength of her arm. People who try to "arm" the ball also have a tendency to "roll" their hitting arm and smother the shot. Sure, the pros will occasionally hit off their back foot, but their coordination and timing must be perfect in order to adjust to the physics at work. They must snap their hips forcefully into the shot in order to generate sufficient power, and if they're early on the hit, their swing tends to cut across their body on a horizontal, rather than follow through toward their target as it should.

To facilitate the forward shift, your child should strive to contact the ball off her front foot (that is, in the direction toward the net) and out away from her body. Teach her to think aggressively and to go after the ball before it gets too close and crowds her into a weak or rushed stroke. The farther away the ball is at contact—providing she can maintain a firm wrist and still feel comfortable—the more power she will get using the same amount of energy. In studying high-speed film of Chris Evert Lloyd, taken from straight above as she hit, I was amazed to see how far away from the ball she actually was at impact, and that her hitting arm was almost straight. This helps explain why she can really pound the ball hard when she wants to, and why opponents claim her forehand travels a lot faster than it appears.

Another reason why I like people to rotate their shoulders and then step into the ball is that the farther they can step forward—and still maintain good balance—the longer they can keep their racket face heading toward the target. This gives them a greater range in which to contact the ball and still produce a successful shot. Conversely, some people don't step forward in to the ball but instead swing from an open stance (one where they face the net during the entire stroke), and they tend to pull across their body when they swing in order to maintain their balance. Again, you may see certain pros hitting from an open stance frequently, but their timing must be perfect—and they have excellent body rotation.

Contacting the Ball

Although the ball is on the racket strings for only an instant (which reminds me of Groucho's line "Hello, I must be going"), a number of crucial factors are at work in the hitting zone, and they need to be reviewed here.

• The racket face must be vertical or near-vertical at impact and traveling sufficiently low-to-high in order to impart effective topspin.

• The player who can keep the racket head and wrist fixed as they reach the hitting zone is the one who will have the best payoff.

• Ideally, the center of the racket strings and the wrist should be on about the same level at impact, since this maximizes the range in which the ball can be contacted properly. However, physical forces actually dictate that the racket head will drop a bit below wrist level, particularly on low balls and when a youngster fails to bend her knees. If a person swings pretty hard on a low ball, the centrifugal force is so great that the racket has a tendency to extend out on the same plane as the arm. If she fails to bend her knees, then her racket may even resemble a golf club going straight down from her arm. There's nothing wrong with that providing she can keep her racket face vertical through the hitting zone and meet the ball squarely; she can actually get more power this way, since the extended arm increases the radius of her swing. But her timing must be perfect.

• As the trunk of the body comes through on the stroke, the player's head should remain steady and her eyes fixed on the point of impact until the follow-through has been completed, because any sudden movement by the head is going to affect the path of the racket. This doesn't mean that the head should remain fixed throughout the swing; it should be going forward and up in sync with the body. The key is to keep the head from abruptly jerking up while the racket is in the hitting zone.

The "Inside-Out" Motion

The natural tendency on forehands is to swing "outside-in." In other words, if viewed from above, a youngster's hitting arm goes out away from her body on the backswing and then back in toward her body (and usually around her neck) on the follow-through. The stroke pattern I teach, however, emphasizes an "inside-out" motion in harmony with the low-to-high one. This means that your child's racket should be pointed to the back fence on the backswing, and then it's forward motion should be "out" away from her body, toward the net post. When you start working on this movement together, she'll likely complain that she's going to hit the ball off the court to the "outside" side (to the right, if she's right-handed), but that's exactly the *feeling* you want her to have. For what actually happens with an inside-out motion is that the racket face ends up parallel to the net at impact and facing the intended target. Most people try to feel that they're knocking the ball straight toward their target; as a result, they get too close to the ball and they often end up hitting to the "inside."

The inside-out motion contributes to a successful forehand (and backhand) in a number of ways:

First, it leads to greater control and consistency by allowing the racket face to remain on line with the target area much longer than with an outside-in swing (which will travel on a horizontal plane rather than low-to-high). When swinging inside-out, if your child's racket face is going toward her target before she strikes the ball, she increases the distance in which she can make contact and still have a good hit; if her timing's off and she's early, she can still hit the ball toward her target. (If she's late, however, nothing can bail her out.) There's little such margin for timing errors with an outside-in swing; the hitter is swinging across her body, and her racket face can only stay on target for an instant.

Second, your child is forced to contact the ball away from her body with

1

2

The "Inside-Out" Concept

Stroking power is related to how far away from the body the ball is contacted. If your child is short, he can play with the power of a taller player by learning to hit with an inside-out forward motion that causes impact to occur well away from his body.

1. From the low position on the backswing, this player concentrates on throwing his upper hitting arm out away from his body in the direction of the net post. This extends the arm and guarantees him that the racket will be comfortably away from his body at impact.

2. Since kids initially fear that hitting this way will send the ball into the side fence, I have them stop their racket where they normally contact the ball and they can see for themselves that the racket is vertical at impact and facing the net, not the net post. Hitting inside-out also increases a player's hitting range, which allows him to be early as he swings into the ball and still contact it on line with his desired target area.

an inside-out motion, which lengthens the radius of her strokes and thus generates more power.

Third, the effort to swing inside-out will help keep her from pulling across her body. The natural tendency on the forehand is for the upper hitting arm to pinch against the ribs just before impact. This braking action (deceleration) causes the lower arm to bend or twist at the elbow and whip across the body, with the racket pulling off to the inside. Check yourself to see what I mean.

Fourth, since the energy flow is toward the intended target and not a side court, the inside-out hitter has an easier time mastering one of the game's toughest plays—the passing shot down the line. Yet she's not restricted from hitting crosscourt against an opponent who's coming to the net. She can control the direction she wants to hit.

If your child can develop a low-to-high stroke, then the key to an inside-out movement is the action of her hips. After her front foot has stepped forward, her weight should be shifting into the ball as her hips are rotating—slightly ahead of her racket swing—so that her back hip turns in toward the target. Ideally, the hip turn should actually stop before impact, since this sudden deceleration will help bring the racket through impact at a faster rate. Once the ball has been hit, subsequent body rotation has no value.

The Importance of Lifting While Hitting

In discussing topspin earlier, I stressed the importance of your child's lifting forward and up as she goes to contact the ball. After all, getting low is futile unless she also comes back up; research has shown that the most efficient swing is one in which the body lifts at the same forward and upward angle as the stroking pattern. So once she starts to shift her weight forward, she should suck her stomach in and lift hard with her thighs and rear end as her hips turn into the shot. She wants to think about "staying over the ball"—by keeping her eyes down on the point of impact as she lifts—so that her back hip can pivot through freely and she can complete her follow-through properly. By doing so, her body, hitting arm, and racket should all be traveling toward her intended target as she contacts the ball. The common error is to fall away from the shot and pull up too soon by leaning (arching) back or by throwing the head back. This "freezes" the hip turn and breaks the kinetic-energy chain. (A good drill is to have your child practice lifting while she keeps her eyes focused on an *X* chalked on the court—or on a coin or similar object placed there.)

If your child really works hard at lifting, her feet may actually come off the ground on the follow-through, but this should occur only after impact. When you watch touring pro Jimmy Connors, notice how often his feet leave the court after he contacts the ball on his groundstrokes—testimony to the powerful forward and upward thrust of his body.

The lifting motion, as we'll see, also pays a dividend on the follow-through. Footwork experts talk about the importance of finishing a stroke with good balance and a high center of gravity, since this facilitates moving quickly to the next shot. Thus, the player who lifts up on the ball will finish high and automatically be ready to break in any direction. On the other hand, the player who stays down with the ball not only has a low follow-through position, but generally lacks good balance.

Synchronizing the Body Movements

Most good players have a synchronized swing; the hitting arm, the racket, and the trunk of the body move in to the ball at the right time and in the proper sequence. Most players of lesser talent are in trouble at impact because they have destroyed that relationship during their swing.

Try the forehand stroke yourself to get this sensation of the different body segments working together. After stepping in to the ball, rotate slowly in to the imaginary ball and notice how your knees and thighs turn and then stop, while the hips continue turning and then stop, followed by the shoulders. Ideally, as the front shoulder stops, the racket will be close to impact (during the inside-out motion), and will come through the hitting zone with an added burst of acceleration. But if there has been excessive wrist action or too long a backswing, the racket will trail behind and lose the positive effects of deceleration-acceleration. Remember the goal: a short backswing but a long step in to the ball. Most people take a long backswing but have very little forward movement. Have your child go through this drill with you so that she, too, can sense how each segment must work in sequence. Then when there's a ball in play, make sure she prepares early so that she has time to put these related elements into effect.

Another key concept that can help with synchronization is the reminder "Play with the palm" (assuming your child is holding an Eastern forehand grip). Many instructors ask youngsters to imagine the racket as an extension of their arm. That's the correct imagery, because a lot of kids have trouble relating to a long, unwieldy object attached to their hand. But I place my emphasis on the palm. Not only is it easier to "feel" the action of the palm and to guide it through the proper stroking pattern, concentrating on the palm will help the racket face travel in sync.

The Follow-Through

When talking about the pros, I often joke that "the follow-through is all cosmetics; all it does is sell tickets." This is true in respect to "guiding" the ball, since the follow-through occurs after the ball is already on its way toward the net. Yet, in reality, a good follow-through (see photo 6 on page 173) is integral to a successful forehand in a number of ways. Here are some pointers:

• I advocate a follow-through that ends with the wrist firm and the hitting arm extended skyward, in line with the intended target. The racket face itself should be directed just to the right of the (right-hander's) target. If your child claims that this causes a rigid and uncomfortable ending, perhaps let her bend her elbow at the end of the swing so the racket comes back toward the shoulder of her nonhitting arm. Just make sure she doesn't twist or roll the hitting arm, since this can lead to tennis elbow. Another potential problem with such a "fluid" ending is that people start relaxing the elbow too early—while still in the hitting zone—and thus another timing variable is introduced into their swing. Ball control comes first, as far as I'm concerned, and then a person's ability to relax on the follow-through. I'd rather have a youngster feel a little stiff in the beginning—and improve her chances of hitting good, consistent shots—than to have her feel fluid but be unable to keep the ball in play, which so often happens. The line I always use with kids is, "After you've won the Nationals, you can add all the fancy follow-throughs you want."

• A good follow-through, when coordinated with the inside-out motion, helps guarantee solid contact by lengthening your child's hitting zone and allowing more leeway for timing errors that involve swinging too early. By keeping her racket face on line with the target before and after impact, she has licked half the question of ball control. (The other half: clearing the net with the right trajectory.)

• Since the average player has a tendency to think she has hit the ball before contact has actually been made, have your child try to see how long she can hang on to her follow-through rather than how quickly she can finish it. This kind of concentration will keep her from pulling off the shot too early, because the brain works first, and the stroke comes second.

• In your quest for consistent stroking patterns, check that your child's follow-through always has the same look, save for extremely high bouncing shots. This will keep her from devising slightly different strokes for balls of different heights. One way you can help is by demonstrating how her body should finish—all the way up and extended, with her weight out on her front foot—whether she has gone for a ball around knee level or chest level. Tell her: "This is how I want you to look. If I see that you haven't finished like this, I'll say, 'Freeze.' Then I want you to get into this follow-through position before you go to hit the next ball." Be persistent and you'll find that she starts going to this desired finishing point automatically, because she gets tired of doing it her old way and having to make the adjustment. She'll also be motivated to work on the rest of her swing to facilitate finishing in this position.

• Use cues to help groove a proper follow-through. For example, have your child wait until her upper arm or shoulder touches her chin before she looks up to see where the ball is going. To encourage her to finish "up and out," point out a follow-through target such as the top of a tree above the opposite back fence; or pick out a cloud moving slowly across the sky and say, "Finish to that cloud." You might even attach targets to the top of the fence.

• Another method to develop a more controlled swing is to catch the throat of the racket with the nonhitting hand on the follow-through. This will keep your child from pulling across her chest and will lead to a better "tracking" motion out toward her intended target. Critics argue that this little trick doesn't allow the body to rotate freely, but research by Dr. Gideon Ariel has now shown that it can actually add some power to the stroke. To understand why, remember the crucial concept: To hit with maximum power and accuracy, a person must let each body segment turn in sync—first the knees, then the hips, and then the upper body. But each part also has to stop in sequence in order for the next one to "go through" faster. When the nonhitting hand goes up to catch the racket, the shoulder turn is automatically stopped and this deceleration leads to greater subsequent racket acceleration.

• I like to stress that a good backswing facilitates a good follow-through. For one thing, when the first half of your child's swing gets the stroke started properly, it's much easier to keep the swing going in the desired direction, on line with the target. (Remember, the racket is traveling so fast on the forward motion that effective last-second adjustments are impossible, even for the strongest pro player.) Some helpful follow-through imagery in turn facilitates a good backswing. When your child knows that her follow-through must "reach toward the sky," she has a greater respect for getting her racket down on the backswing so that she can have a natural low-to-high swing. Taking another perspective: If she's allowed to think she can let her racket go anywhere on the follow-through, then she tends to start her backswing anywhere, with unfortunate results.

How to Evaluate the Forehand Swing

You certainly don't have to be a full-fledged teaching pro in order to detect flaws in your child's swing and then suggest what you hope are appropriate remedies. By knowing the basic elements of a good stroke and some of the common errors, you can evaluate your child as you give a lesson, during practice, or as she plays a match. In the meantime, you should also encourage her to learn to evaluate her own swing and to go after the necessary corrections.

Pay Attention to the Grip

It's easy to get so absorbed in your child's stroking form that you overlook what's happening to her grip. So periodically check to see that she's still holding the proper grip and using the right amount of pressure.

I like my students to hold a firm but relaxed grip—neither tense nor floppy—from the beginning of the swing until just before impact. This helps prevent stiff movements and muscle fatigue while practicing the stroke; the natural tendency for most beginners and intermediates, unfortunately, is to clutch their racket handle tensely from the time they see the ball coming until they complete their stroke. Make sure that your child relaxes her grip between shots to avoid muscle strain, but don't let her fall into the nervous habit of spinning the racket around in her hand. This will hamper her efforts to master a consistent, correct grip. She should "find" her grip as she waits for the ball to arrive, and then keep it—but in a relaxed fashion.

What the Follow-Through Can Reveal

Most good evaluations take place at the end of the stroke. So have your child occasionally freeze on her follow-through and then both of you can look for the following tip-offs:

• Is her weight fully shifted forward on her front foot? Can she lift her back foot completely off the ground and maintain her balance? (If not, she hasn't shifted her weight into the shot properly and she's failing to use the potential power that is generated when all of her body segments work together. Some instructors teach students to end with the top of their racket head pointed at their target, but I discourage this because it requires at least a 45-degree wrist-position change. If a youngster can do this after striking the ball, fine, but most people start thinking about it *before* impact. This habit can lead to timing problems and subsequent inconsistency in ball direction.)

• Is her belly button facing to the outside net post? (If it's facing the net or has twisted even farther around, she is either hitting from an open stance without turning her body on the backswing, or she has failed to control her body rotation properly. Remember, her pivoting front shoulder should stop just before impact so that her racket will go through faster at impact.)

• Has her back knee come up close to her front knee? (If not, she probably hasn't used her hip turn and hit with an inside-out motion. Also, ideally, the back foot should not have moved forward at all, but if it has, it should have moved no farther than the front foot did.)

A good idea is for your child to learn to freeze and take a look at her own follow through if she's having trouble while actually playing a match, especially at the junior tournament level. She'll find that she thus has time to check her swing before she needs to worry about her opponent's return. Self-evaluation of the follow-through like this during the heat of a match may help her discover why the stroke has been giving her grief.

Use a Stroke-Production Chart

You may want to duplicate the checklist on the next page and fill one out every so often, not only to make sure you're teaching and analyzing all the important elements on the forehand, but to give you and your child an objective record—on paper—of the progress being made over a period of time and an indication of where persistent problems might exist. I like the idea of keeping records, but only so long as the information being gathered—and interpreted—is useful to the student and her instructor. Some people become so bogged down with record-taking that they fail to enjoy the sport, so my philosophy is: Keep records until you find yourself not using them; then stop.

How to Deal with Common Forehand Problems

Obviously, you're going to be continually striving to solve problems in your child's technique—some of them easily correctable, others more persistent (such as if she tries to maintain a horizontal rather than a low-to-high stroke or emphasizes a lot of wrist action). I'll present the most common forehand problems in this section and suggest ways you can tackle them by using techniques described earlier. But first, a couple of reminders that should lead to more effective—and enjoyable—problem-solving with your child.

• *Try to focus on just one basic correction at a time, and balance it with a positive comment.* This helps maintain high motivational levels and keeps a youngster from being overwhelmed and discouraged by a constant barrage of technical input.

• *Learn to soften your child's frustration when nothing's going right.* I've found

Stroke-Production Chart
FOREHAND

Name _____   Date _____

FUNDAMENTAL   COMMENTS

- Holds proper grip
- Waits in a relaxed but eager ready position
- Tries to anticipate opponent's shot
- Pivots body and has a quick first step toward the ball
- Activates backswing with shoulder rotation
- Keeps backswing the proper length (with no wrist layback)
- Times loop drop properly
- Lowers racket 12″ below intended contact point
- Has racket slightly hooded at bottom of loop
- Steps in to ball properly
- Bends knees properly and "gets low"
- Transfers body weight properly
- Swings "inside-out"
- Uses palm properly in guidance control
- Provides balance with nonhitting arm
- Synchronizes rotation of knee, thighs, hips, chest, and shoulders
- Keeps firm wrist in hitting zone
- Contacts ball in proper relationship to body
- Maintains vertical racket face at impact
- Contacts ball near center of racket strings
- "Takes ball on rise"
- Lifts body forward and up while hitting
- Keeps head steady and in sync with body
- Keeps eyes down till upper arm touches chin
- Uses nonhitting hand to catch racket on follow-through
- Elevates shots properly
- Completes stroke before returning to ready position

that I can diffuse a lot of pressure in a youngster by simply putting my hand on her shoulder and transferring the "problem" to me. I'll say: "You know something, Amy? You're trying so hard and I know you've got the ability, so I must be doing something wrong here. There are a lot of ways to teach the forehand, and once I find the way that works best for you, then you'll be terrific." I'm never defensive about it, just matter-of-fact. Too often, instructors lay all the blame on their students, consequently causing guilt and loss of confidence.

• *Place your biggest rewards on stroke-production style rather than ball direction.* If you focus too much upon where the ball lands, your child will begin opting for techniques that are initially more successful—and comfortable—but not necessarily correct. For example, she may be able to swing on the horizontal and still hit the ball accurately, if she has extraordinary timing. But why allow these successes to overshadow the fact that she's grooving a stroking style that provides little room for error and will ultimately limit her progress in the game as she begins to face opponents who hit the ball harder?

• *Have your child practice parts of the stroke and the stroke as a whole with her eyes closed.* Show her the desired stroke pattern, which you've fashioned out of cardboard or with tennis balls stuck in the fence. Then, so she can get a better "feel" for what should be happening, ask her, with her eyes closed, to trace just her hitting hand along the stroke pattern, since the palm moves in direct relationship to the racket face.

• *When suggesting a change in technique, encourage your child to exaggerate the desired movement.* Have her overcompensate—go beyond the correct movement—and then work her way back, so that she really understands what the sensation is like. If she isn't bending her knees, for example, tell her to pretend she's sitting in a chair. You have to overcome the fact that most players prefer to make only tiny changes in their technique. If they're bending their knees an inch and you suggest they get lower, they might then try to bend only two inches, or possibly three. Such reticence when adjusting their stroke is why most players fail to improve as much as they should.

Now that you're armed with some psychological weapons, here are some of the problems that may need solving out on the court.

The Student Misses the Ball Completely
The most common teaching approach here is to say, "Watch the ball—you're not keeping your eyes on the ball." This could be the reason for the problem, but, since there are a number of possible influences at work, your child may need more specific advice.

• Remind her that she should focus only on the ball—nothing else.

Have her try to watch the seams rotating as it approaches, and then try to see the racket head coming through at impact. (Just don't let her feel bad if she can't see the seams moving; it's the effort that counts.)

• Concentrate on her head as she swings to make sure she's keeping it steady, not abruptly pulling up at or before impact in her eagerness to see where her shot might go if she could only hit it.

• Ask her to think about only one thing—making contact with the ball. Many beginners have trouble because they're worried about two things simultaneously: hitting the ball, and getting it over the net into their opponent's court.

• You may be overteaching. Try saying: "I'm not going to worry about your footwork or where the ball goes or anything. All I want you to do is simply watch the ball and concentrate on making contact."

• Very likely she needs to shorten her swing, so that her racket can come around in time to meet the ball. What so often happens, particularly with little kids, is that they think they need to take a big swing in order to hit the ball hard. Unfortunately, they lack the strength to control the physical forces at work. They intend to contact the ball in one place, but the weight of the racket and the inertia from their long swing takes the racket off-target. Switching to a lighter racket (or "choking up" slightly on the grip) may help if your child's swing is totally erratic, but it's not going to be the panacea you seek if the swing itself is too long.

• Make sure you're "feeding" her the ball slowly and from an appropriate distance. If the problem continues, shorten the distance between the two of you and slow the ball down even more.

• If your child is controlling her racket and concentrating on contact but still missing the ball, she might have a visual defect. She may be swinging exactly where she actually perceives the ball, even though the ball is at a different level. Have her eyesight checked by an ophthalmologist.

The Student Consistently Hits off the Edge of the Racket Frame

Review the points made above, and remember that most youngsters rarely hit the ball with the center of the racket strings, as is desired.

The Ball Keeps Going to the (Right-hander's) Left

The problem of pulling the ball can generally be traced to a horizontal swing, uncontrolled wrist play, or both. When your child swings on a horizontal level, rotational forces are going to cause her to follow through across her body. This in turn gives her only an instant in which to contact the ball on line with her intended target. By contrast, a low-to-high, inside-out motion allows her racket arm to "track" freely out toward her target. So here are some teaching points to remember:

• Remind your child that the tennis court is a long, narrow sidewalk and that she'll seldom get a chance to use two courts at once when playing an opponent.

• Have her learn to go forward to meet the ball so she can make contact before it gets too close and forces her to pull back or to hit from her heels or her back foot.

• By stepping in to the ball and transferring her weight forward, she'll keep her momentum going toward her target. If her feet remain too close together, she'll tend to pull across on a horizontal in order to maintain her center of gravity.

• When she keeps her hitting palm going toward the intended target during the swing and finishes her follow-through with the racket face still directed just to the outside of her target area and upward, she'll insure a tracking motion that prevents pulled shots.

• If her head suddenly turns or lifts, at or before impact, her body will tend to pull the racket in the same direction.

• Even with a nice low-to-high stroke, a pulled shot will generally result if she starts to roll her wrist.

A good way to help your child learn to keep all of her movements on the proper inside-out line toward her target is to have her stand with her back against a wall or a fence and then take a practice swing. If she can avoid hitting the barrier with her racket on the backswing (when she's not using extra body rotation intentionally) and on the follow-through, she has a good, controlled swing.

The Ball Keeps Going to the (Right-hander's) Right
Anything that causes the racket to come through late on the hit will contribute to the problem here. It could be that your child is slow getting to the ball or is starting her backswing at the last moment. This produces too rapid a backswing and, subsequently, deceleration-acceleration and wrist layback. As a result, when the body turns into the shot, the racket is trailing behind, out of sync. The best solution is to have your child work to get into hitting position early and initiate her loop backswing well before the ball bounces. Also, be sure she's contacting the ball off her front foot and out away from her body.

Of course, even with early preparation and a firm wrist, your child may be contacting the ball late because her swing is too long. Her racket goes back too far and once again her wrist leads the way as her body turns into the shot. So here's another use for the back-against-the-fence drill. If her racket bangs against the barrier on the backswing (when not using extra trunk turn), she'll know she's taking her racket back too far.

The Ball Keeps Going Too Long

Depending on your child's age and ability level, there are three main trouble areas here.

First, the most common problem I see, is the failure to have a vertical racket face at impact; the racket is instead turned under ("beveled"): the bottom edge of the frame is leading the way and the racket face is tilted up. Check to see that your child's wrist position is correct at the beginning of the stroke and remains in that position through impact. Also make sure that her hitting palm is pointed *downward* (slightly hooded) at the lowest point of her backswing. If she has the proper stroke pattern, she should correct the nonvertical-racket problem by facing her palm down more on the backswing and by maintaining the desired wrist position. Don't let her succumb to the natural tendency to change a good overall stroke to accommodate a beveled racket face. (Similarly, if she lifts with her body from low to high, but her shots keep going out because she has an improper wrist position, she should not change the nature of her swing; instead, she must find the wrist position that places the racket face vertical at impact.)

Second, if your child has a vertical racket face at impact, then hitting long may result from having insufficient topspin, in which case she must increase the upward angle of her low-to-high forward swing. This will impart greater rotation on the ball and produce a shorter shot.

Third, it just may be that your child gets more enjoyment out of pounding the ball as hard as she can and gambling for baseline winners than she does from easing off and keeping it in play. There's not much you can do when it's more important to her ego to hit full-force on every shot rather than try to win matches. However, if she wants to win—but lacks the competitive temperament to ease up on her swing—she must learn to impart severe topspin. (When you watch her matches, record where her forehands land when she makes an error; this will bring her problem into perspective in an objective way.)

The Ball Keeps Landing Too Short

Most people think this problem stems from having too short a backswing or too weak a hitting arm, but other factors have much more of a negative influence.

For example, your child may be playing with an isolated arm movement, instead of deriving power from a rotating body trunk. If so, have her work on stepping out toward the ball and turning into the shot with hip rotation and a lifting action by her thighs. She must also concentrate on going out to meet the ball and trying to "take it on the rise," instead of hesitating and "letting the ball play her"—a mistake that can force her to hit off the back foot or while leaning back. Another problem that results from playing basically with the racket arm is that a person falls into the habit of rolling her wrist over as she comes into the ball, thus smothering it and leading to short shots.

Shots that consistently land short may also be caused by (1) a horizontal swing, since gravity causes the ball to begin its descent sooner than a ball hit with the same speed on a higher trajectory, and (2) too much topspin—which is actually a nice problem to have. Hitting the ball hard with topspin doesn't guarantee that it will go deep, so if such shots are falling short, your child must simply decrease the low-to-high angle of her forward swing.

The Ball Keeps Going into the Net

If the ball continually hits the net because your child insists upon hitting hard with a horizontal swing, she'll have to make some major adjustments. But if she's working on a low-to-high motion and her racket face is vertical at impact, then it's likely that her only problem is a backswing that's still too high and insufficient knee bend. You can encourage her by saying: "Hey, you just about have it licked. Your racket face is perfect and you're down to one final thing. You just have to get your racket lower than the intended point of contact so you can lift the ball up over the net." Remember that the key is to lower the racket arm and racket together, *not* to do what's "natural" (simply bevel the racket face under and "chip" the ball over the net).

The Ball Keeps Going All Over the Place

If your child is spraying shots long, wide, short, and into the net, chances are excellent she's using too much wrist play. So that the necessary adjustments can be made, you must discover whether the wrist is going astray on the backswing or while moving in to the ball. Here are several tests you might use:

• It may be that your child's racket is simply too heavy, thus forcing wrist layback (though I find that the real culprit is often insufficient body rotation). Her racket is too heavy if she can't keep the racket head on a level with or slightly higher than her arm as she contacts the ball at about waist level. Physical forces will cause the racket to drop a bit lower when she goes to hit a ball around knee level.

• When practicing her stroke, your child should be able to see her entire racket at the end of her backswing by making just a slight head turn.

Stand directly in front of her as she swings, and if her racket reappears behind her body, very likely (unless her body pivot is excessive) she's laying her wrist back. Another method to check for wrist layback is to have her stand with both feet on a court line and see if her racket moves across this line on the backswing.

• Horizontally attach a yardstick across her racket frame, on a plane parallel with the racket face, and have her try to keep the racket face and the yardstick aimed slightly down on the backswing. The yardstick magnifies any wrist movement and thus helps identify the problem area.

• Ask your child to freeze on her follow-through. Then, with the shoulder of her hitting arm as the only moving part, have her lower the arm back down to where she normally contacts the ball, off her front side. If the racket face is still vertical, you'll know she hasn't turned her wrist on the swing. But if the racket face is pointed up, it was turned under when she hit. Whatever it takes to roll the racket back to a vertical position is the amount it has moved during the swing.

• Even if your child has a firm wrist, the top edge of her racket frame may be leaning forward or backward at impact. So have her work against a wall or a fence, taking practice swings and stopping her racket face at the intended point of contact in order to find the wrist position that produces a vertical racket head. To keep herself honest, she should also try swinging with her eyes closed to help gain that "feel" of keeping her wrist firm.

Additional Forehand Drills

• To help your child practice getting her racket down before starting her forward motion, place an object (a beach ball, for instance, or a chair) at about knee level behind her back leg; then have her make sure her racket hits it as she gets low on her backswing. This is not a natural feeling, but it reflects the position her racket should reach in order to hit with a low-to-high stroke. Hitting the prop with her racket will provide some objective feedback that she's swinging right.

• A good way to develop her stroke and to get her legs in shape as she rallies is to have her intentionally hit balls on the rise—not by simply "scooping" the ball with her racket, but by getting low and lifting up with her torso. This forces her to use her thighs to help lift the ball over the net.

• To help her concentrate on the impact area, have her rally with a friend (or with you), and whenever one person doesn't see her own racket or racket arm going through at impact, that person yells "Stop!" and the rally must start again. At first, these rallies will end after one or two shots, but they will lengthen as both players learn to zero in on the ball.

11/The Backhand

MANY instructors have long treated the backhand as an alien stroke, uniquely different from the forehand, and thus you often hear them saying, "Now we'll get to the all-time tough backhand side." Certainly the backhand presents new challenges, such as having to hit off the nondominant side and the need to concentrate on checkpoints that are different from those on the forehand. But as I stressed earlier: the ideal forehand and backhand have identical stroking patterns and the same basic body movements, for the laws of physics are the same on both sides. Therefore, I tell my students I can make them famous on the backhand if they can master the same four things I taught them on the forehand (plus an important grip change):

First, they must be able to get their racket and racket hand lower on the backswing drop than the intended point of impact with the ball.

Second, they must swing at the ball with a low-to-high forward motion, using body lift and trunk rotation.

Third, they must meet the ball with a vertical racket face in order to impart topspin.

And fourth, they must have their racket face on line with their target area at impact.

Here again, my goal is to have youngsters start out by striving for a stroking pattern that will benefit them the rest of their lives. Eventually their only interest may be to enjoy the game at a recreational or club level—which is fine with me. But if they want to go beyond that into tournament play, they should learn to hit with topspin off both the forehand and backhand sides if they hope to become lethal.

Earlier, I noted the argument by some critics that youngsters lack the wrist strength needed to impart topspin, particularly on the backhand side. "You can't expect to make Lavers out of all these kids," they say. And

1

2

4

The Loop Backhand

1. The student waits in a comfortable, fairly erect ready position as her opponent strokes the ball. She wants to be able to break in any direction with equal ease, the instant she sees where the ball is going.

2. Before the approaching ball even reaches the net, she initiates her backswing by rotating her shoulders, allowing only a slight elbow bend in her hitting arm. Many instructors advocate much more of a bend in the elbow, but remember: the more you bend, the more you must snap back before impact — and this leads to difficult timing problems. Notice that the student cradles the racket throat with her nonhitting hand as she goes back, which helps keep the racket head raised.

3. The player is still watching the oncoming ball, but has turned her trunk to bring the racket the rest of the way back. Since the shoulder housing the hitting arm is at the front, the backhand usually calls for greater body rotation than the forehand. As a result, the racket head often goes around farther than just straight back, as shown here. This longer stroke is fine, but it should stem from a trunk turn, not a big wrist layback. Try to get your own racket in this position and you'll find that the shoulder and torso turn are crucial.

4. By bending her knees, she has properly lowered her racket and non-hitting hand to her back thigh, preparing her to lift forward and up through the ball. Touching the thigh with the nonhitting hand forces her to get low and produces a fully extended hitting arm for greater power. From this position she also has an easier time staying on line toward her target as she swings forward. Notice, too, how the racket face is slightly hooded at this point, which helps insure a vertical position at impact.

5. She contacts the ball with the center of the strings, out in front and away from her body, with her eyes focused at or near the point of impact and her hitting arm rigid. Youngsters need to build up their forearm extensor muscles in order to hit with the arm extended like this. If they can't control their racket in this fashion, they must either use a smaller, lighter racket or learn to hit with two hands (see page 223) until they have the necessary strength.

6. Even though the player is reaching toward the sky on the follow-through, her eyes are still down on the spot where she made contact. Not until she feels the arm fully stretched out like this should she worry about seeing where the ball is going.

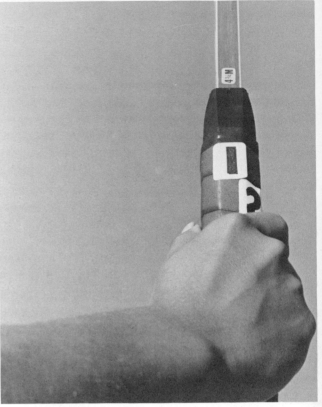

The Eastern Backhand Grip

1. For orientation purposes, here's the Eastern forehand grip again. The center of the palm rests on the outside vertical bevel, parallel with the racket face.

2. To switch to the Eastern backhand grip, your child should turn his hitting palm upward so that an ink spot in the middle of the palm lands on the top bevel of the racket. The knuckle at the base of the forefinger can act as a checkpoint here — it should be on bevel number 1.

3. This side view shows the desired position of the thumb on the racket handle. This position will provide the greatest stability at impact.

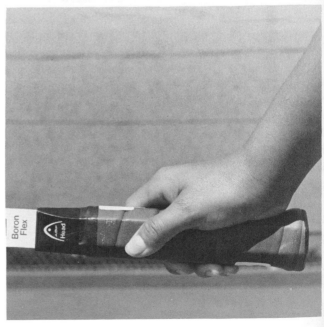

they're right—but that's not what I'm seeking, nor is it what I teach. The fallacy is in thinking that topspin must be generated solely by wrist action that snaps the racket through at impact. Instead, remember that kids can hit topspin with simply a proper low-to-high forward stroking pattern. They may only produce slight topspin rotation at first, but they're working on a weapon that is increasingly necessary in top-flight tennis, from the juniors through the pros. It's also a nice weapon to have in social tennis.

Key New Points on the Backhand

When you begin teaching the backhand, there are several new elements to introduce to your child that differ slightly from the forehand, but not the stroking pattern itself. With this in mind, try to take an enthusiastic approach, putting aside any of your own misgivings, and you'll reduce your child's anxiety considerably. If he's comfortable about learning the backhand, that's a good indication of your mettle as an instructor. (The two-handed backhand will be covered later in the chapter, though again, the basic stroke is the same.)

Switch to the Eastern Backhand Grip

If your child is capable, have him learn to switch to the Eastern backhand grip as he moves into hitting position. This requires a quarter-turn (90 degrees) of his hand on the racket handle, which moves the palm to the top of the handle with the top knuckle of the index finger as shown in photo 2. The thumb should be placed at a downward angle *behind* the handle to provide stability at impact. Your child can practice switching grips one-handed—with just the hitting hand holding the racket—but I encourage all my students to use their other hand as an aid.

At first, the racket face will feel as though it is pointed down, but this grip position provides the most stability and requires the least amount of wrist adjustment in order to produce a vertical racket head at impact. Preventive medicine is also involved. If your child tries to maintain an Eastern forehand grip on the backhand, his stroke will not only suffer, he'll be more vulnerable to tennis elbow, since his wrist and elbow will be leading into the shot. Hold a racket this way and take it through the stroke to see what I mean.

You may want to have your child adopt a one-grip game by using the Continental, thus emulating some of the pros. But remember what I pointed out earlier: A person can learn to switch grips faster than he can take one step, and the Continental demands greater coordination and better timing if he ever plans to hit successfully with topspin. The Continental is fine for hitting underspin on the backhand, but it requires a strong wrist and a roll of that wrist when imparting topspin.

If youngsters are to switch grips between the Eastern forehand and the Eastern backhand — as I advocate — they must learn to do so by feel as they take their first step toward the ball. This girl is practicing changing her grip with her eyes closed to give her confidence that she can do it without looking down at the racket as she plays.

Whatever grip your child holds in the beginning, the extensor muscles on top of his forearm will be unaccustomed to the strain of repeatedly hitting backhands—especially when he's playing with just one hand on the racket—so proceed slowly and carefully. Beginners tend to hold the grip they've been shown steadfastly, in order to concentrate solely on the stroke; they don't want to "lose" that correct grip—but pretty soon their arm is so fatigued they can't even hold the racket up. One good precaution is to have your child take his hand off the racket every two or three hits and wiggle that hitting arm. Taking the hand off the racket periodically is also good practice for relocating the proper grip on one's own. Another precaution is to have your child switch and hit forehands rather than backhands after five or ten minutes so that he uses different muscles. Then, as a longer-range exercise, have him start building up his extensor muscles by taking practice backhand swings with a cover on his racket.

Contact the Ball Farther Out in Front of the Body

More problems are caused on the backhand than on the forehand by letting the ball get too close to the body. In fact, your child must contact the ball 12 to 18 inches farther out in front of his body on the backhand in order to hit through freely with maximum power. This enables his hips to snap through properly (as his body turns into the shot) and then stop just before impact, thus generating greater acceleration by the hitting shoulder and racket arm. When he's late and the ball gets too far back in

To hit the backhand with power and accuracy, your child must learn to go out to meet the ball, so that he contacts it well in front of his body with the hitting arm extended — as this player is doing. If your child lets the ball get too close to his body, he'll be forced into a weak, cramped stroke.

relation to the body, the hips are "frozen" throughout the swing and this prevents the top of the body from gaining sufficient acceleration. The result is a weak, generally ineffective shot.

Since the ball should be contacted farther from the body, early preparation is even more crucial than on the forehand. Have your child learn to initiate his backswing as soon as he sees the ball heading to the backhand side—by rotating his shoulders, not simply by having his arm take the racket back. And encourage him to think aggressively, though the tendency is to think defensively, so that he always goes out to meet the ball before it gets too close and handcuffs him.

"As the Knuckles Go, So Goes the Racket Face"

Just as the palm is the guidance-control factor on the forehand, the *knuckles* at the base of the fingers of the hitting hand help dictate the success of the backhand, for they move in tandem with the racket face (using an Eastern backhand grip). If your child can keep his knuckles on line with his target as his racket comes in to the ball, can keep them aligned straight up and down at impact, and move them out and up on the follow-through, he's going to come close to an accurate placement; his only remaining worry is length. (Still another guidance checkpoint can be the path of his thumb behind the racket handle.)

Think "A.T.A." on the Follow-Through

I've found that these three initials, which stand for "Air the Armpit," help remind kids to finish high on their follow-through, with the racket arm extended upward and on line with the intended target area instead of pulled off toward a side court. When your child is swinging correctly on the backhand, there's a tremendous amount of energy going forward and upward—and the chin isn't there to interfere with the racket arm—so make sure he doesn't let his follow-through end too early.

Key Backhand Details

Following are the important concepts I like to stress on the backhand. As you get into this stroke, remember to refer to the forehand chapter if you need a more detailed explanation of key points that are similar on both strokes.

The Backswing

Early preparation gives your child time to meet the ball properly and generally prevents the negative effects of deceleration-acceleration, which can lead to wrist layback.

Using the loop swing, it's generally impossible to be too early on the backswing, so as your child moves toward the ball, he should rotate his shoulders to take his racket back. This places his side to the net—enabling his body and racket to then move in sync—and keeps the racket arm from "taking a solo" going back. Once he reaches his hitting position, he can rotate his body farther back if he wants a longer swing. Whatever he does, the arm's only real job should be to hold the racket steady in a proper position throughout the stroke, while the body does the work and supplies the power.

If your child gets lazy with his body, a common, chronic error on the backhand can result: bringing the racket back by bending the hitting elbow instead of maintaining an extended arm. When the elbow bends at any point, the wrist has a tendency to loosen and lay back, which causes the racket face to tilt back and the knuckles to face up. This requires a forward rotation of the wrist in order to produce a vertical racket face at impact. A good preventive trick here is to have your child cradle the throat of the racket with his nonhitting hand on the backswing while extending his hitting arm. This forces both shoulders to rotate as a unit and will help keep the racket head up, ready to make its drop on the loop.

A short, controlled backswing is desired, with the racket going back at eye level and traveling only so far as to point to the back fence or slightly beyond. This will not diminish your child's power if he rotates his trunk

*Just as on the forehand, the two-racket
drill can help your child develop sufficient trunk rotation and coordinate it
with her arm motion. Most people think
they turn their trunk on the backhand,
when actually they are simply wrapping
their hitting arm around their body on
the backswing. By having your child
prop a second racket against her non
hitting shoulder — as the player is
doing here — or against any part of her
upper body, she can then take a backhand swing and check her body rotation
by watching whether the rackets turn in
sync and maintain their relationship
until impact, when her front side should
stop rotating in order to generate greater acceleration by the hitting arm.*

well and he goes out to meet the ball properly. It's all right to take the
racket back farther than perpendicular to the back fence (in order to
generate greater power and possibly more topspin if the racket is low
enough)—but only if he rotates his body properly, not by letting his wrist
lay back, as commonly happens.

The Drop on the Loop Swing

When your child learns to "buy time" with an early backswing, he can
pause before letting the racket drop, thus absorbing the negative effects of
deceleration-acceleration. However, once the racket begins to fall, he
must keep the swing continuous, for the fall is what produces significant
kinetic energy gains. Then it's a matter of learning how to time this
lowering of the racket with the bounce of the ball. The best method I've
found is to feed a youngster twenty or thirty balls in a row into the same
area. He can then learn to sense, through repetition and experimentation, where the ball must be before he starts his drop.

To hit with topspin, the racket head should be sufficiently hooded
(facing down) at the lowest point of the backswing. This will assure a
vertical racket face at impact, without any adjustments, if he has a

low-to-high stroke. Conversely, for every degree the racket is faced *up* at this low point on the backswing, your child must turn it over a corresponding amount to produce the correct position at impact (or he'll hit with underspin).

A good checkpoint for your child is to make sure that his top hitting-hand knuckles are pointed to the court as he begins to swing into the ball. Even earlier, he should aim those knuckles down as his racket goes back, because the natural tendency is for these knuckles to be facing up. The nonhitting hand can help out by holding the racket lightly at the throat and keeping the racket face up and in the desired hitting position. The nonhitting elbow should be carried high to help avoid wrist layback.

Get Low with the Body and the Racket

Even though the high net is a visual reality for your child, remember to stress *why* its height influences the way he should always try to swing, even if he grows another foot or two. Just as on the forehand, the lower he can get for every ball—by bending his knees, not by loosening his wrist and dropping the racket head—the easier it's going to be to hit with topspin. By getting his hitting hand and the racket face below the intended point of impact, he'll have a natural pendulum motion and his top knuckles will stay naturally on line with the target. (Have him imagine that he wants to scrape the fingers of his hitting hand against the court on balls below knee level.) Conversely, if he's got the racket on the same level as or higher than the ball at the lowest point on his backswing, rotational forces will cause him to pull across his body as he contacts the ball. My "Sit-and-Hit" drill (pages 188–189) will remind him how much he has to bend his knees as his racket drops and his foot steps out toward the ball.

If your child prefers to go straight back on his backswing, as opposed to taking a loop, make sure he still lowers his racket head properly—by either taking the racket diagonally down, or by going straight back on the horizontal and then adding a little loop drop.

Work on the Body Lift

The key point here is that you want your child to learn to become trunk-oriented. "Use your hitting arm to perfect the stroke pattern and rely on your body to generate power" is what I tell my students. "If you can bend your knees and get your racket low, then a lifting motion by your body and rotating trunk will supply all the power you need."

When you work with your child on this forward lifting motion, start out slowly. Simply bounce the ball to his backhand side and have him try to relax and get the feeling of the proper stroke in slow motion. You want him to learn how easily he can swing and still lift the ball over the net if he uses his body. However, don't let him get lazy; encourage him to exaggerate by getting way down and then going way up on the follow-through, for this exaggerated feeling is actually how he should normally swing. Here's how your coaching patter might go:

"Let your swing flow and just get the rhythm. Don't worry about where the ball goes. I want you to understand what it really means to lift, so exaggerate: as an experiment, try to come right off the ground when you lift—but don't lunge. You want to stretch those stomach muscles and come up on your toes as you hit through the ball. Make the calves and thighs really work for you—*feel* them pull you up. You want to lift the ball, not scoop it."

When working on this lifting motion, teach your child to keep his front shoulder going out in front of his hips, and not to lean back. The common tendency is to turn backwards or fall off the shot, which tilts the racket face back and produces weak, misdirected shots. This is where a long step forward toward the target is helpful. Also, as he lifts forward, make sure his racket is also moving from low to high. I often find that when students have their front shoulder pointed down as they lean into the shot, they think they have their racket down low, but their elbow is actually bent and the racket is high. Take some swings yourself and notice how the shoulder is a radial point that has direct effects on the position of the racket face.

Hit Inside-Out

Just as on the forehand (though the directions are reversed), hitting through the ball with an inside-out motion is crucial. When your child is coiled at the end of his backswing, he should think about turning his front hip "in and then out" toward the target, not around on a horizontal plane. In practicing this, have him focus on his lower body and make his hips push out toward his target as he turns in to the ball.

Minimize Wrist Play

Maintaining a firm wrist position from the beginning of the backswing through impact is even more crucial on the backhand than the forehand, since your child must contact the ball so much farther out in front of his body. If he tries to play with a loose wrist, he'll rarely contact the ball with authority or consistency. The last-second adjustments he'll have to make before impact will force him to rely on "touch" and he'll never know from day to day what kind of player he is, for the fluctuations in his game will be too great.

Obviously, any effort to simulate a "Frisbee-throwing" motion is absolutely destructive to what I teach. Not only does this force your child to rely completely upon snapping his wrist, the implication is that he should slap at the ball on a horizontal plane. Here again, I want to reiterate how topspin rotation is actually imparted. High-speed photography shows that on a properly hit shot the racket face—at impact—is vertical and moving on a low-to-high plane, that it contacts the *back* side (not the underside) of the ball, for only an instant, and that the wrist is as firm as possible in the hitting zone. This holds true no matter how wristy a player might appear.

Impact and Follow-Through

As your child goes to contact the ball, make sure he keeps his head steady and eyes down, and that he tries to remain focused on the point of impact until his hitting arm is extended upward. This will help insure consistent hits near the center of his strings. You might tell him, "Stay with your stroke—don't suddenly pull off the ball, or stop your follow-through, or jerk your head up to see where the ball is going. Just 'A.T.A.' and then worry about the ball. It won't even have reached the net yet and you'll have plenty of time to prepare for your next shot."

A Follow-Through Checklist

When your child is working on his backhand, the two of you can learn a lot about his stroke by having him freeze on the follow-through. Here are some points to look for:

• Can he lift his back foot off the ground without falling backward? If not, he hasn't transferred his weight forward to the front foot.

• If his front foot is perfectly flat or his knees aren't straightened out, he didn't lift up with his thighs and rear end as far as I suggest.

• He should be able to drop a plumb line from the front shoulder to a point ahead of his front foot.

• His racket arm should still be on line with his target, but pointed toward the sky, if he has swung with a proper inside-out motion.

• Did he A.T.A.? If he has really stretched his arm up properly, it should be pointed to about one or two o'clock.

• On a down-the-line shot, the front side of his upper body should finish slightly facing the net, not pulled around. On a crosscourt shot the upper body will end up in a slightly open position, toward the crosscourt corner. (Remember the benefits of deceleration-acceleration. If your child can stop his hitting shoulder abruptly just before impact—when his front side is pointing toward his target—his arm will accelerate and bring the racket through even faster in a whipping action.

• Have him lower his hitting arm back to the approximate point of impact, allowing only the shoulder joint to move. Is the racket face vertical? If not (and if the problem isn't caused by an improper grip), then he

Stroke-Production Chart
BACKHAND

Name _____   Date _____

FUNDAMENTAL   COMMENTS

- Holds proper grip
- Waits in a relaxed but eager ready position
- Tries to anticipate opponent's shot
- Pivots body and has a quick first step toward the ball
- Activates backswing with shoulder rotation
- Keeps backswing the proper length (with no wrist layback)
- Uses nonhitting hand on racket throat to help prevent layback
- Times loop drop properly
- Lowers racket 12″ below intended contact point
- Has racket slightly hooded at bottom of loop
- Steps in to ball properly
- Bends knees properly and "gets low"
- Transfers body weight properly
- Swings "inside-out"
- Uses knuckles properly in guidance control
- Synchronizes rotation of knees, thighs, hips, chest, and shoulders
- Keeps wrist firm in hitting zone
- Contacts ball in proper relationship to body
- Maintains vertical racket face at impact
- Contacts ball near center of racket strings
- "Takes ball on rise"
- Lifts body forward and up while hitting
- Keeps head steady and in sync with body
- Keeps eyes down till hitting arm reaches full extension toward sky
- Elevates shots properly
- Completes the stroke before returning to ready position

hasn't maintained a firm wrist position; whatever it takes to set the racket face properly is the amount he has rolled it during the course of the swing.

How to Deal with Common Backhand Problems

When tackling problems your child might be having on the backhand, you can very likely find solutions in the section on forehand problems (pages 201–208). In addition, you might also watch for the following problems.

The "Slapping Elbow"

This is one of the most common problems on the backhand and can eventually lead to tennis elbow, which sometimes occurs when the elbow leads the way in to the ball. Have your child maintain an extended hitting arm and learn to pivot properly with his body. This will help him keep from laying the wrist back on his backswing, which is what leads to a slapping type of stroke. It's true that a lot of youngsters don't yet have enough arm strength to control the racket properly and to keep the hitting arm extended, but they can compensate by learning to use the power in their body—or by playing with a two-handed grip (as I describe subsequently). Exercises to help strengthen the forearm extensor muscles will also help. I simply have kids put a cover on their racket and take three or four practice swings at a time, making sure they then rest their arm briefly and give it a good shake to prevent muscle strain. An exercise like this is all your child really needs for that part of the arm, and as he's strengthening his muscles he'll also be working on his stroking motion.

Too Long a Swing

Pro players will all tell you that their goal is to shorten their backswing on groundstrokes, in order to hit with efficiency and power. Yet average players, youngsters and adults alike, often work in the opposite direction. They worry so much about getting sufficient power, particularly on the backhand, that they increase the length of their stroke without a corresponding increase in trunk rotation. This can lead to two common problems:

First, the longer the arm movement going back, the more difficult it is to synchronize the action of the arm and racket with the rotating body. This also increases the likelihood of wrist layback, which compounds the problem.

Second, the front shoulder is a radial point, and the farther the hitting arm goes back without sufficient body rotation, the higher the racket tends to rise above the approaching ball (unless the racket is consciously lowered). This forces an undesired adjustment in the forward swing pattern and a tendency to hit every ball on a horizontal plane. Take a racket and see for yourself how it rises as you lengthen your backswing.

This should help you understand why the racket arm itself should travel only a short distance. If your child wants to take it back beyond what I recommend, he should only do so by increasing his trunk turn, not by lengthening the arm swing.

Misangled Stroking Pattern

If your child's racket is vertical at impact but his shots keep going past the opposite baseline, he must work to increase the upward angle of his low-to-high forward swinging motion so that greater topspin will bring the ball down sooner, or else he'll have to use less force. If his racket-head position at impact is correct but the ball keeps going into the net, then he must get his racket lower on the backswing and use more of a body lifting motion. The crucial point to emphasize to him is: "Don't change the position of your racket face to make these corrections. Only change the angle of your low-to-high swing."

Also, remember that a person will normally get maximum efficiency on his groundstrokes if his body and racket face are moving forward and upward together at the same angle. If your child can bring his racket up at a particular angle and turn his body and lift at the same angle, there are no opposing forces.

Pulling across the Body

If your child consistently pulls across his body on the follow-through instead of stroking inside-out toward his target, the problem can usually be traced either (1) to failing to take the racket down low at the end of the backswing, which causes rotational forces to drive him around on the horizontal when he swings forward, or (2) to letting the ball get too close, which forces him to bend his hitting elbow and throw his front hip back in order to make contact—which in turn causes the racket to follow around. Some players seem to program themselves to get too close to the ball or to start their swing too late; they make all the necessary adjustments in their stroke and body position long before the ball comes. So if you're tackling this problem with your child, tell him to imagine that he's going to swing so early that he's going to miss the ball. Even if he makes a conscious effort to do this, he may still swing late—but he'll be better.

The Two-Handed Backhand

If your child has a reasonably supple upper body, you shouldn't have any reservations about letting him learn a two-handed backhand. Suppleness is a requisite, since the shoulders must rotate into the shot in order for your child to hit with power and control. But given this ability, the two-handed stroke offers a number of virtues:

The Two-Handed Backhand

1. This right-handed five-year-old is a two-handed player off both sides. As I recommend, she's waiting for the ball with her two-handed forehand grip (her dominant hand is on top). This means she must switch her nondominant hand to the top, using an Eastern forehand grip, when she goes to her backhand side, in order to avoid hitting cross-handed. Though research must still be conducted into the actual drawbacks of hitting cross-handed, this is what I now teach.

2. She has made the recommended grip change (switching to the Eastern backhand grip with her right hand, as on the one-handed stroke) and is turning her body sideways to the net.

3. With her body turned, she's looking over her front shoulder at the ball. Two-handed players must be encouraged to exaggerate their trunk turn, because many of them think they are rotating properly when actually they are swinging just with their arms.

4. The player has bent her knees and lowered her racket, ready to transfer her weight into the shot as she lifts up through the hitting zone. Notice that her hands are on about the same level as the racket head.

5. As she makes contact, her back leg is extended and she has raised up from the low position at the bottom of her loop backswing. Many two-handed players have a tendency to rest their elbows against the body as they hit, but she is keeping her arms properly extended and contacting the ball out away from her body.

6. On the follow-through, she's looking over her arm, down at the point of impact — just like the big kids. This keeps her head still and her swing smooth.

First, it helps motivate many youngsters to stick with the game, by enabling them to learn a forceful, respectable backhand at a time when they lack the strength to hit with just one hand on the racket.

Second, it emphasizes an important stroking fundamental by asking kids to pivot their body and use its power. They quickly discover that even with two hands they can't simply "arm" the ball over the net and still develop a reliable stroke.

Third, it curbs the tendency to use too much wrist. Kids find they have an easier time hitting with firm wrists. And, they don't have the usual strain on their extensor muscles. (Orthopedic surgeon Dr. Robert Nirschl, one of the nation's experts on tennis elbow, has yet to see this ailment in players who use the two-handed grip.)

Fourth, since the hand that usually doesn't hit generally controls the two-handed backhand, a youngster in effect learns to hit a forehand with his normally nondominant arm; a right-hander therefore learns to hit left-handed and vice versa. This enhances a player's ability to hit topspin off either side against an opponent who's rushing the net or is already there. He doesn't have to meet the ball as far out in front of his body as he does with a one-handed backhand, and he thus has a split second longer to contact the ball and apply extra topspin on crosscourt passing shots.

One argument against the two-handed stroke is that it reduces the reach a person has by roughly half the width of his body. Yet reach isn't the problem for most players. If your child has reasonable reactions and average footwork, he'll get to most of his opponent's shots. So, with one hand or two, the basic problem remains the same: how to hit the ball over the net properly. Moreover, the reduced reach on the two-handed backhand is more than compensated for by the fact that your child virtually has two forehands. In addition, a study by Dr. Jack Groppel at the University of Illinois shows that the good two-handed players reach as far out away from the body as one-handers by simply making a conscious effort to do so.

The Grip

Since your main concern is to have your child's normally nondominant hand and whole upper trunk control this stroke, he should hold an Eastern forehand grip with that "weaker" hand. As for the regular hitting hand, I like people to switch to an Eastern backhand grip. This reduces the chance of tennis elbow, since the wrist and elbow are not leading into the shot as they do when the Eastern forehand is retained, and your child will groove a proper grip for a one-handed backhand, should he one day want to adopt one. On the two-handed backhand, I don't make much of an issue about the dominant hand's grip with little kids, for as soon as they gain the necessary strength and express an interest in playing one-handed, they're still at a young enough age to easily learn the proper grip. But if I'm starting an older youngster (say, ten or over), I explain the drawbacks of retaining an Eastern forehand grip with the dominant hand.

The Swing

The stroking pattern with two hands should match the one-handed pattern. Although most people prefer to have the "weaker" hand dominate the two-handed swing, since it gives them the feeling of having two forehands (instead of a forehand and a backhand), that doesn't reduce the importance of the regular hitting hand in terms of guidance control. By forcing shoulder rotation, the two-handed stroke will encourage your child to swing through the ball, rather than slap at it. But there's no guarantee this will happen unless he also develops a "tracking" motion, out toward the target area, with *both* hands and the front shoulder.

The main problem I see on two-handed backhands is a tendency to bring both shoulders around on a horizontal plane instead of going up and out. This causes a pulled shot, particularly by players who have a supple upper body. So here again, you want your child to learn how to stop his front shoulder from rotating just before impact so that the racket head, through the effects of deceleration-acceleration, can go through the hitting zone faster.

Hitting with Underspin

Despite my preference for topspin, I'm the first to agree that an underspin backhand can provide a useful weapon for experienced players. I've always encouraged advanced junior players to learn the necessary motion, but only after they've developed an efficient low-to-high stroking pattern. My point to them is: "You can reach the finals at Wimbledon 'slicing' the ball, but you're unlikely to get there without using topspin, too."

Here are some reasons why the pros learn to use underspin:

• It allows them to float the ball deep in a baseline-to-baseline rally. Topspin, if imparted by too severe an upward angle on the forward swing, tends to make the ball fall short (although it causes a big kick forward to help offset the error).

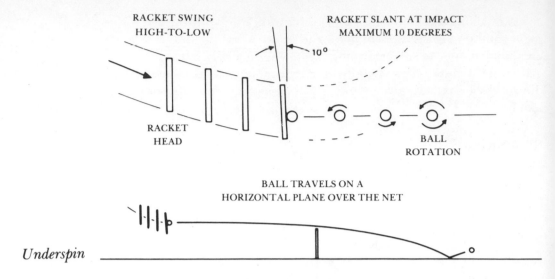

RACKET SWING
HIGH-TO-LOW

RACKET SLANT AT IMPACT
MAXIMUM 10 DEGREES

10°

RACKET
HEAD

BALL
ROTATION

BALL TRAVELS ON A
HORIZONTAL PLANE OVER THE NET

Underspin

• By slowing the ball up, underspin provides the hitter with more time to regain position while possibly upsetting his opponent's rhythm.

• A player can be late and still hit the ball sucessfully with underspin, because the high backswing is already set for the slightly downward hitting motion. A topspin backhand must be contacted well out in front of the body.

• Underspin is more adaptable to the Continental grip, which some pros like to use for both the forehand and backhand.

• Most pros prefer to "chip" the backhand on a high ball, which is fine, but I warn youngsters: "When your arm is strong enough to muscle straight through the ball like that, then I'd do it—but not until you have that strength." Up until then they should stroke high-bouncing balls with an upward swing.

• Many pros feel that underspin is needed to handle low-bouncing balls around knee level, because the racket face is thus tilted back slightly at impact and this helps lift the ball up over the net. Actually, in terms of physics, it's easier to hit topspin on a low ball than a high one, provided there's enough room between the court and the ball to enable the player to start a fairly severe upward and forward lift. Dr. Pat Keating and other physicists have told me that when you really want to topspin a ball, you should let it drop from the peak of its bounce, because the steeper the downward arc of the ball, the easier it is to give it a big lift and thus create topspin. It's difficult to impart topspin when you return a high-bouncing ball—unless you let it drop—because it's hard to keep the racket face vertical at impact.

Some Misconceptions about the Stroke

In teaching your child how to hit underspin, don't be taken in by the common misbeliefs about how the stroke is executed. First of all, despite the implication, underspin is not achieved by "slicing" *under* the ball. That's the feeling people get, and it's what is commonly taught. Even the touring pros talk about how the racket strings should "brush under the ball" to give it underspin. But research shows that as the racket comes down in a slight high-to-low stroking pattern, the racket face actually contacts the *back side* of the ball, barely below the halfway mark.

Second, it's not true that a player must have his racket face angled upward toward the sky as it reaches the hitting zone—unless he wants to send the ball straight up and have it come right back down on his head. In reality, the racket face should be nearly vertical at impact, and it can be beveled (angled upward) no more than 10 degrees if your child wants to hit the ball reasonably hard and keep it in play from the baseline. Here again, newspaper photographs of the pros in action are misleading. They show players on their backswing, with the racket face tilted as much as 90 degrees—pointing toward the sky—in preparation for a "chip" or "slice" backhand. But they don't show that the racket face is then turned back virtually straight up and down as it reaches the hitting zone. Kenny Rosewall has the classic underspin backhand, yet analysis of his swing has revealed seldom more than a 5- to 7-degree racket-face bevel at impact.

Third, the wrist does not go loose nor does the racket head move freely through impact. A pro like Rosewall gives that impression to the naked eye, but on film his wrist is shown to be actually locked in tight and his hitting arm is extended through the hitting zone. Rosewall and other pros must use a lot of forearm rotation to bring the racket head into this position at impact, and must have strong extensor muscles to do so. That's asking too much from the average player, and certainly from youngsters who are taking up the game.

Fourth, hitting with underspin looks deceptively easy, since a player is hitting slightly down on the ball and thus doesn't have to worry about knee bend or getting his racket face below the intended point of contact. However, there are actually more variables to be controlled when hitting with underspin than with topspin, particularly when trying to hit the ball hard. Not only must the player make corrections with the hitting wrist before impact, he must calculate—under pressure—how hard he should contact the ball, how much his racket should be beveled at impact, and the forward and downward angle of the swing. These decisions are completely dependent on the incoming angle at which the ball bounces; if he miscalculates, he may have to go out the gate, retrieve his shot, and then come back in to play the next point.

There's seldom this fear when hitting with topspin. A player can fix his
wrist position and racket at the beginning of the swing and then leave it
alone. He knows that the racket face should always remain vertical at
impact, no matter how the ball bounces off the court, and so he has fewer
variables to worry about. He knows that if he can get the ball over the net,
topspin will work in his behalf. Very few people ever hit the ball hard with
topspin and watch it go over the fence.

Your child will find that topspin allows him to slug away throughout the
match, whatever the pressure, and still keep the ball in play. Underspin
won't allow him this luxury.

12/The Serve

DEPENDING upon your child's age, competitiveness, and learning aptitude, she may be happily challenged by months of hitting forehands and backhands and volleys before tackling the serve. Or, she may want to learn how to serve right away so she can begin to play matches with a friend. Whenever this point comes, remember one of my basic teaching precepts: Introduce the complete stroke and stress the overall motion from the very beginning, even for youngsters five or six years old. After you've demonstrated the key points, let her try it out. Be patient and good-humored, for if the two of you can work through the initial learning difficulties, a solid base will have been laid. (Only if my overall approach proves too difficult and discouraging for your child should you turn to the "lead-up" drills for the serve, discussed on page 94.)

An Overview of the Stroke

After watching service motions around the club or on public courts, your child is likely to share a common perception of the serve—that it involves a maze of wild and intricate movements. So when introducing the serve, let her know that the stroke itself is inherently easy and it's only her image of the stroke that may be complex.

First of all, the serve is the only stroke over which a player has complete control; an opponent doesn't (or at least shouldn't) have any influence on the actual stroke. As I like to remind my students: "You don't have to run to the ball before setting up to hit, it's not coming to you at different heights, and there are fewer things happening that might disrupt your concentration. Just stand comfortably behind the baseline, let your hitting arm relax, and learn to toss the ball exactly to where you want to contact it."

3

6

The Serve

1. The player is preparing to serve, reminding himself to have nice relaxed movements. Since he's not tall enough to hit down on the ball, he's visualizing an imaginary target area above the net. Target points in his opponent's service box are visible only through the squares in the net, and since the body has a tendency to move toward where the eyes are looking, aiming for targets on the court can lead to pulling the serve down into the net.

2. He's now thinking only about the racket-impact point as he starts rotating his trunk away from the net. The racket and the ball-toss hand should go back together on the same level — in this case at waist level, which is fine.

3. The server releases the ball with an upward and outward motion while the racket begins a natural loop behind the shoulders.

4. The player doesn't wait for the ball to fall; ideally, he should be able to complete a continuous loop swing and contact the ball at the peak of the toss. Before the racket reaches the small of his back, his body is opening up and his back shoulder is starting to turn in so that he can make an upward and forward striking motion with his hitting arm. A common mistake is to think, "Scratch your back, then turn in"; that breaks continuity and prevents the player from developing a kinetic-energy chain.

5. Just before impact, the front shoulder should stop rotating, enabling the hitting arm to gain acceleration. Several top servers actually cross their free hand in front of their body to stop this shoulder action. At impact, the server's chin remains up and his eyes are focused on the ball as the forearm pronates and snaps the racket through. There is so much momentum going up and out that the racket actually travels to the outside of the path the ball takes after impact. This player is not up on his toes as much as some purists might recommend, but I prefer to have my students comfortable on the ground and getting good body motion than for them to worry about gaining 2 or 3 inches by straining. I find most youngsters stiffen when they try to get way up on their toes and thus fail to get their body segments turning into the shot.

6. On the follow-through, the player watches the ball in flight and his back foot steps forward onto the court. He's ready either to fall back or move forward toward the net, as determined by prior strategy and how he's hit his serve. In intermediate tennis, he'll want to stay back if his serve is weak — despite his prior intentions. But when he reaches a more advanced level of play, he can't afford to waste time second-guessing his serve: he must hit and attack.

The stroking pattern I teach requires that your child coordinate two simultaneous movements—the ball toss and the action of the racket—while she incorporates the following points:

• a relaxed stroking motion, similar in movment to a baseball pitcher's delivery and stripped of extraneous movements;

• a rotating body trunk;

• a loose hitting arm (especially the elbow);

• a feeling of hitting "up and out," not down; and

• a low toss that enables her to strike the ball at or near the peak of the toss with a racket that has maintained a continuous motion.

Here's basically what ought to happen:

The player should toss the ball to the peak of the racket's reach (when the hitting arm is fully extended), at least one arm's-length in front of her body and well to the side of her head to allow for an effortless, unimpeded motion. Meanwhile, the racket arm should be drawn back between waist and knee level toward the back fence until it reaches a horizontal position. At this point, your child should start to turn into the shot, rotating both shoulders and allowing the hitting arm to bend naturally at the elbow so that the racket falls toward the small of her back. This loop by the racket—if uninterrupted—is one of the primary sources of power on the serve.

Your child should then contact the ball with an upward and forward striking motion while the hitting-arm elbow, forearm, and wrist snap the racket out through the ball. By contacting the ball out in front of her body, off her hitting shoulder, your child can shift her weight forward naturally. She should step forward with her back foot and let her follow-through motion carry her into the court, even if she's planning to remain at the baseline.

Knowing that all these elements go into the desired stroking pattern, you may question my claim that the serve is simplicity in motion. But it is, when you place primary emphasis on a stroking movement that's like a baseball pitcher's throwing motion, for this automatically rotates the body, which in turn generates the greatest amount of power. All that's left is to make sure your child maintains a loose hitting arm as she syncs her "throwing motion" (the racket swing) with the ball toss.

I've found that six-year-olds can develop a natural service motion and generate sufficient power just from their body rotation if they use a racket that's not too heavy and have the ability to throw a ball properly. Two of my coaches, Will and Sue Arias, have a son, Carlos, who had it all together before he turned seven: a full body turn, a perfect toss, and remarkable accuracy. In his first tournament match, he lost to a ten-year-old in two sets, but had only three double-faults.

Key Elements of the Serve

The Grip

Encourage your child to use the Continental grip if she has a good throwing motion, a fairly strong wrist and forearm, and is able to master new concepts quickly. This grip lies halfway between the Eastern forehand and Eastern backhand (see pages 174, 176, 212) and is the eventual goal of all good players, for it facilitates greater ball rotation with less stress on the wrist. However, by placing the face of the racket in an awkward position at impact unless there has been appropriate body rotation the Continental can prove uncomfortable and ineffective for many youngsters. If that's the case with your child, have her start out by using her regular Eastern forehand grip. But have her gradually try to move her palm toward the Continental as she becomes stronger and learns to unwind her body into the shot.

Ready Position

In order to have the best angle for hitting her opponent's backhand corner (which is generally the desired target area at all levels of play), your child should stand as close to the center mark as possible when serving from the right side ("deuce court"), and about three steps from the mark when serving from the left side ("ad court"). This principle applies for both left-handers and right-handers (against a right-hander).

As she prepares to serve from the deuce court, have her stand with her front shoulder pointed out toward the left net post (if she's right-handed), with her feet comfortably spread and her hands and racket held at waist level. When she serves from the ad court, her front shoulder should point toward the right net post. In either case, remember that the shoulder doesn't remain in this position, but turns back.

Remind her that while preparing to serve—and while serving—she should do whatever she can to keep relaxed, so that her muscles never work against her. When she walks to the baseline, even during practice, she should try to shrug her shoulders and shake her arms loose so she doesn't have even one tense muscle. "Tell yourself you're going to have the smoothest swing in the world" is my advice to students. "Exhale, and wherever your shoulders fall, leave them there."

Use Rhythm, Not Brute Strength

With youngsters and adults alike, I stress that it's counterproductive to go through weird, twisting gyrations or a strained muscular effort when trying to serve the ball hard. Instead, it's looseness that counts. The great servers generate their power by synchronizing body, shoulder, and arm movements into a relaxed, flowing motion. You rarely see them strain for power or hear them grunting and groaning. Take Pancho Gonzales, for instance, who I feel had the greatest serve in the history of the game. He hit the ball harder than anyone, but his serving motion was so fluid, without a single hitch or wasted movement, that he never had upper-arm or shoulder problems. Others would tie themselves up in knots trying to hit hard, but Pancho, as powerful as he was, never let his muscles work against him.

Maintain a Continuous Motion and Trunk Pivot

Each little section of the stroke should contribute to a kinetic-energy chain that builds in momentum and reaches maximum speed where it is most meaningful: at impact. Thus, your child should think of her swing as a smooth-running motor that starts slowly and then steadily increases speed without any hesitation. Have her understand that whenever the swing stops or slows down in any way, she must go like crazy and expend extra energy just to regain—if all goes well—the speed and synchronization she was developing. The kinetic forces at work explain why certain players can swing so easily or be short and slightly built, yet hit the ball so hard. Basically, they're relying on their efficiency in moving their body segments, not on flexing their muscles.

Elemental to this effort to have a continuous stroke is an understanding of the baseball-throwing motion. On the serve, most tournament players try to imitate the upper body movements of a pitcher after he completes his windup: he turns most of his back to the batter as he rotates his trunk, enabling him to uncoil his body into the pitch while his arm accelerates.

Similarly, a good server shows the back of her front shoulder to her opponent by pivoting with both shoulders on a horizontal plane. This turns her trunk and sets the kinetic chain in motion, culminating—ideally—in maximum racket speed at impact.

If your child can already throw a baseball properly, she'll understand the importance of turning her body as she serves. She knows that if she tries to throw a ball without using shoulder rotation, she can't throw it very hard or very far because she's using only the power of her arm. The same principle applies on the serve. (A useful drill here is baseball tennis, pages 94, 107).

The Service Toss

I like to have all my students start right out with the so-called advance toss, and ignore the "beginner's toss." Both tosses are difficult to master and in both the player tries to release the ball to the same point out in front of the body, but the advanced toss is preferable because it enables the shoulders to work together in a smooth, rolling motion that leads to more power and rhythm. Youngsters with a good throwing motion actually have a much easier time learning the advanced toss.

In teaching the advanced toss, you want your child to turn her front shoulder and draw her tossing hand back as the racket is going back. She should release the ball with an up-and-out motion so that it arcs out in front of the body—but not until her tossing arm is pointing to the side fence and the hand is at about head level. This keeps the length of the toss short and makes it more consistent. (Students learning the beginner's toss are normally taught to leave the front shoulder fixed and to throw the ball straight up with their arm outstretched, which is more inhibiting than the throwing motion I seek.)

If your child can concentrate on grooving a smooth arm-lift (with her shoulder as the only moving joint) and can just open her fingers to release the ball, she'll be on the right track. Her arm should do the work, not her wrist or palm; that way there won't be drastic variations in the toss. Just a little flick of the wrist can throw the toss off drastically. Also, have her keep the arm moving up in a flowing motion; don't let it suddenly stop as the ball is leaving her fingers. Nor should she have a death clutch on the ball.

Mastering a consistent toss to the desired location is the toughest part of the serve for many people. But your child must understand a basic truth about good tennis serves: It takes a perfect toss to effect a perfect swing. She may develop a beautiful stroke, but she won't have a consistent serve unless she can release her toss to the same place every time. If her toss keeps going to different locations, she will have to adjust her swing accordingly, and such variety will keep her finishing second in a field of two.

Ideally, the target on the toss should be (1) about a racket's length above her outstretched tossing hand, (2) to the right (outside) of her head, and (3) as far out in front of her body as possible, without disturbing the rhythm of her service motion.

Most beginners and intermediates try to throw the toss straight up in front of the body, right in the middle, but on the swing this forces them either to pull the hitting elbow in, arch their back, or make severe wrist adjustments—any of which can cause an unnatural or cramped stroke. By contrast, tossing the ball out on line with the shoulder of the hitting arm will provide these benefits:

• Your child will maintain a natural flowing motion without any necessary "adjustments."

• She'll enhance the ball-trajectory angle off the racket. Geometrically, the closer the racket face to the net at impact on the serve, the less chance she has of hitting into the net.

• She'll be able to stretch out over the baseline when she makes contact, and can thus snap her forearm and wrist in to the ball, out ahead of her body, instead of straight above her head where all real power is lost.

• She'll be in a position that allows her racket to follow through naturally down to the left side of her body, enabling her to move quickly into position for her opponent's return.

Another "myth" that helps destroy good serves everywhere is the teaching advice "Throw the ball high and give yourself plenty of time to swing." This leads to all sorts of problems, starting with people sometimes throwing the ball so high it takes two days to come down—except if it's windy, in which case they may never see the ball again. More seriously, a big problem with a high toss is that people have to wait for the ball to drop, which means that somewhere along the line they slow down their body motion, pause with the racket behind their back, or adjust their swing in some way—thus destroying the kinetic-energy chain. In addition, a high toss, while giving your child more time to prepare for a gigantic effort, actually gives her less time to make a good hit because the ball falls faster through her hitting zone.

Your child doesn't need to gain time by lengthening her toss, she needs continuity. So all she must do is toss the ball to the peak of where she can reach with her racket as she contacts the ball properly. This requires a toss of less than 27 inches from her extended tossing hand. Hitting the ball at its peak not only dictates a smooth, continuous motion, it insures solid contact, since the ball isn't traveling in any direction. Roscoe Tanner and John Newcombe, two of the best servers in history, both hit the ball at that precise instant when it stops moving upward and hangs motionless—a perfect target.

As your child tries to develop a perfect toss to match her desired swing, here are a couple of tips to help her out:

• When she is practicing her serve or serving in a match and she doesn't like her toss, she should let the ball drop and try again. You can remind her, "Your opponent cannot force you to swing at a lousy toss."

• Many people develop a high toss because they refuse to believe what research has shown: that the ball-tossing motion and the swing can occur simultaneously and the racket will still strike the ball before it has started to drop. So make sure your child is taking her racket back as the ball leaves her fingers, even though she may feel that she's not going to have enough time for the racket to complete its loop behind her back and still go up to contact the ball at the peak of the toss.

• This is a good way to help her find the specific spot at which to contact

I'm using a teaching aid here to show this youngster how far she should throw the ball from her outstretched hand on the service toss — to the peak of where she'll reach with the center of the racket face. Most kids incorrectly visualize a toss two or three times higher. You might create a similar teaching device, such as a tennis ball stuck on a 27-inch barbecue fork. Just as my goal is to help mold independent-thinking players, I want to help develop independent, ingenious teachers, too.

the ball: Have her start to serve as you stand on the other end of the court to see where her shots are landing. Tell her to keep her head up as she hits and concentrate only upon where her toss is going and where she contacts the ball. "Never try to see what your opponent is doing out of the corner of your eye. Just watch the racket meet the ball up there. You can actually see the contact on the serve because the ball shouldn't even be moving at impact; it should be at the peak of its arc." Then, as she hits, tell her where the ball is landing so that she can remain focused on her toss and the impact point. When she hears you say "Great serve!" that's her cue to mentally mark the spot at which she contacted the ball and to start to practice tossing to that point every time.

How to Form the Loop

If I could erase one favorite line used by instructors teaching the serve, it would be "Bend your elbow and scratch your back." This kindly advice is intended to help people form a looping motion with their hitting arm, but the fact is, any conscious effort to get the racket down behind the back simply undermines a good service motion. Rather than use the sequential

This father has constructed an arrow to help his son visualize the desired path of the racket head as it contacts the ball on the serve. "Up and out" is the theme. Note the fully extended hitting arm — but remember that this full extension should not occur until the moment of impact, accompanied by the forearm snapping through.

unwinding of key body segments—the hips, followed by the trunk, the shoulders, and the hitting arm—"scratch-your-back" hitters are forced to rely on the power in their arm and on muscular effort. They think they're going to turn in and unleash a gigantic serve, but all of their segments turn at once, in an abrupt forward and upward thrust. By then straining for power, they tighten their muscles and thus oppose their own serve physiologically.

So here's what I teach: From a starting position, your child should take her hitting hand back at about waist level as she pivots horizontally, with both shoulders working together. The palm of the hitting hand should face *down* as the racket goes back and the elbow should remain up. Then, as she starts turning the shoulder of her hitting arm in toward the tossed ball and uncoiling her hips, she should let her arm collapse at the elbow—bending far enough to squeeze a finger held there (while practicing)—and her hitting wrist should relax. The racket head will fall naturally behind the small of her back and the energy generated by the rotating shoulder action will automatically form a perfect loop motion.

To make everything work right, the unwinding of the body must precede the loop. Any intentional effort to force the racket down into a

"back-scratch" position will usually make the arm go rigid, though the goal is to keep it loose and lanky. So have your child try to think of her hitting arm as a rope attached to her racket, and urge her to combine this loose arm with a turning trunk. The arm can actually go spaghetti when she pivots into the shot, for when the trunk unwinds properly, the racket is automatically thrown up and out at the ball (if the ball is properly out in front of the hitting arm's shoulder).

Hit "Up and Out"

In order to hit the ball over the net with speed *and* accuracy, your child must learn to swing "up and out" on her serve, with the racket head moving forward and upward through impact. If she's tall, this may not be the image she has. A lot of tall teenagers think they can "hit down" on the ball and strike fear into their opponents' hearts, but because of the high net they're actually many inches too short to be effective this way. In fact, the center of the racket face must be 10 feet in the air at impact in order to

These two photographs illustrate why kids must always hit "up and out" on the serve and never down if they want to get the ball over the high net and into play.

1. This ten-year-old girl (4'9") stretches up to hit an imaginary serve.

2. Here's a "racket-face view" from the desired impact point. The opponent's service box is not even partly visible above the net; a serve that's hit down can't possibly clear the net tape and land in play.

hit the ball on a straight line, have it clear the net by 1 to 6 inches, and land 1 inch inside the opponent's service line. In theory, a player must be about 6'6" tall to achieve this, but unfortunately the heavy pull of gravity will send the ball into the net.

Still, most players eventually think they're tall enough or good enough to hit down on the serve; or they have a tendency to pull down, with negative results. So I stress, "Keep your chin up and hit up at the ball." When your child allows her chin to drop before impact, her stomach muscles tend to pull down and can bring the racket head down prematurely. Keeping the chin up helps keep the eyes focused on the ball, and research shows—perhaps most importantly—that keeping the chin up automatically stops the unwinding action by the front shoulder before impact. This deceleration creates an accelerated whipping motion by the hitting arm.

Snap the Arm and Follow Through

As your child turns in and her upper body unwinds, she should stretch up to strike the ball at the peak of its arc, with her arm snapping through in a whiplike motion (once she has the strength to do this, of course). If she has started her swing slowly and maintained a kinetic-energy chain, her racket head should be reaching maximum speed as it approaches the ball. In studying her form, you'll know she's generating real speed if the racket is a blur as she makes her loop and contacts the ball. But if the racket comes into focus on the loop, she's swinging too slowly or has hesitated at some point.

Another reason I emphasize hitting *up* at the ball is that this gets the hitting elbow extended, thus slowing it down near the peak of the arm's reach. This in turn allows the forearm, wrist, and racket to gain even greater acceleration. But remember, a loose arm is needed for this action to take place.

An important clarification is needed here. Like most teaching pros, I've always told students that the wrist snap generates most of the power at impact on the serve. However, our high-speed photographs of Arthur Ashe, Ilie Nastase, and other pros show that the real power supply comes from the pronating (rotating) action by the forearm. The major part of the wrist snap doesn't come until the ball is already on its way to the net. Still, that fancy snapping action we all try for is important. If your child really strives to throw her wrist up at the ball, she'll make the racket go faster.

When your child holds a Continental grip—and rotates her trunk properly—her racket face will actually be traveling "inside-out" (left to right, if she's right-handed) at impact, before coming down to the side of her body on the follow-through. Have her experiment with her ball toss to realize how much easier it is for the forearm to pronate naturally when she contacts the ball as far out in front of her body as she can manage while maintaining control. After contacting the ball, she should step forward over the baseline with her back foot to support her shifted body weight on the follow-through and to help maintain good balance. Be careful that this foot doesn't come off the ground before impact, for that can cost her power.

Inhibitions to a Continuous Motion

Most people get into deep trouble on the serve because they fail to maintain a continuous motion by the racket arm. This is an important segment of the desired kinetic-energy chain and it can be broken in several ways:

• Trying to force the racket into the "back-scratch" position in hopes of forming the loop motion will break the flow.

• Too high a ball toss, which forces your child to wait for the ball to drop or to subconsciously build in braking motions somewhere during the stroke, also destroys continuity. Theoretically, if she's serving with a continuous motion and throws the ball higher than the peak of her outstretched racket, she'll (1) miss the ball and (2) realize that her toss needs to be lowered. Unfortunately, this isn't the natural tendency, for most players delay their swing and thus are forced to throw the ball higher. So make sure your child works on lowering her toss instead of adjusting her swing.

• Dropping the hitting elbow while drawing the racket back prevents the necessary loop and halts the kinetic-energy chain. I call this the "chain-puller's syndrome," and the cure is to keep the elbow high and the hitting shoulder up on the backswing. A helpful drill to force continuity is to have your child toss the ball so low that she'll miss it if she drops the elbow and makes her unwanted little hitch. Once she works out this problem, she can raise the toss to its appropriate height (if necessary).

Attack the Net after Serving

Once your child has developed some basic abilities (such as a good serve and a capable volley), encourage her to play aggressively by approaching the net after her serve. To do this, she should bring her back foot forward over

1

2

Footwork after the Serve

A skilled player who wants to attack the net after serving should use this footwork sequence as a guide.

1. On the serve follow-through, the player's back foot has crossed the baseline; he's "fallen in" on his dominant leg.

2. He then takes one full step . . .

the baseline on the serve, take three full steps forward, and then take what is called a stutter-step, or check-step, that brings both feet together momentarily (see photos). This will put her in position to break easily in any direction for her opponent's return, thus increasing her chances of winning the point.

Your child's initial goal should be to reach her check-step position before the ball leaves her opponent's racket. Otherwise, if she's still on the run, she's likely to find herself saluting the ball as it goes by, either crosscourt or down-the-line. When a person is on the move like that, she can't make sudden directional changes in order to meet the challenge of an opponent's return.

Your child will want to remain at her stutter-step position for only an instant as she studies her opponent's return. Her next objective will be to break quickly forward in order to volley that shot from inside her service line. That's what good tennis involves. Her physical development and conditioning will certainly affect her ability to move forward and diagonally, but don't overlook the value of good service form. When she contacts the serve well in front of her body, all of her momentum is going into the shot and this helps give her a faster and more balanced first step. She can also take longer strides, because she's already on the move as her back foot crosses the baseline and hits the ground.

3

4

Variations of the Serve

Since nearly all servers have to "bend" the ball over the high net to get it to land in play, they can rely on either of two methods: (1) hit a "patty-cake serve"—a soft, high-arced shot—and then let gravity do the work (which is the typical choice of beginners and intermediates hitting second serves), or (2) impart ball rotation, which enables a server to hit the ball hard and still bring it down inside the opponent's service box. Of course, many players think there's a third option—hitting the ball hard and "flat" (with minimal spin)—but this isn't a reasonable alternative unless they're about 8 feet tall.

The serve variations that I teach all use nearly the same toss and the same general hitting motion, and all have some amount of spin. So what really distinguishes them is the angle at which the racket face strikes the ball and the amount of ball rotation thus imparted.

The "Flat" Serve
On this serve (if the body turns properly into the shot), the palm and racket head do not travel straight toward the intended target after striking the ball, as is commonly thought. Instead, the racket face contacts the back of the ball and continues forward but slightly toward the outside of the target line (an imaginary line leading from the point of contact to

3. A second full step . . .

4. And then a third full step. At this point he draws his trailing foot forward so that his feet come together momentarily in what is called a check-step, or stutter-step. This leaves him ready to break quickly in any direction for the service return. The player has settled in here for purposes of illustration; under actual playing conditions he will only pause for an instant — poised on his toes or shuffling a bit as he anticipates his opponent's shot. In some cases, when he lands he already knows where he's going next and he doesn't even hesitate. If he finds that the opponent's return is continually coming his way before he reaches his ready position, he should reassess his tactics: he's not hitting his serve well enough to warrant such an aggressive style of play.

the intended target). This imparts a slight amount of horizontal sidespin (commonly known as "slice").

Since this serve creates the least amount of ball rotation of any variation, it offers the smallest leeway for error; the harder the ball is hit, the greater the gamble it will go too far. Trying to hit with an Eastern forehand grip adds even greater limitations, since a player can't make a natural snapping action in the hitting zone in order to apply spin. Thus, she can never rotate the ball hard enough—by brushing the racket face against it—to ever develop a hard, reliable serve.

The Modified Topspin Serve

The ability to hit a modified topspin serve will become increasingly important as your child grows taller and stronger and wants to improve. For example, youngsters aged fourteen or fifteen will often come to me and say: "Vic, what's wrong with my serve? I used to serve better when I was ten or eleven." I look at their technique, and if they're hitting the ball primarily "flat," I tell them: "When you were younger, you could slug the ball swinging like that and it would go in because you weren't as strong and the ball died a little. Gravity also helped you out. Now you're a lot stronger, but you're still too short. You've got to hit up at the ball and make it bend with ball rotation if you want to hit it hard."

The physical principles for applying topspin to the serve are basically the same as on groundstrokes (the racket face must move from low to high and brush the back side of the ball). However, the topspin serve that I advocate—the single most effective serve—is actually contacted on a forward and upward angle about halfway between vertical (which is the American twist) and horizontal (which we call slice). The racket head should rise and move from inside to outside so that when viewed from the baseline it brushes across the top right side of the ball at about a 45-degree angle (or slightly less, closer to horizontal). If your child's right-handed, have her visualize a dot on the back of the ball rotating from the lower left to the upper right, or from about an eight-o'clock position to a two-o'clock position on an imaginary clock. That's the direction the racket head should take, and it's also the way the ball will spin. (For left-handers, it's lower right to upper left—four o'clock to ten o'clock.)

Just as on groundstrokes, you may have heard that the racket face should go *over* the ball at impact in order to impart topspin, instead of continuing "up and out." I'll agree that this feeling of "coming over the ball" is what your child should seek, but only to help produce the correct stroke. Photographic studies of the pros show that their racket heads continue briefly upward after striking the ball and imparting the necessary spin; they don't turn over the ball. This reality about topspin also dictates that impact must occur before the racket head reaches the top of its arc, in order for the racket to contact the ball while moving low-to-high.

The Continental grip is very important on the topspin serve, since it provides greater forearm flexibility than the Eastern forehand grip and automatically places the racket on a plane at impact that facilitates increased ball rotation. However, your child will have trouble mastering the Continental grip until she learns to rotate her body properly. When the upper body unwinds, the hitting arm is "thrown" out naturally toward the outside net post and the palm turns outward (perpendicular to the flight of the ball)—but the racket face contacts the back side of the ball, pointed to the opponent. This may sound crazy, but there are no exceptions for someone who serves well. Conversely, if your child fails to rotate her body (when holding the Continental), she won't have those forces going out and her racket edge will come straight through toward her opponent, while her shots sail into the side fence.

The Slice Serve

The myth about this serve is the belief that a player must try to bring the racket face around the outside of the ball, to impart "slice." Like all serves, the slice is produced by contacting the *back side* of the ball, in this case with the racket face moving from inside to outside on virtually a horizontal path when viewed from behind. When the ball lands, it kicks to the left (for a right-hander) and stays lower than a topspin serve because of its lower trajectory over the net.

If your child can learn a good slice serve, she'll gain a valuable tactical weapon. Few of her opponents will be able to return the ball aggressively, since her serve moves them laterally off the court. If they try to come back crosscourt, she can hit into the open side of the court—often to their backhand. If they want to go down-the-line when returning her slice serve, the pressure is on them to cut the bounce off before the sideward angle gets too wide, and then to "thread the needle" with their return.

If your child's a left-hander, the slice serve is going to be a natural goal. Most of her opponents will be right-handed and the slice serve will go naturally to a right-hander's backhand (usually the weaker side) when hit from either side of the center mark. Left-handers don't develop any special physiological advantages in this regard, just a lot of experience playing right-handers. If right-handers grew up playing primarily left-handers, they would also spend months and years developing the slice, since they could then hit to the left-hander's backhand and pull her wide when serving from the right side of the center mark.

The American Twist

This serve is contacted with a severe upward lift of the racket face that produces almost vertical forward rotation on the ball, and thus a high kick when it lands. Although this high kick makes for a difficult return on the junior level, I never teach this serve, for two basic reasons:

First, it is ultimately limiting in big-time tennis, because it loses too much speed. In the quarter-finals at Wimbledon in 1978, for instance, Pam Shriver was employing a big kick serve to Sue Barker's backhand (and weaker) side, but Sue would simply move back one step and then "run around" to hit a powerful forehand. She had time to wait for the ball to come down and then to place it where she wanted.

Second, the American twist places too much strain on a person's back and the elbow of the hitting arm. Ideally, on this serve the ball must be tossed directly overhead or a bit behind the hitter's back, thus forcing her to bend backwards in order to fix the racket face on a horizontal plane before it goes forward and up. This backward bend "freezes" the desired shoulder rotation and forces her (1) to rely on the strength of her arm to supply all her power as she turns in to hit the ball and (2) to contact the ball with a sophisticated wrist and forearm snap. Placing these excessive pressures upon an elbow that is already in a twisted position can lead to long-term damage.

Aiming and Using the Different Serves

Once your child can get her serve into her opponent's service box, she should try to become target-oriented, even before she has the kind of control that calls for. Her guiding principle should be: "Always try to serve to the opponent's side that will produce the weakest ball in return." Then, as she learns to attack and volley, she'll also want to try to produce the highest return she can. This means she'll find herself aiming for her opponent's backhand corner the great majority of times, for three basic reasons:

• Most players have less accuracy and power—and thus less confidence —hitting from their backhand side, particularly under pressure against a strong serve. (These weaknesses tend to lessen in top-flight tennis.)

• Opponents have to react faster on the backhand in order to meet the ball out in front of their body and hit flat or with topspin. The odds are good that they will fail to get into position fast enough, and will thus have to hit with underspin.

• Since opponents are likely to be hitting with underspin, the chances are excellent that they'll turn under the ball and return it higher than when hitting a forehand. If your child is attacking the net, a high service return gives her a much easier volley. A lower return that is dipping over the net with topspin may force her to hit from a lifting position below net level, thereby costing her a tactical advantage.

As she develops control on the serve and gets into stiffer competition, she may question this strategy of concentrating on the backhand side: "Yeah, Mom, but I like to serve to the forehand and mix things up. If I always go to my opponent's backhand, she's going to be waiting for me and I'm going to get killed." Your answer could be: "Why let your opponent off the hook? If you're winning your serve by attacking her backhand, why go to her forehand and give her a chance to regain some confidence?" Even if an opponent knows your child will be serving to her backhand side, the question still remains: Can she hit a backhand? If she can't, then knowing in advance won't really help.

The only times your child should try to serve to an opponent's forehand are (1) when she knows her opponent has a strong backhand, (2) when her opponent is leaving herself vulnerable to an ace—an untouchable serve—by "cheating" (moving over) excessively to her backhand side, (3) when your child has such a strong serve that she can use it as a way of nullifying an opponent's particularly strong forehand, and (4) when she's positive she can force a weak return by driving her opponent off the court. For example, when an opponent is trying to protect a weak backhand by positioning herself to hit her forehand at every opportunity, it may sound suicidal to serve into her strength on purpose. But remember, very few players can hit outright winners in baseline rallies, especially when they've been pulled off court. So by hitting a slice serve that stretches her opponent wide to hit a forehand return, your child opens up the court and can then hit her next shot deep to the backhand corner, forcing her opponent to go with that weaker stroke on the run.

The topspin and slice serves are both important weapons and should be mixed judiciously once your child has the ability to do so. Since slice has a lower incoming trajectory and the ball stays close to the court surface, it can be particularly effective against tall players who hate to bend and those who are slow in moving to the ball. High-bouncing topspin proves troublesome to short players, forcing them to hit from up around shoulder level, where power is more difficult to achieve.

The Second Serve

A player gets two chances to hit his serve into play before losing the point, but I like all my students to understand that the first and second serves should not involve two different kinds of swings. Both of them should be forceful but controlled efforts with identical stroking patterns —despite the additional pressure that exists on the second attempt.

Ideally, the only difference between them is a matter of changing the ball rotation (increasing or decreasing the amount of spin on the ball) rather than a reduction in the speed of the swing. You'll give your child a lifetime gift if you can convey this concept and not let her fall into the trap of trying to bomb her first serve and, if it fails (called a fault), then to poke a little helium ball over the net. To me, it's a terrible feeling to have to swing softly under pressure on the second serve, when you really want to hit hard. Plus, you're giving an opponent the edge by allowing her to move in closer to the net for her return.

Therefore, have your child learn a topspin serve so that she can swing hard on the first serve and, if she "faults," hard on the second too—but with control. Her stroke will remain the same and all she must alter is the upward angle at which she contacts the ball. For example, if her first serve goes long, she must increase the spin on the second serve by swinging harder but with the racket traveling on a more vertical low-to-high angle. This gives the ball a greater arc and brings it down into play more quickly. The ball doesn't travel faster (the more spin, the less speed) but she's allowed to swing faster. She will learn through experience that she doesn't have to "adjust" her second serve by swinging slowly.

Once into match-play competition, she may wonder, "How do I keep from choking on my second serve?" If she has a good stroke and is following your advice about hitting out, her problem is a mental one. But I've found over the years that most people choke because they don't have the basic stroke, and that's where the work should begin. Also, if she begins telling you, "I'd be terrific if I just had a second serve," question whether she's being realistic. She may be blaming the wrong stroke: if she already had a strong first serve, she wouldn't be so dependent on the second.

Other Service Tips

Here are some additional service pointers:

• When your child is preparing for her first serve, she should plan on serving only one ball. She doesn't want the second ball to become a crutch.

• Remind her to concentrate on each serve and to take her time: "No one can run in and grab your toss."

• If she thinks about her service motion up at the line, she should be more concerned about rhythm and letting everything flow rather than about isolated movements of the body.

• She should try to serve deep and avoid hitting the net. She may get some lucky line calls. Deep serves will also give her more time to advance

Stroke-Production Chart
SERVE

Name _____

Date _____

FUNDAMENTAL

COMMENTS

- Holds proper grip (strives for Continental)
- Stays relaxed in original stance
- Positions feet properly
- Activates backswing with shoulder rotation
- Starts hitting arm slowly, finishes fast
- Uses continuous hitting-arm motion
- Bends elbow sufficiently on the loop
- Lets racket loop naturally behind the back
- Synchronizes ball toss with the hitting-arm motion
- Tosses ball to the proper height
- Tosses ball in the proper direction
- Tosses ball to the proper distance in front of body
- Keeps overall swing rhythmic
- Properly executes kinetic-energy chain
- Keeps wrist and forearm loose
- Hits "up and out"
- Snaps (pronates) forearm properly
- Brings back foot forward on follow-through

behind her serve and to react to her opponent's return. Plus, she prevents her opponent from attacking the net.

• Statistics show that there are two times in a match when an average player is likely to lose her service: on her first serve of the day (because she hasn't warmed up sufficiently) and when leading 5–4 in a set, because she's thinking, "If I win this game, I'll win the set," instead of concentrating on each attempt sequentially.

Practicing the Serve

As the single most important stroke in the game, the serve demands a lot of practice if your child hopes to master a swing that will hold up under pressure. Here are some guidelines to incorporate into practice sessions on the serve, as well as some common problems to watch for and suggested solutions.

• Most recreational players never really practice their serve, except when they're warming up before a match. Yet the serve is the easiest stroke of all for your child to practice, alone or with a friend or a parent. Repetition of a good stroking pattern is the key when practicing, so make sure she has a bucket of practice balls handy. She should hit balls repeatedly—but with a purpose in mind for every serve. She should try to develop positive habits in practice that will become second nature in a match.

• Use on-court targets to help provide greater incentive and challenge, to make practicing more fun. Place tennis cans, a pile of tennis balls, or balloons (taped to the court) in appropriate corners of the service box and see if she can hit them. You want her to become target-oriented, because good tennis involves a person's ability to hit a target area under stress.

• Emphasize that she should always strive to hit deep, even if she's wild. In a match, it's easier to learn to bring a long serve down in bounds by increasing topspin rotation than it is to lengthen a serve that keeps going in the net. When practicing, see how many balls she can serve without hitting the net—and never let her finish practice with a serve that hits the net.

• If her serve is going long consistently (and she's getting the proper forearm and wrist snap in to the ball) she must throw the ball farther forward off her hitting shoulder, or must brush up against the ball with more of a vertical angle, or both.

• If her serve is falling too short or going into the net, she's probably trying to swing down on the ball, letting her chin drop, or throwing the ball too far in front of her hitting shoulder—or perhaps a little of all three.

• If your child wants to master an ideal bread-and-butter serve that she can use effectively on both her first and second attempts, she should groove that 45-degree, forward-and-upward hitting angle. This gives her an effective compromise between the spin of the American twist and the slice serve, and the speed of the "flat" serve. One practice reminder: Make sure your child has a low-enough toss so she can contact the ball at its peak while the racket is still rising.

• If your child is holding the Continental grip and her serves are traveling toward the left fence, the cure is better shoulder rotation and a conscious effort to turn the palm out while snapping the wrist. If your child is using an Eastern forehand grip and her serves are traveling too far to this side, then she's unwinding her body improperly and the ball is going to travel naturally in that direction.

• As her serve improves—and she shows an interest—have your child practice taking three steps forward (after following through) and bringing her feet together momentarily on the stutter-step, ready to break toward her opponent's return. You don't want her falling into the habit of automatically staying back if she has the ability to begin attacking the net. Here, too, is where you can also work on your own tennis game—by acting as the service returner—while providing instruction.

13/The Other Important Strokes

One of the nice things about tennis is that it allows children options. Once they get into competition—simply among friends or in tournaments—they can stay on the baseline and develop a sound defensive game or they can learn to rush the net and become good offensive players. For sure, as Bjorn Borg would say, they can go a long way just with deep, consistent groundstrokes, a reliable serve, and competitive zeal. As I used to remind my students, "Chris Evert Lloyd goes to the net every April but visits the bank every week." Now I use that line in regard to Tracy Austin (although she's actually an excellent net player as well). Even if your child has a less cosmic goal than being ranked No. 1 in the world—like working on a suntan—he can camp on the baseline all day and have a lot of fun. Who's to knock that?

Yet fortunately tennis also offers a more diversified, full-court challenge, built around the approach shot (which is used to gain a position at the net), the volley, the overhead, and the lob. If your child is motivated to become a better player, he may find he can win many matches by outlasting opponents in baseline rallies, but increasingly he's going to find himself caught in a trap: the better he becomes, the more he's going to be forced to improve his other strokes.

There's an interesting chain reaction at work (for those who wish to go along), which dictates that as a person becomes a better server and learns to rush the net, he's going to get more chances to volley. And as he becomes a better volleyer, he's going to encounter more lobs as opponents try to drive him away from the net by hitting over his head. This is going to force him to develop a more effective overhead stroke. Meanwhile, before he can capitalize on the first short ball in a baseline rally, he must know how to advance after hitting a deep approach shot—and how then to maintain his tactical advantage with his ability to volley and hit overheads. In addition, he will need a good lob himself to counter net-rushing opponents. And as he faces better servers, he will have to develop his service return as a sound stroke in itself.

Although I think it's fun to know what lies ahead in tennis, all these strokes and tactical options may sound a bit overwhelming at this point if you and your child are still trying to figure out how to keep score. In fact, even as he improves he may not want to play the game offensively; he may be happier staying around the baseline and trying to win from there. So don't push an aggressive style of play when his interest isn't there. Your only responsibility is to explain why the net position is strategically important and how strokes other than his forehand and backhand can help him win matches. That's my purpose in this chapter.

The Approach Shot

An approach shot is actually any shot that a player uses to help him move up and gain control of the net, whether he hits it after the ball bounces or before it touches the court. In most cases, however, it's a stroke that is executed while he's on the run, near the service line, and it's aimed for a deep baseline corner. The player then continues forward to his desired waiting position, ready to break forward to cut off a passing shot or to quickly retreat against a lob.

At any level of play, the closer a youngster can get to the net after a good approach shot, the greater his chances of winning the point (given that he can also volley). For one thing, geometry is in his favor. He can't push people around hitting from the baseline in baseline rallies; unless he gets a lucky angle, he can only run an opponent three steps to either side. But from midcourt he can force an opponent to run laterally as many as five to seven steps, and from up near the net he can angle the ball sharply away from the fastest player around. In addition, when he gets good position close to the net, he tightens the pressure on his opponent by reducing his opponent's effective options to two: a lob or a passing shot.

Many players tend to overlook the approach shot, since it comes late in the normal teaching sequence. So I teach my students right away that this will become a fundamental shot for them as they advance in tennis. The opportunity to hit this shot is what the pros are waiting for in baseline rallies or on second serves, for it gives them an almost unbeatable edge up at the net—providing they hit it deep, as I'll explain.

Find Your Child's "Short-Ball Range"
Most approach shots are set up by an opponent's weak groundstrokes, though soft second serves also present numerous opportunities in

The Approach Shot

1. A successful approach shot begins with anticipation — based on an awareness that in beginning and intermediate tennis most balls hit during a baseline rally are going to land short rather than deep. This player is expecting that a ball will land in his "short-ball range." He is ready to break forward with a quick first step.

2. The overall swing itself — on both the forehand and backhand — is short and compact, with a forward stroking pattern that's a slight high-to-low-to-high arc (see photo on page 278). As the hitter runs in, he tries to keep his head still and he doesn't worry about getting sideways for the hit until he nears the ball.

3. When contacting the ball, he tries to keep his head very still and the racket head high. He also tries to run through the shot smoothly so that he can quickly reach his volleying position at the net. Some critics say it's best to stop running in order to hit this shot, but I've found that when a player stops on the approach shot just before impact, the racket head and the body tend to do the same thing as a car that brakes suddenly: the front end goes down and the back end goes up. In tennis, the result is often a ball that travels into the net or one hit very short to the opponent.

4. Notice that the racket finishes high on the follow-through, which encourages the desired overall stroking pattern and deeper shots. The nonhitting arm can either be left at the side or extended for better balance.

3

4

intermediate tennis. Whether your child should hit an approach shot on a particular ball depends on how weak and shallow the opponent's hit is and on your child's "short-ball range." This is an area on the court from where he can hit an approach shot and run forward in time to reach a ready position (X) halfway between the service line and the net before (or as) the ball gets to his opponent's racket. To fix this radius, have him hit approach shots from different points on the court while you act as his opponent on the opposite baseline. Connect those starting points from which he can reach his X before you yell "Now!" as you contact the ball, and this will define his short-ball range.

Have your child think about this radius and refine it in practice so that during a match he'll only try an approach shot when he sees that he'll have time to reach his X ready position.

The Stroke

When your child moves up against a short ball, he should try to advance as close to the net as possible. Thus, he should turn slightly sideways to the net and "run through" his approach shot, contacting the ball off his front shoulder so that body energy can supply most of his power while momentum carries him forward. Although many people are taught to stop as they hit their approach shot, I believe this destroys the rhythm they seek and introduces a negative effect of deceleration-acceleration. When a person suddenly stops running, his upper body continues to move forward and down, forcing his racket arm to go down. The usual result is a shot that falls too short or travels down into the net.

To help insure consistency at impact, your child should strive for a compact stroke, fixing his wrist and letting his body and racket arm do the work as a unit. His backswing should be short (his racket should always be in sight out of the corner of his eye), and he should hit with a slight high-to-low-to-high motion (see photo on page 278) and with a slight racket-face bevel in order to produce underspin (unless he wants to hit flat). The resulting trajectory makes the ball stay low when it hits the court, thus forcing an opponent to bend down as he hits, increasing the chances of a high return, particularly off the backhand side. Remember, however, that it's the incoming trajectory of the shot—not the spin of the ball—that dictates this low bounce. Underspin actually produces a higher initial bounce than topspin when the incoming trajectories are the same.

Although your child is swinging down slightly in order to impart underspin, his racket should travel on nearly a horizontal plane through the hitting zone and then finish up and out toward his target area. This high follow-through helps insure a stroking pattern that keeps the ball from landing short or going into the net.

Anticipation, Footwork, and Positioning

If your child is to gain control of the rally by hitting a deep approach shot, he must learn to reach the ball before it bounces lower than waist level; his goal will be to contact it around chest level. This requires anticipation, quick but controlled footwork, and a readiness to think and react offensively rather than defensively. Remind him that once he has some trusty weapons (an approach shot and volley) and his opponent hits the first short ball in a rally, he has been given a gigantic opportunity. So instead of thinking "Hit and stay back" when he's on the baseline, he should stay on his toes, ready to get a quick jump forward as he watches his opponent swing. With experience, he'll learn to sense a short ball coming before it reaches the opposite service line and he'll break forward, striving for good body balance while on the run so he doesn't have to pause as he hits.

After hitting the ball, he should keep moving forward toward the side of the center line to which the shot travels—arriving at a point halfway

Approach-Shot Tactics

After hitting an approach shot to his opponent's backhand, the player in the foreground has advanced to his X — a momentary ready position that puts him equidistant between the passing shots his opponent can hit either down-the-line or crosscourt. From here he will want either to move forward to volley or turn and run back for a lob.

between the service line and the net, and within 3 feet of the center. His actual X should be midway between where his opponent can hit passing shots (groundstrokes) down-the-line or crosscourt. So the only time he should stand on the center line is when he has hit the ball straight down the middle. (In terms of imagery and incentive, it can help to chalk in the ideal X position on the court—3 feet to the right side of the center line for a right-hander and 3 feet to the left for a left-hander).

When my students first try to position themselves correctly after hitting to their opponent's backhand (assuming both players are right-handed), they often feel as though they've exposed a "wide-open" area on their own backhand side. But I assure them that if they have good reactions and a decent volley, there are few players around who can hit past them on the backhand side. Even the pros have a difficult time hitting a crosscourt backhand safely away from an opponent at the net. "So stop worrying about the extraordinary shot," I tell my students. "Be much more concerned about what realistically is possible. By positioning yourself correctly, your opponent can now only go to your right or over your head with his backhand. You have just cut off thirty-three percent of his real opportunities."

When your child reaches his X, he should use it only as a ready position for his next shot. He should stop momentarily by bringing his feet together with a little check-step—as or before the ball reaches his opponent's racket strings. This will enable him to break quickly in any direction for his next shot. He wants to be light on his feet, asking himself "Drive or lob, drive or lob?" as he studies his opponent's swing. If he sees that it's going to be a drive (a passing shot), his goal is to move two steps forward. If it's a lob, he wants to turn and run back three steps. Whatever, the key is to move instinctively, without standing on his X trying to decide.

Placement and Strategy

If your child is to be successful playing an attacking type of game, keeping the ball in play is not enough—he must try to advance after hitting a deep approach shot. When he can land the ball within about 5 feet of his opponent's baseline, he (1) pins his opponent deep, (2) reduces the angle at which his opponent can hit a crosscourt passing shot, and (3) gives himself more time to reach his X and then to react to his opponent's shot.

Conversely, if he hits his approach shot short, anywhere into the midcourt area, he gives his opponent an excellent opportunity to win the point with a passing shot to either side. (When your child does hit a weak approach shot from his short-ball range, he should still move forward aggressively, instead of retreating, since his presence up near the net can distract some opponents. In addition, he should look for cues in his opponent's stroking pattern or body position that will help him anticipate where his opponent is going to hit the ball. If cues are lacking, a pro will guess and break either right or left; at least he has a 50-50 chance. Standing in the middle of the court and waiting for the ball to leave his opponent's racket won't leave him enough reaction time to program a move.)

Here's a drill to illustrate my rationale about depth. Stand on the baseline as your child hits approach shots from inside his short-ball range (say, just behind the service line), and check how far he advances before you yell "Now!" as you hit your return. He can see for himself that a deep shot allows him time to reach his X easily, while a short ball leaves him on the dead run as you are hitting. In a match, he'll discover that he doesn't even have to hit the ball hard to maintain his tactical edge as long as he hits it deep. (When his shots are going too long, he should still have a good feeling, because it's easier to make the necessary adjustments; playing pros are much more upset when they start hitting the ball too short or into the net.)

Even as your child is learning to use the approach shot, have him strive to aim for his opponent's backhand corner—specifically, a 4-foot target area inside the baseline and the sideline. He may only be able to hit this corner by accident, but this is going to be his target for the rest of his life unless he plays an opponent whose forehand is weaker than his backhand. Just as on the serve, he should concentrate on the side that will most likely produce a high return—and thus an easier ball to volley.

To reinforce this concept, have your child stand behind the baseline as you hit balls deep into his backhand corner from the opposite service line. He'll quickly realize—or be reminded—how it feels to be penned in against an opponent who advances to the net after hitting a deep approach shot.

If your child can get this constant target clearly fixed in his head as he moves up to hit his approach shot, it will reduce the variables he has to contend with and leave him free to hit. Most people, by contrast, debate with themselves about what to do: "Should I hit to the forehand or go to the backhand? Maybe I should go down the middle and play it safe?" This kind of debate is usually academic, since the ball tends to wind up in the net.

Practicing the Approach Shot

The best approach-shot drill for a two-person practice session goes like this:

Mark off 4-foot target areas in both baseline corners on your side of the net (using chalk, white tape, or rope) and then start hitting short balls to your child that land around his service line. His goal is to run in from his baseline, stroke the ball toward a corner target area, then move forward to his X. (He should practice hitting into both corners because he'll be playing right-handers as well as left-handers, who of course have different backhand sides.) Set tennis cans inside these corners; they will provide a nice sensation when knocked over or sent flying. This drill will help your child realize how high he must hit the ball over the net in order to have it land deep, and will demonstrate just how much he needs to work on the stroke. It's certainly not an easy matter to land many shots in either corner. (Target areas will also help you know if your child has too much wristiness. A wristy player will hit an occasional good approach shot, but the variations are great when he misses. A firm-wrist player has much more consistency.)

You can also improve your own approach shot as you work with your child by setting up tennis-can targets in all four corners and then rallying together. Whenever a short ball is hit, the person on the receiving end should rush in and hit toward one of the corners. For fun, see who's the first to knock over a can.

The Volley

When your child achieves his first goal—to gain control of the net after hitting a deep approach shot—he places enormous pressure on his opponent to execute perfectly. But to hold down the fortress, he must also know how to volley.

The Grip

Although the common advice is to play a one-grip game at the net by holding a Continental, I recommend hitting with the regular Eastern forehand and Eastern backhand grips—all the way through junior tennis and into the pro game. As I've mentioned, youngsters can learn to switch grips as they're taking their first step toward the ball; and besides, the Continental requires greater coordination and talent. For example, when a player holds this grip and tries to hit a forehand volley down-the-line—attempting to contact the ball properly, slightly out in front of his body—the racket face is automatically angled toward the opposite side of the court, and the face is tilted slightly back. This forces some undesired

3

4

The Volley

Stroking technique on the volley is basically the same on either side of the body, except that the backhand — just as on groundstrokes — must be contacted farther out in front of the body than the forehand. Volleys can be hit with either one or two hands on the racket handle.

1. This left-handed player may look a little stiff with her elbows out, but her shoulders are relaxed and she's ready to break in any direction.

2. She's rotating her shoulders to take the racket back and using her nonhitting hand to keep the racket from laying back. This enables the racket face to stay on line with the ball throughout the stroke and helps insure a shortened swing; most people make the mistake of having a racket that's 2 or 3 feet farther back at this point.

3. Her swing is short, mostly a blocking or punching motion, but she steps in to the ball to gain power. By contrast, the common problem here is for a player to "freeze" the body and swipe at the ball with a longer, wristy swing while standing flat-footed.

4. On the follow-through, notice that she carries the racket high. A conscious effort to finish high helps insure a stroke that keeps the ball out of the net and leaves the player ready for the next volley. Many volleyers err by finishing with the racket down.

adjustments in order to go down-the-line. If, instead, he's late on his swing, the racket face will be properly set—but he won't be able to hit crosscourt without severe adjustments.

The Stroke

Since accuracy and consistency are more important on the volley than the speed of the ball, your child should try to master a short, punching motion rather than an actual stroke. On the forehand side, his racket should go back only as far as the shoulder of the hitting arm, because the greater the length of his swing, the greater must be his talent. You might tell him, "Instead of a backswing, think of your palm reaching out to intercept the ball, as if you were catching a baseball." The same stroking philosophy applies to the backhand volley, but with different checkpoints: the racket should be drawn back to the shoulder of the nonhitting arm and your child should visualize his knuckles going out toward the ball.

The instant he sees the ball coming, he should turn his shoulders to get his racket into position, and then step forward to meet the ball. On the forehand, he should contact the ball when it is even with his front shoulder and at eye level, thus requiring appropriate knee bend for low balls. Backhands should be contacted 6 to 10 inches in front of the body. At impact, the racket face should be vertical or slightly beveled and well above wrist level, with the top of the racket pointing upward—as much as 45 degrees, if possible. Keeping the racket head up like this is doggone tough against low balls, which is why I have kids work hard not to let their opponent's shot drop below net level when they go to volley. Although little follow-through is needed, show your child how to build in a safety margin for getting the ball over the net by punching through the ball and carrying the racket up and out toward his intended target. Have him think of an ear-to-chin-to-ear motion with the racket face and don't let him fall into the habit of pulling the racket down or across, or letting it suddenly stop. He should always finish high, whether he is contacting the ball at shoulder height or below net level.

On high volleys people have an overwhelming tendency to pull down on the ball, either because of (1) stress, (2) a fear of hitting the ball over the opponent's baseline, or (3) incorrect visualization. Go out onto a court and see for yourself just how close you must get to the net before you can actually see the opposite baseline by looking *over* the net. Despite this physical reality, I frequently see adults swinging down on the ball from near the service line while trying to hit their opponent's service box. It just can't be done.

Now try to view the volley in terms of an average-sized ten-year-old youngster. The net tape is almost on a level with his racket, and thus he

1   2

Testing Volley Technique

A short swing is desired on volleys (and service returns) because the ball is coming fast and the objective is to make a clean, solid hit in the desired direction. Extra power should be sought not by lengthening the swing, but by stepping in to the ball properly and having a forward body movement at impact. A fence can be a teaching pal by reminding your child that he may be going back too far with his racket.

1. This is as far as your child should take the racket back on the forehand volley. If he imitates the player here and lets his elbow (not his wrist or racket) touch the fence, he will find that the racket face is already on line with the oncoming ball. Notice how the player uses his free arm for balance.

2. When hitting a backhand volley, the player uses his nonhitting hand to help keep the racket head from laying back, so it stays fixed in its proper position, facing the oncoming ball. Once your child masters the feeling of holding the nonhitting elbow high, have him move away from the fence and practice turning his trunk.

must swing "up" on virtually every ball in order to clear the net safely. So remember what I tell coaches who teach at my tennis college: "The goal is to hit the ball deep, but your emphasis should be on a high finish, because when a person finishes his volley up here, the ball goes deep and it's crisp. But if his follow-through finishes below the tape of the net, he's going to be in bad trouble. Even if the ball does go over the net, it may fall short."

Another crucial point is for your child to fix his racket with a firm wrist and to keep his hitting arm extended. (When he's working hard to do this in a practice drill, his hitting arm can quickly tire, so avoid too many consecutive hits without a chance to rest briefly.) Sufficient power will come through the forward movement of his body and the speed of his opponent's shot when it rebounds off the racket strings. It just kills me to see kids try to volley with a soft wrist or by laying the racket head back in order to snap their wrist in to the ball. Playing with wristiness may supply a bit more power, but it requires people to judge—under pressure—how and when to snap their wrist so that they can contact the ball properly. That's putting too much faith in "touch" and timing.

Just as on the forehand groundstroke, your child can prevent wrist layback by maintaining a high, slightly bent hitting elbow that leads the racket on the backswing. Then, as he goes out to volley, he should keep his palm and the face of his racket directly in line with the oncoming ball so that his opponent sees only his racket strings, never the butt of the handle. Also, make sure he keeps his hitting elbow out away from his body, for when his elbow comes in too close, the wrist will usually lay back.

On the backhand side, your child can use his nonhitting arm to keep his racket from laying back. The hand should cradle the throat of the racket on the backswing, with the elbow held high and out away from the body so that the racket face is always on line with the ball.

Some stroking tips:

• If your child is going to play a successful attacking type of game (or compete in doubles), he must learn to volley from a deep position, back around the service line. He'll get these midcourt opportunities when he's charging in behind his serve and his opponent returns the ball high. Instead of letting the ball bounce, he should go for the volley and continue moving forward. Of course, volleying from a deep position takes greater talent than does volleying up at the net. He must learn to hit out and almost lift the ball; if he swings down even slightly, the ball will go into the net.

• People rarely hit the ball deep enough on any volley, even when the ball arrives at head level or above. They're so afraid of hitting it over the baseline that they overcompensate by snapping down severely with their racket.

• The closer a person gets to the net, the more he has a tendency to relax and swing down. So have your child work at keeping the racket head up and going out—unless he's absolutely on top of the net. Then he can hit the sharp angle.

• When he's volleying softly hit balls from below net level, he especially must guard against letting the wrist and the racket go limp on the shot or he'll dump the ball into the net.

• Against hard-hit balls, when you see your child's racket head dropping after impact instead of staying above the level of his wrist, you have to discern what actually is taking place. He may have bad technique, but it could be that the force of the ball hitting the racket is knocking the racket head down. You might be telling him, "You're dropping the racket head when you hit," and he might respond: "Really? I don't feel it. I'm trying to keep my wrist firm." Perhaps he doesn't yet have the strength in his wrist needed to counteract the forces of a baseline drive from his opponent. Here's where a two-handed stroke could prove useful, especially on the backhand side. Extensor muscle drills will also help (see page 222).

• In running for the ball and stretching to make a hit, he should keep his hitting arm up and the face of the racket high, no matter how late he might be. Even on a desperate lunge, he'll still have a chance to catch the ball on the strings and return it over the net.

• Have him learn to treat easy shots and difficult ones with the same respect. When an opponent hits a weak drive from the baseline, the tendency is to relax and forget about moving forward to cut it off early. Then suddenly the ball loses speed and drops below net level, forcing a defensive volley.

Anticipation, Positioning, and Footwork

Acquiring good volleying form is certainly important, but it's not going to make your child famous at the net until he (1) learns to anticipate his opponent's shot, and (2) can then react aggressively, even instinctively. As I often tell my students: "The reason many pros can volley so well is that they start moving before (or at the same time as) their opponent contacts the ball. This enables them to volley close to the net. The average player hesitates until the ball is already on its way, and as a result the ball either goes by him totally or gets below the level of the net and forces him into a lunging defensive effort."

Therefore, early in your child's volleying experience, help him develop the attitude that it's fun, even if he guesses wrong, to anticipate whether an opponent is going to drive the ball or lob it—and then to break quickly in the appropriate direction. Point out that most players fail to disguise their baseline shots and that if he concentrates, his guesses will soon

1   2

The "Two-Steps-Up" Concept

A player must get as close to the net as possible to increase her volleying success. This takes anticipation, fast reactions, and quick footwork.

1. The player in the foreground has correctly anticipated her opponent's drive and has taken two steps forward from the X ready position before the ball leaves the opponent's racket. She is now ready to break either left or right.

2. Remember, few players can hit a hard crosscourt backhand that lands in bounds ahead of the 65'9" diagonal shown on the court, even if they hit with topspin. So with just one good step toward the ball, the player at the net can stretch over and volley back her opponent's passing shot. In effect, taking two steps forward has nullified the opponent's crosscourt shot as a sensible option. Even one step forward is valuable.

become educated ones as he learns to "read" his opponent's racket face. For example, if the opponent's racket face approaches the hitting zone on about the same level as the ball, the shot is normally going to be a drive (since there's insufficient time to drop the racket suddenly and lob). But if the racket head has been dropped below the oncoming ball with the face tilted back, then the shot's likely going to be a lob.

When your child is at the net and studying his opponent's swing, he should be in a ready position—physically *and* mentally—that facilitates a fast first step. Instead of settling in flat-footed, he should bring his heels off the ground just before his opponent contacts the ball. This forces your child into action, and allows him to push off his toes in any direction. I like to tell youngsters: "Don't let your feet fall asleep. They've got to get you to the ball in time to allow you to look great."

Meanwhile, your child should be asking himself "Drive or lob, drive or lob?" as his opponent takes his swing. If it's going to be a drive, his goal is to take two steps straight forward before the hit is made. When he sees where the ball is going, he should then step diagonally in that direction— toward the net post—to volley. The closer he can get to the net, the tougher it is for any opponent to hit past him on either side. He cuts off the angle and he gives himself a higher ball to volley, making it easier to end the point. If, instead, he runs parallel to the net, balls that are sharply angled will simply get farther away.

The question is: Can your child make that quick move to the net every time? Even one step diagonally forward will put him ahead of the average player, who tends to back away from the net as an opponent goes to hit from the baseline.

Placement and Strategy

In most cases, top players try to volley the ball on a short diagonal, because this either ends the point outright or forces an opponent well off the court and out of position for a return shot. However, trying to force short-angle shots can very often lead to errors. So teach your child to be aggressive when he comes to the net, but not impatient. If he's not positive that he can end the point with a short-angle volley, he should just strive for depth and, with experience, the baseline corners. This will still keep the pressure on his opponent and enable him to move closer to the net if he has to volley again.

Taking this attitude—"Volley deep and in play"—should also help him relax, since he's not regarding the shot as an all-or-nothing effort. In fact, the farther away from the net he is (near the service line, say), the more this philosophy should apply. Even in tournament tennis, going for the angles from far back is a low-percentage gamble.

1

The Half-Volley

Your child may not want to work much on the half-volley, an ugly-duckling shot that must be hit from down around his sneakers, just after it bounces off the court. But he's going to need this stroke as an intermediate when he finds himself inadvertently caught in the midcourt area, and also as a more advanced player when he tries to follow his serve to the net. If his opponent has worked hard on a service return, he will try to land the ball at your child's feet and your child will have to know how to half-volley it deep if he wants to play a successful serve-and-volley game (one in which, ideally, he advances toward the net after hitting a strong first serve, in hopes of volleying his opponent's returns before they hit the court).

The Stroke
The half-volley is basically a truncated forehand or backhand, requiring the same basic stroking pattern. So your child should try for a short backswing, good knee bend, and a low-to-high lifting motion with a racket

2

3

The Forehand Half-Volley

Most people are afraid to hit the half-volley, but their confidence increases when they realize that the desired stroking pattern is the same as for groundstrokes, just shorter.

1. Moving in for this shot, the student is carefully tracking the ball, with his racket faced slightly down. Most important, he's bending his knees to get his body down to the ball and he's going to take a very compact swing.

2. The key here is to contact the ball while on the run, if possible — but it must be contacted in front of the body, as shown. Your child will get in trouble if he lets the ball get behind him (which forces him to stop) or crosses his legs as he goes to hit. The hitting hand should stay level with the ball, which is possible only with sufficient knee bend, and the racket face should be near-vertical at impact.

3. Although the player's made the hit, his head is still steady and his eyes remain on the point of impact. Also, the racket and thighs have come up and he's continuing on his way to the net. In reviewing this sequence, notice how he has kept his body movement smoothly coordinated, without bobbing up and down.

The Backhand Half-Volley

On the backhand half-volley, just as on the forehand, this player using a two-handed grip strives to bend down and lift up, contacting the ball out in front of her body with a vertical racket face. Getting low like this isn't easy, but it's essential if your child wants to play a successful all-court game.

face that is vertical or just slightly closed (faced downward) at impact. This enables him to lift the ball up over the net and, with the help of gravity, still have it come down safely deep in his opponent's court.

Not surprisingly, most people try to execute the half-volley by staying high with their body and simply lowering their racket head with the face beveled back (faced upward) to "scoop" the ball up over the net. That doesn't help them become too famous. Instead, your child must learn to lower his hitting arm and his body almost to the court, keeping his wrist position firm, and then use his thighs and the lift of his body to supply the power. He should hit the ball immediately after it has bounced, keeping his eyes down on the point of racket impact. If he lifts his head up too early, out of sync with the racket, he will tend to scoop the ball. (When you teach your child this stroke, have him swing easily against soft shots at his feet so he can practice different upward angles and get a feel for what he wants to do.)

Whenever possible, he should contact the ball with little or no pause in forward motion so that he won't lose time moving to his *X*, on the side of the center line to which he hits the ball (same as on the approach shot).

In singles play, hs goal is to hit the ball deep and thus gain more time to reach a good volleying position close to the net. Even an opponent in the backcourt can easily move in against a short half-volley attempt and give your child a "fuzz sandwich."

In doubles, your child should keep the half-volley as close to the top of the net as possible, so that an opponent isn't handed an easy volley opportunity on a high ball. The pros try to hit a "soft" shot that goes over the net and dies, forcing their opponents to bend low and volley up.

The Drop Shot and Drop Volley

Once they get into competition, most kids are tempted to use the drop shot when they're 5 or 6 feet inside their baseline and they've run their opponent way off court or close to the back fence. The shot is an off-speed groundstroke, hit deliberately short, just over the net, with little or no forward bounce. (An underspin stroking pattern is thus desirable.) However, my observation has been that "temptation shots" generally lead to a second-place finish in a two-man field. Even among the pros, the drop shot from backcourt is a gigantic gamble and a difficult play. The hitter must choose wisely and execute perfectly. If he fails to hit an outright winner, the ball either goes into the net or bounces up and gives his opponent an easy put-away.

The effectiveness of a drop shot depends on how soon the other player starts toward the net. I've found that if a person can "read" shots and get a quick first step—if he's prepared to go forward on every ball and thus is never caught unaware by a drop shot—then it's almost a physical impossibility to make the shot work against him. Roscoe Tanner learned this lesson against Jimmy Connors when he tried a drop shot at a crucial point in one of their matches, only to have Connors race to the net and hit a winning passing shot. "The drop shot was a dumb shot," Tanner admitted afterward. "But Connors was so far back that I thought it might work." (Tanner is an outstanding player because he learns by his mistakes and he's not afraid to admit them.)

I advise juniors to save the drop shot for when they're playing on slow surfaces such as clay, and never to hit the shot unless they *know* it will win the point or they're trying to tire an opponent by repeatedly bringing him to the net.

One caution here: When reading or listening to advice about the drop shot, make sure the person is talking about a ball hit from near the baseline (after it has bounced once)—and not the drop volley, which is contacted before it bounces. The drop volley is certainly a finesse shot, but one your child will eventually want to master up near the net. He should execute the drop (or "stop") volley not by dropping or angling the racket head just right, but by loosening the grip just before impact. Without any real force coming forward into the shot, the ball will simply drop off the racket.

The Service Return

In my opinion, the service return is the second-most-important shot in the game (after the serve), but I've placed it at this point in the chapter because the stroke itself—in good tennis—is basically identical to the one used on the approach shot and volley. The main difference comes when the serve is slow enough to allow the returner to take a slightly longer backswing, or even a regular groundstroke.

I consider the service return so important because if the serve goes in, the return determines the nature of the point from there; your child's second, third, and fourth shots in a rally become important only if his return is effective. Moreover, an opponent's serve becomes much less decisive when your child can return the ball consistently. He forces an opponent to beat him with other strokes and he doesn't allow him to win by being a "one-stroke artist."

The service return can also become an effective psychological weapon. When your child plays an opponent whose ego is wrapped up in his serve, he can quickly demoralize that player by hitting his best serves back into play. Meanwhile, he puts all the pressure on his opponent to keep from making the first mistake.

The Stroke

As a beginner, your child will have time to hit his regular forehand and backhand groundstrokes on the return. But as he progresses in competition and begins facing faster serves, he'll find it necessary to strive for a shorter, more compact stroke. Fortunately, he will already be familiar with the desired motion and this should make for an easier transition— physically and mentally.

On the forehand return, this is the overview you want to keep in mind:

The most common problem against fast serves is that people try to take a full swing, only to get caught late when the ball arrives. To avoid this excess motion, your child should strive for a blocking motion, with the racket fixed, the wrist firm, and the face of the racket always on line with the approaching ball. If he can make a clean hit out in front of his body, the speed of the serve when it rebounds off his racket strings and his forward motion will supply all the necessary power. So once he detects the direction of the serve, he needs to turn his shoulders, keep the elbow of his racket arm raised and slightly bent (to keep the wrist from laying back), and then hit through the ball on an almost horizontal plane. The racket face should be nearly vertical at impact. The racket should finish high—never down—to help insure a return that safely clears the net and travels deep. This high follow-through won't lift the ball, since it has already left the racket strings, but it helps insure a level stroke through the hitting zone. Finishing with the racket up is also a compensatory move, since the racket has a natural tendency to come down when a person slows or stops to hit.

On the backhand service return there's even more of a demand for fast reactions, quick footwork, and a compact stroke to insure a properly positioned racket face at impact, well in front of the body. To help shorten the backswing and also to prevent wrist layback, your child should cradle the racket throat with his nonhitting hand and keep the elbow of his hitting arm raised, up and away from his body. Then, as he moves forward into the ball, he can impart underspin by having a slight high-to-low stroke with a slightly beveled racket face. Once again, make sure he finishes with a high follow-through, out toward his target.

Some playing pros advocate a downward "chopping" motion in order to produce extra underspin and to take speed off the ball. However, this effort to start high and finish low calls for much greater talent and requires considerable wrist and arm strength to maintain racket control. Also remember that the pros don't always do what they say they're doing as they stroke the ball. Research using high-speed photography shows that although they appear to start high and swing down sharply, they are actually hitting straight across in the impact area and then lifting up on the follow-through—often finishing with their heels off the ground.

Here are other stroking pointers on the service return:

• When waiting for the serve, your child should hold his regular Eastern forehand grip, and then switch to his Eastern backhand if necessary. Most people are slower shifting from the backhand grip to the forehand. Twirling the racket handle in his hand as he waits is a bad habit, for he must then "find" his grip, even if the ball comes to his forehand side.

• Tightening the third and fourth fingers (ring and little finger) just before impact will help insure a firm grip and will allow a player to make a fairly clean return even if he hits off-center.

• A common mistake off both sides is to let the racket head lay back, instead of keeping the racket face on line with the ball throughout the stroke. (The farther the racket goes back, the greater the need for good timing.)

• Check to see that he doesn't let the racket head drop below the level of his wrist.

• He should keep his eyes glued on the ball as long as possible and then focus on the point of impact until his follow-through is complete. Keeping his head down will help him hit much more consistently near the center of the strings, and concentrating on the ball will help him avoid becoming distracted by an opponent who is attacking the net.

Anticipation, Footwork, and Positioning

If an opponent is consistently getting his first serve into play, your child can usually establish his waiting position fairly early in the match: a point near the baseline, halfway between the distance the server can stretch him to his forehand and to his backhand. In advanced junior play, he'll usually stand at the baseline and straddle the singles sideline when receiving on the deuce (right-side) court; but until he begins facing opponents who can slice the ball wide and force him off the court, he can stand several steps closer to the center mark. Against a right-hander, he can also often stand closer to the center mark when receiving on the ad (left-side) court, because the right-hander's serve usually curves to the left, limiting his serving range. Prior charting or scouting of an opponent is recommended in tournament play so that this range is known beforehand.

Your only other worry about the ready position should be to find the posture that will let your child get to the ball the fastest. A lot of players are obsessed with getting into a low crouch as they wait for the serve, but research shows that they could move faster to the ball by standing fairly erect so that their first move is lateral or diagonal, not upward. If your child crouches in a low position (especially if he's tall), his center of gravity is low, which makes it hard to get a fast first step in laterally or diagonally. A low crouch may help him go straight forward, like a sprinter coming out of the blocks, but that isn't reality in good tennis. It's also true that some pros crouch in their ready position—but they stand almost straight up just before the serve is hit. They know that most returns must be hit at chest or shoulder level.

Against a hard server, your child's speed afoot is no more important than his ability to "buy time" by (1) anticipating the direction of the serve and then (2) getting a fast first step toward the ball, preferably on a diagonal. He should do all his backing up *before* the serve has been hit so that his first step can always be forward.

Just as on the volley, an aggressive attitude is crucial on the service return, as well as a willingness to guess wrong about a fast serve. To keep your child from settling in on his heels, have him learn to bounce up on the balls of his feet as the ball is served, so that his weight is forced forward. Telling himself "It's a forehand!" or "It's a backhand!" will help him start moving to the ball with short, rapid steps before the ball has even bounced.

Strategy and Placement

Strategically, your child should always give the service return the respect it deserves by thinking of it as his main shot of the rally. Everything follows from that. Even in junior tournament play, if he can get ten out of ten returns back into play, he'll be surprised at how many easy "sitters" his opponent misses. But no matter how far he advances in the game, he'll still have a harder time controlling his service return than any other shot; against a hard, deep serve, his only real option will be to scramble, get the ball in play, and fight for the point.

When he has the opportunity and ability to "control" his service return, he has a choice of two objectives:

First, if his opponent remains at the baseline after serving, he should strive for depth on the return to keep the opponent away from the net. The rally will then generally boil down to the question of who has the better groundstrokes.

Second, if the server rushes the net, your child should lob or else keep the ball low and ideally down at his opponent's feet (by hitting flat or with underspin) so that he's forced to bend and scoop for a half-volley or volley. Remember, it's the trajectory of this shot that keeps the ball low after it bounces.

In addition, when your child has some experience and his opponent hits a weak second serve, he should never stay back on the return. He should intimidate the server by moving in, hitting an approach shot, and then taking the net. This will put even greater pressure on his opponent to get his first serve in play.

Here's some information your child can use when he's facing an opponent with a high-bouncing "kick" serve. If you've always wondered why an American-twist serve gives people trouble, even when they know it's coming, Dr. Pat Keating offers this insight. His research shows that it's not just the high bounce that causes trouble for most players, but also the optical illusion caused by the arc of the approaching ball. The ball is arcing so much that people tend to think it's coming slowly, so they base their timing accordingly. Yet in reality this high ball is rotating with topspin and actually traveling fast. Thus, when it kicks up, people are caught unaware and forced into jabbing at the ball. Therefore, your child should react just as quickly for a high arcing ball as he does for a low hard serve.

This mother is helping her son practice the desired forward stroking pattern for typical service returns, volleys, and approach shots that are contacted at about chest level. She has painted an inverted bow on a piece of construction paper. The youngster has taken his racket back at eye level with a shoulder turn. This facilitates a proper stroking pattern that is initially slightly downward, but the racket should actually travel almost straight across in the hitting zone before it finishes high. The number-one error on the service return, volley, and approach shot is to start high with the racket and continue downward — sending the ball either too short or into the net. Thus, the mother wants her son to practice finishing high on the follow-through, in order to groove a stroke that keeps the ball safely over the net and landing deep. A high finish also leaves the player ready for his next shot.

Practicing the Return

Important as the service return is to good tennis, I rarely see it being practiced. One reason most people overlook the need for special practice drills is their belief that the return is simply a forehand or backhand groundstroke; if they get blown out by a strong server, they blame the server's speed rather than their own lack of a reliable return stroke. Another problem is the overly optimistic notion some people have about what they can do with their service return. I've heard junior tournament players talk about how they aim their service return for an opponent's shoelaces, but very often I find that they have trouble just getting the ball back into play—let alone hitting a specific target area.

Here are some ways to help improve your child's return:

• Either serve the ball yourself as he practices his returns, or find another youngster who wants to practice these strokes. One can serve until he's tired while the other strives to return every one, and then they can alternate.

• Set up practice targets and target areas: (1) for deep, down-the-line returns against a server who is staying back or rushing the net; (2) for crosscourt passing shots, and (3) for short "chip" shots that force an attacking server to hit half-volleys.

• At the high-school and college levels especially, a player must be able to move in against a high-kicking second serve before it gets higher than his shoulders. So, if possible, have your child practice against a ball machine that can bounce the ball high and give him experience returning such serves (when he's reached an appropriate level).

• When he plays a match, have him shorten his backswing and try to move in against every serve, no matter how fast it comes, instead of automatically stepping back and waiting for the ball. He'll be amazed at how many balls he actually returns, and at how much quicker he can learn to react and move toward the ball when he sets his mind to the task.

The Overhead

In order to rush the net effectively, your child will need an overhead stroke that he can consistently hit hard and deep when he's driven back by an opponent's lob. He should always regard the overhead as a power play and—against a short lob—as his "home-run opportunity"; he's in control of the point and here's his chance to end it with a big bomb. However, this is also a stroke that demands careful attention during a match, for a missed overhead seems to trigger more frustration than any other missed shot, while giving one's opponent a big lift. On big points, young players seem to "choke" on overheads more than any other shot. The overhead is a "confidence" stroke that requires a great deal of practice, for I've observed that generally there's no in-between: a player either has a good overhead or a crummy one.

The Stroke

Although the overhead introduces several new sensations and challenges, the basic stroking motion is identical to the serve. The only important difference is that your child should shorten his overall backswing on the overhead by taking the racket head back at about eye level rather than around waist or knee level. This gives him the time he needs to combat lobs hit with topspin or to prepare for a ball that is falling from a greater height and at a faster speed than his service toss.

Before starting his backswing, he needs to position himself quickly and then strive for a continuous throwing motion as he goes up to meet the ball—out in front of his body, on line with his hitting shoulder. Just as on the serve, any deliberate effort to reach a "back-scratch" position on the loop will nullify the fluidity he seeks. As his body turns forward he simply wants to let his racket loop naturally behind his back as his shoulders rotate into the shot. Check to see that he keeps his chin up throughout the stroke and, ideally, that he "tracks" the oncoming ball with the bent elbow

1

2

Pointing on the Overhead

1. When learning to hit an overhead stroke, youngsters are often taught to extend their free arm and point a finger at the dropping lob in order to help them track the ball. Unfortunately, as the little girl shows here, pointing the finger inhibits the proper upper-body rotation that turns the back of her front shoulder toward her opponent. As a result, trunk motion — which should supply the main power — is absent and she must rely entirely on her hitting arm for power. This is especially destructive for kids who don't yet have the arm strength to hit the ball forcefully.

2. Instead, I like to have players point toward the dropping ball with the bent elbow of their non-hitting arm, then, as they swing, point their finger with a roll-out type of motion. This automatically produces the desired shoulder rotation.

of his nonhitting arm. This turns the front shoulder back and promotes a smooth, baseball-pitcher's coiling and uncoiling motion.

Anticipation, Footwork, and Positioning

One common reason why people get into trouble on their overhead is that they loaf on their footwork, and thus let the ball get behind them or drop too low in front of them as they go up to hit. So have your child realize that an effective overhead demands perfect positioning, which is set up by good anticipation, a fast first step, and proper footwork.

If he's up at the net, an aggressive mental approach begins with the question "Drive or lob, drive or lob?" as he studies his opponent's stroking motion and the position of his racket face as it nears impact. When he sees the lob coming, he should turn and run back naturally—like an outfielder in baseball chasing down a fly—or backpedal very quickly. I personally think the turn-and-run system is faster, and more natural for most people, but test your child to see which method works best. If he runs to the ball, he should take long steps to reach the general striking area, then short, quick steps to position himself for the hit.

In working with your child on this stroke, you'll very likely have to overcome his tendency to become "paralyzed" at the net as he contemplates his opponent's shot. Most players, young and old alike, want to confirm their judgment before they move; they can make fantastic mental decisions—"That lob's going to land a foot from the baseline"—but they fail to make an appropriate physical response. Good tennis doesn't allow for this kind of hesitation. The instant your child smells a lob, he should turn and get those three or four steps back while looking up to see where the ball is. If the lob is short, he now has plenty of time to get into position. If it's going over his head, he's already on the dead run and he can keep right on going toward the baseline.

Strategy and Placement

Normally, overheads should be hit before the ball has bounced. This shortens the time an opponent has to get back in position (if, for example, he has lobbed from off the court) and increases the angle for hitting an outright winner. However, lobs that are going to land near the baseline or those hit extremely high that are dropping at a steep angle may be allowed to bounce, since timing the stroke is difficult.

When hitting overheads from behind the service line, depth and accuracy are the crucial goals. Only if your child is right on top of the net does he want to go for short-angled winners; very few players can do this consistently from a deep position. Have him just become comfortable with hitting deep, and nobody will be able to return the ball offensively.

Since the natural tendency on the overhead and serve is to pull down and hit the ball short or into the net, I like my students to establish a pattern of hitting long and then gradually shortening their shot if necessary. "Don't be afraid to hit two or three balls beyond the baseline early in the match, trying to find your overhead range," I tell them, "because once you find it you'll be lethal. When you get into pressure situations you'll have the confidence to hit hard the way you should." Most people start out hitting short—and never adjust. Then when the pressure's on they're afraid to hit deep because they haven't tested that area near the baseline.

If your child keeps hitting too long but has good form, very likely he's letting the ball get too far behind him as it comes down. To adjust, he must continue to hit up through the ball while he strives to contact the ball farther out in front of his hitting shoulder. What he doesn't want to do is try to hit down on the ball (a destructive concept) or ease off and start aiming the ball for midcourt. This gives his opponent a reprieve and also the incentive to keep lobbing, since he knows he can't really get hurt by an overhead.

Should your child persistently hit his overheads into the net, there could be a number of causes: a flaw in his stroke (for instance, pulling his chin down before impact and thus lowering the racket head), letting the ball drop too low, or simply getting careless. Even the pros dump easy overheads when they fail to concentrate. I also find that players of all ages tend to be misled because in adopting a service motion as they hit their overhead from near the baseline, they unconsciously think of the distance they must hit on the serve. They tend to visualize their target area as the opponent's service box, instead of realizing they can aim for a spot anywhere on the opponent's court, up to 18 feet beyond their opponent's service line. Even when hitting overheads from near the service line, there is still more distance to play with than on the serve. Yet, instinctively, players mistakenly feel that they have a smaller target available to them and that they must shorten the length of their shot by hitting down on the ball. So remind your child that when he hits an overhead from the backcourt, he must swing up and out at the ball in order to keep it deep.

If your child is to become a threat with the overhead, he must also develop a willingness and an ability to "deck" the ball—to hit it hard, whatever the psychological pressure. Not that you want him to slug away recklessly and go for the line—but you do want to emphasize taking a full swing while staying in control. If he can learn always to treat the overhead as an offensive weapon, he'll find it much easier to avoid "choking" when the match tightens up, and he'll know he can hit hard with his normal swing instead of having to ease off. Also, though he's stroking the ball like

The Approach Shot–Volley–Overhead Drill

Here's a group drill to give your child practice in hitting three different strokes in quick succession, just as they might arise in an actual match. In this photograph, the instructor (foreground) feeds balls successively to three spots on the court. The player at position 1 starts by hitting an approach shot. He then runs to position 2 at the net and volleys back a second ball, then moves back on a diagonal to position 3, where he attempts to hit a third ball using an overhead. Much of the success of this drill depends on how accurately the instructor can feed the balls for each shot. Also, as shown here, a proficient instructor will keep the action moving at a brisk pace by hitting a ball to a new player at position 1 while the ball is still in the air heading to the player at position 3. For added fun and challenge, the instructor can set up appropriate target areas on her side of the court.

a serve, he's nearly always closer to the net, with wider and deeper target areas. He should capitalize on this advantage. If, instead, he falls into the habit of poking the ball into the middle of the court with his overhead, he lets his opponent off the hook and leaves himself stuck in no-man's-land. He would be better off just to let the ball land, hit a groundstroke, and then run back to the baseline and wait for his opponent's return.

The Lob

Most people hit the lob as an afterthought. When they're in deep trouble during a rally or looking for a way to catch their breath, they think, "I may as well lob." Not surprisingly, they don't have much of a shot because they've never learned to hit it properly on offense, nor do they spend any time practicing it. Before your child falls into this trap, have him realize that the lob is not a passive or desperate kind of stroke—hit only when an opponent is at the net—but a weapon to use at any point during a rally. If he prefers to blast the ball from the baseline, remind him that Jimmy Connors, as hard as he hits, isn't bashful about throwing up a lob, nor was another big hitter, Pancho Gonzales. In the women's game, Tracy Austin uses the lob as well as anyone to "start the point over" when she's been run off the court by an opponent's shot.

The Stroke

Although your child should elevate the ball more on the lob than on groundstrokes, he doesn't have to learn a new stroke. His forward stroking motion should be the same low-to-high one he uses on forehands and backhands and he should use the same Eastern grips. His biggest problem will be to learn to judge the speed of the ball and then to determine, under pressure, (1) how much to tilt his racket face at impact in order to gain the necessary trajectory, and (2) how much speed to take off his swing in order to keep the ball in play. In adjusting his swing, however, he must make sure he completes his follow-through and thus avoid jabbing at the ball.

As he gains experience, he should try to disguise his planned lob as a drive by turning his front shoulder, stepping into the ball, and taking a loop swing identical to the one on his groundstrokes. When he can conceal his intention to lob until the very last instant, his opponent must "freeze" at the net, which delays his first step toward the ball.

Strategy and Placement

Here are some ways a well-timed, well-executed lob can help your child against any type of player:

• A lob can be used offensively to try to win the point outright.

• A lob can be used to break up an opponent's rhythm and the pace of a rally. On groundstrokes, most players like to face a ball that's coming to them at around waist height every time. Nobody likes to encounter an arcing lob that clears the net by about 20 to 25 feet, lands deep, and forces a shot that must be contacted at about shoulder level.

• A high lob enables your child to "buy time" for getting back into position after scrambling off-court to make a play.

• As a tactical weapon, a lob drives an opponent away from the net and allows your child to move in and gain control.

• If an opponent continually comes to the net and has a strong volley, a lob forces him to win with other strokes, such as an overhead from backcourt. He can't stay at the net and win with his volley.

• Lobbing against an opponent who attacks the net can have a tactical conditioning effect on him. It will help wear him out by forcing him to retreat and to stretch up to hit overheads, or it will force him to change his strategy by staying back and trying to win from the baseline.

The most common mistake on the lob is to hit shallow and thus give an opponent the easy overhead kill. So here's the approach I advocate for when people get into competitive play: In warming up, your child should try to hit at least ten lobs and work on having the ball land within 5 feet of his opponent's baseline. If the ball goes too long, he should consider that a positive step and practice adjusting the upward angle of his swing and the bevel of his racket face. He can then go into the match with some confidence about his stroke. Once play begins, he should hit a lob early—assuming there's a good opportunity—trying to land it as close to the baseline as possible. If it's long, he should hit the next lob with the same speed but a steeper forward-and-upward stroking motion, as practiced, in order to bring the ball down a little shorter.

This approach will keep your child from falling into a ruinous trap on the lob. When most people hit their first lob of the match too long—unintentionally, and without sufficient warm-up—they tend to overcompensate on the next one and invariably they hit a weak little pop-up. In effect, they lose two straight points as a result of trying to lob (unless their opponent flubs the return), and very often they're afraid to lob again the rest of the match.

The tendency to lob short can result from several other factors: First, if your child looks at his opponent out of the corner of his eye as he goes to lob, he may unconsciously slow up his stroke. Second, if he fails to compensate when he runs to the ball laterally or toward the back fence, his momentum away from the direction of his lob will rob it of energy.

When youngsters practice the lob, a high barrier such as this 10-foot-high rebound net can be helpful in several ways. First, you can easily change the upward angle at which you want your students to hit — to practice either high defensive lobs or topspin offensive lobs — by moving the barrier closer or farther away. Second, you force them to use the desired low-to-high swing. And third, you provide immediate feedback: students can begin to see the relationship between the height of the barrier, the upward angle of their swing, and where they see the ball land. Of course, even a rope strung across the court can be used to serve the same purpose as a rebound net.

And third, if he jabs at the ball instead of taking a full swing, he'll lose power.

In addition to concentrating on lobbing deep, your child should work the following aspects into his lob as experience dictates:

• If he lobs successfully over his opponent's head and forces him back to the baseline, he should match him step for step by moving forward to gain control of the net.

• If it's sunny and the game's outdoors, he should try to lob so that he forces his opponent to look up into the sun.

• If he's near one of his baseline corners, he should try to lob on the diagonal—especially to the opponent's backhand corner—to gain extra distance. From baseline to baseline, the distance is 78 feet down-the-line, but it's 82½ feet along the diagonal.

Practicing the Lob

I like my students to understand why there are very few good lobbers in the game: simply because people fail to pay their dues by going out and practicing the shot. It takes hard work and experience for players to learn how much to adjust their upward stroking angle and to bevel the racket face at impact when lobbing against different types of shots.

The key is to practice under realistic conditions, but without the pressure of a match (just as you want to do on all the strokes). So when your child is first learning to lob, lay the ball down the middle so he can simply concentrate on his stroke and gain some confidence. But then gradually force him to run laterally along the baseline (and sometimes backwards) to make the play, and feed him balls at different speeds and trajectories so that you simulate match-play conditions. To give him a challenging target area, stretch a rope across the court horizontally about 5 feet inside the baseline. He can also practice on his own by just bouncing the ball and hitting a lob, but make sure he forces himself to run in both directions along the baseline, and backwards.

When your child can learn to venture forward from the baseline—not simply by accident or with a prayer, but with a tactical plan in mind and an arsenal of sound strokes—he's going to find that the game becomes more challenging, enjoyable, and rewarding, with greater texture and nuance. Even if he remains a nontournament player, he's going to get more out of the game by knowing the various strokes, practicing them, and trying to hit them at the appropriate moments when he competes.

14/Getting Into Competition

SOME youngsters are content to become lifelong rallyers, but I find that most kids want to be competitive once they learn a few strokes and the basic idea of tennis. They're convinced they can beat *somebody* and they want to start playing matches to see where they stand. Yet still, as widespread as competition has become in America today, adults have a responsibility to let a youngster's competitive desire surface naturally, of her own volition, without biasing her. In fact, most troubles arise when parents or teaching pros start encouraging and even emphasizing competition before a youngster is psychologically ready for a game— particularly at the singles tournament level, where there's always a winner and a loser, and where teammates can't help shoulder a defeat. I see such overemphasis on competition. Parents might tell their youngster, very expectantly, "Hey, why don't you play Lisa and see how well you do?" Some kids will respond favorably to the idea, but those who don't are forced either to disappoint their parents by saying no, or to go along with something they're not very keen about yet.

In my opinion, when a youngster begins to show an interest in the rules of the game and in how to keep score, a parent should present the options available and then let the child make her own decisions. For example, you might tell your child: "What's nice about this game is that you can play it any way you want. You can play people or you can hit against a backboard or a garage door. You can enter tournaments or you can rally and never play a match in your life. If you have fun rallying and you find somebody else who enjoys it, that's super. If you get good and want to play in tournaments, you'll have fun traveling to different towns and competing against a lot of other kids and meeting new people. So you can do whatever you want. It just depends on what you like to do best."

Once your child understands the options, your responsibility is to remain open-minded and accept whatever actually motivates her to pursue the game beyond her lessons. If you've been teaching her for months and you thrive on match-play competition, but she prefers simply to hit with friends, don't chastise her by saying: "All you ever do is rally—doesn't it get boring? When are you going to start playing some matches?" Very likely she's getting some good exercise, developing muscle tone, improving her flexibility and hand-eye coordination—and having fun—so why be distressed that she doesn't want to compete? Besides, she'll receive enough subtle pressure from people she encounters outside the family. For instance, she'll come off the court and invariably somebody will ask, "Who won?" When she responds, "Oh, it wasn't a match, I just rallied," the questioner may even increase the pressure: "Really? You mean you didn't *play* anybody?"

On the other hand, if your child is motivated by a competitive approach during practice (for instance, if she responds positively when you set up target areas and run her through special drills that simulate match-play situations) and if she's openly eager to start playing her friends, then you should encourage this instinct, for it can heighten her enjoyment of the game. When Tracy Austin was just five, there was no denying her competitiveness, whether it was in a private lesson or as part of a group. She wanted to be the best in her tennis class at the Kramer club and she begged to take part in Saturday-afternoon drills that included college kids. Even then, she had a great hunger to succeed in tennis—so she was provided with appropriate competitive activities.

Develop a Wholesome Competitive Ethic

When your child begins to challenge her friends to a match or gets involved in junior "ladder competition" (in which players challenge one another to establish their ranking within a particular age group), the pressure is on; nobody can convince her that winning isn't important to her sense of accomplishment or her self-esteem. Nor should anybody try to deny the human instinct that values winning, providing it is kept in perspective—tempered with the idea that tennis is a game, not a life-and-death drama. I like the motto that appears on a plaque in the Palestra, the University of Pennsylvania's basketball arena: "To win is great, to play the game is greater, to love the game is greatest."

My goal is to help youngsters develop a realistic approach to competition that will help insure their lifetime enjoyment of tennis or any other sport, regardless of how well they eventually learn to play. I stress that they should always strive to win, and should never feel guilty about winning, because that's the object of the game. At the same time, losing doesn't make them lesser people, nor should they try to hide in a dark corner if they fail to win an important match. "Never feel bad about losing when you know you played your heart out," I tell them. "Whatever the score, if you can look me in the eye and say you hustled and you gave your best effort, then you're still a winner in my book."

I want youngsters (and their parents) to know that a "winning-is-everything" philosophy is the surest way to ruin a beautiful game like tennis. Sure, it's fun to beat an opponent who has equal or greater talent, but if a youngster must always win a match to be happy, then tennis is going to be endlessly frustrating. I'm not saying she has to learn to enjoy losing, but she has to be realistic: half the kids who play in competition every day are "losers," and only one player goes home the "winner" in a sixty-four-person tournament. A youngster who grows up believing that winning is the only real measurement of success could be making unbelievable gains as a player—in terms of her own natural ability—yet nevertheless regard herself as a failure simply because she doesn't win a junior tournament or even advance past the quarterfinals.

Of course, coaches themselves can easily fall into the same kind of blind reverence for winning. Not only are they always working hard to help kids gain the skills that will produce more victories, their students' ability—and their own ability to teach—is in a sense measured very clearly by a tennis match: one kid wins and the other one loses. Thus there can be a tendency to view a youngster's performance in black-and-white terms, instead of recognizing that vast gray area in between that can be mined for positive and rewarding feedback regardless of the outcome of a match.

My objective is to have parents, instructors, coaches, and children alike get wrapped up in self-improvement and individual growth—and to have them place their major expectations and rewards there. Striving for improvement is all your child should expect of herself in tennis (or anything else, for that matter), and this emphasis should begin when she's first learning her strokes. As I suggested earlier, you want to set goals together and keep records that will measure her improvement in terms of "What can I do today that I couldn't do last week, or last month, or six months ago?" You'll also want her to understand, at the appropriate time, that once her improvement starts to level off—even with regular practice sessions—and she reaches her basic capabilities, she should then learn to gain her enjoyment and rewards through playing the game at whatever level she has attained.

Once she begins to play matches, measure her success not necessarily by whether she wins or whom she beats (though this can be one indication of her progress), but rather by how much she improves the different areas of her game from match to match and month to month, imperceptible as that improvement might seem at times. Help her recognize that in every match she ever plays there will be certain things she does well and certain things that are weak. You'll know you're making headway when, after a loss, she's able to tell you something like: "Well, I served better today, but my approach shots were too shallow. We've got to work on that in practice this week." Youngsters who lack this sort of realistic perspective can easily get down on themselves when they lose week after week, especially in tournament play; they begin to think there's no hope, that they're always going to be "crummy" at tennis. They can easily lose sight of the fact that they're actually improving and that this improvement will eventually pay off—if only they have the right perspective.

If you and your child can learn to approach her tennis game in terms of self-improvement, and not really worry about wins and losses, everything will tend to fall into place. She'll eventually find herself beating most of the players who beat her in earlier months, for the simple reason that most people fail to practice their strokes. Thus, their natural athletic ability takes them to a certain level, and then they stagnate.

Of course, as your child improves she'll find herself playing against stronger competition, particularly in tournament play, and she could wind up losing as often as she wins. But if you've helped instill the right attitude, she'll know how to be honest with herself after a match. For example, I've found that champions have flexibility: they can adapt to losing situations and learn from them. Instead of sulking or moaning about their bad luck or looking for excuses, they go out and work on the strokes that gave them trouble. They concentrate on the future by improving their strokes today, instead of simply dwelling negatively on past mistakes. In a similar sense, youngsters who are open-minded will often learn more from their losses than from their wins. Their mistakes and weaknesses are generally more clearly etched by a defeat, whereas a victory can often gloss over areas that need work (particularly if the match hasn't been "charted"—monitored by an instructor or a friend who keeps an objective written record).

In trying to counteract society's obsession with winning, I'm certainly not trying to promote a losing syndrome in youngsters or a noncompetitive approach to the game. I love to see a kid who has spunk, who wants to win, and who has set some goals—as long as she's learning how to handle victories as well as defeats as she goes along. It's important for a youngster not to feel guilty about being a hard-nosed competitor. If you have a child who does, you might talk to her along these lines: "Competition itself is a healthy kind of thing; it's beautiful to have the talent to beat somebody, because one objective of competition is to establish a winner. Not that you should beat a person with crazy antics or humiliate her for any reason—you have to play hard and fair. You can love your opponent but you certainly don't have to apologize for winning 6–0, 6–0. Besides, if you're talented, you should expose the world to that talent. Just do so graciously."

As a parent in this situation, you, too, shouldn't feel guilty if your child wants to win and you love to see her win—providing your wishes don't go beyond her enthusiasm. The prevailing principles should be that your child's internal system will dictate the intensity of her competitive involvement in tennis. In other words, if she's competitive and you're competitive, that's great, just as long as the two of you can handle the situation positively. But if she's competitive and you're cool to the idea of tournament tennis, you should let her get into tournament play if she wants and be careful that your attitude doesn't dampen her enjoyment. After all, it's *her* sport. Conversely, if her internal system rejects competition and you think it's a great idea, proceed carefully and sensitively, for you could drive her out of a game she otherwise enjoys.

Maintain a Perspective on Winning and Losing

Here are some other ways you can help your child develop positive attitudes about competition that will help her enjoy the game beyond winning and losing.

• If you've been teaching her the game, you've already set the emphasis on stroke production and simply trying to play to the best of her ability (while having fun). Remember, she should focus on playing the ball, not her opponent; when she goes out to compete she should "reward" herself for how well she actually hits the ball, regardless of the eventual score. Tell her: "The very best you can do is get into position to hit the ball and take the best stroke you can under the circumstances. That's all you can ask of yourself." I also like to have youngsters aim at target areas throughout the match, for this emphasizes stroke production and can give them success experiences as they play, while also helping their concentration.

• Always keep in mind my golden rule: "If you're thinking something good about your child, say it. Don't save it for later." Kind words reward her not only for the improvement you see her making as a tennis player, but also for her effort and intensity when she plays. More important, you can help shape her growth as an individual by reinforcing desired behavior—such as controlling her temper, showing good sportsmanship, and learning to schedule her time. These are the kinds of habits and traits that really count in the long run.

• Just as with losing, you should help your child put winning in perspective. If she continually wins, congratulate her after a victory—especially for being a gracious winner. If she has instead acted boorishly, remind her how important it is to be considerate of losers. Not that you have to tell her, "Be careful—you may be in the same boat one day"; but perhaps suggest, "Put yourself in the loser's place for a moment and tell me how you would feel." Don't let victories blind her to the fact that there's always room for improvement, but be careful with your suggestions. Parents of a talented youngster are sometimes so concerned with keeping her ego in check that they inadvertently spoil everything by failing to give her justified praise for a good winning effort. Instead, they brush off the victory and go straight to what the youngster did wrong, emphasizing all the work that needs to be done at the next practice session. Pretty soon she's thinking, sometimes desperately, "What do I have to do to satisfy my parents?" However successful she becomes, she still wants and needs parental credit and recognition for what she is achieving.

• Early on, and throughout your child's junior-tennis experience, you need to question your own approach to competition and how it might be influencing your child. For instance, think about the way you handle your own emotions in sports and the example you set. When your child is watching, how do you respond if you're losing badly in the first round of a club tournament? In the finals? Do you bang your racket against the fence in frustration, berate yourself loudly and needlessly, and use abusive language when you think your opponent is cheating you on line calls? After losing, are you able to calm down quickly and act civilly toward your opponent—and your child? When you discuss the match, can you avoid the common excuses and simply display the sort of objectivity and sense of humor you expect from your child?

Another area to explore is the attitude you display in regard to your child's own competitive efforts. For example, how do you respond in the stands when she's winning—or losing? Do you brag to your neighbors when she wins, but avoid the subject when she loses? Do you criticize her when she loses? Do you have punishments? Do you reward her with an ice-cream cone when she wins? If so, why not when she loses? Are you supportive and understanding regardless of the final result? Or must she start every match thinking, "I've got to win because my folks are in the stands"?

• Get in touch with the attitudes your child has formulated about competition. I find that most kids have formed strong opinions about winning and losing by the time they're five or six. They've learned through personal experience, with reinforcement from parents, older siblings, neighborhood friends, and televised sports, that winning is a lot of fun and there's not much joy in losing. Everywhere they turn they're hit with the direct and subtle pressures to be a "winner."

For example, consider what happens in many households when a youngster returns from her tennis match. Usually the parent's first question is "Did you win?" If the poor kid lost, she must now lose a second time, for the parent has made it clear that the outcome of the match is the most important issue, even if the child happened to play well in losing. This instinctive question from parents partly results from not knowing another way to launch the conversation. So think about other questions, such as: "Did you have fun? Which strokes were working best? Did you see how deep you could keep the ball? How was your second serve? Did you hit soundly off the center of the strings? How did you do when you came to the net?"

By taking this approach when you can't attend your child's match, you'll let her reveal the final score naturally, without feeling pressured. Meanwhile, you're reinforcing the idea that striving to reach her potential and enjoying doing so is what counts. Obviously, if your child comes bounding through the door and announces that she finally beat her nemesis, don't be reticent with your praise. Just try to take an approach in which you say: "Hey, that's really nice—good for you. How did you hit the ball? What stroke worked best? Were you hitting your target areas? Did you feel the pressure when you got to match point?"

In trying to effect this perspective on competition, you may find yourself going against some of your own ingrained attitudes. In fact, you may actually have to rehearse what you're going to say when your child comes home. I'm serious; these new questions won't come naturally at first. You can tell yourself, "Don't ask her if she won—ask her if she tried anything new"; but the moment she walks in the door, your first words automatically may be "Did you win?" So you'll have to work on this.

Playing against Your Child

When the day comes that your child wants to play a set or two against you, a ticklish situation arises if you're a much stronger player than she is: You don't want to crush her confidence by using your strength and experience to win easily, but it isn't much fun to dump balls into the net on purpose so that she can win a couple of games.

My advice is to play her fair and square, even if this means winning 6–0, 6–0—but let her beat herself. Never give away points and don't play an overly aggressive game by rushing the net and ending the point quickly or by trying to hit shots she can't reach. Instead, just take a little speed off the ball and try to get every shot back into play—which is not as easy a task as it sounds—so that whenever she loses a point, it's the result of *her* error. Even if you still win easily, you'll have some long rallies together, you yourself will get good practice as you concentrate on trying not to miss a shot, and your child will be reminded how important it is to keep the ball in play.

I think most kids know, perhaps subconsciously, when an adult is intentionally missing a shot, and they resent it. When you take the approach I've suggested, make it clear to your child that when she finally beats you, she'll know that she's done it honestly and legitimately—that you will have given it everything you had while hitting your best shots. This will be a great feeling for her—to beat one of her parents in a sport and to know that she's earned her victory. You can even tell her, "The day will come when you can get the ball back more times than I can, and that's when you're going to destroy me." Believe me, if she sticks with the game, that day is going to arrive faster than you ever expected. You're then going to want to know how to lose graciously to a twelve-year-old. So you had better enjoy your winning now, because you'll want to have some nice memories.

Tournament Tennis

Frenzied as the competition has become at certain levels of play, junior tournaments can still provide a beautiful growth experience for a child, starting before she is ten and continuing through high school. It's important, however, that the youngster herself is allowed to determine if and when she wants to try tournament play, that she—and the adults around her—avoid falling into the winning-is-everything syndrome, and that they can all keep tennis in perspective, properly balanced with the other aspects of the child's life.

Obviously, most children are going to venture into tournament tennis unaware of the pitfalls that actually lie ahead—dealing with their competitive nature under stress, saving face among peers, meeting self-imposed goals, and trying to measure up to the expectations (real and imagined) of parents and coaches. So it's incumbent upon the adults involved to step in and help youngsters handle the inherent pressures, and not contribute to them. Otherwise, the increasing stress can drive even the most promising young player out of the sport.

The decision to enter tournaments may come easily if your child is a gung-ho competitor and she starts asking you, "When can I play in a tournament?" If you don't belong to a tennis club (where, ideally, a junior program will already be in existence), you can find out about local junior events through your municipal recreation department. There are a number of organizations that arrange junior tournaments, such as the United States Tennis Association, the National Public Parks Tennis Association, and the American Tennis Association. Check for listings of local affiliates in your phone book, or call your local tennis club.

However, what if your child has been playing competitively for a year or two—maybe longer—and has some talent, but hasn't shown any real interest in tournament play? You don't want to push, but you may be thinking: "I'm the parent and I'm supposed to know what's best for my kid. I think she would enjoy herself and it would be good for her to get some tournament experience."

You may be right about your child; we all know that parents often have the right instincts about giving their children a hard push in a particular sport or activity. I've heard a number of professionals admit, "If my parents hadn't forced me, I would have never stayed with tennis, and now I'm really grateful to them." Prodding your child to try tournament play may be fine, but you have an obligation to consider some key questions: Have you been doing all the suggesting? Have you perhaps been so eager or persistent about the idea that your child's afraid to disappoint you by saying no? Why do you really want her to play? Have you given her a realistic idea of what she would be getting into? And can you meet your responsibility to help her get to practice sessions and tournaments?

The risk you always take here is that an initial push becomes a constant shove—to take lessons, to practice more, and not to quit. If your child doesn't share your enthusiasm for improvement or for the game, your approach may produce lifelong negative attitudes toward a sport like tennis and can adversely affect the relationship between the two of you. So the key here, if you feel your child needs a nudge, is to analyze carefully the variables involved and then to assure her that she has an "out" if she ever wants it. It's very important for her to know that if she's not enjoying herself playing tournament tennis, she's free to give it up without any sense of guilt.

Though I've pointed out the potential dangers of junior tournament tennis, such competition can nevertheless provide youngsters with many valuable experiences. Here are some of the virtues I've seen over the years:

• Youngsters have the opportunity to travel to other cities and towns (or in some cases to other areas of their own city that they've never visited). Out of town, they often stay in private homes, thus gaining insights into how other families live and learning how to get along with different people—peers and adults alike.

• They learn to set goals and what it means to strive to achieve these goals by practicing hard, organizing their free time, setting priorities, and learning self-discipline. Since their spare time is pretty well filled by their involvement in junior tennis, they have no real reason to hang out on street corners.

• Through tournament competition, kids learn the value of controlling their emotions, concentrating under pressure, never giving up, showing good sportsmanship, and having a sense of integrity about themselves. These are the traits I stress as a coach (though several of the top players in the game have obviously failed to learn them, much to the detriment of youngsters in junior tennis who follow their example).

• Children and adolescents alike need sports and recreational activities they can share with friends so they develop mutual skills they can talk about. If your child plays tournament tennis and thus meets other kids who play the game, there's an immediate bond of camaraderie and a comfortable starting point for conversation.

• Since junior tennis is basically an individual sport, youngsters don't have teammates to share in a victory or to blame for a defeat. They learn to accept responsibility for their own actions out on the court and this sense of self-reliance can help them in other areas of life. Their self-image is enhanced and they feel good about themselves.

Once your child expresses an interest in entering a tournament, do all you can to help make it a positive experience, but then step back. Let her know that you're ready (within the limits of your time and financial ability) to provide whatever help she might need for future tournaments —such as transportation, entry fees, lessons, practice sessions—but make it clear that it's her decision whether to continue.

If she grabs at every tournament opportunity, and you discover that she has a determination to play championship tennis and is willing to make sacrifices toward that goal—whether it's the city championship, the national junior title, or Wimbledon—respect her desire. But don't let her (or yourself) become so obsessed with winning matches and improving her ranking that you overlook her personal growth, on and off the tennis court. Throughout this book, my goal is not only to help her learn to play tennis to her potential but also to have tennis help her grow as a self-confident, independent person who can cope effectively with life. As I've always told the kids I've coached: "You can be the Number One player in your area—or in the world—but if you get injured and can't play again, you're going to have to make it in the outside world on what's inside you as a person: your heart, your mind, and your personality. Just being Number One in tennis isn't going to pave the way any longer."

Watching Your Child's Match

Whatever the competitive level, I believe that responsible parents should have the right to watch their youngsters play a match, and that when a good parent-child relationship has been established, the youngster will enjoy having her parents in the stands. You certainly should never feel guilty about having an interest in what happens to your child in tennis and wanting to stay closely involved with her progress, even if you stop providing the instruction and coaching yourself. In my opinion, not to stay involved cuts back communication and creates an empty relationship. There are, however, some implied obligations on your part as a parent/spectator.

First, put your child at ease by stressing that the real idea in tennis is to "laugh and hit," that it's the striving to win and to improve that's important. You might remind her before she goes out to play, "Just give it your best shot and have some fun." She'll then be free to go right out, bust her tail, and accept whatever happens—win or lose—because she knows you're supporting her all the way.

Second, if you can't say something encouraging from the stands, don't say anything at all. Sideline criticism places too much pressure on a youngster, who must compete and please her parents at the same time. Besides, second-guessing your child from the stands won't help her. You may think you can detect what she should be doing, but this might not have any relationship to what's actually happening down on the court from your child's perspective. (And verbal coaching isn't allowed in tournament play.)

Third, when the match is over, try to dwell on the positive things that happened and save your critical comments for later (and then express them as positive suggestions for improvement). If she's won, give her time to savor her accomplishment and join in rehashing the highlights. After a tough loss, perhaps you can comment: "Boy, that was a fun match to watch. It was frustrating for you, I know, but I liked the way you were hitting out, right to the end. You really kept the pressure on her. And remember how you lost your temper last week? Well, you stayed cool today, even though you were losing, and that's really nice to see. I think it helped you play better, too."

Once a match is under way, you can sit and watch as an interested spectator who applauds the good shots of *both* players—or you can play the role of a coach and "scout" your child's performance. Here are some ways you can help out:

• By charting the match, you can provide an objective review of how well she has hit her various strokes. This will give the two of you a record for comparing her performance in earlier matches, and a statistical basis

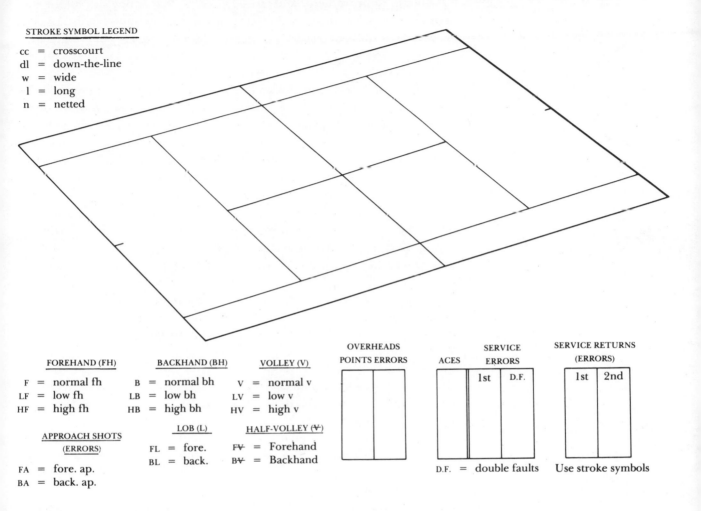

STROKE SYMBOL LEGEND

cc = crosscourt
dl = down-the-line
w = wide
l = long
n = netted

FOREHAND (FH)	BACKHAND (BH)	VOLLEY (V)
F = normal fh	B = normal bh	V = normal v
LF = low fh	LB = low bh	LV = low v
HF = high fh	HB = high bh	HV = high v

APPROACH SHOTS (ERRORS)

FA = fore. ap.
BA = back. ap.

LOB (L)

FL = fore.
BL = back.

HALF-VOLLEY (V̶)

F̶V̶ = Forehand
B̶V̶ = Backhand

OVERHEADS
POINTS ERRORS

SERVICE
ACES ERRORS
1st D.F.

D.F. = double faults

SERVICE RETURNS (ERRORS)
1st 2nd

Use stroke symbols

Match-Play Recording Chart

To use the match-play recording chart, sketch a blank court and place the appropriate symbol for each error at the exact spot on the court where the error was committed. For example, the letters LFccn placed inside the forehand singles sideline corner would mean the person being charted hit a low forehand (LF) crosscourt (cc), and the shot landed in the net (n). Thus recorded are the stroke, the ball direction, and the zone in which the ball landed. Most players chart errors only, because there are so few placements (outright winners) during a match; clusters of errors reveal weaknesses that need attention in practice sessions. Service, service return, and overhead errors are simply tallied in the boxes provided, since such errors are usually numerous.

for noting improvement and specific areas that need attention. For example, you'll know the percentage of first serves she got in play, the number of unforced errors off her forehand and backhand ground-strokes, the percentage of serves she returned, and her efficiency on the overhead and lob.

• Observe how well she tackles her trouble areas. Does she go for the shot she knows she should hit, at the risk of losing the point? Or does she opt for expediency by avoiding her weaker strokes whenever possible (for instance, by "running around her backhand" to hit a forehand, by letting overhead-stroke opportunities drop so that she can hit a safe ground-stroke, or by retreating to the baseline instead of advancing to the net after coming in for an opponent's short ball)?

• Watch for traits such as hustle, competitive spirit, sportsmanship, and good etiquette that have value far beyond the outcome of a particular match. This perspective is crucial, because it's easy to become fixed on your child's negative performance and to overlook her quiet, positive actions.

• If you discussed a "game plan" with your child before the match (a recommended aspect of prematch preparation), try to note whether she's following what she set out to do in the way of overall strategy, tactics, and shot selection.

By getting involved as a "scout," you'll have numerous areas to discuss with your child—in an objective fashion and at the appropriate time—once the match is over. You'll be able to move past the final score and talk positively about the match she played, thus reaffirming your insistence that the outcome of a match is only incidental to your interest in her tennis game. Of course, this doesn't mean that you want to take the fun out of her victories by coming up with your charts and telling her right off: "I don't know how you managed to win—you only got twenty-eight percent of your first serves in play. And you made thirty-three unforced errors with your forehand." She deserves her chance to feel good about the victory. Plus, her adrenaline will be flowing so intensely that her mind can't really focus on charts and statistics. As you gain some insight into your child the competitor, you'll discover the most effective time to rehash the match together—to cover what worked, what didn't, what was learned, and what should be highlighted in the next practice session.

Similarly, your child often may need time by herself to recover from a defeat in her own way (even if you both agree that "winning" isn't the most important issue). Again, you'll learn to sense when she needs space, when she needs your arm around her shoulder, and when she needs verbal support. One of the nice things about scouting her match with a constructive purpose in mind is that this will always provide tangibles you can praise if she loses. Remember, a youngster who loses often has a tendency to think she's all bad, and it's your responsibility to help identify those things that she has done well, or where she has improved in terms of her own previous performances. For example, when you check your charts you may discover that she got more first serves in play than in any of her four previous matches. And although she may have had an inordinate number of errors from the baseline, she hit six out of eight overheads for winners, whereas just a couple of months ago the stroke was a real handicap.

Ultimately, you want your child to know that you're not judging her by the number of matches she wins, but by how hard she works to improve, by her willingness to experiment with her strokes, by her attitude as she plays, and by the way she controls her emotions. This is what will make the time she spends playing tennis—and the time you spend with her—a treasured experience for both of you.

15 / Match-Play Strategy, Tactics, and Psychology

LIKE many parents, you may be overly concerned about the relationship between your child's success on the tennis court and his grasp of strategy, tactics, and psychology. Certainly these aspects deserve close attention as he works to get the most he can out of his strokes and his ability to cover the court. Shot selection and "mental toughness" can, in fact, prove decisive when he's playing under pressure or against a player of comparable skills. But don't let all the sophisticated theories obscure a basic truth about tennis: Winning ultimately boils down to who has the best strokes under pressure. Your child may develop an intricate, sinister strategy for handling a particular opponent—but does he have the weapons to put this plan into effect? You can talk to him about the virtues of positive thinking, but if he has a lousy forehand and a lousy backhand, the most positive attitude in the world can't bail him out; it will just make it easier for him to lose with a grin.

Jimmy Connors typified the attitude most pro players have about strategy and tactics when he told me: "We all know where the ball's going—where we want to hit it and where our opponent is going to try to hit it. The problem is, Can you make the shot?" The pros know, for example, that when they're on the baseline and their opponent comes to the net on an approach shot, the tactical options are clearly defined. They can either hit to the opponent's left, to his right, over his head, or at his navel. Reduced even further, the only option is to drive or lob. Even the pros don't have to be brilliant strategists in this situation, because the real question is: Do they have the basic weapons?—the ability to hit a down-the-line passing shot, a sharply angled crosscourt shot, or a deep lob that forces their opponent back.

Sound basic strokes rather than complex strategy or tactics are also what's crucial on the serve. A good server will generally aim for his opponent's backhand corner because that is normally his weaker side.

The opponent knows this, and the server knows that his opponent knows, but he still aims for the backhand side because that's his best tactical option. So once again the issue becomes: Does he have the essential weapon (an accurate serve)? And, if so, does his opponent then have the essential weapon (a good-enough backhand to get it back)?

Since the basic strokes themselves are what matter most, you can relax when you start talking to your child about strategy (which is his overall game plan) and tactics (the methods he uses to implement the strategy). There are many interesting areas to explore together, but neither of you should become intimidated by the notion that there are countless untapped horizons to worry about. There are only four basic concepts in strategy that I teach, and they determine how the game is played at every level of competition:

- Keep the ball in play.
- Keep it deep.
- Hit it away from the opponent—if possible—so that he can't return it or is forced to hit on the run.
- Hit it to his weakest side.

In the early stages, that's all one really needs to worry about. The only thing that changes is a player's ability to master these concepts by becoming adept at using variations in shot trajectory, ball rotation, and ball speed. Tracy Austin did such a great job of grooving her ground-strokes, with the help of her second coach, Robert Landsdorp, that not until *after* she had won the U.S. Nationals in 1979 did she feel she had to start developing an all-court strategy—in her quest to become No. 1 in the world.

Throughout this book I've placed my emphasis upon developing the best possible stroke production, for I know that everything else—strategy, tactics, and match-play psychology—will then tend to fall into place when your child goes out to play. So now the key factor is to work on a simplified, sensible strategic approach to the game that has two basic goals: teaching your child (1) to select his shots intelligently and (2) to block out the external stimuli and extraneous thoughts that can inhibit his swing and keep him from taking his best stroke. Instead of trying to find new things he can think about that might help him win, you should worry about reducing the mental clutter so that he's free to concentrate on the hit. Remember, there are actually very few variables to manipulate—mentally or physically—during a match. All the analyzing should be done beforehand, during practice sessions and in review sessions.

And as I've stressed, always remind your child that the best he can do is to make a strong effort and have some fun while he's competing. If he can get wrapped up in self-improvement, winning will take care of itself.

Keep the Ball in Play, Down the Middle and Deep

Whether your child is a beginner or has ideas of going to Wimbledon, he needs to worry about only two basic concepts when hitting during a baseline rally: (1) keep the ball in play, and (2) aim it down the middle and deep (until he can control his shots into the corners). He may complain that this sounds like a dull way to play tennis, but you can assure him that he'll never get bored with winning. In all the years that I've been in the game, I've never heard anyone complain, "Nuts, I won again."

The more successful your child becomes, the more he'll realize that exotic but low-percentage shots and unique stratagems seldom bring fame and fortune. He'll discover the truth of what Jack Kramer has always said: "Tennis is giving your opponent one more chance to take gas." Even in pro matches charted over the years, unforced errors (such as hitting the ball into the net or beyond the boundary lines) end the point more often than placements (shots hit so accurately that an opponent cannot reach them with his racket) and forced errors—in which an opponent gets his racket on the ball but has insufficient time to execute the swing properly. In beginning-to-intermediate-level tennis, there are often twenty or thirty errors for every outright winner, which explains why players at this level can more easily recall their great shots than advanced players can.

When your child first goes out to play a match, his only real strategy should be to strive for as much depth as possible while trying not to miss. You might tell him, "Don't try anything fancy—just see how many balls you can hit over the net without missing." Right away he'll begin to appreciate the fundamentals you've been working on in practice, such as concentrating on the ball and getting into position quickly, and he'll realize the reality of tennis: You beat yourself, or the other person loses to you.

In baseline rallies, once your child gains some control over his groundstrokes, have him begin aiming for an imaginary semicircle with a 10-foot radius in front of the center mark on his opponent's baseline. Help him learn to visualize this target by marking off the area for him in practice. Then gradually shrink the target area to a semicircle with a 5-foot radius. Going "down the middle and deep" is hardly an easy task—try it yourself when you go out to play—but it gives your child a system that is easy to remember under pressure and that offers a number of virtues. For example:

• The net is about 4½ inches lower in the middle than at the singles sideline, thus providing a greater safety margin.

• It keeps his opponent from returning the ball at a sharp angle; he'll have to hit from behind the baseline and at most he can run your child laterally about three or four steps in either direction.

1   2

• Your child greatly increases his chances of receiving a short ball, which is his goal in good tennis.

• By concentrating on depth, he will hit the ball too long at times, but he may get an occasional lucky line call. He can't get lucky when his shot lands in the net.

• Instead of worrying on each shot about where he should hit the ball, he can concentrate on one constant target area.

If your child asks you, "Who can I beat playing that way?" you can tell him, "Almost anybody in the world." I've yet to see a player who couldn't win by keeping the ball in play. Marita Redondo wasn't afraid to admit that she used this strategy to beat Chris Evert Lloyd in a World Team Tennis match. "I was trying to keep the shots deep on her," she said. "You can't give Chris the angles because she'll come back and hit a better angle. So mostly I tried to hit the ball down the middle." (I would add that this is exactly how Bjorn Borg plays most of the time.)

One drawback with this down-the-middle system is that an opponent doesn't have to run or stretch for the ball along the baseline. Also, an opponent with a particularly weak forehand or backhand can step around and hit from his stronger side. However, if your child can keep the ball deep, he's not going to get pushed around. And once he has learned to hit a straight ball consistently down the center, he can move his target area into his opponent's weak-side corner by making just a slight adjustment in the direction of his swing and follow-through.

Target Practice

1. This instructor (foreground) has fashioned a 5-foot-radius semicircle out of white cards to help her students practice my "down-the-middle-and-deep" concept for baseline rallies. A rope or a chalked line can serve the same purpose. Without a visual target area, some youngsters think they are hitting the ball deep, though their shots are actually landing near the service line. A good instructor will always have such objective techniques for measuring progress.

2. Once your child has learned to hit her groundstrokes consistently down the center — and as deep as possible — you can shift the semicircle into the corners for down-the-line shots (as shown here). She can also practice hitting from the middle of the baseline toward an opponent's weak side, remembering to visualize hitting down a long, narrow sidewalk.

Another reason your child may scoff at this system is that it requires a lot of patience. Instead of trying something fancy to end the point quickly, he's being asked just to keep the ball in play and try to "outsteady" his opponent. He may not have this kind of frustration threshold. Perhaps his instinct will be to think: "Hey, the ball's gone over the net three times. I've got to do something big to win this point." So he tries a drop shot, or he bombs the ball into a corner, or he goes in for an approach shot on a ball that's coming too deep—and that's when he tends to lose.

A similar problem arises among developing junior players who, as they gain some strength, like to hit the cover off every ball, even if they lack control. They can't get very excited about just hitting the ball back down the middle, so instead of providing their opponent with an opportunity to beat himself, they give him a helping hand by attempting too many shots that are statistically unsound or beyond their ability. They think they can push their opponent around the court by hitting with wild abandon and unbelievable accuracy from the baseline, but very few players have ever been able to play with this kind of control. "Going for the lines" sounds gutsy, but it's also foolhardy, for the hitter puts all the pressure on himself; if he's slightly off on his swing, he hits his ball out. Even Jack Kramer—the originator of the "serve-and-volley," attacking type of game—played everything for position and percentages. "Deep and safe" was his advice.

Attack the Net

Unless your child has a long fuse and can learn to hit extraordinary groundstrokes like Bjorn Borg, the day will come when he can't afford to simply camp at the baseline and ignore his opportunities to attack the net—if he hopes to keep advancing in junior tournament play. This is particularly true beyond the twelve-and-under division. He'll need to acquire the strokes and mental aggressiveness essential to operate between the baseline and the net, either as part of his own strategic design, or in response to opponents who force him to come up.

Of course, an eagerness to come to the net may not be your child's problem. Instead of spending time developing a steady baseline game, he may want to attack before he has learned the necessary strokes or how to sense the right opportunities. This is a common problem among intermediates who know a little about the game and who hate extended rallies. They feel they can somehow win without any real strokes by having a keen knowledge of tactics, so they say: "Hey, Vic, how do the pros play? That's how I want to play." I tell them, "Well, most of them serve and attack on fast surfaces." So these intermediates get into a match and they try to attack—but they beat their own serve to the net. If they stay up there and try to volley, their opponent has an easy time hitting the ball past them or giving them a "fuzz sandwich."

Therefore, whatever your child's ability at the baseline and despite his temperament, he can't simply run up to the net and expect to win points. He must learn in stages how to work his way up there, without losing respect for the baseline. Former champions such as Jack Kramer, Pancho Gonzales, and Ted Schroeder have all said that they first learned to keep the ball in play as youngsters, and then developed their big strokes as they matured.

Starting out, your child must build his defense at the baseline by developing sound groundstrokes. When his shots go deep, he denies his opponent a short-ball opportunity and increases his own chances on the return. A strong baseline game also gives him something to rely on when his offense isn't working. A lot of offense-minded youngsters who neglect their groundstrokes are dismayed at how their game just falls apart when they're having trouble with their serve and volley.

Once your child starts to work on his approach shot, volley, and overhead, he must learn to think and react aggressively in order to capitalize on short-ball opportunities. Most intermediates have trouble making the transition to an attacking type of game because they're accustomed to reacting defensively—physically and mentally—during a baseline rally. So, though they're waiting for the first short ball, when it comes they move in, hit the ball, then automatically back up. Or, they stand flat-footed on the baseline until the last moment instead of getting a fast first step forward. You can help your child avoid this trap by reminding him that statistically the next ball is likely to be short, because very few intermediates have learned to keep the ball deep—otherwise they'd be more-advanced players.

As your child's serve improves, he can also begin to advance toward the net after his first serve instead of simply staying back and waiting for the first short ball. But first he must have:

• A hard first serve. If he's getting hit in the back of the head with his own serve as he tries to go in, he must stay back.

• A well-directed serve. He should only advance behind a serve he knows is going to produce a weak return. If he doesn't know where it's going but he advances anyway, his gamble is much greater.

• Proper footwork after the follow-through on the serve.

• A strong volley. Coming to the net is, in most cases, a wasted effort if he can't end the point outright or keep the pressure on his opponent with a deep volley.

• A body that's in good shape. If he's looking for oxygen after the first four or five games, his subsequent performance is going to suffer as he tires.

Select Shots Intelligently

At any competitive level, the winners are nearly always those who strive for consistency by playing the percentages. They stick to the shots they control best and save the temptation shots for practice sessions. The losers are those who take all the risk by trying to end the point with shots they don't really "own."

In order to play with this concept in mind, your child must have a realistic idea of how well he can control his different shots. One way to do this is for you to chart his matches by recording where his errors occur and on what strokes (see page 299). Another method is to mark off target areas at practice and then see which ones he can come closest to most of the time hitting a particular stroke. Those are the shots he should hit in a match, when he has a choice. (Ultimately, if he really "owns" a shot, he should be able to land the ball inside a 6-foot-diameter circle—when fatigued and under pressure. A lot of players are great at 9:30, but often the match doesn't start until 10:00—and they have no shots once the pressure is on.)

As I've said, your child at first will simply want to concentrate on going "down the middle and deep" in a baseline rally. Any other thoughts about strategy or tactics are counterproductive at a beginning level. But let's say he improves and you want to test his groundstrokes against a net-rusher (assuming he has practiced hitting such passing shots). You should stand on that imaginary X on the court (halfway between the net and the service line and 3 feet to either side of the center line) and then feed balls to his backhand and forehand. See how well he can hit the ball past your outstretched racket—going down-the-line and crosscourt—and how effectively he can lob. Also make sure you give him balls at different speeds and trajectories and that you make him run and hit along the baseline.

What you learn together should help make him much more realistic about his shot selection during a match. For example, he may realize that his best option is to simply drive the ball at his opponent and at least force him to win the point with a good volley. This realization should help clear his mind so that he can focus on stroke production rather than also worrying about tactical variables ("Should I lob? . . . or should I go down-the-line?"). Similarly, if his opponent has hit to the backhand corner and is approaching the net, and your child's best return shot is a crosscourt drive, he should go with his strength. Even if it's the same shot all through the match, he at least forces his opponent to make a play instead of handing him a weak down-the-line attempt or a shallow lob. He can then work on these weaknesses in practice.

Here are some related concepts to help your child learn to select his shots intelligently:

• I've come to the conclusion that variety ruins more people on a tennis court than anything else, so have your child take pride in hitting his high-percentage shots, keeping them inside the boundaries and letting his opponent do all the gambling. Statistics show that someone is always about to make an error. Better the opponent than your child.

• When he's on the defensive or in trouble (pulled off the court, for instance), he should always hit the shot that has the highest probability of simply getting him out of the hole. If he can just get the ball back into play—instead of trying for a miracle shot—his opponent may surprise him by dumping the ball into the net.

• When in control of the point, your child should continue to rely on the shots that have put him there. If he tries to end the point outright by getting fancy, then the pressure's on him to execute perfectly; if he misses, he could give his opponent a big boost and create a loss of confidence for himself.

• For when the pressure's on, the best system I know was promulgated by Rod Laver: Hit the shot that should be played, regardless of the score. When your child gets into a tight situation (once he has some control of his different strokes), he shouldn't let the pressure dictate a change in his normal, logical shot selection. If he's one point away from losing the first set and he gets an approach-shot opportunity, his tendency might be to think, "I just want to play it safe and down the middle and then get back to the baseline." Instead, he should try to hit the ball crisply to his opponent's backhand corner and follow it in. Even if the ball goes long, he can compliment himself for hitting the shot that was dictated by the situation. And you'll want to pat him on the shoulder after the match because he showed some class and he's developing a habit that will enable him to play well under pressure. A youngster who adapts a logical "go-for-it" philosophy will also find it easier to adjust to close defeats, for he can only second-guess his execution, not his shot selection. (If he keeps missing a shot he elects to hit under pressure, try to determine if it's actually his best shot in that tactical circumstance. If so, are you working on it in practice? If he hits it well in practice but it fails him during a match, obviously something is interfering psychologically. One reason could be that although he has developed a good stroke, he knows it breaks down under pressure and he's thinking about *that* instead of execution.)

Don't Freeze under Pressure

Your child should accept the idea that he's going to get nervous, even fearful, during a tight match—it's a natural sensation for everyone. The real question is: Can he keep himself from becoming thrown by the psychological circumstances of a match (when he's playing in front of an audience, say, or trying to beat a particular rival)? Fear and stress can inhibit movement and, in turn, have a catastrophic effect on stroke production and court coverage.

For instance, your child may want to lob deep, but if he is nervous, his fear can inhibit appropriate muscle movement and produce a short lob that gives his opponent an easy putaway. I've also found that when a youngster is feeling the pressure or is beginning to lose his confidence, he tends to let the ball get too close to his body, which cramps his swing and leads to choppy, ineffective groundstrokes that usually land short. To counter this tendency (especially on the backhand), encourage your child to be aggressive under stress by going out to meet the ball and "hitting out." Also remember to reward him when he does this. Pressure can also cause a player to swing on a horizontal plane as he feels that "choking" sensation. So make sure your child doesn't forget the importance of lifting and contacting the ball with a low-to-high forward motion, whatever the score.

Another important concern in pressure situations involves moving to the ball. If your child succumbs to the tension or is fearful of making mistakes, he will rarely go with his initial impulses, especially when he's up at the net or should be moving in against a short ball. By contrast, all the great champions I've known have been adventurists who love the excitement of having to make the big play at crucial moments in the match—win or lose. Pressure seems to ignite their reflexes.

Thus, I always advise my students that when they're in trouble or involved in a pressure game, they should remind themselves to "get off the pad" and always try to move forward, in to the ball, as they go to hit. If they start moving defensively by heading laterally, along the baseline or at the net during volley attempts, they're going to have trouble pulling off the victory. Another hint comes from Arthur Ashe, who used to write himself a note—"Keep your feet moving!"—and leave it at the umpire's stand as a reminder to himself when he passed it on the crossover (when players switch courts every two games). When watching your child play, check that his feet don't go to sleep under pressure; he can't afford to stand flat-footed on the baseline or fail to get a fast step toward the ball on key points.

Keep Your Style Flexible

One of the similarities good players share is their willingness—and ability—to make adjustments in their playing style during a match. Not that they start experimenting with unproven shots; but they continually look for ways to apply Pancho Segura's theory "Give 'em what they hate."

For example, when your child runs into a player who loves to pound the ball from the baseline, he may be tempted to show that he, too, can blast the ball. A sounder tactic would be to break up this opponent's timing with a mixture of change-of-pace groundstrokes, low lobs that land deep and bounce high, and strong drives. Hard-hitters often have a short fuse and a liking for balls that come in about waist high and at about the same speed every time, enabling them to maintain a nice rhythm while cracking their hips into the ball. But when the ball starts arriving at different heights and speeds, they can never get in the groove—and their stroke production begins to falter while their frustration mounts.

This same tactic of varying the shots also works well against players who rely on a lot of wrist action. Wrist-rollers can generally be identified by the way their racket face comes well behind their body on the backswing as they lay their hitting wrist back, and by occasional shots that go over the back fence when their timing's off. They like to think of themselves as "finesse" players, but they're vulnerable against anyone who can apply the axiom "Never give wrist-rollers the same-paced shot twice in a row." When the ball always arrives at relatively the same speed, they can learn just when to roll the wrist. Their groundstrokes start unraveling, though, when the balls come fast, slow, medium, fast, medium, slow, slower . . . and so on.

Facing another type of opponent, your child might even use his flexibility to deviate from his normal hitting pattern. Say he's come across the tall, stiff player who hates to bend down for groundstrokes. If possible, your child should keep his shots low (by hitting flat or with underspin) so that his opponent is continually forced to bend down—thus wearing him out and, very likely, driving him to frustration.

Conversely, against a short opponent, your child should try to have his groundstrokes land deep and bounce high, either by hitting low lobs or shots with heavy topspin. When a player is forced to contact the ball at around head level, he has a difficult time getting his body weight behind the shot and is forced to use just his hitting arm. In fact, nobody likes to hit a ball that lands near the baseline and bounces high, especially on the backhand side. Yet when I suggest using the high-bouncer as a deliberate tactic, some juniors tell me: "Yeah, but that's a chicken way of playing. That's how a dinker plays." My answer is: "Explain what's chicken about it.

Your opponent is going to have a tendency to hit down on the ball, thus giving you a short ball that you can attack. You also force him to rely on strong forearm extensor muscles, and even if he's got them, he's still not going to be able to hit with real power."

The key is for youngsters to become flexible in all areas of the game, not just tactics. As I tell my tournament-level players: "When you enter a tournament, you have to be prepared to play against any style of player, from the kid who camps on the baseline to the kid who just loves to come to the net. Not only that, you have to be able to adjust to all the different court conditions today. So you won't make it to the top of a lot of events if you're not flexible."

Probe and Exploit an Opponent's Weaknesses

Your child should learn to be observant as he plays—without losing his concentration—for this will help him detect patterns in his opponent's play that he can take advantage of, thus improving his shot selection as the match progresses. He'll find that most players exhibit a certain style of play and seldom deviate from it; if they react a certain way under stress on a particular shot, they will usually respond the same way when that shot comes up again. Knowing this, your child may be able to improve his anticipation and hit an important winner, especially when playing at the net or while approaching it.

For example, suppose your child stays alert and notices that his opponent is beginning to tire. Here are some of the consequent weaknesses that often begin to surface—and how your child can try to exploit them:

• A tiring player is going to start hitting more short balls from the baseline, providing greater approach-shot opportunities. He's also going to hit weaker second serves, which means your child should be ready to move in, not hang back.

• Weariness in an opponent generally leads to his using less knee bend, and thus a flatter backhand. So your child should attack the backhand side in such a case, since his opponent is going to start raising the ball more, thereby providing easier volley opportunities.

• When a youngster tires, he often starts reprimanding himself for the errors he makes. All this talking out loud is usually an indication that he's edgy and is losing confidence. Your child should keep the pressure on by going for the shot that needs to be hit, while striving especially hard to keep the ball in play so that his opponent makes most of the errors. Since a tiring opponent tends to lose his patience, the longer the rally, the greater his temptation to go for the big winner—and muff it.

Remind your child that these weaknesses are likely to show up in his own game as the match wears on, and that a smart opponent is going to be searching for them. So even if your child gets hot under the collar when he blows a shot—despite your efforts to produce the right perspective on competition—he should keep his feelings to himself. Otherwise, he'll begin to telegraph his fears near the end of a tight match and give his opponent an edge. On the other hand, if your child appears calm and fights for every point, whatever the score might be, an opponent who is a little impatient could be tempted into thinking that the only way he can win is to do all the gambling himself by hitting high-risk shots. I liken this situation to Las Vegas, where the losers play the slot machines and the winners own the machines—because they stick to the percentages.

With experience and some control of his shots, your child can learn to keep an opponent from compensating for a severe weakness—thus increasing your child's chances of beating such a "one-stroke artist." For example, if an opponent has a powerful forehand but a pathetic backhand, your child won't always be able to direct the ball into that backhand corner because his opponent will probably be accomplished at "running around" to hit his big forehand. How to trick him? At the right opportunity, your child should first drive the ball wide to his opponent's forehand to pull him off the court. If he gets it back, your child can then go straight to his backhand side and he'll have no choice but to hit his crummy backhand. It may seem foolhardy to hit deliberately to the opponent's forehand, but remember: he can't put your child on the defensive from behind the baseline.

A corollary to exploiting an opponent's weaknesses is adjusting for his strengths. Your child should try to "overplay" his court position when there is a distinct pattern to the direction of his opponent's strong shots. For instance, let's say your child rushes the net after hitting an approach shot to the backhand corner. If his opponent obviously prefers to go down-the-line returning this shot, your child should shift his normal ready position and "overplay" (slightly favor) the court on that side. This forces his opponent either to hit right to him or attempt a shot that he tends to hit less successfully.

Work on Concentration

There are a number of ways you can help your child develop his ability to concentrate properly during a match and thus rule out distractions such as the wind, the sun, comments from spectators, people playing on the adjacent court, disputes over line calls, thoughts about winning and losing, and movements, antics, or idiosyncrasies of his opponent. Yet as

I've stressed throughout the book, the lasting emphasis should be on the fact that tennis really boils down to the ball and a player's relationship with that ball.

Obviously your child is going to be conscious of his opponent, but the more he thinks about that person during the match—instead of focusing intensely on the ball—the more trouble he's going to have executing his strokes. Take a tip from Betty Stove, who told reporters after defeating Tracy Austin, then fourteen, at Forest Hills in 1977: "I really played well against Tracy. A lot of people were psyched out by her when they saw her across the court. I never saw Tracy. I just played the ball. That's all I did."

Taking this concept a step further, here's another crucial reminder for your child: Treat each shot with respect. The better players try to concentrate solely on the shot they are making, viewing it as a total entity in itself; they take each shot in sequence and give each one the respect it needs, without worrying about the past or thinking ahead to what they're going to do with their opponent's return. For example, when such players prepare to advance against a short ball, they know they'll want to reach as good a net position as possible if they have to volley—but first they concentrate only on hitting a deep approach shot. What I like to tell my students is "Take good care of each shot—it may be your last." The tendency is to think there will be a tremendous number of shots on every point, and thus people talk about how they like to set their opponent up with a variety of shots. Or they may think to themselves as they play, "I know I'm crummy now, but on the eighth shot I'll be great." Unfortunately, statistics show that a point will rarely last that long. Even in the pro game, on a fast surface the ball crosses the net an average of only 2.6 times before an error is made.

The smart players also treat each point and each game as tremendously important, while those who worry instead about the overall score fall into a dangerous trap. For example, a lot of players who get ahead 40–love are tempted to take wild chances—like trying drop shots from near the baseline—and very often they miss, giving their opponent a reprieve and often changing the momentum of the game. Then there are those tennis buffs who theorize that the seventh game or the ninth game of the set is the most important in a close match—which may lead them to play with less intensity and concentration early in the set.

Your child may not give much thought to concentration until he realizes he's playing poorly or carelessly, at which point he might begin banging his racket against his body while admonishing himself, "Concentrate, dummy, concentrate!" If you haven't discussed this with him beforehand, he may assume the trick to better strokes is simply to apply himself to thinking hard about the task—but then all he's doing is concentrating on *concentration*, which is actually distracting. Instead of focusing on the ball and taking care of each shot, he's simply reminding himself that he's playing terribly. And, as the visual-imagery experts tell us, that negative image is what he'll have on his next shot. The game is tough enough without making it tougher. So here are some ways your child can learn to concentrate solely on the shot he is making:

• He can develop little checkpoints on his swing that keep him involved in the present. For example: "Hit with the palm" on the forehand; "Knuckles down and A.T.A." on the backhand; "Chin up" on the serve; "finish high" on the volley.

• Whenever he finds his mind wandering, he should refocus on the ball, with a reminder to himself such as "Here comes my friend." I find this is a less threatening phrase for kids than "Watch the ball!"

• Between points, some people try to find a thought, image, or mannerism that relaxes them under pressure and helps keep external stimuli from intruding. Your child might want to see what works best for him—perhaps focusing on his breathing. I know that when you count to four as you breathe in and again count to four as you exhale, it's very difficult to think about anything else.

• If your child is to treat the shot he is making with respect, he must avoid dwelling on the volley he just dumped into the net or on a questionable line call. The unfair calls and the crummy shots tend to "even out" on both sides in a close match. He should expect such minor setbacks as part of the game and not let them pull him apart.

• Just *thinking* too much out on the court—about strategy, the score, or the opponent—is a trap to avoid. I've found that the pros do very little intellectualizing during a tennis match, because they want to be totally free to concentrate on hitting the ball. "When I start to think too much on the tennis court," Ron Laver once told me, "that's when I know I'm going to lose." So as you watch your child play, try to sense whether he's thinking about too many things. Some kids get so overwhelmed with details about stroke production and tactics that it detracts from their play—and their enjoyment. If this is happening to your child, talk to him about it after the match. Then, before he goes out to play again, tell him: "Forget everything that you've been working on in practice. Just go hit the ball and have some fun."

Prepare to Win Whether You Lead or Trail

Ideally, the overall principles I've been discussing in this chapter should be applied by your child throughout the match, whether he's serving in the opening game or at 5-all in the third. Of course, this doesn't happen in real life. People think, react, and play differently depending on the situation—when the score's 40–love as opposed to deuce, when they're comfortably ahead in the match rather than far behind, or when it's the first set instead of the third. We've all seen or heard about the player who can do no wrong until he gets close to winning, when suddenly his game begins to unravel. And we know about the opponent whose game, in shambles, suddenly pulls together. Though it happened about thirty-five years ago, I can still remember the Junior Davis Cup match I won after my opponent missed an easy overhead when he had reached match point. (The final score was 0–6, 7–5, 6–0.)

There are a number of tactical and psychological factors you can work on with your child that will help him build competitive toughness and an awareness of what's going on in the match so that he can maximize his chances of finishing off an opponent when he's ahead, or fighting his way back when he falls behind. The thinking is actually interchangeable in many cases, but I'll first isolate those situations that apply when your child is ahead.

How to Hold On to the Lead

• Your child should never feel guilty about winning, especially if he gets into junior tournament play. I'm not trying to promote a "killer instinct" in young players, whereby they enjoy humiliating an opponent, but I like an attitude that says, "The rules of competition are that one person wins and one loses—and I'd rather not lose." To me, this means going all out to win by the best score possible, fair and square, without any regrets. As I like to tell juniors: "It's important for you not to apologize for wanting to win and for wanting to defeat somebody. If you are good enough to beat an opponent 6–0, 6–0, you should do it, to be true to yourself. If you start giving him a couple games to make him feel better, you are not recognizing your responsibility to the sport, nor his. His responsibility is to get only what he earns and yours is to allow him only what he earns."

Some kids then ask me, "But what if I'm playing my best friend?" I tell them, "You can be a generous friend right after you've won the last point." One thing I've always liked about many of the Australian players is that they're the greatest of friends—until they go out to play each other. Then it's survival of the fittest. But afterward, win or lose, they go right back to being friends.

• Your child can play relaxed, but he should never ease up when he has an opponent in trouble. If he feels sorry for his opponent and proceeds to give him breaks on line calls, or just keeps the ball in play when he could end the point with an outright winner, his opponent may suddenly find new life, turn the tide, and wind up winning. In the same vein, let's say your child is winning nearly all of his points by hitting to his opponent's backhand, and his opponent is rapidly losing all of his confidence. Yet suddenly your child decides to "keep things balanced" by hitting to his forehand—and the opponent promptly knocks off a big winner and starts making a comeback. This is a common occurrence in junior tennis, so tell your child: "Stick with your best-percentage shots. If you're winning two out of three points, you can never lose a match in your life."

• If your child's aggressive playing style is controlling the match, he shouldn't change that style unless his control is beginning to slip away, or has ceased. When your child gets way ahead in an important match, he may be so startled at his good fortune or so unsure of himself in that position ("What am I doing beating this guy?") that he tends to start playing conservatively, hoping he can quietly close out the match before his opponent wakes up. But by playing "close to the vest" when he senses a victory, he's not the same player who piled up that big lead, and it can quickly evaporate. Momentum is an elusive element and often impossible to retrieve once lost.

• To help keep his eagerness to win from ruining his concentration when victory is near, your child should let his opponent do all the extra thinking while he just takes care of each shot. Most youngsters have trouble playing well as they come close to winning because they get emotionally involved and their minds increasingly wander. They tend to dream of victory, instead of reminding themselves: "I've been winning by concentrating on each shot. If I stick to this system, I'll probably keep winning, and that's the best I can do. All these other thoughts just mess me up." For example, if a child breaks his opponent's serve and goes ahead 5–3 in a set, he often makes a fatal mistake by thinking, "Now I've got him if I can just hold serve," instead of simply concentrating as he has been doing all along. He has avoided thinking about winning or losing, and he should continue to do that. He may want to focus on a simple checkpoint such as "Chin up, watch the ball." However, if a person is really playing well, he shouldn't have to focus on stroking checkpoints. He should just hit, having grooved those checkpoints in practice.

• Though your child should maintain the aggressiveness that has brought him close to winning, he shouldn't forget about patience. If he gets overconfident ("I've got this match in the bag!") or overeager for the kill, he may try to polish off his opponent too quickly by hitting shots he doesn't "own." He'll be tempted to go for the exotic but low-percentage shots instead of calmly maintaining his winning system, and the resulting errors can very often help his opponent gain his momentum.

• Good tennis is a game of "closing out the point" at every opportunity, and not letting an opponent keep playing. Although this seems to contradict my basic advice to keep the ball in play deep and let the opponent make an error, there comes a time when one common denominator among most winners is their ability to find ways to win a point by seizing the initiative. This is often the deciding factor when two opponents of relatively equal ability square off. Basically, a player closes out the point with his volley and overhead, since outright winners from the baseline are rare. His effectiveness depends partly on anticipation and aggressiveness, and partly on good technique, for not only must he learn to crowd the net for excellent volleying position and to retreat quickly for the overhead, he must hit both shots hard and deep—and not be content with simply keeping the ball in play (assuming he has gained some skill with these strokes).

How to Come from Behind

When your child falls behind in a match, there should be only a couple of modifications in his strategy and outlook that differ from when he's ahead.

• When he's winning and playing well, he probably shouldn't change his rhythm or the pace of the game; but if he's losing, he should try to disrupt his opponent's tempo and get him out of that winning groove. One good method is to increase the time the ball is in the air, either by lobbing during a baseline rally or by taking the pace off his groundstrokes while keeping them deep. This increases the anxiety level in a short-fused opponent by forcing him to think longer about his next shot. Off-speed shots can also frustrate an aggressive opponent who thrives on hard-hit balls.

• Another possible way to upset an opponent's winning pattern of play and make a comeback is to increase the number of variables that he must confront. For example, when your child rushes the net at every opportunity, he increases the chances that his opponent will take his eyes off the ball as he swings (especially if he lacks confidence in his passing shot). Even if your child has a weak volley, just the fact he's coming to the net may bother his opponent. Most players don't like to be attacked; many want to sit back at the baseline and wait for an error to occur. When they see their opponent coming to the net, they know that they must execute—right now—or it's all over. (You'll occasionally see players who are losing take time between points to tie and retie their shoes, obviously hoping they can disrupt their opponent's momentum. Not only is this against the rules—play must be continuous—it's the sign of a con artist more than a tennis player. If a player's trying to use his shoes to pull him out of a hole, he's in deep trouble.)

• If your child loses the first set, he shouldn't automatically junk his primary game plan unless he knows his only hope is to try a new approach that can stall his opponent's momentum. When he's playing well and he's convinced his plan can still work—that the real problem is an opponent who's hitting great shots, or getting some lucky breaks—then all he can do is hang in there, keep the ball in play, and hope his opponent will revert to his natural ability level. By learning to analyze a match in this way, and not panicking when he gets behind, he'll often find himself pulling ahead ultimately. Here's where advance charting and study of an opponent's strengths and weaknesses will really pay off. If your child knows that his opponent is able to camouflage certain weaknesses only until he starts to tire or crumbles under persistent pressure, then he can confidently stick to his original game plan even after losing the first set. Against a hard-hitter who likes to go for outright winners, for example, if your child can just keep getting the ball back until his opponent starts to miss more frequently, the opponent will very often fall apart.

I advise junior tournament players to keep a notebook of observations about all the opponents they play. Many of these kids will be playing one another for years in local competition, and if they update their scouting reports as new strengths and weaknesses are noted, they'll be able to devise more meaningful game plans while improving their ability to predict what an opponent is going to do in a particular situation in terms of shot selection.

• Patience is a crucial factor for the player who's behind. Often the temptation is to try to catch up quickly by taking all the risks, but that's just a faster route to losing. Your child has to take the long view and focus on just one shot at a time—the high-percentage shot—and one point at a time. There's no other formula, short of a default by his opponent.

• Finally—and this is perhaps the most important tip of all—have your child take pride in never giving up, no matter how far he falls behind. If he keeps fighting for every point, he's going to find himself winning matches that seemed hopelessly lost, for the simple reason that virtually every player in the game is susceptible to a sudden, seemingly inexplicable collapse in stroke production and confidence. Even with his back to the wall in a runaway match, your child should always play with the realization that just one little incident can upset his opponent and trigger a turnaround. A questionable line call, a careless volley into the net, consecutive double faults when the score is deuce, a lucky "wood" shot off your child's racket frame that goes in for a winner—these events can so infuriate a youngster that his attitude deteriorates and completely destroys his performance. In fact, just a little bit of "giving up" by the opponent may be all your child needs to climb back into contention—provided that he hasn't himself already given up psychologically.

When your child has a reputation as a fighter, especially on the junior tournament level, his opponents can never relax. Even if it seems they have the match locked up, they still have to work for every point and every game. The pressure's always on, because they're always thinking, "I can't let up—this kid's a fighter." They know that if their game falters even slightly, your child may still come back and pull ahead. And when a fighter gets ahead, he's even tougher to play against because he doesn't want to give up the lead. With all this in mind, the opponent often tends to psych himself right out of the match.

Since an opponent can get flustered and fall apart, it's important that your child strives constantly to "get the ball back one more time." He may be on the brink of extinction, but just one good effort might prove pivotal. For example, he might run and stretch for a ball that seems hopelessly out of reach and knock it back in, causing his opponent to blow his concentration—and the point. I've interviewed many pros over the years who have singled out a specific point in a particular match and said, "That was the turning point—when I won that long rally; it gave me a big lift and it seemed to take the starch out of my opponent."

The "go-for-it" concept can also play a crucial role in your child's comeback attempts. One reason Rod Laver was such a great player is that he never let being behind dictate his shot selection. If he was down at match point, he took pride in always going for the fundamental shot that needed to be hit—not the fancy one—and very often he came up with a winner that got him back into the match. And if he missed, you would rarely hear him moaning afterward. He'd say, "I made the shot I had to hit and I just missed it by an inch." That was his reward and that's the perspective every player should try to develop.

Psychological Warfare

In my first book, I had some fun talking about the psychological gamesmanship found in tennis, particularly at the club level. Today, as when I first addressed the subject, a lot of players are more interested in trying to build a winning game around clever psych jobs than upon sound strokes. And my advice remains the same: "Winners rely on stroke production while losers rely on psychological ploys." Bjorn Borg is perhaps the greatest psych artist in the game—not because he walks to the baseline thinking of some mental trap he can spring on his opponent, but because he just concentrates on hitting the same old boring winner time after time, letting the adversary psych himself out.

So when talking to your child about the game, remind him that he can read all the books he wants about sports psychology, but the best way to destroy an opponent mentally is by overwhelming him with good performance. Solid strokes will beat one-upmanship any time. This doesn't mean your child shouldn't learn to watch for weaknesses in an opponent and exploit these vulnerabilities, for this is an intriguing aspect of head-to-head competition. What I'm against is the youngster who continually uses rude tactics that will give him a psychological advantage by unfairly irritating, distracting, or unnerving his opponent. Besides, I've found that the more time a youngster spends on psychological ploys during a match, the less confident he is about his game and the less successful he is at winning matches. A great player, in my book, is one who doesn't have to fall back on psychological gimmicks because he's working on his strokes—and coming out on top.

I have an old-school belief that the true "champions" are those who act like champions—whatever the level of play. When they lose, they don't throw rackets, rage about the court, swear loudly, make obscene gestures, try to intimidate the linesmen, or throw sit-down tantrums. They simply show a lot of style and class, reflecting the philosophy exemplified by the great Australian players such as Rod Laver and Kenny Rosewall: "Keep your mouth shut and let your racket do the talking." When the Aussies go out to play, they don't dwell on "ego outs" or set up excuses for losing ("The weather's lousy" . . . "The court's not clean" . . . "I didn't get enough sleep" . . . "My knee is hurting" . . . "I hate to play left-handers"). If they agree to play, they act 100 percent ready; they swallow their little aches and pains, and if they lose, they don't complain. If they are sick or they feel that playing could aggravate an injury and perhaps permanently ruin their career, they don't agree to go out on the court in the first place.

Champions, as I try to have all my students realize, can accept disappointment and play the game as it was intended to be played. "If you're a champion," I tell them, "you can play anyone, against any style, under any conditions, and on any surface—and still have fun." I want kids to appreciate that tennis is one of the few sports in which two people can play a game and when one comes out the winner, the loser comes up to the net smiling, shakes hands, and says, "Congratulations, you were better than me today—and I'm looking forward to getting you the next time."

16/Beyond the Teaching Relationship

THE best reward any instructor can hope for is a happy, well-motivated, independent student. This should be the goal from the start for both you and your child, and it should come as no shock or disappointment when your role as the instructor has to end, for whatever reason. Even in an ideal instructor-student relationship, there may come a time when your teaching is blocking her advancement as a player, and the two of you will have some decisions to make.

Your child's feedback is always important, and never more so than at this stage. If you've enjoyed a productive and rewarding time with your child, make sure you aren't sticking to teaching for your own needs and satisfaction rather than for her ultimate good. She may feel hesitant about wanting to take lessons from a pro, anxious about making a new serious commitment, or afraid that she'll hurt your feelings (or your pocketbook) by asking for professional lessons. Talk about the options open to her and stress that you don't want to stand in the way of her improvement, no matter how much fun you're having. Ideally, you'll continue to play together and you'll stay involved in her tennis program, but you may be doing her a big favor—in terms of her tennis game—by tactfully stepping aside and letting a pro take over.

Of course, your child's success on the court is not always the reason for stopping your teaching involvement. It may be that the problems and strain of working with your child outweigh the joys. One or both of you may feel dissatisfied with the way your lessons are going and, after an honest try, decide that it would make sense to end your instructor-student relationship amicably. Teaching isn't for everyone, and without the pressure of instruction, the two of you can take a more relaxed approach to the game.

This chapter will alert you to indications that your teaching relationship isn't working optimally. It also offers hints on how to bow out gracefully and try a new tack. But no matter what your reasons are for finding a professional teacher, it's important to find a qualified instructor with the right approach for your child. I've included some suggestions in that area, as well as advice on how you can remain actively involved in your child's tennis progress and enjoyment.

Warning Signals: Is It Time to Step Aside?

• Dedicated as you might be to teaching your child tennis, the most important obligation you have is to remain a good parent and share positive experiences with her. The prevailing attitude should be, "Let's have fun and grow together." So when you find that your teaching style is arousing heated feelings on the court or that your role as instructor is creating a negative environment at home, it's time to find an instructor who can make it fun for your child.

• I think you should end the teaching relationship when learning isn't taking place—if you've tried different approaches but your child isn't motivated to improve. You should also stop when some learning is taking place but your child's behavior is making you so miserable that you can't enjoy the relationship (assuming that you've tried different ways to change her behavior patterns). In such a situation, you have a tough enough role being the parent and trying to guide your child in other areas, much less be her tennis instructor.

• When it comes to the language you use while giving lessons, I take a hard-and-fast stand. If you happen to swear at your child or use abusive and degrading language after a dreadful day at the office, you can set a good example by apologizing to her and then working hard to keep your temper under control. But if you repeatedly find you cannot curb your language on the court, you should get out of the situation immediately. Learning tennis is a leisure pursuit, not a life-and-death experience, and a youngster should never be expected to accept any kind of verbal abuse in the guise of "motivation."

• A primary goal should be to have your child learn tennis for herself and to play it for her own satisfaction. It's nice for kids to want to please their parents, but if you sense that parental approval is your child's primary goal, then priorities are out of kilter and the two of you need to have a frank discussion.

• Similarly, your role as an instructor is not to try to get gratification from your child's verbal acknowledgments of your effort; these will come naturally in a good relationship. But if you find that you thrive on these thank-yous and they are a necessary part of the motivation you need to continue teaching, you have an unhealthy situation that ought to be terminated.

• How do you handle the situation when your child, after talking to other people about tennis (which is something you should encourage), begins to challenge what you've been teaching? Do you feel threatened when she says, "You know, Mr. Schott told me I should be hitting my serve like this, but this isn't what we've been doing"? Do you scoff defensively at what Mr. Schott has told her—"Aw, what does he know about tennis?"— or can you take a positive tack by first asking her, "What do *you* think about that?" By eliciting her response, you avoid influencing her thinking. Then you can add your thoughts, such as, "Well, it sounds interesting; let's put it to the test and see if it can work for you." If you start discovering that you're teaching your child a lot of incorrect techniques (that won't happen if you follow the advice in this book), then you shouldn't be teaching. Either you're not doing your homework or you're in over your head, and your child is the one who will suffer.

• You also need to ask yourself how you respond when your child starts asking questions about technique that you can't answer or you haven't even thought about. For example, suppose she asks you, "How much power do you get by rotating your hips on the serve?" Would you respond positively by replying, "I don't know, but that's a good question. Let's try to find the answer." Or, would you belittle her question by answering, "That's not important—you're having enough trouble just with your toss, so don't worry about your hips"? Once again, if your child's questions are exposing your limitations, you either have to do your homework or bow out.

• If you have a strong suspicion that your child no longer wants you to be her instructor (or her coach, if she's at the junior tournament level), and you sense that she can't bring herself to tell you because she doesn't want to make you feel bad, try to give her an easy out. Ask her in a nice way or set it up by saying: "Well, we've worked a long time together and everything's fine, but maybe it's time to move on to another instructor? I'm just taking a look at the situation, but what do you think?" If she doesn't grab at this opportunity and instead says, "No, Mom, we're really getting into it now and I like it," then fine. But if she hesitates and says, "Well, maybe you're right," then I'd peel out of there fast—but in a nonemotional, predetermined fashion. It may be that your lessons have become an extension of the home, and she doesn't want that extension any longer. She may want some new experiences, with other people, and you have to respect those feelings.

• Most kids who get involved in tournament play will eventually beat their instructor or coach, whether it's their parent or a professional teaching pro. So that in itself is not a reason to end the teaching relationship with your child. In fact, you'll want her to know—without putting her under pressure—that the day will come when she will beat you, fair and square. The real question is whether the two of you together see a strong value in the relationship, irrespective of your relative playing abilities.

• If your child openly discusses securing a new instructor, it shows you've instilled trust in her; she can be open with you and you will respond by doing what is best for her. Keep in mind that when she goes to another instructor, she may discover that you are twice as good a teacher as that person and that she would like to come back and start lessons again with you. So always leave that door open.

When the time comes to find another instructor, don't think of yourself as having failed. If you've made every effort to develop a positive and productive relationship on the tennis court, and it just hasn't worked out, you've still met your obligation as a parent by introducing your child to a fun and challenging lifetime sport. Besides, though she's now moving forward with another instructor, there are many ways you can still help her thrive in tennis, as I discuss later in the chapter.

How to Select a Teaching Pro

When choosing a tennis pro for your child, you must do some careful scouting. As I've stressed throughout this book, an instructor can wield enormous positive or negative influence on your child—on her self-esteem and values, not to mention her playing ability and attitude toward the game. Since your child may idolize her pro, you'll want to know that he deserves her adulation. So really investigate an instructor's teaching philosophy, how he works with kids, the stroking styles he advocates, and the kind of person he is. What you've learned here about teaching will give you invaluable insights into the kind of instructor who will work best with your child—and you'll know which instructors to avoid.

Following are a number of ways you can evaluate any teaching pro—before you commit your money, and your child:

• *Sit near the court and study the way he gives a lesson to a youngster or a group of youngsters.* (If he acts threatened by your prior inspection, keep searching for an instructor who has confidence in his teaching methods.) Try to sense whether your child would respond positively to his personality and his teaching style. Also notice how effective he seems to be in giving his students a sound understanding of technique. For example, is he able to justify and explain the stroke being taught, based upon the physical laws and principles described in this book? If he can't do this, you're taking a big gamble, for physical laws dictate where the ball goes, not a coach's "unique" theory. Moreover, remember that talented pros never offer their students a get-rich-quick approach to the game. They know that good strokes are built by working hard on the proper fundamentals, but they try to keep it fun.

What about the pro's ability to communicate in general? Does he seem to talk too fast or too slowly? Is he inarticulate or too technical? Monitor his chatter and try to sense whether it's effective by watching how his students respond. Kids want action with the talk, so I'd look for a reasonable amount of talk with lots of action. Some pros keep their comments in rein, especially if things are going well—which is fine—while other pros are too nervous to do that; they feel that unless they're saying something all the time, they're not doing the job right. But that can turn kids off.

How does the pro you're studying treat his students? Is he friendly? Is he patient and enthusiastic, even with those who stumble every time they walk across the baseline? Does he motivate with positive reinforcement? In short, is he obviously concerned about his students feeling comfortable out on the court? You may equate a stern, no-nonsense approach with getting your money's worth, but I've always maintained that an instructor can be a nice, lovable human being—and also an excellent teacher.

Since your child is the one who's going to be affected most by the pro, she should go along when you do your evaluation and should help you make the final decision. Solicit her impressions; she may tell you right away that there's something she doesn't like about the pro. For instance, some kids just don't like a person's voice.

• *Talk to the pro.* Find out about his teaching background and his philosophy about working with kids. What experiences or training has he had that might affect how well he works with youngsters? What is his overview about the game and about technique—and does it make sense to you? If not, will he be successful in getting through to your child? Is he defensive—even hostile—in answering your questions, or does he encourage them? Remember, you want an instructor who will encourage open-ended discussion with your child.

If the pro has a busy schedule and you hate to steal his free time between lessons, offer to buy him lunch in order to have time to ask him your questions—or simply pay for a thirty-minute session so that the two of you can just talk. That may seem extravagant, but for fifteen dollars you may discover that you never want to see the guy again, even though he has developed some top players in your area. On the other hand, if you like him and sign your child up for lessons, you can be sure he'll take good care of her because he knows your concern is genuine.

I believe that every teaching pro should be required to distribute his credentials to the parents of prospective students. Not the fact that he played on the pro tour at one time or a list of the tournaments he has won, but something that says: "I studied this game under the following people and my basic philosophy about teaching kids and my approach to competition are as follows. . . . If you don't share this philosophy, let's talk." One problem with tennis instruction today is that too many people who learn to hit a backhand can immediately hang out a shingle that says TENNIS PRO and begin charging fifteen or twenty dollars an hour. To me, it's far more important that a pro have a sound theory of learning and some knowledge about teaching skills. When he lacks these insights, he isn't teaching—he's just hoping people learn.

• *Talk to the parents of a youngster who's taken lessons from the pro.* Have some questions in mind, such as: "Did your child like the pro? Did the pro motivate him to stay with the game? Did the pro love to teach? Was he fun to be around? Was he considerate of individual differences? Did he seem to know what he was talking about? Was he always on time for the lesson? Did he spend too much time on idle chatter? Did he set a good example? How did he dress—was he clean, and did he have good personal hygiene?"

• *Talk to kids who are taking lessons from the pro.* I've found that if you listen very carefully, they will give you the best insights possible. But don't start out by asking them directly how they liked the pro. Just say, "Can you tell me about the lessons you took?" and pretty soon everything will start coming out. A youngster may say, "Boy, he was mean; I was really shaking," and you can then ask, "Why were you shaking?" Also find out what the youngster actually learned about the game. If she can tell you more about the pro's background than about tennis, that's the sign of a pro who's talking too much about himself.

• *If the pro has a junior development program, try to watch the worst players in action at a practice session.* If they have a good idea about how to play the game and what they're striving for—even if they can't really stroke the ball the way they want yet—and they're enjoying themselves, then that's the measure of a great coach. He's really digging in and trying to help every student, and he's not simply coasting by basing his reputation on his talented players.

(By the way, in defense of high fees—which can range upwards of forty dollars an hour for junior tournament players in some areas—it's important to understand that many instructors must pay court rental fees out of what they charge for each lesson. Moreover, if a coach has impressive personal qualities and can really teach your child the game, he's probably worth whatever he charges. I encourage pros to explain why their fees are reasonable.)

When choosing a new instructor, decide with your child whether you're going to opt for private or group lessons. For example, if your child is already into tournament play, she may want to have private lessons (if you can afford them) in order to concentrate on honing her stroke production. Also, you may have no other choice but private lessons at your local club. Some pros must have a one-on-one relationship to be effective, and a few just don't want to work as hard as they must to give good group lessons. (The best pros, however, will work equally hard in private and group lessons, and will put in effort between lessons.)

If your child ends up taking public group lessons or tries a junior program at a club rather than going the public route, you shouldn't worry that she will miss something (other than some long, concentrated work on a particular weakness). When the group instructor knows what he's doing and has the right attitude, your child will get nearly all the coaching she needs and valuable social and competitive experiences as well. Good tennis begets good tennis: if she's highly motivated and around stronger players, it will really be hard for her not to be pulled upward by this positive peer pressure.

Ending the Relationship with a Pro

Prior evaluation of the pro will certainly insure a rewarding experience, but even after all your "scouting," you and your child may discover that he's unsatisfactory in some way and decide you want to sever ties with him. If you follow the basic guidelines I recommend for ending a parent-child teaching relationship, this decision should never come as a real surprise or shock to the pro, and the parting will be amicable.

Basically, what you and your child owe the pro is complete honesty as you go along. As I tell my students (and their parents): "All I expect is an open discussion of my strengths and weaknesses. Let me know where I stand and give me a chance to correct any problems I have that might be interfering with your learning or spoiling your fun." In my own case, for instance, my hands are always moving when I teach, and occasionally I'll notice that a youngster looks away while I'm talking because she's distracted by my gestures. It helps me a lot when students point out this quirk so I can work on it.

You do the pro a disservice by being his humble servant. When you're dissatisfied with his teaching—if, for example, he's rude to your child, insensitive to the little things she's doing right, or is trying to push her too fast—let him know that you want to talk about what's bothering you. Or let's say that as you seek feedback from your child about her lessons, she starts telling you that she's not learning much each week and indicates that she's beginning to think negatively about the pro: she's constantly challenging his concepts—in a nice way—but he's not showing a willingness to consider her opinions seriously. Maybe you even see things about your child's technique that are wrong, but the pro isn't noticing them or isn't working on them. You should raise all of these issues, and if the pro doesn't appear concerned about improving his teaching approach or his knowledge of tennis technique, I think you have every right to end the relationship.

Your honesty will also give the pro a chance to get some things off his chest. You may think he's stealing your money, but he might point out that he's spending a lot of time thinking about your child between lessons and trying to come up with ways that will help her improve, even though she's not responding with an honest effort herself: she's not practicing on her own, say, or even working hard during her lessons; she wants to do everything "her way" and won't even try to see if his advice can possibly work for her. Whatever comes out, at least the air has been cleared, and perhaps you'll gain a better perspective on your child.

Ideally, if your child has spent a lot of time with the pro, their parting will be as friendly as possible. I think this is important, since the pro may work at the club where your child happens to play; the two of them should be able to say hello and continue to discuss her tennis game even when she is working with somebody else.

How to Contribute as a Nonteaching Parent

Whatever your playing ability or knowledge of the game, I think it's a big mistake to think, "I'll put everything in the hands of the pro," and then avoid any real involvement in your child's lessons, practice sessions, and matches. There's so much more you can contribute, especially with the perspective you have as your child's first instructor. When you handle your role properly, your child will appreciate your interest and will feel comfortable about having you on the sidelines.

One way you can help everybody involved get more out of the tennis experience is to monitor lessons and matches and take notes. But check with both the teaching pro and your child beforehand. As mentioned earlier, most good instructors will enjoy having you observe from nearby the court—providing you keep your comments under control. My rule has always been that parents may watch the lessons I teach as long as they (1) don't say anything negative or critical that detracts from the lesson, and (2) offer support to their youngster, however well she plays. But once they start criticizing or yelling in any way ("You can do it, Mary—just listen to what he's telling you!") then they have to leave. It's just too hard—and it's unfair—for a youngster to have to try to serve two coaches.

Here's an involved parent who's taking notes as his son takes a lesson. After the workout he might suggest: "You're keeping your head still on your groundstrokes and your eyes are focused on the point of impact. That's good, but I think you can afford to get a little farther away from the ball. If you can extend your swing a bit by hitting out away from your body, you'll get more power without swinging any harder." The idea is to contribute positively, yet honestly, as your child's sideline observer.

Also, in a group lesson disparaging comments from the sidelines embarrass a youngster in front of the other kids and rattle her concentration.

As a nonteaching observer, you should have an open discussion with your child before the first lesson. Find out where she'd like you to sit when you watch, since it may make her nervous to have you too close. Some kids have told me that they try too hard to please the parent when he's sitting next to the court, but they can relax when he's a little less obvious. You should also explain the purpose of your note-taking, that it's a positive contribution you're trying to make and not a vehicle for negative criticism or punishment after the lesson is over. Then there are no surprises for your child and she's not going to worry when she sees you taking notes.

Instead of thinking, "Oh no, what am I doing wrong now?" she'll have the attitude, "Oh boy, Dad's found something that can help me improve." You should emphasize that sometimes you'll be writing down how great she's hitting the ball or how hard she's working—to tell her afterward—so that she doesn't associate your writing only with criticism but also with praise. Occasionally, you should give her your notes and let her read them herself, to break the pattern of you always reading them to her. Finally, agree when the two of you will discuss your notes and observations, either right after the lesson or later at home.

Of course, constant note-taking can become intimidating to some youngsters, but if you've established positive lines of communication with your child, she'll tell you when she doesn't enjoy it. You may decide to stop before that point if you find your notes are becoming repetitive and you have the same list of corrections and comments week after week. You can even give her the option to stop by saying, "Maybe you're tired of hearing my notes."

In your prior discussions with the pro, you should establish how the two of you are going to communicate as the parent-pro relationship evolves. You might say: "I'm going to be taking notes and watching my child closely during practice, so when I see things happening, how do you want me to present them? Do you want them in a list? Or do you want me to talk to you once a week and give you a five-minute summary?" This can be a nice system if the pro is receptive and you stay closely in tune with what he is teaching.

Whether or not you regularly attend your child's lessons or practice sessions—and you need not be there for every one—you can provide valuable objective information for both her and the pro by charting her matches whenever possible (see page 299). Once again, confer with both of them beforehand to determine what specific information they might want so there's a purpose behind your paperwork. And remember, effective charting can be hard, tedious work—you must watch every point—and this absorption can take a lot of enjoyment out of watching your child play. You may want to compensate by charting only the first set or just key games, such as when crazy things begin to happen under pressure. Whatever approach you take, be careful not to overdo your charting and note-taking. Some parents tend to rely too much on statistics—and overlook the human element.

If you don't want to chart matches completely, you might ask about specific aspects of your child's technique that you can watch for in particular. If she says she's having trouble with her follow-through, have her show you how she wants to look when she finishes correctly, and then note the times she doesn't as you watch her play. Perhaps she's working hard to get her racket face below the intended point of impact on groundstrokes, or trying to keep her head down at impact, or striving to initiate her backswing by rotating her shoulders before the approaching ball crosses her opponent's service line. You can watch for all these checkpoints on her swing even if you don't have a trained eye, and in doing so you can help her make some beautiful gains.

You can also contribute in a tactical sense. For example, if your child says, "Gee, I'm hitting my approach shot too short," have her show you where it should be landing; then you can draw an empty court and put a dot to indicate where each of her approach shots lands during a match. This is the kind of perspective most teaching pros miss, since they're generally at home earning a living by giving lessons while their students are off playing in a tournament. So you can really help the pro structure some realistic practice sessions for your child by bringing back a "scouting report" from her matches and giving him some insight into how she actually played under pressure. I know that I've always relied on parents to report back—and not only about their child's playing performance, but also about her attitude. If she acted like a jerk when she lost, I want to know so that I can bring it up with her in a nice way before her next match. Then my tennis lessons can become an arena for personal growth as well as better strokes.

There are still more ways you can help improve your child's playing ability and expand her understanding of the game:

• Even if nobody seems interested in your charting, keep your own little notebook and try to analyze why your child is winning or losing from week to week if she's competing. Don't be afraid to talk to the coach if your child won't really listen. Get involved and let your child know that you're making a serious study of the game in general—and of her game particularly—and you'll probably never hear her say: "What do you know about it, Dad? You're not a coach."

• Volunteer as her practice partner. If you can't rally with her, you can still feed her balls to hit from the baseline or up at the net. Moreover, you can help her document what's taking place by setting up targets and target areas, by using a stopwatch to see which footwork style is fastest for her when moving sideways along the baseline or when retreating from the net for a lob, and by watching for key checkpoints on her swing.

• Take her out to a pro tournament or a top amateur event and bring along a clipboard and a pair of binoculars so that the two of you can keep statistics, write down observations, and focus tightly on a particular player's stroking form. Instead of getting wrapped up in the ball going back and forth across the net, notice how the players move to the ball, how they select their strokes, and where they aim their specific shots. It's also instructive to notice that the ball lands deep in a good baseline rally, that most players try to capitalize on the first short ball (but often hit a weak approach shot), and that on fast surfaces the ball is usually hit only a few times before an error occurs.

• If your child is motivated about tennis, try to get her involved at the ground level by becoming a ball girl for a pro tournament. You can call the local tournament committee and find the person who trains kids for this job. If your child qualifies (prerequisites are generally an ability to move quickly, "good hands," and some knowledge of the game), she'll get right down on the court with the top players. This is a super experience for young kids, providing the pros treat them civilly (which is not automatic behavior by all pros, I'm afraid).

If all of what I've been suggesting sounds like too much time and effort just for something like tennis, think about your responsibility as a parent. If you have only a limited amount of time each week for recreation, and you prefer to spend that time playing tennis or some other sport with adult friends, perhaps you should ask yourself whether you're spending enough time with your child doing something *she* wants to do. At first you may not want to spend your time with your child on a tennis court, but it could be that tennis becomes her number-one interest in life outside of her school, her friends, and her family. It could even provide one of the most powerful influences in her life before she leaves the roost. I know that in my own life, in addition to the fact that I had great parents, it was tennis that provided me with enormous opportunities that had a far-reaching impact. So try to get involved with your child and explore what this great game is all about.

Glossary

This alphabetical listing explains the basic tennis and teaching terms used in this book, as well as some others you and your child may encounter as you get involved in the game. I've also included some slang expressions—those preceded by an asterisk (*)—many of which were picked up in my pro tour days with Jack Kramer and Myron McNamara. (You might want to spice up your teaching by including some of these terms in your lessons.) In addition to the brief definitions here, the parts of the racket are identified in the diagram on page 61, and terms pertaining to the court are illustrated on page 71.

ACE   A ball served so well it goes untouched by the opponent's racket.

AD   An abbreviated form of the word *advantage*.

AD SERVICE COURT   When serving or returning serve, the left side as a player faces the net. *See court diagram in chapter 6.*

ADVANTAGE   A scoring term referring to the lead held by the player or side who wins the first point after deuce—e.g., "advantage Borg."

ALL   A scoring term that refers to an equal (tied) score for both players or sides—e.g., "30–all."

ALLEY   The 4½-foot strip on each side of the court used during doubles play. The two doubles alleys enlarge the court from a 27-foot width for singles to a 36-foot width for doubles. *See court diagram in chapter 6.*

*AMAZON   A player of gigantic physical proportions who possesses little regard for percentage tennis and a high regard for smashing tennis balls.

AMERICAN TWIST   A special serve for advanced players that creates a high and irregular bounce that's generally most effective when hit to an opponent's backhand. (Hitting this serve can lead to tennis elbow.)

ANGLE   The direction of a player's shot in relation to the baseline (measured in degrees).

ANTICIPATION   The ability to make educated guesses as to the type, speed, direction, and elevation of an opponent's shot before the shot has been made.

APPROACH SHOT   Any shot used to approach or gain position at the net, but typically a ball hit from near the midcourt area, after which the hitter continues forward toward the net.

*A.T.A.   "Air the armpits"—a checkpoint on the backhand to remind a player to finish the stroke with his hitting arm extended upward.

ATTACK   To take the offensive rather than play defensive tennis. Most offensive tennis involves moving in from the baseline at every opportunity—attacking (rushing) the net—and quick, aggressive net play.

AUDITORY TEACHING   A method of instruction that employs the student's sense of hearing—e.g., describing how a stroke is executed.

BACKCOURT   The area on the playing court bounded by the service line, the baseline, and the sidelines. *See court diagram in chapter 6.*

BACKHAND   The stroke used by right-handers to hit balls on their left side and left-handers to hit balls on their right side. The body pivot automatically turns the back side of the hitting hand toward the net.

BACKHAND CORNER   The corner of the playing court to which one must run to hit a backhand.

BACKPEDDLE   To run backward while facing the net.

BACKSPIN   *See* UNDERSPIN.

BACKSWING   The beginning part of a stroke: the movement of the hitting arm and racket backward to a position from which the downward or forward motion begins.

BASELINE   The boundary line at each end of the playing court, located 39 feet from the net. *See court diagram in chapter 6.*

*BELL-RINGER   A server who, as the racket begins to drop behind his back, suddenly drops his elbow against his body as though pulling a chain (which inhibits fluidity).

BEVEL (OF RACKET)   Any of the eight planes at the base of the handle that constitute the outside surfaces of the racket grip. *See photos on page 174.*

BEVELED RACKET FACE   One that's aimed upward as it moves forward. Also called an *open racket face.*

BODY LIFT   The torso's forward and upward movement (ideally at the same angle as the racket swing) on groundstrokes.

BREAK POINT   The situation reached when the server is within one point of losing the game in which he is serving.

BREAK SERVE   To win a game in which the opponent is the server. *See also* HOLD SERVE.

BUTT (OF RACKET)   The very end of the handle. *See racket diagram in chapter 5.*

*BUTTERFLIES   Term used to describe nervousness before or during competition—e.g., "I've got butterflies in my stomach."

*CANNONBALL   An extremely hard serve.

CENTER LINE   The playing-court line on both sides of the net (and perpendicular to it) that separates the service courts. *See court diagram in chapter 6.*

CENTER MARK   The short slash ("hash mark") on the playing court that bisects each baseline. *See court diagram in chapter 6.*

CENTER STRAP   A strap placed at the middle of the net and anchored to the court to maintain a 3-foot net height at the center line.

CHARTING   Gathering and recording statistics on errors, placements, and other pertinent details of a match. *See Match-Play Recording Chart in chapter 14.*

*CHEAP-SHOT ARTIST   A player who continually hits lucky shots off the racket frame and the net.

CHECK-STEP   *See* STUTTER-STEP.

CHIP   The short, high-to-low forward motion of the racket as it contacts the lower back side of the ball to impart underspin. Also, a shot hit in this manner, or to hit such a shot.

*CHIP-SHOT ARTIST   A player who usually hits with underspin.

CHOKE   To play poorly in a critical situation as a result of fear or severe nervousness.

CHOKE UP ON THE GRIP   To grasp the racket closer to the throat for more control (which results in less power).

CLOSED RACKET FACE   *See* HOODED RACKET FACE.

CLOSED STANCE   A hitting position in which the feet and the belly button point toward the side fence.

CLOSE OFF THE POINT   To move aggressively and hit offensive shots at the right opportunity (e.g., when an opponent is out of position) in order to end the point quickly.

CONCEAL SHOTS   To hit shots without revealing their intended speed, direction, or elevation in advance.

CONTINENTAL GRIP   *See page 176.*

COURT   The playing surface. *See court diagram in chapter 6.*

CROSSCOURT SHOT   A ball hit diagonally from one corner or side of the court, over the net, to the opposite corner or side (rather than down-the-line or down-the-middle).

CROSSOVER   The periodic switch of players from one side of the court to the other during competition to equalize the effect of sun, wind, and other peripheral factors.

CUT OFF THE ANGLE   To move forward quickly (when volleying) against an opponent's crosscourt shot in order to hit the ball before the angle gets wider or the ball moves deeper into your court.

DECELERATION-ACCELERATION   The relationship between two moving body segments or between a body segment and a racket part. When one segment stops, the related segment or part normally speeds up (as dictated by the laws of physics).

*DECK IT   Kill the ball! Hit it hard.

DEEP SHOT   A groundstroke or volley that bounces in bounds near the opponent's baseline, or a serve that lands in play near the service line.

DEUCE   A scoring term that refers to a game score of 40–40 or any tied game score beyond that point.

DEUCE SERVICE COURT   When serving or returning serve, the right side as a player faces the net. *See court diagram in chapter 6.*

*DING-A-LING   A player who plays without purpose, continually loses, and seldom attempts to change his losing style.

*DINKER   A player who intentionally and continually hits high, soft shots to keep the ball in play and to disrupt an opponent's timing and patience.

*DINK SHOT   A ball intentionally hit very softly and relatively high in order to insure that it lands in bounds.

DOMINANT HAND   The hand that a nonambidextrous individual uses most effectively (a right-hander's right hand, a lefty's left one).

DOUBLE-FAULT   To lose a point by making two consecutive unsuccessful serves (the unforced error is called a *double fault*).

DOUBLES   A contest in which four players compete—two on each side.

DOUBLES SIDELINE   The outermost side boundary on each side of the playing court, located at the ends of the baseline and perpendicular to it. Used in doubles only. *See court diagram in chapter 6.*

DOWN-THE-LINE SHOT   A ball hit from near a sideline that travels along that line rather than down-the-middle or crosscourt.

DOWN-THE-MIDDLE SHOT   A ball, usually hit from the midcourt or backcourt, that travels along the center of the court rather than down-the-line or crosscourt.

DRILL   A practice technique or activity that demonstrates or grooves proper strokes, usually through repetition.

*DRILL IT   Kill the ball! Smash it!

DRIVE   An offensive groundstroke (usually in a baseline rally).

DRIVE VOLLEY   A high volley hit very hard with an unusual amount of backswing.

DROP SHOT   An off-speed groundstroke, hit in such a manner that it drops just over the net with little or no forward bounce. This shot is designed to win a point outright or to tire an opponent who is behind the baseline or off to one side of the court.

DROP VOLLEY   A volley hit in such a manner that it drops just barely over the net with little or no forward bounce. Also called a *stop volley*.

*DRUM MAJOR   A player who unnecessarily twirls his racket while awaiting an opponent's shot.

EARNED POINT   A point won as a result of a forced error.

EASTERN GRIP   *See page 174.*

*EAT FUZZ   To be hit in the mouth with a tennis ball during competition.

*EGGS   Tennis balls.

ERROR   A mistake (forced or unforced) that costs a player a point.

EXTENSOR MUSCLES   The muscles used to extend the arms or legs.

FACE (OF RACKET)   The hitting surface formed by the intersecting strings. *See racket diagram in chapter 5.*

FAKE SHOTS   To make an opponent believe you are hitting to a location other than your intended target.

FAST COURT   A playing surface such as cement that causes the ball to skid off it quickly.

FAULT   An unsuccessful serve—usually one that fails to land inside the proper service court. *See also* DOUBLE-FAULT; FOOT FAULT.

F.B.I.   "First ball in" on the serve will count (i.e., more than two faults are allowed) when a player is serving for the first time in the match. Never acceptable in official tennis.

FIFTEEN   In scoring, the first point scored by a player or a side. Also called *five* erroneously.

FIVE   *See* FIFTEEN.

FLAT SHOT   A ball hit with very little spin.

FLUIDITY   Smooth, regular stroking motion that's free of extraneous movements.

FOLLOW-THROUGH   The last part of a stroke, after impact.

FOOT FAULT   A serve that's disallowed because of improper foot movement. Foot faults are usually committed by stepping on the baseline or onto the court before the ball has been contacted, but can also be committed by running along the baseline before serving.

FORCED ERROR   An error that is induced by one player's strong play, such as failing to return a shot that has been hit so hard or at such a sharp angle that there's insufficient time to respond with a normal stroke.

FORECOURT   The area on each side of the playing court bounded by the net, the service line, and the sidelines. *See court diagram in chapter 6.*

FOREHAND   The stroke used by right-handers to hit balls on their right and by left-handers to hit balls on their left.

FOREHAND CORNER   The corner of the playing court to which one must run to hit a forehand.

FORTY   In scoring, the third point won by a player or side.

FRAME (OF RACKET)   The overall structure, exclusive of the strings and tape. *See racket diagram in chapter 5.*

*FUZZ SANDWICH   A shot that lands in a player's mouth.

GAME   A tennis contest that is complete when one player or side wins at least four points while holding a minimum two-point lead over the opposition. Also, an organized competitive activity to give kids practice and make lessons fun. *See also* SET.

GAME PLAN   *See* STRATEGY.

*GARBAGE SHOTS   Shots that are lucky winners—e.g., balls hit off the frame.

*GLUE POT   A player who can't seem to start running until after the ball has hit the court on his side of the net.

*GO SPAGHETTI   A teaching term used to remind a student to relax the muscles of his hitting arm as he goes to hit a serve or overhead.

GRIP (OF RACKET)   The covered part of the handle that is grasped by the hitting hand. *See racket diagram in chapter 5.*

GRIP (STYLE)   The manner in which a player grasps the racket handle—e.g., the Eastern forehand or backhand, the Continental, the Western, or the semi-Western.

GROOVE STROKES   To develop uniform, consistent strokes—ideally, proper ones that can be relied upon under pressure.

GROUNDSTROKE   A shot in which the ball is hit after it has bounced (as opposed to a volley).

GROWTH-AND-DEVELOPMENT SCHEDULE   The normal height, weight, strength, and agility expectations for various age categories.

GUT   A type of racket string made from the intestines of animals (as opposed to nylon).

*GUT IT   To try to hit the proper strokes under severe stress. A player who "guts it" attempts to hit the shot that is called for in a particular circumstance, whether he's nervous or not.

HALF-VOLLEY   A stroke in which the ball is contacted only inches away from the court's surface after it has bounced. (It probably should have been named a "half-groundstroke.")

HANDLE (OF RACKET)   The long part, between the butt and the throat. *See racket diagram in chapter 5.*

HEAD (OF RACKET)   The oval part that houses the strings. *See racket diagram in chapter 5.*

*HELIUM BALL   A high shot from the baseline that takes three days to land.

"HIT DEEP"   To hit groundstrokes that consistently land in play near the opponent's baseline.

"HIT OUT"   To make a complete and uninhibited swing at the ball, whatever the pressure. *See also* "INSIDE-OUT"; "UP AND OUT."

HITTING ZONE   The short distance in the racket path just before and including the impact point during which the ball can be hit on line with the intended target. Also called the *impact area.*

"HIT UP"   To hit the ball on an upward trajectory (on groundstrokes, serves, and overheads).

HOLD SERVE   To win a game while serving. *See also* BREAK SERVE.

HOODED RACKET FACE   One that's aimed downward as it moves forward. Also called a *closed racket face.*

IMPACT AREA   *See* HITTING ZONE.

IN PLAY   A term that describes a valid shot, hit in bounds, that will win the point unless returned by the opponent.

"INSIDE-OUT"   A forward motion by the racket and racket arm, out away from the body and toward the outside net post. (An inside-out swing is one important characteristic of players with strong forehands and backhands.)

*JOHNNIE RAY   A player who constantly cries about bad line-calls by the umpire or his opponent.

*JUNK ARTIST   A player who counts on lucky shots to win matches and is upset when he doesn't get them.

KINESTHETIC TEACHING   A method of instruction that employs the student's sense of touch—e.g., guiding his arm through the proper stroking pattern.

KINETIC-ENERGY CHAIN   The properly synchronized sequence of body-segment movements that results in maximum power. *See also* DECELERATION-ACCELERATION.

LEARNING CURVE   A graphic depiction of the rate and amount of learning.

LEARNING EXTINCTION   The condition that exists when knowledge is no longer being acquired.

LEFT SERVICE COURT (OR BOX)   *See* AD SERVICE COURT.

LET BALL   Any point that is played over because of interference of some nature (such as a ball that rolls across the court from an adjoining one).

LET SERVE   A serve that touches the net tape before landing in the proper service box. Let serves are replayed and do not count as a fault.

LINE CALL   An announcement that a shot has landed out of bounds.

LOB   A groundstroke hit sufficiently high to pass over the outstretched racket of an opponent at the net. Used primarily to drive an opponent away from the net or to "buy time" to get back into position on the court.

LOB VOLLEY   A shot hit high into the air from a volleying position.

LONG BALL   A shot that lands out of bounds beyond the baseline.

LOVE   A term that refers to the score of a player who has either won no points in a game or no games in a set.

LOW-TO-HIGH   The forward stroking motion of the racket needed to impart topspin, from a point closest to the ground on the backswing to its finishing point toward the sky on the follow-through.

*MARBLE COLLECTOR   A player who seeks tournaments that have weaker players just to win more trophies for his display case.

MATCH   A contest between two opponents (or two pairs of players) that is complete when one side wins a specified number of sets (normally either two or three).

MATCH POINT   The situation reached when one player will win the match if he can win the next point.

*MEATBALL   A player who understands nothing of tennis strategy.

MIDCOURT   The area on each side of the playing court near the service line. *See court diagram in chapter 6.*

*MR. CLEAN   A player who would rather lose points than stretch for shots that might result in a fall and dirty clothes.

MIX UP SHOTS   To change the speed, elevation, and spin of shots constantly to confuse an opponent's anticipation and rhythm.

MUSCLE-MEMORY   A nonscientific term used to describe the fact that people have a strong tendency to form repeated patterns in their physical movements. This phenomenon can have both positive and negative effects in terms of mastering reliable tennis strokes.

*NAVEL COMMANDER   A player who always points his belly button to the net when stroking the ball.

NET   The mesh fabric strung horizontally across the center of the court as a barrier.

NET BALL   A shot that hits the net and falls back on the same side as the hitter.

NET PLAYER   One who has gained position at the net and is prepared to volley.

NET POST   The pole on each side of the playing court that supports the net.

NET TAPE   The strip of canvas or plastic band at the top of the net.

NONDOMINANT HAND   The hand that a nonambidextrous individual uses least effectively (a right-hander's left hand, a lefty's right).

NOSE (OF RACKET)   The outermost tip of the head. *See racket diagram in chapter 5.*

OFFENSIVE LOB   A ball hit just above the racket reach of an opposing net player, normally driven hard with topspin.

*ONE-SHOT ARTIST   The player who tries to slug his first shot on every point—either his serve or his service return—but who hardly ever gets a chance to hit a second shot. He either wins or loses very quickly.

*ONE-STROKE ARTIST   A player who puts all his faith in one basic stroke, such as his serve or his forehand.

OPENING   An opportunity to hit to where the opposing player has left a wide gap.

OPEN RACKET FACE   *See* BEVELED RACKET FACE.

OPEN STANCE   A hitting position in which the feet and belly button point toward the net (which prevents a player from stepping in to the ball).

*OUTITIS   A compulsive tendency of some players to call "out" on all close line-shots hit by their opponents.

OVERHEAD   A forehand stroke hit while the ball is higher than one's head.

OVERHEAD SMASH   An overhead that's hit extremely hard.

OVERHIT   To tend to put too much force into each shot by hitting hard without corresponding control.

OVERPLAY   To favor one side of the court, generally as a tactic against a particular opponent, but also to compensate for one's own particular weakness—such as to overplay the forehand or backhand side.

PACE   The speed of the ball.

PASSING SHOT   A ball hit in play from the baseline that passes beyond the reach of a player at the net or approaching it.

PATTERN TENNIS   A sequence of shot-selections that has been planned before the match and that is repeated frequently. For many players, this helps reduce the need for excessive thinking during a match.

*PATTY-CAKE SERVE   A ball served so slowly that the receiver has time to eat a sandwich.

*PEEL THE ORANGE   To impart severe sidespin on a volley so the ball drops quickly at a sharp angle. The racket face contacts the side of the ball in a "peeling" motion.

*PILLS   Tennis balls.

PLACEMENT   A shot hit so accurately (and usually with good pace) that it goes untouched by the opponent—e.g., an ace.

PLAYABLE   Any shot within reach of a player.

POACH   In group drills, to move improperly into another player's territory.

POINT   The smallest unit of scoring in tennis, won by a placement or an opponent's error. *See also* GAME.

RACKET   *See racket diagram in chapter 5.*

RALLY   To hit balls back and forth across the net in the course of playing a point. A rally includes all shots other than the serve, but usually refers to when both opponents are at the baseline—e.g., "a long baseline rally."

READY POSITION   The relaxed posture a player should assume as he awaits his opponent's hit so that he can take the fastest possible first step toward the ball.

RECEIVER   The player to whom the ball is being served.

RETRIEVE   To reach an opponent's well-placed shot and get it back over the net and in play.

REWARD SYSTEM   Favorable comments or facial expressions used by an instructor to provide wholesome motivation to a student.

RIGHT SERVICE COURT (OR BOX)   *See* DEUCE SERVICE COURT.

ROLL THE HITTING ARM   To rotate the hitting arm forward in the hitting zone unnecessarily in an attempt to impart topspin on groundstrokes.

RUN AROUND A SHOT   To intentionally avoid hitting a particular stroke.

RUSH THE NET   To move in aggressively from the baseline and try to capitalize on an opponent's weak shot. *See also* ATTACK.

SAFETY MARGIN   The distance by which the ball clears the net tape.

SERVE   The stroke that puts the ball in play on every point. The server is given two chances to land the ball in his opponent's service court; failing that, he loses the point. *See also* FAULT.

SERVER   The player initiating play.

SERVICE COURT (OR BOX)   The rectangular area on the court in which a serve must land to be valid. The boundaries of the four service courts are formed by the net, the singles sidelines, the service lines, and the center line. *See also* AD SERVICE COURT; DEUCE SERVICE COURT; *court diagram in chapter 6.*

SERVICE LINE   The back boundary of the service courts, which runs parallel to the net. *See court diagram in chapter 6.*

SERVICE RETURN   The stroke used to return a serve.

SET   A contest made up of a group of games that is complete when one player or side wins at least six while holding a minimum two-game lead. *See also* MATCH; TIE-BREAKER.

SET POINT   The last point needed to win a set.

*SET THE CALENDAR   To make up your mind about when you might think about running a little harder.

SET-UP   A ball hit so softly and close to the net that after it bounces the opponent is "set up" for a certain winner. Also, a weak lob that gives a player an easy overhead smash opportunity near the net.

SHORT-ANGLE SHOT   A ball that clears the net traveling crosscourt, away from the opponent, and (normally) falls within the service court. (This shot can be hit hard, but most players take the speed off.)

SHORT BALL   Any shot except the serve that lands less deep than intended, generally giving the opponent an offensive opportunity.

SHORT-BALL RANGE   The distance on the court a player can cover after hitting an approach shot and still reach his desired *X* position (see separate entry) as or before his opponent strikes the ball.

SIDELINE   *See* SINGLES SIDELINE; DOUBLES SIDELINE.

SIDESPIN   Ball rotation on a vertical axis that causes the ball to veer to the left or right and kick after bouncing. *See also* SLICE.

SINGLES   A contest in which two players compete—one on each side.

SINGLES SIDELINE   The innermost side boundary on each side of the playing court, perpendicular to the net and running the entire length of the court. Used in singles play. *See court diagram in chapter 6.*

SLICE   On the serve or the overhead, a ball struck by a racket face that is moving sideways as it contacts the outer back side of the ball, thus producing sidespin.

SLOW COURT   A playing surface such as clay that causes the ball to rebound slowly and rather high.

SPIN   Rotation imparted to the ball that affects how it curves and bounces.

*STEEL ELBOW   Excessive nervousness that prevents a player from swinging normally. (Pros will sometimes say, "I had the 'steelies' out there.")

STOP VOLLEY   *See* DROP VOLLEY.

STRATEGY   A player's master plan for winning, carefully formulated before a match to give him the best chance at beating a particular opponent. *See also* TACTICS.

STRINGS (OF RACKET)   The intersecting cords that form the hitting surface (face).

STUTTER-STEP   A footwork technique used when attacking the net that involves bringing both feet together momentarily as the player determines the direction of an opponent's shot. Also called a *check-step.*

SUCCESS EXPERIENCE   Anything that gives a student an emotional lift (and positive reinforcement) as he learns to play.

TACTICS   The strokes and methods (such as "overplaying") used in a match to execute one's strategy.

*TAKE GAS   To lose by a horrible score.

"TAKE TWO"   A term used following an interference in play; a courteous opponent will suggest that the server "take two"—start the point over with two serve attempts allowed.

*TANK JOB   The performance of a player who quits trying in a match.

*TAP CITY   Where you're at when there's no hope left to win.

TAPE   *See* NET TAPE. Also, the cloth or metal lines used in place of chalk or paint on clay courts.

TARGET LINE   A straight line between the hitter's racket and his intended target.

TELEGRAPH SHOTS   To inadvertently reveal to an opponent the intended speed, direction, or elevation of one's shots before hitting them.

TENNIS ELBOW   A painful condition caused by excessive stress in the elbow region.

THIRTY   In scoring, the second point won by a player or side.

*THREAD THE NEEDLE   To hit a shot that requires precise accuracy, especially when hitting from the baseline.

*THREE-SHOT FREDDIE   A player who hits three beautiful shots and then "dies."

THROAT (OF RACKET)   The part that connects the handle and the racket head. *See racket diagram in chapter 5.*

TIE-BREAKER   A scoring method commonly used in tournament play to end a set when the score reaches 6–6. The most widely accepted version is the 12-point system, in which the winner is the first player to win 7 points and be ahead by at least 2 points. The player whose turn it is to serve initiates the first point, and thereafter the opponents alternate the serve after every two points.

TOPSPIN   Ball rotation on a horizontal axis that causes the ball to arc downward and bounce high.

T POSITION   The place on each side of the playing court where the center line meets the service line. *See court diagram in chapter 6.*

*TURKEY   A social and athletic failure who continually talks about his great feats.

*TURTLE   A player who refuses to run after balls hit to the corners.

*TWO-INCH-EYES   A player who on all balls hit close to the line says, "Sorry, but your shot was out by just two inches."

UNDERSPIN   Ball rotation on a horizontal axis imparted by contacting the lower back side of the ball with a racket moving from high to low. Also called *backspin*.

UNEARNED POINT   A point won as the result of an unforced error.

UNFORCED ERROR   An error that is the result of one player's weak play rather than an opponent's skill, such as a set-up that's knocked into the net.

"UP AND OUT"   An important concept on the serve and overhead: the racket head should be going skyward and away from a player's head as it approaches the ball and after impact.

VERTICAL RACKET FACE   A racket hitting surface that is straight up and down at impact (as if resting on its edge on a table), on a plane parallel to the net.

VISUAL TEACHING   A method of instruction that employs the student's sense of sight—e.g., having a student look at a diagram or film, or watch a desired stroke or movement as it is performed by someone else.

VOLLEY   A shot in which the ball is hit before it has bounced (as opposed to a groundstroke).

WEIGHT TRANSFER   The shift of one's body weight from a position primarily over one foot to a position over the opposite foot.

WESTERN GRIP   *See page 177.*

*WINGER   A player who throws his racket on the court or against the fence when angry.

WOOD SHOT   One in which the ball hits the racket frame rather than the strings. (The term originated in the days before metal rackets.)

WRIST LAYBACK   Excessive and undesired wrist movement on the backswing, which usually causes the racket head to be late on the forward movement into the ball.

WRIST-ROLL   The unnecessary turning of the wrist in such a manner as to cause the racket face to "roll over" in the hitting zone, which creates severe timing problems at impact.

X POSITION   The spot on the court a player wants to reach after hitting an approach shot—located several feet to either side of the center line, in the direction of the shot and halfway between the service line and the net. This *X* position places the volleyer about halfway between where most opponents can hit passing shots either down-the-line or crosscourt.